Equal Employment Opportunity and the AT&T Case

Contributors

Bernard E. Anderson is Associate Professor of Industry, The Wharton School, University of Pennsylvania

Philip Ash is Professor of Psychology, University of Illinois at Chicago Circle

Orley Ashenfelter is Professor of Economics and Director of the Industrial Relations Section, Princeton University

Barbara R. Bergmann is Professor of Economics, Univeristy of Maryland and Director of the Project on the Economics of Discrimination

Kenneth E. Boulding is Professor of Economics, Institute of Behavioral Science, University of Colorado

Jill Gordon King is an economist at Mathematica, Inc.

Judith Long Laws is Assistant Professor of Sociology and Psychology, Cornell University

Felix M. Lopez is president of Felix M. Lopez and Associates, New York

Jack E. Nelson is a consultant in Washington, D.C.

Ronald Oaxaca is Assistant Professor of Economics, University of Massachusetts

John Pencavel is Associate Professor of Economics, Institute For Mathematical Studies In The Social Sciences, Stanford University

Phyllis A. Wallace is Professor of Management, Massachusetts Institute of Technology

Equal Employment Opportunity and the AT&T Case

edited by Phyllis A. Wallace

The MIT Press
Cambridge, Massachusetts, and London, England

This book was set in IBM Composer Press Roman
by CCI Compositors,
printed on Finch Title 93,
and bound in MBL-4265
by The Colonial Press Inc.
in the United States of America

Library of Congress Cataloging in Publication Data
Main entry under title:

Equal employment opportunity and the AT&T case.

Includes index.
Appendices (p.   ): A. Consent decree: Equal Employment Opportunity Commission et al. vs. American Telephone and Telegraph Company et al., January 18, 1973. B. Twenty-five jobs with greatest number of employees in thirty SMSA's. C. Consent decree: Equal Employment Opportunity Commission et al. vs. American Telephone and Telegraph Company et al., May 31, 1974. D. Summary of supplemental agreement, May 13, 1975.
1. Discrimination in employment—Case studies—Addresses, essays, lectures. 2. American Telephone and Telegraph Company. I. Wallace, Phyllis Ann.
HD4903.3.T3E65   331.1'33   75-34095
ISBN 0-262-23073-9

To William H. Brown III and all who worked with him on the AT&T case. Their work resulted in a "quantum jump" for equal employment opportunity.

Contents

III Personnel Assessment

IV The Institutional Environment

Preface

This volume is intended for those who are interested in a variety of perspectives on equal employment opportunity. The essays draw heavily on the materials made available during a two-year public hearing on the employment patterns of the American Telephone and Telegraph Company (AT&T), the largest private employer in the country. We have examined the past in order to improve our knowledge of management of human resources in the future.

I am deeply indebted to a number of persons who have provided helpful suggestions. As Chairperson of the Ad Hoc Advisory Panel to the EEOC on the AT&T case I worked for more than two years with William H. Brown, III (former chairman of the US Equal Employment Opportunity Commission), David Copus, and William O. Wallace. I am especially pleased that they were inclined to support my effort to report the AT&T story to a wide audience. Of course, I am grateful to all of the contributors to this volume who revised their original reports on the case.

Although I accept full responsibility for the manuscript, several persons have read drafts of selected chapters: Lotte Bailyn, Glenn Cain, William Enneis, Peggy Griffiths, and Alice Kidder. I am indebted to Thomas Bentley, Ronald Ferguson, and Glenn Loury for research assistance. Carole LaMond helped with the editorial chores and prepared the index. At an earlier stage Ineze Patterson served most effectively as the Administrative Assistant to the Ad Hoc Advisory Panel. Frances Moy typed the final manuscript.

I have tried to present a balanced view of a highly complex issue. Perhaps other researchers will be encouraged to expand upon this report.

List of Tables and Figures

Chapter 14

Book Appendix B

Book Appendix D

Equal Employment Opportunity and the AT&T Case

1 Introduction

Phyllis A. Wallace

On January 18, 1973, a consent decree between the American Telephone and Telegraph Company (AT&T), the Equal Employment Opportunity Commission (EEOC),
the United States Department of Labor, and the Department of Justice was approved
by the US District Court for the Eastern District of Pennsylvania.[1] The agreement
ended a two-year effort to bring the AT&T and twenty-four subsidiary operating
companies (the Bell System) into full compliance with federal equal employment
opportunity requirements. A remedial wage adjustment of 38 million dollars[2] was the
largest and most comprehensive civil rights settlement ever agreed to in this country.
Moreover, the projected implementation of the agreement over a six-year period implies a major restructuring of personnel and industrial relations procedures within the
Bell System and therefore will affect large numbers of workers not covered under
employment discrimination laws.

In the words of the courts,

this Consent Decree goes to the very heart of the system—money, goals, timetables,
affirmative action programs, employee information programs, compliance monitoring, pay adjustments, new transfers and immediate promotion options. Estimates of
this landmark settlement are conservatively projected to cost AT&T $38,000,000—
$15,000,000 allocated as back wages to the victims of AT&T's purported discrimina-
tory employment practices, and the remaining $23,000,000 to be expended for ad-
ditional benefits created by the Decree.[3]

The Bell System, with nearly 800,000 workers, is the largest private employer in
the country. In 1970, when the EEOC had petitioned to intervene before the Federal
Communications Commission (FCC) in a proceeding involving a long distance telephone rate increase proposed by AT&T, the EEOC lacked strong enforcement powers under Title VII of the Civil Rights Act of 1964. That Act had prohibited discrimination in employment on the basis of race, color, sex, national origin, and religion.
Three of the major types of discrimination prohibited under Title VII—race, sex, and
national origin—were at issue in the AT&T case. The FCC, the regulatory agency for
the telephone industry, provided a quasi-judicial forum for adjudicating the charges

1 In the United States District Court For the Eastern District of Pennsylvania: *Equal Employment Opportunity Commission, James D. Hodgson, Secretary of Labor, United States Department of Labor and United States of America vs. American Telephone and Telegraph Company
et al.* (Civil Action No. 73-149, January 18, 1973)
2 The actual experience of the company in the first year of the implementation of the agreement
was that some 45 million dollars was expended. See Chapter 13.
3 In the United States District Court for the Eastern District of Pennsylvania: *Equal Employment Opportunity Commission et al vs. American Telephone and Telegraph Company et al.*
(Civil Action No. 74-149), October 5, 1973.

of employment discrimination by the AT&T. The hearings were of national scope, with representation from every geographic area of the country.

During the two years of administrative litigation, social scientists, lawyers, and experts on employment discrimination analyzed the voluminous materials provided by AT&T. These studies examined employment discrimination from several perspectives—economic, psychological, and social. The experts dealt with the problems of large urban labor markets from which many industries were moving to suburban locations; the impact of technology; child care for working mothers; mobility options for women managers, and personnel assessment techniques. When these labor market activities are perceived and examined as elements of a larger social system, we may be able both to make advances in social theory and to better understand the dynamics of employment discrimination.

The documents from the hearings on the AT&T case have now been deposited in the National Archives of the United States. With one exception (Chapter 2), all of the essays included in this volume draw in a significant way on this data base. The researchers had access to the materials provided to the federal government and subsequently testified and were cross-examined during the hearings. Their revised studies, other reports from the hearings, and the consent decree of the federal court, are the focus of this book.

These essays investigate the subtleties and consequences of institutionalized employment discrimination within the context of the AT&T case, but are ultimately concerned with larger issues such as: (1) Can equity be achieved in the workplace? (2) How are individuals allocated to occupational roles? (3) What kinds of trade-offs between efficiency and equity can be tolerated as different kinds of workers are assimilated into the workplace? (4) How can the present manifestation of past discrimination against some groups be minimized without imposing an unjustifiable burden on others? (5) What are the mechanics of the internal labor market that may facilitate or hinder achievement of equal employment opportunity?

Kenneth Boulding's essay (Chapter 2, "Toward a Theory of Discrimination") presents a conceptual framework within which the different perspectives on employment discrimination may be explored. Boulding distinguishes three sources of discrimination—the desire for monopoly power, personal prejudices, and role prejudices. Following this, the economists Ronald Oaxaca, Barbara Bergmann, Jill King, Orley Ashenfelter, and John Pencavel measure the effects of discriminatory employment practices. Oaxaca (Chapter 3) develops a measure of sex discrimination in the telephone industry that is based on wage differentials between males and females of similar characteristics. After controlling for a number of demographic variables (education, experience, industry, health, marital status, regional location, and number of children for the women workers), Oaxaca finds substantial gross wage differentials and concludes that although female workers may have had the same worker characteristics when compared with their male counterparts, the women are found overwhelmingly in the lower-paying occupations. "The reason why females received less than the wage predicted on the basis of the male wage structure has more to do with the types of jobs they hold than with unequal pay for equal work."

The Bergmann-King paper (Chapter 4, "Diagnosing Discrimination") analyzes occupational segregation by race and sex. In the absence of discrimination, each race-sex group would eventually approximate the same share in the jobs of each occupation as they have in the qualified pool for that occupation. From the quarterly status reports of the Bell companies Bergmann and King have "extracted the percentages which white women and blacks of both sexes were of total employment in each of 16 occupations in each (operating) company as of December 31, 1970." Their analysis reveals that black males had been excluded from white collar and craft jobs in AT&T. The authors have also projected the share of employment of every job in each company that each of three race-sex groups will have in 1980.

Ashenfelter and Pencavel (Chapter 5) construct a model to determine the average cost of discrimination associated with sex-segregation of jobs. Male-female wage differentials are estimated (removing the effect of schooling, experience, unionism, marital status, and industrial class, then cross-classifying by occupation and region) for the communications industry. Ashenfelter and Pencavel found that AT&T could make significant savings (2.3 percent of costs) by substituting females for males, without affecting profitability.

These three papers reach the conclusion that employment discrimination within the Bell System was by occupation and not by wage within occupation. The jobs in the lower paying occupations were reserved for women and minorities while jobs in the higher wage occupations typically went to white males. Thus, ending discrimination within AT&T had to be accomplished by removing occupational barriers rather than by merely altering wage structures.

Two significant segments of the AT&T work force protected under the fair employment laws are women and black workers. In Part II of this book Judith Long Laws and Bernard E. Anderson undertake detailed studies of these groups. (The limited information available on the Hispanic worker is included later in Chapter 12.) Laws surveys the psychological literature on theories of work motivation and discusses the status of women workers in the Bell System. Anderson investigates equal opportunity and black employment in the telephone industry.

In Chapter 6, Laws focuses on how the pervasive sex labeling of jobs affects the aspirations and achievement motivation of women. The work motivation model that assumes the centrality of work appears to apply mainly in professional occupations, and "research shows that women professionals do not differ from men in what they put into their work, nor in their productivity." Achievement motivation has two important components: the desire for the goal (incentive value) and expectation of attaining the goal (expectancy). At present our knowledge about the dynamic process by which the work orientation of women is formed is both superficial and fragmentary. However, "neither sex differences in interests nor in abilities seems to provide an explanation powerful enough to account for the discrepant experiences of women and men in the labor force."

In her analysis of data from AT&T (Chapter 7), Laws concluded that "sex discrimination was the primary organizational arrangement with the Bell System, with racial, ethnic, and age discrimination superimposed upon it. Every aspect of employment, from recruitment through pay and promotion was managed within sex-segregated limits." Sex discrimination at the entry level (operators) in the Bell System had its parallel at management levels as well. Although women comprised the majority of Bell employees, they accounted for barely one percent of career management personnel in 1970. A company-sponsored study of the utilization of women in management had revealed both structural and attitudinal obstacles which were detrimental to women's careers in management.

"Despite the avowed commitment to fair employment reflected in the public statements of management officers," Anderson states that "the performance of the Bell System in hiring and upgrading minority group workers was, until very recently, far less than satisfactory by any reasonable standard of equal opportunity. Under the combined effects of labor market conditions and government pressure, the industry has shown an increase in black employment since 1968 that exceeds in number and occupational scope any gains registered by blacks in the telephone industry at any comparable period in the past."

Anderson, in Chapter 8, documents the trend of black employment in the telephone industry from the turn of the century through 1970 and notes that the recent black employment gains continue to be heavily concentrated among women. A disproportionate number of the black women who received the bulk of expanding job opportunities were telephone operators. The pressures from federal enforcement agencies, civil rights groups, and others to reduce employment discrimination were largely responsible for the reversal of past trends in the black hiring practices within the Bell System. Anderson concludes that this transformation far exceeded in both size and scope the gains experienced by blacks in most other industries.

In Part III, the psychologists Philip Ash and Felix Lopez investigate testing and other characteristics of the Bell personnel selection strategy. Their analyses are based largely on test validity studies prepared by the AT&T personnel research unit or by some of the operating companies. Psychological tests to select potential employees and to upgrade workers had been widely used in the Bell System prior to the issuance of federal guidelines on selection procedures. A personnel research unit located at AT&T headquarters was assigned the responsibility of development and validation of tests to ensure System-wide compliance with the testing guidelines.

In Chapter 9, based upon his testimony before the FCC, Ash concludes that the Bell craft test batteries rejected a vastly disproportionate number of black applicants. "The disadvantage blacks suffer because of low 'intelligence test' scores far outweighs the disadvantage inflicted by the Bell System's educational prerequisites." The criterion used by AT&T for validation of the selection tests was a work simulation programmed instruction test, the Learning Assessment Program (LAP). Ash contends that the LAP was not a good surrogate of performance either in training or on the job.

Lopez (Chaper 10) focuses on the nonmanagement personnel selection strategy of the Bell System. AT&T's selection strategy "operated, deliberately or not, to create a pattern of sexual and ethnic segregation and discrimination." Lopez contends that Bell's employment selection strategy did not emphasize those criteria of job effectiveness that guaranteed the most satisfactory achievement of business objectives. Evaluations by Lopez and Ash of the Bell System testing programs are consistent. In addition to AT&T's psychologists, many distinguished psychologists and psychometricians supported the Bell testing program.[4] Although the consent decree did not "exonerate the AT&T testing procedures," it did not resolve these issues.[5] The decree neutralized the testing issue in that it permits AT&T to continue the use of tests but mandates that test results be ignored if they obstruct meeting the affirmative action requirements of the settlement.

In Part IV I describe the institutional environment within which the administrative litigation was conducted. Here are discussed the legal processes and strategies of intervention by the federal officials, and perspectives of the Bell corporate management and of federal compliance agencies on the meaning of equal employment opportunity. Both views are based on a detailed analysis of the voluminous documents presented in the hearings. The final chapters outline the consent decree and note some of the consequences of the AT&T case. The fallout from the decision may be significant. Since the frontal assault on employment discrimination was based mainly on sex discrimination, equal employment opportunity has become a priority item for many employers. The fact that one of the largest corporations "with high visibility in American society" was willing to revamp its entire employment process in order to comply with a federal fair employment law has disturbed the status quo in personnel and industrial relations for employers with fewer resources. This change in focus and direction provides a new perspective on equal employment opportunity.

The Appendices include the consent decrees. These documents may help to shape the external environment of employers far beyond the six years of the initial agreement. Statistical data on the twenty-five telephone jobs with the greatest number of employees in thirty Standard Metropolitan Statistical Areas (SMSA's) are also included as an appendix. Current information (1975) on the implementation of the 1973 Consent Decree is reported in Appendix D.

4 See the testimony by Dr. Brent Baxter and Dr. Robert M. Guion, FCC Docket No. 19143.
5 Interview with William H. Brown III, August 6, 1974.

I Economic Perspectives

2 Toward a Theory of Discrimination

Kenneth E. Boulding

Discrimination is a phenomenon which is so pervasive in all human societies that there is no doubt at all that it exists. It is not, however, a unitary phenomenon but a complex of a number of related forms of human behavior, and this makes it not only hard to define but frequently difficult to comprehend fully.

The history of the word itself is a strange one as it has two almost entirely opposite meanings, one very good and one very bad. On the good side, it means a correct appraisal of complex issues and valuations, as in the expression "a discriminating taste." A person who has a discriminating taste is supposed to be able to reject what is meretricious and to discount what is only superficially either attractive or repellent, and is thus able to exercise true judgment not only in matters of aesthetics but presumably in all other fields in which judgment applies. To say that a person has discriminating taste is indeed a high compliment, but like most high compliments it has a slightly ironic edge to it, implying perhaps that a person is a little too much above the common run of mankind.

At the other end of the scale the word discrimination in a bad sense means precisely the opposite of the discriminating taste, that is, a failure to make correct judgments, especially of other people. The consequence of discrimination in the bad sense, then, is illegitimate differences, that is, differences in the treatment or rewards of different individuals which are not in accord with some standard of equity. We can distinguish at least three sources of discrimination in the bad sense in which it will be used in the rest of this essay. One is the desire for monopoly power; this has been particularly stressed by Lester Thurow.[1] The second is personal prejudice, the theory of which is particularly associated with the name of Gary Becker.[2] The third is role prejudice, which is particularly significant when it comes to sex discrimination.

Any form of exercise of monopoly power implies some capacity to exclude persons from some occupation or activity. The excluded persons may be defined as those who would prefer to be in this occupation with the existing structure of rewards if they were not prevented by some essentially artificial means, usually supported or created by the people who are enjoying the benefits of the monopolized occupation. Monopoly power may be exercised in a great many ways. There may, for instance, be legal restrictions on entering into some occupation, created, for instance, by licensing or immigration restrictions, often obtained as a result of the political power and political pressures of those who are already in the occupation. There may be contractual restrictions—usually depending, of course, on a legal basis for the contract, such as

1 Lester C. Thurow, *Poverty and Discrimination* (Washington, D.C.: Brookings Institution, 1969).
2 Gary S. Becker, *The Economics of Discrimination*, 2nd ed. (Chicago: University of Chicago Press, 1971).

trade union restrictions on entry through closed shops, restrictive hiring practices, and so on. There may also be quite informal and customary restrictions of which prejudice in terms of culture, race, class, sex, religion, or any other distinguishing feature is the most striking example. Unfortunately, any occupational group which develops prejudice is likely to be rewarded by some rise of income as a result of monopoly power. From this point of view it does not matter in the slightest who is kept out as long as somebody is kept out. The excluded may be females, males, blacks, whites, Catholics, Jews, Protestants, tall people, short people, red-haired people, black-haired people, people with strange accents or peculiar customs. The more kinds of people excluded, indeed, the easier it is to keep people out of the occupation and the easier it is to obtain some sort of monopoly power. Often the most effective form of discrimination is familistic. In some cities I understand it is virtually impossible to become a plumber unless one has at least an uncle in the trade. At the extreme this becomes a caste system in which everyone is excluded from an occupation who cannot claim descent from somebody in it.

Monopoly discrimination need have no particular effect. It is not necessary at all to hate or even to dislike the people who are excluded. They may indeed be liked very much as long as they do not try to enter the occupation. In practice, however, exclusion frequently goes along with dislike simply because this is the easiest way to justify it. Excuses are nearly always more important than reasons, especially when the reasons, like the desire for monopoly power, are a little shady and hard to justify in strictly ethical terms. Under these circumstances, excuses are multiplied, and the simplest excuse is that the excluded party is in some way inferior, undesirable, immoral, dirty, uncouth, or in general someone with whom one would not wish to associate. Monopoly discrimination, therefore, frequently has a tendency to be reinforced by personal prejudice, but the two sources of discrimination should be kept intellectually distinct.

Personal prejudice, which is the second principal source of discrimination, may arise, as we have seen, out of the attempt to excuse monopoly power. Nevertheless, it has other sources and it has a certain independence of its own as a source of discrimination related to "taste." The taste for discrimination may, as Gary Becker has pointed out, actually result in a diminution of the income of those who practice the discrimination. In this sense it may have quite opposite effects from the exercise of monopoly power. The taste for discrimination, however, has a number of different origins and may take several forms. Its most defensible form is a simple taste for homogeneity in surroundings and associates. There may be quite real costs of heterogeneity in terms of information and learning costs in dealing with widely different varieties of persons and circumstances. Homogeneous environments are easier to adapt to and to behave in than heterogeneous environments. The taste for homogeneity, therefore, cannot be wholly condemned as irrational, although like many other tastes it often becomes addictive, and then it can be damaging to all parties.

There are difficult questions of social ethics involved here. If people of the same race have a taste for being together, at what point does this become illegitimate? We have a similar problem in the case of sex. The taste for sexual segregation may be quite strong, as is often observed at parties, where the men gather at one end of the room and women at the other. Similarly, there may be tastes for men's colleges and women's colleges, men's drinking clubs and women's sewing circles. At what point these become illegitimate is also hard to say. It seems clear that the extremes are worse than the middle. Something would be lost if no gathering were ever allowed to take place which did not contain both sexes, and even more would be lost if there were no gatherings at which the sexes mingled on equal terms. In the middle, however, is the famous Aristotelian mean—though where it lies is a matter of judgment which is hard to decide.

We have similar problems in educational prejudice. Educated people and professional people tend to gather together; so do the uneducated. Homosexuals segregate themselves and one would certainly hesitate to argue that every homosexual gathering should have an appropriate quota of heterosexuals. It is clear that this is an area where there are no simple rules. It is easy to postulate that there are optimum structures of heterogeneity and homogeneity. The principle of self-determination in the international system, for instance, suggests that within political units a certain amount of homogeneity is a positive good. On the other hand too much homogeneity leads to dullness and stagnation and a lack of human development and learning. Where the optimum in this case lies, however, is clearly beyond the powers of operations research or even of the present state of human wisdom.

Just as the exercise of monopoly power does not necessarily involve any distaste for the excluded, so the exercise of taste for homogeneity does not necessarily imply a distaste for the "other." We see this, indeed, in the ideology of toleration, which indeed can easily put a positive value on variety so that we can actually rejoice in the contemplation of suitably separated differences. We see this especially in the United States in the ideology of religious toleration: "You go to your church and I'll go to my church and we'll walk along the road together." This treats religion as a taste rather than as a burning conviction of the truth, though this raises problems of religious identity. Nevertheless, when, as in the past, burning convictions have often led to the burning of people, the philosophy of mutual toleration seems to have much to recommend it, even if it leads to some loss in intensity. A similar toleration for cultural and linguistic separation is even easier to justify. One may contemplate the rich variety of human languages and cultures with great satisfaction, especially as long as one does not have to go outside one's own language and cultural group. The concern for richness and variety of species which leads us to seek to protect the whooping crane and the whale from extinction should also apply to the Amish, the Hari Krishnas, the Fijians and the Hungarians, without any of which the whole world would surely be poorer.

However the record of history is all too grim: differences often lead not to toleration and joy in the contemplation of variety but to mutual distrust and hatred, and situations in which everybody becomes worse off. The separation of the human race into different nations, classes, cultures, linguistic groups, races, and so on has had a strong tendency to lead to disruptive conflict which has been strongly adverse to human welfare and development. The control of these conflict processes is indeed one of the high priorities of the human race. Indeed, they threaten to destroy the human race altogether if they are not controlled. The study of these processes would carry us far beyond the scope of this book. One can suggest, however, that a good deal depends on the nature of the identity of the persons and communities involved. Where the basic identity is a "positive identity" built around certain positive values in the culture and the person, it is much less likely to result in destructive conflict. When we have a "negative identity" built around "not being" the enemy, conflict easily becomes pathological. One sees this, for instance, in the extraordinary contrast in regard to religious conflict between Northern Ireland and the Republic of Ireland. In the north of Ireland Protestants organize their identity about not being Catholic and Catholics about not being Protestant, no doubt as a result of a long, unfortunate history of conquest, displacement, and settlement. By contrast, in the south of Ireland with a somewhat different, though no less unhappy history, Protestants and Catholics have a more positive identity and hence do not feel the acute need for conflict. There is something indeed in the "I'm OK, you're OK" doctrine. An accepting attitude toward differences certainly leads to the diminution of pathological conflicts.

A third source of personal prejudice is false generalizations which lead to a failure to discriminate in the good sense of the word. Generalizations of the form "all A are B" are very dangerous, because usually only some A are B. If we dislike B, perhaps for legitimate reasons, then if we make the false generalization that all A are B we would dislike all A, whereas we should only dislike some. This might be described as a "cue problem." Our impressions and judgments about the world are inevitably derived from cues, all of which are more or less misleading. There may indeed be some rational grounds for believing false generalizations and forming images with imperfect cues if the cost of improving the generalizations is too great. This may be so in the case of highly complex realities, where ignorance, if not bliss, is at least cheap. This problem emerges very clearly in the assessment of persons, each of whom is an extremely complex reality. It becomes particularly acute in hiring practices. Judgments as to whether individuals are as suited for particular jobs are often made on the seemingly most irrelevant cues such as a facial expression, body posture, trace of accent, and, for all we know, even unconscious perceptions of body odor, simply because the reality about any individual is so complex that it is almost impossible to discover. Not even psychological tests and measurements have done much to alleviate this problem. It may be indeed that job and career discrimination against people with funny faces is more severe and harder to deal with than discrimination against people of different races.

One has an uncomfortable feeling sometimes that the really important categories of humankind are quite unidentifiable, and that the most intractable discrimination is against those people who have the bad luck to fall into one or other of these unidentifiable categories. A corollary of this proposition, however, is that the obvious categories of race, sex, class, and culture are often not the significant ones from the point of view of real abilities. In trying to eliminate these false forms of discrimination, then, what we are really trying to do is to improve the "cue process" by which images of people, especially, are derived from fragmentary and imperfect cues. By eliminating some of the false cues, at least we have some hope of improving judgment in regard to the really significant cues.

A third source of discrimination may be called role prejudice. This is similar in some respects to personal prejudice, but it is sufficiently different to deserve being placed in a separate category. Role prejudice involves processes in the upbringing of children, and even the training of adults, which predispose them to certain skills and roles and exclude them from others, even though these predispositions have no foundation in genetic differences. Thus, the adult brought up under a system of role prejudice may be actually unfitted for certain roles because of the processes of nurture, education, and training, so that denying access to such roles would not involve simple personal prejudice but would be a mere recognition of the facts of the distribution of skill and ability as they exist at the moment. Personal prejudice involves denying people opportunities for roles for which they are in fact fitted at the present time. Role prejudice involves the unfitting of persons for certain roles because of their life experience and not because of any genetic differences.

Role prejudice may be present in all forms of discrimination. In class discrimination, for instance, even though the genetic differences between the upper and the lower class may be very small, the rearing practices of the lower class are designed to produce individuals who will fit into it and who will not, therefore, have the skills of the upper class. A caste society is perhaps the extreme form of role prejudice. All the educational influences on individuals compel them to conform to the practices and occupations of the caste. Class differs from caste only in the degree of mobility; the difference may not be very great. Thus, we see role prejudice as one of the aspects of inheritance through the family. Children are much more likely to be culturally similar to their parents than they are to anybody else.

When some very obvious characteristic of the person such as skin color or sex becomes the basis of what is essentially a class structure, then the role prejudice which is characteristic of class structures likewise becomes identified with these other distinguishing characteristics. What we call "race" is mainly a combination of varying degrees of caste and class, for the genetic differences between the races are really much smaller, for instance, than the genetic differences between the sexes. Men are genetically far more different from women in general than blacks in general are from whites. Both race and sex, however, are strongly associated with role prejudice. Sex discrimination is undoubtedly the most flagrant case of it. All societies tend to form stereotyped roles for men and women. Men are supposed to be "masculine" and women are supposed to be "feminine," although the content of these roles differs very widely from society to society, suggesting that they are determined in large part at any rate by cultural rather than by genetic inheritance.

Some genetic differences between men and women are, of course, important in determining role structures and the comparative advantages of the two sexes in different roles. Men tend to have more muscular strength than women, though there is a very wide overlap between the weakest man and the strongest woman. Women have an overwhelming comparative advantage in having babies and providing them with milk, and this no doubt is the origin of the primitive division of labor between men and women. In a developed society, however, women do not have to spend very much time on child rearing by comparison with what they have to do in primitive societies with high infant mortality. And the combination of the virtual abolition of infant mortality together with the technical revolution in the household, largely as a result of electrical appliances, has enormously diminished the need for relative difference in role structures between men and women.

Role prejudice in regard to sex may be compared with role prejudice between the left- and the right-handed.[3] Genetic factors produce populations in which a certain percentage of the people are strongly left-handed, physiologically, and perhaps a somewhat larger percentage are strongly right-handed, but in which most of us occupy the middle ground so that we could easily learn to be ambidextrous. Social pressures, however, force most people in most societies into being right-handed and indeed actually discriminate against the left-handed. The emancipation of the left-handed is a phenomenon by no means dissimilar to the emancipation of women in that it represents the correction of fallacies of social learning. There has been strong tendency in many societies, indeed in almost all societies, to overgeneralize the genetic predominance of right-handedness into the false generalization that right-handedness is "right" (how significant the language is at this point!) and that left-handedness is "wrong." Truer appreciation of reality can undo the damage caused by this false generalization and release resources for human betterment.

Prejudice in all forms can be regarded as a kind of "mine," a natural resource which can be mined or used up by suitable activity in the production of better states of the world. Alternatively it can be thought of as a burden which prevents the human race from achieving levels of satisfaction which are feasible for it. Like any other mine, however, it has to be discovered and identified before it can be utilized through its diminution. Just what the optimum degree of role differentiation is we cannot easily determine. There is certainly a case for some role differentiation between the sexes, a very much poorer case or no case at all for role differentiation between the races and classes. Where indeed there is a waste of human resources, this is clear evidence of

3 See Rodney Needham, ed., *Right and Left: Essays on Dual Symbolic Classification* (Chicago: University of Chicago Press, 1973).

prejudice that could be "mined," that is, diminished to the benefit of all. Furthermore, there is a strong case for having prejudice against prejudice. The dynamics of human learning almost ensures that we will have too much prejudice rather than too little, just as we tend to learn to have too much hostility and malevolence. Techniques, however, by which prejudice can be diminished have to be learned, just as the techniques of mining have to be learned, and it is clear that we still have a great deal of learning to do. Research in prejudice reduction indeed is likely to be one of the most profitable of intellectual activities, parallel in many ways to the research in the discovery and utilization of natural resources.

3 Male-Female Wage Differentials in the Telephone Industry

Ronald L. Oaxaca

Introduction

The answer to the hypothetical question of what female workers would earn on the average if they were treated the same as male workers is pertinent to the issue of sex discrimination in the telephone communications industry. Of particular interest is the wage position of females employed as telephone operators. This chapter examines the wage and employment status of female telephone workers and provides estimates of the impact of sex discrimination in the industry. Objections to the methods described herein raised by AT&T consultants will also be considered. The Appendix to the chapter presents the mathematical methods used in this study.

A Measure of Discrimination

A simple measure of discrimination is given by the proportionate difference between the observed male/female wage ratio and the ratio that would exist in the absence of discrimination. This proportionate difference is referred to as the discrimination coefficient, and larger positive values of the coefficient imply greater discrimination against females (negative values imply discrimination against males).[1] In the absence of discrimination the coefficient would equal zero. The usefulness of the discrimination coefficient hinges upon our ability to form an estimate of the male/female wage ratio in the absence of discrimination. A nondiscriminatory labor market would be one in which males and females face a common wage structure. For the purpose of this study it is assumed that this common wage structure would be identical to the currently observed male wage structure. This assumption implies that the male/female wage ratio in a nondiscriminatory labor market could be estimated as the ratio of the currently observed average male wage to the average wage females would earn if they were treated as males.[2]

In order to estimate what females would earn if they were treated as males, it is necessary to arrive at a general formula for males that treats the hourly wage as a function of various worker characteristics. Given a sufficiently large sample of

1 That is, $D = \dfrac{[(w_m/w_f) - (w_m^o/w_f^o)]}{(w_m^o/w_f^o)}$, where D = the discrimination coefficient, (w_m/w_f) = the currently observed male/female wage ratio, and (w_m^o/w_f^o) = the male/female wage ratio in the absence of discrimination.

2 That is, $D = \dfrac{[(w_m/w_f) - (w_m/w_f^o)]}{(w_m/w_f^o)} = \dfrac{(w_f^o - w_f)}{w_f}$, assuming $w_m^o = w_m$.

workers, the wage equations can be estimated by multiple regression techniques. The predicted average wage of female workers treated as males is obtained by evaluating the estimated male wage equation for the female averages in the selected worker characteristics. This predicted wage can also be interpreted as the wage that would be received by males who possess on average the same values for these worker characteristics as the females.

It is clear from the definition of the discrimination coefficient that the magnitude of the male-female wage differential per se is not indicative of the extent of discrimination. The observed wage differential is the combined effect of different wage structures for male and female workers and male-female differences in the average values of worker characteristics: the former differences are regarded as discriminatory sources of the wage differential, and the latter are viewed in some sense as justifiable sources of the differential.

Data Source

Since a random sample of personnel records from the files of the various Bell companies was not available for this study, it was necessary to examine data gathered from a household survey. The source of the data was the 1967 Survey of Economic Opportunity (SEO). The Bureau of the Census conducted the SEO on behalf of the Office of Economic Opportunity. The SEO covered some 60,000 individuals distributed across approximately 30,000 households in the United States. For the most part, the survey represented a random sample of households drawn from much the same sampling frame as the Monthly Current Population Survey; however, the SEO also included a special supplementary sample drawn from predominantly nonwhite areas in order to improve the statistics on nonwhites.[3]

For the purpose of this study, a special subsample was lifted from the overall SEO sample. The subsample consists of all urban workers who were sixteen years of age or older, who reported their race as either White or Negro, and who reported their weekly wages or salary and hours worked during the week preceding the survey. The urban subsample contains 12,020 males (8,123 whites and 3,897 blacks) and 8,464 females (4,962 whites and 3,502 blacks). Within the subsample there are 92 males (80 whites and 12 blacks) and 124 females (97 whites and 27 blacks) who were employed in the telephone communications industry.

The wage equations were estimated on the basis of the total urban subsample and then evaluated with respect to the average values of the characteristics of the telephone workers in the sample. The characteristics singled out as determinants of the hourly wage are the following: experience, education, class of worker, industry of

3 A more complete description and documentation of the Survey of Economic Opportunity can be obtained from either the Office of Economic Opportunity or the University of Wisconsin Data and Computation Center.

employment, occupation, health, part time versus full time employment, migration status, marital status, population size of urban area, and regional location. In the case of females an additional characteristic is the number of children ever born to the female worker. I selected the natural logarithm of the hourly wage as the dependent variable. The semilogarithmic form allows interpretation of the estimated partial effects (coefficients) of the worker characteristics as percentage effects on the hourly wage.[4] The regression results are reported in the Appendix to this chapter. Although this study makes little use of the wage equations estimated for females, they are reported in the Appendix for purposes of comparison.

Average Sample Values

Table 3.1 shows the average sample values of telephone worker characteristics that are expressed as continuous variables. Special features of some of these variables are discussed here.

Each worker's hourly wage was computed by dividing the hours worked during the reference week into the wages or salary received for the same period. The geometric mean was selected as the measure of central tendency for the hourly wage. Accordingly, the mean wage for each subgroup of telephone workers was calculated by summing the natural logarithms of the hourly wages, dividing this sum by the number of workers in the given subgroup, and taking the antilog of this last figure.[5]

For the purposes of this study, migration is defined as a move of more than fifty miles occurring after the age of sixteen. The continuous form of the migration variable is defined as the number of years since the worker last migrated.

Work experience, whether defined in reference to time spent in the labor force or time spent with the current employer, is expected to be an important determinant of wage rates. Since the SEO data did not contain direct information on past work experience, a measure of potential experience was used. I have calculated potential experience as the worker's age minus his or her level of education minus six years. Basically, potential experience measures the length of time since the worker left school. In the case of males this is a reasonable estimate of years spent in the labor force. On the other hand, potential experience could overstate the labor-force experience of females to the extent that some labor-force time is lost due to child-bearing. For this reason the children variable was introduced as a correction factor.

Squared terms for the education, experience, and migration variables were included in most of the wage regressions. The average values of these squared terms

4 For a more detailed discussion of the wage model adopted see Ronald L. Oaxaca, "Male-Female Wage Differentials in Urban Labor Markets" (Ph.D. dissertation, Princeton University, 1971).

5 This is expressed by $w = \exp \dfrac{\sum\limits_{i=1}^{n} \ln(w_i)}{n}$, where w = the geometric mean wage.

Table 3.1 Average Sample Values of Telephone Worker Characteristics (Continuous Variables)

Group	N	ℓn(Wage)	Wage	Education	(Education)^2	Experience	(Experience)^2	YRSM[a]	(YRSM)^2	Children	Age
White Males	80	1.3394	$3.82	12.6	162.4	19.3	515.4	5.5	106.9		37.9
White Females:											
Total	97	0.7858	$2.20	11.9	143.1	15.3	427.2	3.2	55.8	0.9	33.2
Telephone Operators	51	0.7645	$2.14	11.6	138.6	15.2	464.1	2.3	48.6	0.8	32.8
Black Males	12	0.9745	$2.65	10.7	122.2	16.2	433.8	2.7	36.2		32.9
Black Females:											
Total	27	0.7871	$2.20	12.1	147.4	8.9	145.4	1.4	13.3	1.1	27.0
Telephone Operators	19	0.7847	$2.19	12.2	149.8	8.2	137.4	1.2	7.1	1.2	26.4

[a]Years since last migrated

Source: 1967 Survey of Economic Opportunity

Table 3.2 Average Sample Values of Telephone Worker Characteristics (Qualitative Variables)

Characteristics	White Males		White Females				Black Males		Black Females			
			Total		Telephone Operator				Total		Telephone Operator	
	N	%	N	%	N	%	N	%	N	%	N	%
Union Membership	42	52.5	50	51.5	28	54.9	8	66.6	18	66.6	15	78.9
Health Problems	10	12.5	5	5.1	2	3.9	0	0.0	2	7.4	2	10.5
Part-Time	1	1.2	7	7.2	5	9.8	0	0.0	0	0.0	0	0.0
Migration	39	48.7	40	41.2	18	35.2	4	33.3	7	25.9	6	31.5
Marital Status:												
Spouse Present	73	91.2	46	47.4	23	45.1	8	66.6	14	51.8	12	63.1
Spouse Absent	0	0.0	3	3.0	1	1.9	0	0.0	1	3.7	0	0.0
Widowed	0	0.0	6	6.1	4	7.8	0	0.0	0	0.0	0	0.0
Divorced or Separated	0	0.0	3	3.0	1	1.9	0	0.0	3	11.1	1	5.2
Single	7	8.8	39	40.5	22	43.3	4	33.3	9	33.4	6	31.7
City Size:*												
Urban Non-SMSA	14	17.6	19	19.7	11	21.5	1	8.3	1	3.7	0	0.0
SMSA < 250	11	13.7	11	11.3	2	3.9	1	8.3	0	0.0	0	0.0
SMSA 250 - 500	8	10.0	13	13.4	8	15.6	0	0.0	1	3.7	1	5.2
SMSA 500 - 750	5	6.2	7	7.2	3	5.8	1	8.3	1	3.7	1	5.2
SMSA 750+	42	52.5	47	48.4	27	52.9	9	75.0	24	88.8	17	89.4
Regional Location:												
North East	23	28.7	21	21.6	11	21.5	3	25.0	9	33.3	5	26.3
North Central	18	22.5	20	20.6	12	23.5	4	33.3	9	33.3	7	36.8
West	22	27.5	18	18.5	10	19.6	1	8.3	3	11.1	2	10.5
South	17	21.3	38	39.3	18	35.4	4	33.3	6	22.3	5	26.3

*The population ranges of the Standard Metropolitan Statistical areas are given in thousands.

Source: 1967 Survey of Economic Opportunity

Table 3.3 Predicted Wages and Estimated Effects of Discrimination[a]

Wage Structure/Group Characteristics	$\ln(G+1)$	G	$\ln(w^{o})$	w^{o}	$\ln(D+1)$	D	$\ln(D+1) \div \ln(G+1)$	J
White Male Regression/White Female Telephone Operators	0.5749	0.77	0.9735	$2.64	0.2090	0.23	0.3635	0.44
White Male Regression Without Occupational Controls/White Female Telephone Operators	0.5749	0.77	1.0576	$2.88	0.2931	0.34	0.5098	0.32
White Male Regression Without Occupational Controls/Total White Females	0.5536	0.74	1.0876	$2.97	0.3018	0.35	0.5452	0.29
Black Male Regression/Black Female Telephone Operators	0.1898	0.21	0.9666	$2.63	0.1819	0.20	0.9584	0.01
Black Male Regression Without Occupational Controls/Black Female Telephone Operators	0.1898	0.21	0.9827	$2.67	0.1980	0.22	1.0432	-0.01
Black Male Regression Without Occupational Controls/Total Black Females	0.1874	0.20	0.9539	$2.59	0.1668	0.18	0.8901	0.02
White Male Regression/Black Female Telephone Operators	0.5547	0.74	1.0878	$2.97	0.3031	0.35	0.5464	0.29
White Male Regression Without Occupational Controls/Black Female Telephone Operators	0.5547	0.74	1.1673	$3.21	0.3826	0.47	0.6897	0.19
White Male Regression Without Occupational Controls/Total Black Females	0.5523	0.74	1.1531	$3.17	0.3660	0.44	0.6627	0.20

[a] G = Gross male-female wage differential
w^{o} = Predicted wage
D = Discrimination coefficient
J = Justifiable wage differential

are given in Table 3.1. As is evident from the figures, the average of the squares of numbers is not generally equal to the square of the average of these same numbers.

Given our definition of experience, average age can be directly calculated from the figures on average experience and average educational level. Although age did not explicitly appear as a variable in our wage model, average ages are given in Table 3.1.

Table 3.2 displays information of a qualitative nature in the form of the numbers and percentages of telephone workers who fall into various classifications. Although most of these categories are self-explanatory, some points of clarification will be discussed.

In the wage regressions the class of worker variable consists of subcategories defined for union members, private wage and salary workers, government workers, and the self-employed. Because the present study focuses upon telephone workers in the communications industry, only the union/nonunion (private wage and salary worker) distinction is relevant.

The health problems category refers to those workers who reported a health impairment that affected the kind or amount of work they could perform.

Those who worked less than thirty-five hours a week were considered to be part-time workers.

The migration category refers to workers who migrated at least once since the age of sixteen.

Analysis of the Data

The effects of discrimination are revealed by the magnitude of the discrimination coefficient and by its magnitude relative to that of the gross (observed) male-female wage differential. Consistency with the semilogarithmic specification of the wage equations requires that the effects of discrimination be calculated in terms of natural logarithms; however, the results turned out in most cases to be nearly the same when either the logarithmic or nonlogarithmic forms of the discrimination coefficient and gross wage differential were used.[6] Table 3.3 presents the results of the calculations. For purposes of calculating predicted wages and the effects of discrimination, the average values of the independent variables given in Tables 3.1 and 3.2 were carried out to four decimal places.

---

6 Let $G = \dfrac{(w_m - w_f)}{w_f}$ where G = the gross wage differential; then $\ln(G+1) = \ln(w_m/w_f)$. It follows from the definition of the discrimination coefficient that $\ln(D+1) = \ln(w_m/w_f) - \ln(w_m^o/w_f^o)$. Now set $w_m^o = w_m$, then $\ln(D+1) = \ln(w_f^o/w_f)$. We find that $\ln(D+1)/\ln(G+1) \cong D/G = (w_f^o - w_f)/(w_m - w_f)$.

The case of white female telephone operators will be examined first. The gross wage differential between white males and white female telephone operators was 77 percent. These telephone operators earned an average hourly wage of $2.14/hour in 1967, but the calculation predicts that they could have earned $2.64/hour had they faced the male wage structure as clerical workers not restricted to the occupation of telephone operator. Another way of viewing this result is to imagine that the telephone industry decides to employ white male clerical workers with the same average worker characteristics as the white female telephone operators. Then the average wage of these male clerical workers would be $2.64/hour. The estimated discrimination coefficient tells us that the white female telephone operators should have received an hourly wage 23 percent higher than what they were paid. The results indicate that at least 36 percent of the gross wage differential in logarithmic terms can be attributed to the effects of discrimination. With the restriction of female telephone operators to clerical type jobs, the justifiable male-female wage differential would be about 44 percent.[7]

The above findings for white female telephone operators were based on the prediction of their wage rate from a male wage regression that controlled for occupation. The difficulty here is that occupational barriers are likely to be a significant source of the discrimination against females. Consequently, occupational controls mask an important aspect of sex discrimination. In an attempt to deal with this problem, I have estimated a separate set of wage equations that do not include occupational variables. As expected, the estimated effects of discrimination are larger. The findings indicate that white female telephone operators could have earned $2.88/hour on average had they faced the same wage structure as males without restrictions to the clerical occupations. Or what amounts to the same thing, white males with the same average worker characteristics as the white female telephone operators would have earned $2.88/hour. The discrimination coefficient indicates that in the absence of occupational barriers white female telephone operators could have earned an hourly wage 34 percent greater than their actual wage. Without occupational controls, discrimination accounts for 51 percent of the male-female wage differential (in logs). These figures imply that a male-female wage differential much in excess of 32 percent cannot be justified.

The gross wage differential between white males and the entire white female sample (which includes telephone operators) was 74 percent. The white females earned an average of $2.20/hour, but they could have earned $2.97/hour had they

---

7 The justifiable wage differential (J) was calculated, in terms of natural logarithms, from the difference between the gross differential and the differential attributable to discrimination:

$\ln (J+1) = \ln (G+1) - \ln (D+1) = \ln (w_m/w_f^o)$. Thus it follows that $J = \dfrac{(w_m - w_f^o)}{w_f^o} = \exp$

$\ln [(G+1)/(D+1)] - 1.$

been treated as white male workers with no occupational restrictions. Or, again, white males with the same general worker characteristics as the white females would have received an average wage of $2.97/hour. According to the estimated discrimination coefficient, this predicted wage is 35 percent higher than what the white female telephone workers were actually paid. The results suggest that discrimination accounted for 55 percent of the male-female wage differential (in logs) and that the justifiable wage differential is 29 percent.

The gross wage differential between black males and black female telephone operators was 21 percent. Instead of earning an average of $2.19/hour, the black female telephone operators would have earned $2.36/hour had they faced the black male wage structure as clerical workers. According to the estimated discrimination coefficient, black female telephone operators restricted to clerical jobs should have received an average wage 20 percent in excess of their actual wage. Discrimination accounted for about 96 percent of the wage differential between black males and black female telephone operators. In this case virtually no wage differential could be justified.

Now suppose that no occupational restrictions were imposed on black female telephone operators. If they were treated as black males, they could have earned $2.67 or 22 percent more than they actually earned. That is to say, the industry would have paid black males an average of $2.67/hour if they possessed the same general worker characteristics as the black female telephone operators. Since the black male average wage ($2.65/hour) was less than the wage predicted on the basis of black female telephone worker characteristics, the proportion of the (log) differential due to discrimination slightly exceeds 100 percent. Thus, no differential in favor of the black male vis-a-vis black female telephone operators could be justified.

The gross wage differential between the black males and the entire sample of black females was 20 percent. Had the black females been treated as black males they would have earned $2.59/hour rather than $2.20/hour. In other words, black males with the same worker characteristics as the black females would have earned $2.59/hour. The discrimination coefficient estimated in this case indicates that black females should have earned 18 percent more that they did. With 89 percent of the gross wage differential (in logs) attributed to sex discrimination, a wage differential of only 2 percent could be justified.

An important comparison is that between the wages of white males and black females. The average hourly wage of the white males exceeded that of the black female telephone operators by 74 percent. Holding the black female telephone operators to the clerical occupations, we find that they could have earned $2.97/hour had they faced the same wage structure as white males. Thus the industry would have paid white male clerical workers $2.97/hour if they possessed the same general worker characteristics as the black female telephone operators. In the present context the discrimination coefficient reflects both race and sex discrimination. It shows that the black female telephone operators restricted to clerical occupations should have earned an hourly wage 35 percent higher than their actual wage. This degree of discrimination accounted for 55 percent of the gross wage differential (in logs), and the justifiable wage differential worked out to be 29 percent.

The predicted wage of black female telephone operators treated as white males without occupational restrictions is $3.21/hour. This is the wage white males would earn if they possessed the same worker characteristics as the black female telephone operators. The larger discrimination coefficient estimated in this case tells us that the black female telephone operators should have received an average wage 47 percent greater than their actual wage. The proportion of the (log) differential attributable to discrimination rose to 69 percent, and the justifiable differential fell to 19 percent.

The gross wage differential between white males and the total black female sample was 74 percent. Treating black females the same as white males would have raised the black female wage to $3.17/hour. This predicted wage is what white males with the same average worker characteristics as the black females could expect to earn. The estimated discrimination coefficient shows that black female telephone workers, in the absence of race and sex discrimination, could have earned an average wage 44 percent higher than what they actually received. Furthermore, 66 percent of the gross wage differential (in logs) between white males and black females can be attributed to discrimination. In this case a 20 percent wage differential is all that can be justified on the basis of different worker characteristics between white males and black females in the telephone industry sample.

As was mentioned earlier, the wage equations estimated for females included a control variable for the number of children ever born to the female worker. This variable was intended to pick up the effects of lost experience due to childbearing and the resulting deterioration of skills. This information was not used in the preparation of Table 3.3 because the Table 3.3 figures were derived from applying the male wage regressions to the general characteristics of female telephone workers. Naturally, the male wage equations do not include the children variable; nevertheless, the figures in Table 3.3 can be adjusted to take into account the effects of childbearing on the predicted wage of females and on the estimated effects of discrimination. The adjustment procedure consists of multiplying the average number of chidlren ever born per female telephone worker by the estimated (partial) effect of childbearing on the hourly wage of female workers, and then subtracting the absolute value of this product from the logarithm of one plus the discrimination coefficient.

The regression results for white females reveal that their hourly wage was reduced by about 2 percent per child when occupation was controlled for and 2.5 percent per child when there were no occupational control variables. Given that the average number of children ever born per white female telephone worker was less than one, we cannot expect the adjustment procedure to reduce the estimated effects of discrimination by very much. In the case of no occupational controls, the adjustment procedure reduced the proportion of the wage differential due to discrimination from 55 percent to 50 percent for the total white female telephone worker sample and from 51 percent to 47 percent for white female telephone operators. When occupation was controlled for in the case of white female telephone operators, the adjustment procedure reduced the proportion of the wage differential due to discrimination from 36 percent to 34 percent. Of course, it could be argued that the effects of lost work experience due to childbearing is in some part a reflection of discrimination. Looked at in this way, the modest adjustments we made may be too large. For black females there was virtually no effect of childbearing on their hourly wage after controlling for other factors; therefore the attempted adjustments produced no change in the estimated effects of discrimination.

The results of this study hint at a difference in the relative attractiveness of "telephone operator" as an occupation for white females and black females. White females who are not telephone operators earn more relative to telephone operators than is the case for black females. This difference in relative attractiveness of the telephone operator job becomes more apparent when one notes that the predicted wage of females in the absence of discrimination is greater for all white females as compared with white female telephone operators, whereas the predicted wage for all black females is less than that of the black female telephone operators. The average level of schooling was higher for white females who were not telephone operators than for those who were (12.2 versus 11.6 years). For black females the average level of schooling was lower for those who were not telephone operators than for those who were (11.8 versus 12.2). These findings could indicate that "telephone operator" is a better job with higher standards for black females as compared with the other jobs open to black females in the telephone industry. Where white females are concerned, "telephone operator" may not be as good a job and may have lower standards than other jobs open to them in the industry.

To place our findings in perspective, we will briefly examine the average effects of discrimination across all industries.[8] The national estimates of the effects of discrimination are based on the entire urban SEO sample discussed earlier in the paper. In 1967 the gross male-female wage differential was 54 percent for white. The female wage rate predicted from the male wage regression with occupational controls implied that 53 percent of the differential (in logs) could be attributed to sex discrimination in the labor market. From the white male wage regressions without

8 Ronald L. Oaxaca. "Male-Female Wage Differentials in Urban Labor Markets." (*International Economic Review,* October 1973).

controls for occupation, industry, and class of worker the predicted wage of white females implied that 78 percent of the (log) difference in wages could be attributed to discrimination. For blacks the male-female wage differential was 49 percent. The black female wage rate predicted from the estimated black male wage structure without occupational controls implied that 50 percent of the wage differential (in logs) was the result of sex discrimination. Sex discrimination accounted for 89 percent of the wage difference when the black female wage rate was predicted from black male wage regressions without control variables for occupation, industry, and class of worker. In summary, the national gross male-female wage differential for whites was smaller than the corresponding differentials in the telephone industry; however, the proportions due to discrimination were larger nationwide. The male-female wage differential for blacks was larger nationwide than in the telephone industry, but a smaller proportion of the national differential was due to sex discrimination.

Eliminating Discrimination in the Industry

There is a wide spectrum of possibilities for raising the relative wages of females to nondiscriminatory levels. One possibility is to lower the wages of male employees, but this is neither necessary nor desirable. Our focus is on adjusting the male-female wage ratio by raising female wages. This is a straightforward procedure in those cases in which women are paid less than men performing substantially similar work: simply pay females the male wage rate. In such cases, back pay would accrue to the women workers involved.

A good deal more is involved where discrimination takes the form of unequal job opportunities for men and women, as in the Bell System. The potential of each female employee for traditionally male jobs within the Bell System could be assessed on the basis of general characteristics much like some of those introduced in this study. Those who are found potentially qualified on this basis should be encouraged to move into these jobs. Naturally, the issue of compensation would be present for those who were denied opportunities for advancement to better paying jobs. The qualification of females with the appropriate general worker characteristics for male dominated jobs would largely take place through on-the-job training (OJT). The economics literature on human capital investments indicates that OJT is the most important source of job preparation and qualification among skilled craft occupations. Rarely would it seem that formal schooling is all that is needed to enable one to step right into industry and successfully perform assigned tasks. The point is that women can qualify for skilled jobs in the same manner that men commonly prepare for these jobs. In addition, males seeking employment in the Bell System should have full access to jobs previously restricted to females.

Criticisms Raised by AT&T

A frequent criticism was that the analysis presented here had not controlled for enough worker characteristics in the wage regressions. It is very important to recognize that it is neither necessary nor desirable to control for all possible sources of wage differences among workers when investigating the extent of discrimination. To do so would virtually eliminate discrimination as an explanation of the observed male-female wage differential. Ths is because we treat all sex differences in the means of the selected variables as justifiable sources of the wage differential. Thus if women encounter occupational barriers which lead to their concentration in lower paying jobs, then to control for occupation would be to treat male-female differences in occupational attachment as voluntary responses in the absence of discrimination. The more detailed the occupational breakdown, the greater the underestimate of discrimination. The other extreme is to regard all sex differences in the relevant characteristics as the products of labor market discrimination. This approach is tantamount to controlling for nothing and assuming at the outset that the entire male-female wage differential is the product of employer discrimination. Fortunately, the approach discussed here avoids assuming either extreme. The possibilities of either all or none of the wage differential being attributed to discrimination are just special cases under this procedure.

We are in effect measuring discrimination as the wage differential between males and females of similar characteristics, and not merely as the wage differential between males and females who perform substantially similar tasks. It is clear that the choice of characteristics to serve as control variables implicitly defines what we mean by labor market discrimination. I maintain that this operational definition of discrimination is in accord with the intents of the Equal Pay Act of 1963 and the Civil Rights Act of 1964. When the issue is looked at in this way, it does not make much sense to talk about "correct" or "incorrect" specifications of the wage equations from the standpoint of measuring discrimination. The procedures and variables used contextually define discrimination, and different researchers have in effect different definitions of discrimination. The basic problem, from a policy oriented point of view, centers on which varieties of differential treatment in the labor market we wish to brand as unjustifiable on the grounds of equity.

It was noted by an AT&T consultant that the measure of experience used increases the earnings of men more than women.[9] The implication was that the proxy experience variable is somehow biased toward finding discrimination. Certainly the experience variable increased the earnings of white males more than white females because the white males in the telephone worker sample had, on average, four years more potential experience than white females. However, this difference reduced, rather than increased, the differential due to discrimination since dif-

9 See the testimony of Dr. Lewis Perl, FCC Docket No. 19143.

ferences in the selected characteristics were treated as justifiable sources of the wage differential. For purposes of a rough comparison with my figures, the AT&T consultant introduced a table which listed the mean years of employment covered under Social Security for various age groupings by sex in 1960.[10] The mean years of covered employment corresponding to the average ages of the white males and females in my telephone worker sample were 15.5 and 11.0 years, respectively. These figures are almost exactly four years less than those calculated for the experience variable. To the extent that individuals may work at some point in their lives in situations not covered by Social Security, the Social Security figures would understate the actual years of work experience. At any rate it is interesting to note that the male-female experience difference using Social Security data is 4.5 years, which is virtually identical to the difference I calculated for whites using my own estimate of experience.

The experience variable does contribute to the estimated effects of discrimination insofar as the estimated coefficients on experience were different between the sexes. The pattern of differences in these coefficients implies some combination of differences in investment in on-the-job training and in the rate of return to such investment. If at one extreme we assumed that males and females invested to the same extent, then the coefficient differences would imply that the rate of return to OJT was higher for males. If, at the other extreme, we assumed that the rates of return were the same for both sexes, then the implication would be that males invested in OJT to a larger extent than females. The mere possibility of the latter case was viewed by the AT&T consultant as prima facie evidence of the absence of labor market discrimination with respect to the effects of experience. From this he deduced that it is reasonable to dismiss the contribution of these coefficient differences to the estimated effects of discrimination. I contend that this is anything but reasonable. Even if the rate of return to OJT were the same for males and females, and there is no evidence that this is the case, it does not follow that discrimination is absent. It could be that the lower returns to female investment in OJT caused by discrimination are sufficiently offset by lower opportunity costs stemming from the same discrimination. Under these circumstances the rate of return would turn out to be the same as for males, yet discrimination clearly was present.

Occupational barriers deny women access to OJT, and this denial of equal job opportunities prevents them from investing to the same extent as men. The consultant assumes that the observed investment behavior of female workers is voluntary in the sense that this same pattern would exist in the absence of discrimination in the labor market. There is no reason to suppose that this would be the case. If one wished to speculate that the investment patterns of males and females might

10 US Social Security Administration, Office of Research and Statistics. *Workers Under Social Security, 1960: Annual and Work History Statistics* (Washington, D.C.: US Government Printing Office, 1968), p. 94.

differ somewhat even in the absence of discrimination, the question would have to become one of how much of the estimated differences in the coefficients could be attributed to voluntary behavior in the absence of discrimination.

The foregoing suggests a drawback of this approach. The procedure does not take into account feedback effects from labor market discrimination. The very reasonable expectation by females of labor market discrimination can give rise to male-female differences in the determinants of wages. Yet our procedure treats all differences in the selected characteristics as justifiable sources of the wage differential. Thus, contrary to the claim that I have not controlled for enough characteristics, I may have controlled for too much.

To briefly summarize, it would appear that the male-female difference in the experience measure used herein reasonably approximates the actual difference. This measured difference in favor of males reduces the amount of the wage differential attributable to discrimination. The estimated male-female difference in the response of wages to experience confirms what is obvious to all—that the work experiences of males and females are qualitatively different. Some combination of differences in the amount of investment in OJT and the rate of return to this investment is exactly the consequence one would expect from role differentiation in the labor market; therefore, these differences contribute to the measured effects of discrimination.

Commenting on another aspect of the wage equations given in the Appendix to this chapter, the AT&T consultant suggested that the estimated smaller male-female wage differentials in large urban areas stem from lower costs of job search in densely populated areas. Women presumably take advantage of these lower search costs, and the result is a narrowing of the wage differential. It should be pointed out that this explanation is not inconsistent with the hypothesis that sex discrimination is less in large urban areas. Job search costs would be higher for women if employers were reluctant to advertise openings in traditionally male jobs as being available to women. This would be especially likely for job recruiting through informal information networks. If attitudes toward female employment are more liberal in large urban areas, we would expect that better job opportunities are relatively more plentiful for females. This too would imply a smaller male-female wage differential in the large urban areas.

AT&T consultants have suggested that Bell's employment record where females and minorities are concerned should not be judged with reference to their proportion in the labor force or gross population. Rather, the reference should be the proportion of females and minorities who possess the traits (other than race or sex) required by Bell in its various jobs. While this may sound reasonable, it would be wise to investigate the extent to which these various job entry requirements are relevant to the performance of the jobs in question. It could be that employers exploit male-female and white-nonwhite differences in certain characteristics in order to exclude females and minorities from jobs not considered socially appropriate. Though differences in these characteristics may stem from past patterns of discrimination, employers could impose entry requirements which are not relevant to job performance but which they know will favor the entry of whites and males.

The AT&T consultant cited statistics which show a different distribution in high school and college courses taken by males and females. We argue that the anticipation of labor market discrimination leads to different preparations and career paths for males and females. The feedback from the labor market is surely an important determinant of these distributional differences. Furthermore, we are led to believe that Bell craft jobs are somewhat unique in American industry. If these jobs are so dissimilar from skilled jobs in other industries, the value of high school vocational courses to the performance of these jobs is questionable. That is to say, it would not appear that high school vocational training is adequate to prepare one for specific tasks in the Bell System. Rather, it seems that OJT is the more important means by which one acquires the requisite skills. It is this component of career preparation that we believe women are denied by employers, including the Bell System.

The same AT&T consultant has developed a theoretical model that seeks to explain away the entire male-female wage differential by appealing to sex differences in the supply of labor to different occupations. The model assumes the following: (1) there are only two occupations; (2) the labor demand schedules for the two occupations are identical; (3) the labor supply schedules are independent between occupations; (4) the male labor supply schedules to the two occupations are identical; and (5) the females exhibit a preference for one of the occupations relative to the other. This constellation of assumptions yields a wage differential in favor of males which is entirely the result of a voluntary concentration of females in one of the occupations. It is not that women prefer low paying jobs, but rather this concentration of females in a particular job lowers the wage in the one occupation relative to the other. Within each occupation there are no wage differentials. The model is then generalized to more than two occupations. It is shown that a wage differential in favor of males would arise if the female labor supply were less responsive to wages and if for females the ratio of the variation in tastes and other factors to their response to wages exceeded the corresponding ratio for males.

If we accept the underlying assumptions of the model, the analysis is formally correct; however, it is no real feat to concoct a model embodying a set of assumptions that will lead to a desired result. For example, one could easily produce a model whose assumptions lead to the conclusion that the entire male-female wage differential is the product of employer discrimination. The analytic possibility that none of the wage differential is attributable to employer discrimination is not in question here. The point is that the model is not operational in its present form and is not of direct relevance to the issue at hand, i.e., the employment practices of the Bell System. We can agree that women are not attracted to low paying jobs, but we also maintain that the occupational crowding which depresses the wages in the female dominated occupations is the result of employer adherence to a policy of role differentiation.

Males and females can be viewed as noncompeting groups. Barriers to entry into male dominated jobs effectively remove, or at least reduce, the incentive of women to expend very many resources on preparation for entry into such jobs. Consequently, the high wages in certain male dominated jobs hardly qualify as realistic incentives where women are concerned. This is in contrast to the AT&T consultant's suggestion that the concentration of women in low paying jobs reflects "voluntary" immobilities such that the response of females to pecuniary incentives is less than for males. The consultant also argues that because women spend a smaller proportion of their lives in the labor force, they are less willing to make the necessary investments that would lead to better paying jobs. If this is true, the question is why do women spend a smaller proportion of their lives in the market sector? I have argued that in the last analysis it is the existence of occupational barriers that reduces the incentive of women to spend much time in the labor force pursuing careers. The payoff to women who contemplate the scale of investment actively typical of men of similar characteristics is therefore reduced by employer discrimination.

Reliance on the possibility of differential supply responses of males and females seems to open the door to the conclusion that all of the male-female wage differential is the result of voluntary decisions reflecting the tastes and preferences of females. The logic seems to be that women are doing what they like to do otherwise they would not be doing it. We maintain that women and minorities are making the best of a bad situation. A certain wage structure is imposed, and the resultant labor market behavior of women reflects their adaptation to the biases of the labor market. The adaptation of women to these biases produces sex differences in on-the-job training, length of working lives, and other characteristics which can only be viewed as rational responses under the circumstances. The alternative is to attempt to change the wage structure via changes in employment practices, which is presumably what the AT&T case is all about.

The AT&T consultant has introduced a theoretical model that is not subject to testing with data of any kind, let alone with data pertaining to telephone workers. Thus, the model does not serve as a useful guide in reaching any conclusions in the AT&T case. We know that the concentration of females in certain jobs leads to a male-female wage differential. This concentration represents occupational immobilities and is interpreted as the consequence of differential responses between males and females to pecuniary incentives. Why do there appear to be differential responses? The answer proffered by AT&T is that it is a matter of voluntary behavior on the part of women. I maintain that the use of the word "voluntary" is strained in the present context. The complete absence of any reference to the ubiquitous role differentiation by sex immediately renders their approach as suspect. I must conclude that the testimony offered by the AT&T consultant is highly speculative, and his model may be nothing more than wishful thinking.

Summary and Conclusion

The empirical results in this study suggest that a substantial portion of the male-female wage differentials within the telephone industry is the result of discriminatory employment practices. This inference derives from the exercise of using the average worker characteristics corresponding to a given group of female telephone workers to predict what they would earn if they faced the male wage structure. This predicted wage is also an estimate of what the industry would pay males with the same average characteristics as the females. The reason why females received less than the wage predicted on the basis of the male wage structure has more to do with the types of jobs they held than with unequal pay for equal work. I have not shown that the entire male-female wage differential among telephone workers is the product of employer discrimination. Only a portion of the differential has been attributed to discrimination. Although this portion may be less than the national average, we believe it is still substantial and merits correction.

In conclusion, it should be noted that the 1967 wage figures can be converted into current wages by adding a percentage wage change component to the logarithm of the hourly wage in order to reflect the secular increase in money wages. If this component is the same for all groups in the industry and wage structures are unchanged, the estimated effects of discrimination would also remain the same.

Appendix to Chapter 3

Mathematical Addendum

The wage equations used in this study were estimated by ordinary least squares and have the semilog functional form

$$(1) \quad \ln(w_i) = Z_i' \beta + u_i \qquad i = 1, \ldots, n$$

where

w_i = the hourly wage of the ith worker,

Z_i' = a vector of individual characteristics,

β = a vector of coefficients, and

u_i = a disturbance term.

Table 3.4 presents the regression results for all four race-sex groups of urban workers in the 1967 Survey of Economic Opportunity. The industry and occupation variables were defined by census two digit categories. Table 3.5 reports the regression run without occupational controls. Coefficients were not estimated in the following instances: (1) the variable served as a reference group; (2) there were no observations in a particular category; (3) the same observations were found in another category; or (4) the variable was left out because of poor results from a previous regression.

A method of decomposition of the gross male-female wage differential into justifiable differences and differences due to discrimination is described below. From the property of ordinary least squares we have

$$(2) \quad \ln(\bar{w}_j) = \bar{Z}_j' \hat{\beta}_j \qquad j = m \text{ (male)}, f \text{ (female)}$$

where

$\bar{w}_j$ = the geometric mean wage,

$\bar{Z}_j'$ = the vector of mean values of the variables, and

$\hat{\beta}_j$ = the vector of estimated coefficients.

The gross male-female wage differential can be expressed in logs as

$$(3) \quad \ln(G+1) = \ln(\bar{w}_m) - \ln(\bar{w}_f) = \bar{Z}_m' \hat{\beta}_m - \bar{Z}_f' \hat{\beta}_f.$$

Table 3.4   Wage Regressions

Dependent Variable
  log (hourly wage)

	White Males	White Females	Black Males	Black Females
Independent Variables:				
Constant	.0365	—.1024	.0953	—.3851
	(.77)	(—1.34)	(1.71)	(—6.35)
Experience				
Experience	.0176	.0138	.0117	.0067
	(13.89)	(8.19)	(7.73)	(4.38)
Experience **2	—.000288	—.000248	—.000204	—.000122
	(—12.22)	(—7.31)	(—7.59)	(—4.33)
Education				
Education	.0082	—.0118	—.0308	—.0175
	(1.27)	(—.98)	(—4.60)	(—1.98)
Education**2	.00169	.00194	.00300	.00245
	(5.92)	(3.53)	(8.23)	(5.26)
Class of worker				
Union	.1113	.1500	.2129	.0719
	(9.39)	(6.70)	(14.15)	(3.11)
Nonunion Private wage and salary	—	—	—	—
Government	.0646	.1445	.1328	.1263
	(3.15)	(5.89)	(5.44)	(5.19)
Selfemployed	—.1290	.1137	—.0128	—.3437
	(3.51)	(1.22)	(—.15)	(—2.67)
Industry				
Agriculture	.1285	.2847	—.0067	—.0190
	(1.81)	(1.09)	(—.08)	(—.21)
Mining	.3604	.4112	.0697	—
	(6.83)	(2.02)	(.40)	
Construction	.2997	.2444	.2729	.0395
	(13.72)	(3.80)	(10.54)	(.22)

Table 3.4   Continued

Dependent Variable log (hourly wage)				
	White Males	*White Females*	*Black Males*	*Black Females*
Manufacturing—durable	.2398 (13.76)	.2562 (8.39)	.2101 (9.15)	.2590 (6.46)
Manufacturing—non durable	.2086 (11.03)	.1968 (6.60)	.1679 (6.85)	.2305 (6.46)
Transportation	.2332 (9.81)	.3154 (5.54)	.2182 (7.39)	.5463 (5.73)
Communications	.2370 (5.62)	.2290 (4.56)	.1555 (1.78)	.2657 (3.71)
Utilities	.2414 (7.32)	.2451 (2.83)	.1433 (3.45)	.7026 (2.76)
Wholesale Trade	.2039 (8.45)	.1979 (4.74)	.1204 (3.76)	.3065 (4.34)
Retail Trade	—	—	—	—
Finance	.2224 (8.25)	.1761 (5.65)	.0184 (.47)	.1593 (3.22)
Business and repair services	.1385 (4.44)	.1525 (3.24)	.0766 (2.10)	.1326 (2.31)
Personal services	—.0618 (—1.71)	—.0183 (—.50)	—.1055 (—3.22)	.0118 (.40)
Recreation	.0488 (.97)	.1527 (1.97)	.0020 (.04)	.1019 (1.29)
Professional services	—.0629 (—2.53)	.0528 (2.01)	.0633 (2.13)	.1181 (4.45)

Table 3.4 Continued

Dependent Variable log (hourly wage)	White Males	White Females	Black Males	Black Females
Public administration	.1970 (6.58)	.2165 (4.86)	.2374 (6.75)	.2170 (5.61)
Occupation				
Professional workers	.1563 (6.62)	.3736 (10.25)	.2144 (4.62)	.4631 (10.80)
Managers	.1822 (8.27)	.2759 (6.85)	.0810 (1.49)	.2792 (3.53)
Clerical workers	—.0639 (—2.68)	.1665 (6.03)	.0208 (.54)	.1509 (4.50)
Sales workers	—	—	—	—
Craftsmen	.0275 (1.28)	.0932 (1.31)	.0733 (1.99)	.1297 (1.97)
Operatives	—.1064 (—4.92)	.0128 (.37)	—.0271 (—.77)	.0236 (.62)
Private household workers	—.1900 (—1.03)	—.3060 (—5.46)	—.0458 (—.28)	—.1432 (—3.58)
Service workers	—.1358 (—5.19)	—.0219 (—.72)	—.0998 (—2.84)	—.0164 (—.53)
Farm laborers	—.4750 (—5.38)	.1579 (.43)	—.1421 (—1.36)	—
Laborers	—.1540 (—5.59)	—.0166 (—.15)	—.0537 (—1.77)	.0317 (.37)
Health Problems	—.1001 (—6.08)	—.0710 (—2.70)	—.0811 (—3.79)	—.0270 (—1.31)

Table 3.4   Continued

Dependent Variable
  log (hourly wage)

	White Males	*White Females*	*Black Males*	*Black Females*
Part-Time	—.1874	—.0445	—.1117	.0034
	(—9.14)	(—2.64)	(—4.80)	(.21)
Migration				
Migration	—.0356	—.1073	.0052	—.0361
	(—2.48)	(—5.03)	(.44)	(—1.94)
YRSM	.0072	.0087	—	.0025
	(4.22)	(3.33)	—	(2.73)
YRSM°°2	—.000140	—.000147	—	—
	(—3.08)	(—2.14)	—	—
Marital Status				
Spouse				
Present	.1841	.0883	.1211	.0995
	(11.88)	(4.51)	(6.43)	(5.13)
Spouse				
Absent	.1124	.0852	.0446	.1050
	(1.72)	(1.39)	(.79)	(2.38)
Widowed	.1030	.0687	.0920	.0980
	(2.37)	(2.21)	(2.13)	(3.47)
Divorced	.0793	.0933	.0396	.0607
	(2.74)	(3.38)	(1.53)	(2.72)
Never				
Married	—	—	—	—
Children	—	—.0198	—	—.0007
	—	(—4.51)	—	(—.24)
Size of Urban				
Area				
Urban, Non				
SMSA	—	—	—	—
SMSA 250	.0332	.0920	.0523	.1458
	(1.98)	(3.86)	(1.54)	(4.19)
SMSA 500	.0727	.0956	.1098	.1833
	(3.89)	(3.65)	(2.83)	(4.61)
SMSA 750	.1411	.1524	.1349	.1316
	(7.30)	(5.46)	(3.55)	(4.46)

Table 3.4   Continued

Dependent Variable
  log (hourly wage)

	White Males	White Females	Black Males	Black Females
SMSA 750+	.1745	.2186	.2079	.3643
	(12.57)	(11.21)	(6.46)	(10.92)
Region				
North East	.0738	.0882	.1366	.1724
	(5.63)	(4.69)	(7.86)	(9.24)
North Central	.0749	.0646	.1479	.1376
	(5.85)	(3.52)	(9.37)	(8.00)
South	—	—	—	—
West	.1200	.1389	.2452	.2612
	(8.51)	(6.83)	(12.48)	(12.07)
Years of experience at which the hourly wage peaks	30.6	27.8	28.7	27.5
R^2	.43	.33	.46	.56
S.E.E	.4034	.4510	.3493	.3560
NOBS	8123	4962	3897	3502

Table 3.5 Wage Regressions Without Occupational Controls

Variable	Whites		Blacks	
	Male	Female	Male	Female
Constant	-.1321* (-2.91)	-.1165 (-1.56)	.0340 (.68)	.3035* (-5.03)
Experience				
Experience	.0205* (15.30)	.0156* (8.78)	.0136* (8.63)	.0073* (4.54)
Experience**2	-.000309* (-12.84)	-.000275* (-7.95)	-.000228* (-8.43)	-.000128* (-4.43)
Education				
Education	.0097 (1.49)	-.0254* (-2.18)	-.0435* (-6.66)	-.0563* (-6.52)
Education**2	.00235* (8.35)	.00353* (6.76)	.00410* (12.00)	.00540* (12.71)
Class of Worker				
Union	.0764* (6.49)	.1335* (6.02)	.2047* (13.42)	.1072* (4.66)
Nonunion Private Wage and Salary	-	-	.	-
Government	.0518* (2.47)	.1614* (6.45)	.1336* (5.40)	.1859* (7.48)
Self-Employed	-.0365 (-.99)	.1906* (2.01)	.0523 (.61)	-.1811 (-1.38)
Industry				
Agriculture	-.1719* (-4.12)	.4160* (2.19)	-.0679 (-1.32)	.0202 (.22)
Mining	.3435* (6.39)	.4891* (2.35)	.0849 (.48)	-
Construction	.3119* (14.81)	.3193* (4.96)	.3011* (12.49)	.0960 (.52)
Manufacturing-Durable	.2191* (13.09)	.2758* (10.63)	.2362* (11.03)	.2710* (7.60)
Manufacturing-Non Durable	.1855* (9.95)	.2163* (8.88)	.1759* (7.49)	.2377* (8.02)
Transportation	.1937* (8.22)	.3643* (6.44)	.2148* (7.48)	.5576* (5.91)
Communications	.2834* (6.61)	.3180* (6.44)	.2195* (2.50)	.3286* (4.59)

Table 3.5 Continued

Variable	Whites		Blacks	
	Male	Female	Male	Female
Utilities	.2191* (6.61)	.3301* (3.77)	.1410* (3.43)	.6546 (2.49)
Wholesale Trade	.1862* (7.56)	.2763* (6.83)	.1323* (4.22)	.3398* (4.82)
Retail Sale	-	-	-	-
Finance	.2262* (8.24)	.2504* (8.58)	.0269 (.69)	.2139* (4.37)
Business and Repair Services	.1361* (4.33)	.2255* (4.82)	.0964* (2.65)	.1771* (3.07)
Personal Service	-.1018* (-2.83)	-.1405* (-4.87)	-.1249* (-3.87)	-.0762* (-3.70)
Recreation	.0490 (.96)	.2246* (2.86)	.0237 (.44)	.1425 (1.76)
Professional Services	-.0676* (-2.80)	.1434* (6.21)	.0769* (2.69)	.1522* (6.30)
Public Administration	.1524* (5.11)	.2795* (6.42)	.2438* (7.08)	.2564* (6.91)
Health Problems	-.1122* (-6.65)	-.0785* (-2.92)	-.0860* (-3.97)	-.0314 (-1.47)
Part-Time	-.2200* (-10.53)	-.0706* (-4.14)	-.1147* (-4.89)	-.0264 (-1.61)
Migration				
Migration	-.0247 (-1.68)	-.1066* (-4.89)	.0052 (.44)	-.0319 (-1.66)
YRSM	.0072* (4.07)	.0088* (3.27)	-	.0020* (2.13)
YRSM**2	-.000143* (-3.08)	-.000140* (1.98)	-	-
Marital Status				
Spouse Present	.2160* (13.73)	.0996* (4.98)	.1275* (6.71)	.0932* (4.65)
Spouse Absent	.1233 (1.84)	.0859 (1.37)	.0429 (.75)	.0996* (2.19)

Table 3.5 Continued

Variable	Whites		Blacks	
	Male	Female	Male	Female
Widowed	.1276* (2.87)	.0605 (1.90)	.0978* (2.24)	.0868* (2.97)
Divorced	.0852* (2.88)	.0965* (3.42)	.0443 (1.68)	.0534* (2.31)
Children	-	-.0251* (-5.60)	-	-.0027 (.91)
Size of Urban Area				
Urban, Non SMSA	-	-	-	-
SMSA < 250	.0353* (2.05)	.1027* (4.21)	.0637 (1.85)	.1530* (4.24)
SMSA 250-500	.0759* (3.96)	.1009* (3.76)	.1168* (2.96)	.1917* (4.67)
SMSA 500-750	.1571* (7.93)	.1692* (5.93)	.1406* (3.64)	.1864* (4.42)
SMSA 750+	.1852* (13.03)	.2373* (11.92)	.2218* (6.80)	.3700* (10.73)
Region				
North East	.0642* (4.78)	.0923* (4.80)	.1478* (8.40)	.1764* (9.17)
North Central	.0700* (5.33)	.0639* (3.40)	.1469* (9.16)	.1464* (8.25)
West	.1090* (7.56)	.1201* (5.78)	.2359* (11.84)	.2503* (11.24)
F Statistic	139.68*	53.38*	83.27*	103.80*
R^2	.40	.30	.44	.53
Standard Error of Estimate	.41	.46	.36	.37
Number of Observations	8123	4962	3897	3502

[a] 't' values in parentheses.

* Significant at the 5% level.

Now define

(4) $\Delta \bar{Z}' \equiv \bar{Z}'_m - \bar{Z}'_f$

(5) $\Delta \hat{\beta} \equiv \hat{\beta}_f - \hat{\beta}_m.$

Upon substituting $\hat{\beta}_f \equiv \Delta \beta + \hat{\beta}_m$ into (3), we have

(6) $\ln (G+1) = \Delta \bar{Z}' \hat{\beta}_m - \bar{Z}'_f \Delta \hat{\beta}.$

If it is assumed that the current male wage structure would apply to both males and females in the absence of discrimination ($w^o_m = \bar{w}_m$), then it can be shown that the "justifiable" differential is estimated as follows:

(7) $\ln (J+1) = \ln (\bar{w}_m) - \ln (w^o_f) = \Delta \bar{Z}' \hat{\beta}_m.$

Similarly, the differential attributable to discrimination is estimated as

(8) $\ln (D+1) = \ln (w^o_f) - \ln (\bar{w}_f) = - \bar{Z}'_f \Delta \hat{\beta}.$

We have thus decomposed the gross wage differential (6) into the differential due to male-female differences in the selected characteristics (7) and the differential attributable to discrimination (8). An alternative decomposition results from the substitution of $\hat{\beta}_m \equiv \hat{\beta}_f - \Delta \hat{\beta}$ in (3):

(9) $\ln (G+1) = \Delta \bar{Z}' \hat{\beta}_f - \bar{Z}'_m \Delta \hat{\beta}.$

The decomposition given by (9) corresponds to the assumption that the current female wage structure would apply to both males and females in the absence of discrimination ($w^o_f = \bar{w}_f$). The differentials attributable to male-female differences in the selected variables and to discrimination are respectively

(10) $\ln (J+1) = \ln (w^o_m) - \ln (\bar{w}_f) = \Delta \bar{Z}' \hat{\beta}_f$ and

(11) $\ln (D+1) = \ln (\bar{w}_m) - \ln (w^o_m) = - \bar{Z}'_m \Delta \hat{\beta}.$

The above procedure was developed to handle the case in which the groups for whom we wish to look at the effects of discrimination are also the groups for whom we have estimated separate wage equations. For example, the estimated effects of discrimination for the entire urban SEO sample were derived from the wage equations estimated on the basis of the entire sample. In the case of telephone workers, their numbers in the SEO sample were too few to allow estimation of separate wage equations. Therefore, we had to predict the wages of female telephone workers in the absence of discrimination from the wage regressions for all males in the urban SEO sample. These regressions include a dummy variable for the communications industry. The modification adopted means that condition (2) will not in general be satisfied. In effect condition (2) has been replaced by

$$(12) \quad \ln{(\overline{w}_{tj})} \cong \overline{Z}'_{tj} \, \hat{\beta}_j = \ln{(w_{tj})} \qquad \begin{array}{l} j = m, f \\ t = \text{telephone workers} \end{array}$$

Table 3.6 gives the differences between the actual average log of the wages and the average predicted by applying the wage structure estimated for the entire SEO urban sample to the average characteristics of the telephone workers in the sample. These differences turned out to be quite small, ranging from virtually no difference for black females to a difference of about 5 percent for black male telephone workers.

Table 3.6   Actual and Predicted Wages in Natural Log Form

Group	Actual (1)	Predicted (2)	$\Delta \ln$ (WAGE) (3)=(1)-(2)
White Males	1.3394	1.3080	+0.0314
White Females: Total	0.7858	0.8046	-0.0188
Telephone Operators	0.7645	0.7903	-0.0258
Telephone Operators*	0.7645	0.8065	-0.0420
Black Males	0.9745	0.9230	+0.0515
Black Females: Total	0.7871	0.7818	+0.0053
Telephone Operators	0.7847	0.8113	-0.0266
Telephone Operators*	0.7847	0.7991	-0.0144

*Predicted wages derived from wage regressions with occupational control variables.

The pattern which emerges reveals that the wage equations slightly underpredict for the males and slightly overpredict for the females. This implies that actual male-female wage differentials among the telephone workers exceed predicted differentials. The actual and predicted wage differentials in logs are respectively

(13) $\ln (G_t + 1) = \ln (\bar{w}_{tm}) - \ln (\bar{w}_{tf})$

(14) $\ln (G_t + 1) = \ln (w_{tm}) - \ln (w_{tf})$.

Upon subtracting (14) from (13) and rearranging terms we obtain

(15) $\Delta \ln (G_t + 1) = \Delta \ln (w_{tm}) - \Delta \ln (w_{tf})$

where $\Delta \ln (w_{tj}) = \ln (\bar{w}_{tj}) - \ln (w_{tj})$ $j=m, f$

The values of $\Delta \ln (G_t + 1)$ are reported in Table 3.7.

Estimates of the discrimination coefficient were derived from

(16) $\ln (D_t + 1) = -\bar{Z}'_{tf} \Delta \beta$.

The justifiable differential was calculated as a residual:

(17) $\ln (J_t + 1) = \ln (G_t + 1) - \ln (D_t + 1)$.

If we had used the predicted rather than the actual gross wage differential in (17), the estimated proportions of the gross differential attributable to discrimination would have been larger.

Table 3.7 Differences Between Actual and Predicted Male-Female Wage Differentials

Male-Female Wage Differential	$\Delta \ln (G_t + 1)$
White Male-White Female Telephone Operator	+0.0572
White Male-White Female Telephone Operator[*]	+0.0734
White Male-Total White Female	+0.0502
Black Male-Black Female Telephone Operator	+0.0781
Black Male-Black Female Telephone Operator[*]	+0.0659
Black Male-Total Black Female	+0.0462
White Male-Black Female Telephone Operator	+0.0580
White Male-Black Female Telephone Operator[*]	+0.0458
White Male-Total Black Female	+0.0261

*Predicted wage for telephone operators derived from wage regression <u>with</u> occupational control variables.

4 Diagnosing Discrimination

Barbara R. Bergmann and Jill Gordon King

Our work on discrimination has convinced us that most acts of discrimination by employers take the form of segregation of occupations by race and sex. Employers tend to view certain occupations as "fitting" for black males, others as "fitting" for black females, and still others as appropriate to white females or white males. Exceptions are occasionally allowed, and the occupations thought appropriate to each group vary somewhat geographically. There is also some variation over time: the occupation of telephone operator, once the exclusive province of white males, and then of white females, is now apparently thought "fitting" for black women; they are now overrepresented there, having been very much underrepresented in most parts of the country in 1960.[1] Nevertheless, there has been remarkable stability in the racial and sexual classification of most jobs through time and across the country: craftsmen's jobs and the upper echelons of managerial ranks are reserved for white males; certain clerical jobs have been the preserve of white women; black men and women are thought to be "in their proper place" when doing jobs involving cleaning.

The results of discrimination through occupational segregation have been to cast severe disadvantages on white women and on blacks and members of other minorities of both sexes. Because the demand for their services has been artificially curtailed due to their exclusion from a large part of the labor market, the wages of women and blacks in those jobs to which they have been relegated have been lowered from a parity with the wages of equally qualified white males. Occupational segregation has also had the effect of increasing the unemployment rate among blacks and women. Lower wages when working and a higher chance of unemployment for blacks and for women have had a significant part in creating the persistent poverty problem in the United States and in fomenting the feelings of anger and injustice so prominent on the national scene today.

Research by several economists has indicated that firms which are sheltered from competition tend to discriminate more than firms which are subject to the full force of competition.[2] Companies which are sheltered from competition either because of their large size relative to the market or because they are in a field where regulation takes the place of competition seem to have the opportunity to ignore sources of black and female labor with impunity. Thus regulation of companies such as those in

1 For a survey of past practices in the telephone industry, see Bernard E. Anderson, *The Negro in the Public Utility Industries* (Philadelphia: University of Pennsylvania Press, 1970). See also Anderson's study, Chapter 8 of the present volume.
2 W. G. Shepherd, "Market Power and Racial Discrimination in White Collar Employment," *The Antitrust Bulletin* 14 (spring 1969) : 141–161. See also William S. Comanor, "Racial Discrimination in American Industry," Stanford University School of Business, Technical Report No. 5, August 1971.

the Bell System tends to create a sheltered environment in which discrimination by race and sex has the opportunity to flourish. It is incumbent on the Federal Communications Commission, in whose hands the regulatory power has been placed, to insure that the fact of that regulation not be permissive of employment discrimination, which is outlawed by federal statute.

In examining the employment records of the Bell companies, we were concerned with four questions:

1. Where did each company stand in terms of current numbers of employees by occupation and by race and sex?
2. What are appropriate goals for employment in each occupation by race and sex for each company?
3. How rapidly did each company appear to be moving towards these appropriate goals?
4. What changes in hiring practices would be necessary if progress towards appropriate goals were to be reasonably rapid?

Partial answers to the first question—where the companies stood—are to be found in the quarterly status reports for 1970 submitted to the Equal Employment Opportunity Commission by the companies. From these documents, we have extracted the percentages which white women and blacks of both sexes were of total employment in each of 16 occupations in each company as of December 31, 1970. This information is contained in Table 4.6 (See Appendix A to this chapter), and is shown as the second line for the three race-sex groups.

In order for information on employment composition to be meaningful, a comparison must be made with some benchmark. The benchmark must indicate on a realistic basis the fair share of each group in employment in a particular occupation. On what basis can such a "fair share" be computed? One principle with considerable appeal is that if for each occupation we can delimit the group in the labor force which is qualified for that occupation, then each race-sex group (white Anglo men, white Anglo women, black men, black women, Spanish-surnamed men, Spanish-surnamed women, etc.) would eventually have approximately the same share in the jobs of that occupation as they have in the qualified group. For example, if a job legitimately requires a college degree, and if Negro males constitute three percent of the group in the labor force with college degrees, then it seems reasonable, lacking information about other requirements, to say that Negro males should have three percent of jobs in that company of that particular type. Of course, job requirements which could be construed as altering the computed target based on labor force proportions alone must pass the test of relevance to actual job performance.

On this principle, and using data on population and education in each company's geographic area together with information on educational requirements for each type of job, we have computed targets for each occupation in each company for the three race-sex groups. The details of the methodology used to make these computations are contained in Appendix B. The results for each job and each company are shown on the fourth line in Table 4.6 for each race-sex group.

When we come to try to answer the question, "Where did the companies stand?" with respect to blacks, we must be careful to use an appropriate benchmark. In the New Jersey Bell Telephone Company, for example, 4.4 percent of the telephone craftsmen were black males. There are two possible benchmarks which can be used to judge whether this employment share represents discrimination. One is to be found in Table 4.1, where the percentage which black males were of all male employees is compared to the percentage of black males in the pool of male eligibles. This table shows that for New Jersey Bell, black males constituted 8.0 percent of males eligible for telephone crafts jobs. On this basis, New Jersey Bell had only 55 percent of the black male telephone craftsmen it would have had in the absence of discrimination against black males as against white males. A second possible benchmark is the "target" for black male telephone craftsmen shown in Table 4.6, which has been computed on the basis that allows black men a share equal to their share in the pool of eligibles, including female eligibles. That "target" value, which represents an estimate of what the situation will be when discrimination against blacks of both sexes and white women has ceased, is a 5.1 percent share of telephone crafts jobs for black males. On this basis, New Jersey Bell had 86 percent of the black male telephone craftsmen expected in the absence of all discrimination.

Which of these two benchmarks is most appropriate to use in judging whether New Jersey Bell has been discriminatory in hiring black males for telephone crafts jobs? We would argue that the past performance of the companies with respect to black males must be judged on the basis of their share in the pool of eligible males. After all, the companies have not kept the craftsmen jobs away from black men in order to give them to women—these jobs have been kept away from black men for the benefit of white men. This does not mean that the targets for telephone crafts jobs shown in Appendix A are irrelevant to the problem, and we shall return later to the question of their use in properly conceived affirmative action plans.

Black men have, of course, been denied entry to jobs traditionally considered "women's jobs," and some of these jobs, especially those largely monopolized by white women, have paid higher wages than some of those jobs allotted traditionally to black men. Thus, in trying to sort out the pattern of discrimination against black men, a comparison of their representation in the traditional women's occupations with the targets as shown in Table 4.6 is relevant.

With this in mind, we have compiled Table 4.2, which shows in a schematic way the pattern of discrimination against black males. For each company, for each job group, a "d" has been entered in the table if the black male share in total employment in that job was below 75 percent of the target share in Appendix A or if the

Table 4.1 Black Employment Share and Black Share in Qualified Workers of the Same Sex, by Bell Company and Occupation

	Offls & Mgrs	Accnt Audit	Engineers	Staff Specl	Technicians	Sales Mgt	Sales Nonmgt	Secry Mgt
New England Tel & Tel								
Black Males								
70 blk emp as % of male emp	.3	.6	.3	.8	.0	1.2	.0	.0
% of qualified males	1.3	1.2	1.2	1.2	1.7	1.4	1.4	1.7
Black Females								
70 blk emp as % of female emp	1.6	.0	.0	1.9	5.3	.0	3.8	.3
% of qualified females	1.5	1.5	1.5	1.5	1.9	1.5	1.5	1.9
Southern New England Tel								
Black Males								
70 blk emp as % of male emp	.4	.0	.5	1.7	3.4	.9	4.7	.0
% of qualified males	1.7	1.1	1.1	1.1	4.0	2.1	2.1	4.0
Black Females								
70 blk emp as % of female emp	3.2	6.9	.0	4.2	.0	.0	6.9	1.9
% of qualified females	2.2	1.7	1.7	1.7	4.8	2.6	2.6	4.8
New York Tel								
Black Males								
70 blk emp as % of male emp	1.4	.5	1.3	1.3	12.8	2.0	5.3	25.0
% of qualified males	4.3	2.9	2.9	2.9	7.8	5.3	5.3	7.8
Black Females								
70 blk emp as % of female emp	12.8	2.9	1.9	10.2	12.3	6.3	14.3	6.0
% of qualified females	6.3	5.1	5.1	5.1	9.8	7.1	7.1	9.8
New Jersey Bell								
Black Males								
70 blk emp as % of male emp	1.2	.0	1.3	2.0	15.1	2.0	4.9	.0
% of qualified males	3.2	2.1	2.1	2.1	8.0	3.9	3.9	8.0
Black Females								
70 blk emp as % of female emp	5.0	3.7	.9	5.6	9.1	.0	.0	4.3
% of qualified females	5.1	4.6	4.6	4.6	9.6	5.5	5.5	9.6
Bell of Pennsylvania								
Black Males								
70 blk emp as % of male emp	1.0	.0	.5	2.1	.0	1.9	7.4	.0
% of qualified males	3.3	2.3	2.3	2.3	7.3	3.9	3.9	7.3
Black Females								
70 blk emp as % of female emp	3.5	1.9	2.7	3.9	7.5	.0	.0	.0
% of qualified females	4.9	4.5	4.5	4.5	8.7	5.1	5.1	8.7

Table 4.1 Continued

	Cler & Steno	Tel Oper	Super S.A.	Service Reps	Bldg & Mtrvh	Tel Craft	Opera-tives	Service Workers
New England Tel & Tel								
Black Males								
70 blk emp as % of male emp	3.0	.0	.0	.0	1.8	1.6	2.8	4.4
% of qualified males	1.7	1.7	1.7	1.4	1.7	1.7	1.7	1.7
Black Females								
70 blk emp as % of female emp	2.9	4.6	3.4	2.0	.0	3.7	.0	2.4
% of qualified females	1.9	1.9	1.9	1.5	1.9	1.9	1.9	1.9
Southern New England Tel								
Black Males								
70 blk emp as % of male emp	5.8	.0	.0	.0	4.1	4.2	7.9	17.5
% of qualified males	4.0	4.0	4.0	2.1	4.0	4.0	4.0	4.0
Black Females								
70 blk emp as % of female emp	13.4	19.7	10.2	5.1	.0	.0	.0	7.1
% of qualified females	4.8	4.8	4.8	2.6	4.8	4.8	4.8	4.8
New York Tel								
Black Males								
70 blk emp as % of male emp	28.6	.0	.0	20.6	9.9	8.8	23.8	41.1
% of qualified males	7.8	7.8	7.8	5.3	7.8	7.8	7.8	7.8
Black Females								
70 blk emp as % of female emp	27.4	44.1	40.4	16.3	.0	14.3	18.8	19.1
% of qualified females	9.8	9.8	9.8	7.1	9.8	9.8	9.8	9.8
New Jersey Bell								
Black Males								
70 blk emp as % of male emp	10.5	.0	.0	50.0	5.2	4.4	22.5	20.4
% of qualified males	8.0	8.0	8.0	3.9	8.0	8.0	8.0	8.0
Black Females								
70 blk emp as % of female emp	16.4	26.4	19.6	5.6	.0	.0	.0	3.6
% of qualified females	9.6	9.6	9.6	5.5	9.6	9.6	9.6	9.6
Bell of Pennsylvania								
Black Males								
70 blk emp as % of male emp	5.9	.0	.0	.0	5.3	4.6	16.3	37.4
% of qualified males	7.3	7.3	7.3	3.9	7.3	7.3	7.3	7.3
Black Females								
70 blk emp as % of female emp	9.6	18.2	10.7	8.1	.0	10.5	.0	26.8
% of qualified females	8.7	8.7	8.7	5.1	8.7	8.7	8.7	8.7

Table 4.1 Continued

	Offls & Mgrs	Accnt Audit	Engineers	Staff Specl	Technicians	Sales Mgt	Sales Nonmgt	Secry Mgt
Chesapeake & Potomac Tel								
Black Males								
70 blk emp as % of male emp	1.7	.8	.9	1.9	.2	.5	3.1	33.3
% of qualified males	6.4	6.9	6.9	6.9	18.1	6.0	6.0	18.1
Black Females								
70 blk emp as % of female emp	5.9	1.2	.7	6.0	9.4	.0	7.7	5.3
% of qualified females	12.6	13.9	13.9	13.9	21.0	11.8	11.8	21.0
Southern Bell								
Black Males								
70 blk emp as % of male emp	.1	.0	.3	.4	.0	.0	.2	.0
% of qualified males	6.1	5.6	5.6	5.6	23.6	6.4	6.4	23.6
Black Females								
70 blk emp as % of female emp	.8	.0	.7	.8	3.4	.0	2.0	.0
% of qualified females	11.4	14.6	14.6	14.6	27.7	9.3	9.3	27.7
South Central Bell								
Black Males								
70 blk emp as % of male emp	.2	1.2	.3	.8	.0	.0	.0	.0
% of qualified males	6.4	5.9	5.9	5.9	22.8	6.8	6.8	22.8
Black Females								
70 blk emp as % of female emp	.5	.0	1.6	1.4	.8	.0	.0	.4
% of qualified females	12.2	15.4	15.4	15.4	27.2	10.2	10.2	27.2
Ohio Bell								
Black Males								
70 blk emp as % of male emp	2.8	4.5	1.2	3.3	1.7	3.6	7.6	.0
% of qualified males	3.6	2.7	2.7	2.7	7.7	4.1	4.1	7.7
Black Females								
79 blk emp as % of female emp	8.6	1.7	3.7	6.0	11.7	.0	6.1	2.6
% of qualified females	5.2	5.0	5.0	5.0	9.1	5.3	5.3	9.1
Cincinnati Bell, Inc								
Black Males								
70 blk emp as % of male emp	.8	.0	.0	2.4	5.3	3.1	.0	.0
% of qualified males	3.6	2.7	2.7	2.7	7.7	4.1	4.1	7.7
Black Females								
79 blk emp as % of female emp	2.1	.0	.0	2.1	.0	.0	.0	.0
% of qualified females	5.2	5.0	5.0	5.0	9.1	5.3	5.3	9.1

Table 4.1 Continued

	Cler & Steno	Tel Oper	Super S.A.	Service Reps	Bldg & Mtrvh	Tel Craft	Opera-tives	Service Workers
Chesapeake & Potomac Tel								
Black Males								
70 blk emp as % of male emp	24.3	.0	.0	25.0	30.0	5.5	48.1	79.1
% of qualified males	18.1	18.1	18.1	6.0	18.1	18.1	18.1	18.1
Black Females								
70 blk emp as % of female emp	19.1	29.1	16.7	12.5	.0	.0	100.0	89.1
% of qualified females	21.0	21.0	21.0	11.8	21.0	21.0	21.0	21.0
Southern Bell								
Black Males								
70 blk emp as % of male emp	6.1	.0	.0	.0	18.7	2.6	38.7	96.4
% of qualified males	23.6	23.6	23.6	6.4	23.6	23.6	23.6	23.6
Black Females								
70 blk emp as % of female emp	5.0	19.6	8.1	4.4	.0	1.7	.0	9C.7
% of qualified females	27.7	27.7	27.7	9.3	27.7	27.7	27.7	27.7
South Central Bell								
Black Males								
70 blk emp as % of male emp	5.1	.0	.0	.0	24.1	2.6	52.7	35.0
% of qualified males	22.8	22.8	22.8	6.8	22.8	22.8	22.8	22.8
Black Females								
70 blk emp as % of female emp	4.5	15.6	4.7	3.6	.0	1.5	.0	98.7
% of qualified females	27.2	27.2	27.2	10.2	27.2	27.2	27.2	27.2
Ohio Bell								
Black Males								
70 blk emp as % of male emp	15.2	.0	.0	.0	12.6	5.8	41.0	55.1
% of qualified males	7.7	7.7	7.7	4.1	7.7	7.7	7.7	7.7
Black Females								
70 blk emp as % of female emp	19.1	21.8	15.9	8.6	.0	6.5	50.0	45.7
% of qualified females	9.1	9.1	9.1	5.3	9.1	9.1	9.1	9.1
Cincinnati Bell, Inc								
Black Males								
70 blk emp as % of male emp	6.8	.0	.0	.0	4.2	3.4	23.1	28.8
% of qualified males	7.7	7.7	7.7	4.1	7.7	7.7	7.7	7.7
Black Females								
70 blk emp as % of female emp	8.1	24.6	16.9	5.4	.0	13.3	.0	13.8
% of qualified females	9.1	9.1	9.1	5.3	9.1	9.1	9.1	9.1

Table 4.1 Continued

	Offls & Mgrs	Accnt Audit	Engineers	Staff Specl	Technicians	Sales Mgt	Sales Nonmgt	Secry Mgt
Michigan Bell								
Black Males								
70 blk emp as % of male emp	1.8	.0	1.4	2.8	6.9	4.8	.0	.0
% of qualified males	4.1	3.0	3.0	3.0	8.7	4.9	4.9	8.7
Black Females								
70 blk emp as % of female emp	10.6	14.8	.0	7.1	8.5	16.7	15.4	2.6
% of qualified females	5.9	5.3	5.3	5.3	10.3	6.4	6.4	10.3
Indiana Bell								
Black Males								
70 blk emp as % of male emp	1.3	.0	2.7	1.4	.0	2.2	2.3	.0
% of qualified males	2.5	2.1	2.1	2.1	5.4	2.8	2.8	5.4
Black Females								
70 blk emp as % of female emp	4.0	9.1	.0	1.9	.0	14.3	17.6	.0
% of qualified females	3.8	3.8	3.8	3.8	6.5	3.9	3.9	6.5
Wisconsin Tel								
Black Males								
70 blk emp as % of male emp	.4	1.4	.0	.8	16.1	.9	.0	.0
% of qualified males	1.2	1.2	1.2	1.2	1.8	1.2	1.2	1.8
Black Females								
70 blk emp as % of female emp	1.4	.0	.0	3.1	8.3	.0	.0	.0
% of qualified females	1.2	1.2	1.2	1.2	2.1	1.3	1.3	2.1
Illinois Bell								
Black Males								
70 blk emp as % of male emp	2.4	.5	1.0	2.2	48.3	1.2	7.1	.0
% of qualified males	4.8	3.6	3.6	3.6	9.7	5.7	5.7	9.7
Black Females								
70 blk emp as % of female emp	8.3	1.2	2.3	7.7	23.3	20.6	21.0	.0
% of qualified females	7.0	6.4	6.4	6.4	11.7	7.4	7.4	11.7
Northwestern Bell								
Black Males								
70 blk emp as % of male emp	.4	.0	.1	.9	.0	.0	3.3	.0
% of qualified males	1.0	1.0	1.0	1.0	.9	.9	.9	.9
Black Females								
70 blk emp as % of female emp	.9	.0	2.2	2.2	1.9	.0	4.1	1.1
% of qualified females	1.0	1.1	1.1	1.1	1.0	1.0	1.0	1.0

Table 4.1 Continued

	Cler & Steno	Tel Oper	Super S.A.	Service Reps	Bldg & Mtrvh	Tel Craft	Opera-tives	Service Workers
Michigan Bell								
Black Males								
70 blk emp as % of male emp	9.7	.0	.0	.0	11.6	5.2	20.3	25.2
% of qualified males	8.7	8.7	8.7	4.9	8.7	8.7	8.7	8.7
Black Females								
70 blk emp as % of female emp	18.2	23.3	23.5	13.8	.0	26.3	50.0	35.4
% of qualified females	10.3	10.3	10.3	6.4	10.3	10.3	10.3	10.3
Indiana Bell								
Black Males								
70 blk emp as % of male emp	5.1	.0	.0	.0	9.4	5.4	53.1	50.0
% of qualified males	5.4	5.4	5.4	2.8	5.4	5.4	5.4	5.4
Black Females								
70 blk emp as % of female emp	9.7	10.7	5.4	5.2	.0	.0	.0	47.5
% of qualified females	6.5	6.5	6.5	3.9	6.5	6.5	6.5	6.5
Wisconsin Tel								
Black Males								
70 blk emp as % of male emp	.7	.0	.0	.0	5.5	1.7	9.1	10.5
% of qualified males	1.8	1.8	1.8	1.2	1.8	1.8	1.8	1.8
Black Females								
70 blk emp as % of female emp	5.2	6.2	5.0	2.0	.0	6.3	.0	6.0
% of qualified females	2.1	2.1	2.1	1.3	2.1	2.1	2.1	2.1
Illinois Bell								
Black Males								
70 blk emp as % of male emp	13.4	100.0	.0	100.0	7.3	7.2	22.6	65.0
% of qualified males	9.7	9.7	9.7	5.7	9.7	9.7	9.7	9.7
Black Females								
70 blk emp as % of female emp	17.7	23.5	12.7	18.3	.0	23.2	.0	52.8
% of qualified females	11.7	11.7	11.7	7.4	11.7	11.7	11.7	11.7
Northwestern Bell								
Black Males								
70 blk emp as % of male emp	2.5	.0	.0	.0	4.2	1.1	5.0	12.0
% of qualified males	.9	.9	.9	.9	.9	.9	.9	.9
Black Females								
70 blk emp as % of female emp	2.7	2.1	1.5	1.2	.0	6.3	.0	5.1
% of qualified females	1.0	1.0	1.0	1.0	1.0	1.0	1.0	1.0

Table 4.1 Continued

	Ofls & Mgrs	Accnt Audit	Engineers	Staff Specl	Technicians	Sales Mgt	Sales Nonmgt	Secry Mgt
Southwestern Bell								
Black Males								
70 blk emp as % of male emp	.4	.0	.5	.3	.0	.0	1.9	.0
% of qualified males	4.1	3.3	3.3	3.3	10.3	4.6	4.6	10.3
Black Females								
70 blk emp as % of female emp	1.5	.0	.8	2.4	3.2	.0	4.0	.5
% of qualified females	7.0	8.0	8.0	8.0	12.4	6.4	6.4	12.4
Mountain States Tel & Tel								
Black Males								
70 blk emp as % of male emp	.6	.0	.1	.0	.7	1.0	.6	.0
% of qualified males	1.7	1.3	1.3	1.3	1.7	2.0	2.0	1.7
Black Females								
70 blk emp as % of female emp	.7	.0	.0	.8	1.6	.0	.0	.4
% of qualified females	2.0	1.8	1.8	1.8	1.9	2.1	2.1	1.9
Pacific Northwest Bell								
Black Males								
70 blk emp as % of male emp	.7	.0	.1	.7	2.2	2.2	1.5	.0
% of qualified males	2.1	2.1	2.1	2.1	1.5	2.2	2.2	1.5
Black Females								
70 blk emp as % of female emp	2.6	.0	.0	3.2	.0	.0	5.1	2.9
% of qualified females	2.0	1.9	1.9	1.9	1.6	2.1	2.1	1.6
Pacific Tel & Tel								
Black Males								
70 blk emp as % of male emp	1.4	.4	.4	1.3	5.8	1.4	4.5	33.3
% of qualified males	4.8	3.9	3.9	3.9	5.4	5.5	5.5	5.4
Black Females								
70 blk emp as % of female emp	4.5	3.2	1.0	3.4	5.0	3.4	6.0	1.8
% of qualified females	5.7	5.1	5.1	5.1	6.4	6.1	6.1	6.4

Table 4.1 Continued

	Cler & Steno	Tel Oper	Super S.A.	Service Reps	Bldg & Mtrvh	Tel Craft	Opera-tives	Service Workers
Southwestern Bell								
Black Males								
70 blk emp as % of male emp	5.0	.0	.0	.0	35.4	3.0	44.5	70.5
% of qualified males	10.3	10.3	10.3	4.6	10.3	10.3	10.3	10.3
Black Females								
70 blk emp as % of female emp	5.8	16.6	5.0	3.5	.0	2.0	.0	60.0
% of qualified females	12.4	12.4	12.4	6.4	12.4	12.4	12.4	12.4
Mountain States Tel & Tel								
Black Males								
70 blk emp as % of male emp	2.6	7.7	.0	.0	6.5	1.1	7.8	16.0
% of qualified males	1.7	1.7	1.7	2.0	1.7	1.7	1.7	1.7
Black Females								
70 blk emp as % of female emp	2.6	3.7	1.9	1.0	.0	1.4	.0	22.9
% of qualified females	1.9	1.9	1.9	2.1	1.9	1.9	1.9	1.9
Pacific Northwest Bell								
Black Males								
70 blk emp as % of male emp	5.6	.0	.0	.0	1.3	2.1	8.7	8.5
% of qualified males	1.5	1.5	1.5	2.2	1.5	1.5	1.5	1.5
Black Females								
70 blk emp as % of female emp	5.3	4.1	2.5	1.7	.0	19.4	.0	15.0
% of qualified females	1.6	1.6	1.6	2.1	1.6	1.6	1.6	1.6
Pacific Tel & Tel								
Black Males								
70 blk emp as % of male emp	9.5	9.4	.0	12.5	3.5	4.0	11.8	25.5
% of qualified males	5.4	5.4	5.4	5.5	5.4	5.4	5.4	5.4
Black Females								
70 blk emp as % of female emp	12.6	12.3	10.2	6.8	.0	5.2	8.1	29.0
% of qualified females	6.4	6.4	6.4	6.1	6.4	6.4	6.4	6.4

Table 4.2 Summary of Employment Pattern of Black Males by Occupation and Company (1970)*

	Offls & Mgrs	Accnt & Audit	Engineers	Staff Specl	Techni-cians	Sales Mgt	Sales Nonmgt	Secry Mgt	Cler & Steno	Tel Oper	Super S.A.	Service Reps	Bldg & MtrVh	Tel Craft	Opera-tives
New England Tel and Tel	d,1	d	d,1		d		d	d	d	d	d	d			
Southern New England	d	d,t	d,t			d,t		d	d	d	d	d			
New York Tel	d	d	d	d,1		d		d	d	d	d	d			
New Jersey Bell	d	d	d,t			d,t		d	d	d	d	d	d,t	d,t	
Bell of Pennsylvania	d	d	d,1		d	d,t		d	d	d	d	d	d,t	d,t	
Chesapeake and Potomac	d	d	d	d,1	d	d,1	d	d	d	d	d	d		d,1	
Southern Bell	d	d	d	d	d	d	d	d	d	d	d	d		d	
South Central Bell	d	d	d	d	d	d	d	d	d	d	d	d		d	
Ohio Bell	d,1	d	d	d	d			d	d	d	d	d			
Cincinnati Bell	d	d	d	d,t		d		d	d	d	d	d	d,t	d	
Michigan Bell	d,1	d	d,1		d		d	d	d	d	d	d		d,t	
Indiana Bell	d,1	d		d,t	d			d	d	d	d	d			
Wisconsin Bell	d,1	d	d				d	d	d	d	d	d			
Illinois Bell	d,1	d	d	d		d		d	d	d	d	d		d,t	
Northwestern Bell	d,1	d	d		d	d		d	d	d	d	d			
Southwestern Bell	d	d	d		d	d		d	d	d	d	d		d	
Mountain States Tel	d,1	d	d	d	d		d	d	d,1	d	d	d			
Pacific Northwest Bell	d	d	d			d	d,t	d	d,1	d	d	d			
Pacific Tel and Tel	d	d	d	d,1	d	d	d	d	d	d	d	d	d,t	d,t	

*"d" indicates evidence of discrimination, "d,1" indicates evidence of discrimination but also of improvement, "d,t" indicates that although the targets in Appendix A were substantially met, racial discrimination is evidenced. (See text for details.)

black male share in male employment was less than 75 percent of the black male share of male eligibles as shown in Table 4.1.[3]

In Table 4.3 we have compiled a similar picture of discrimination against black women. Here again, data from Table 4.1 and from Appendix A have been used. For discrimination against white women, pictured in text Table 4.4, only data from Appendix A have been used.

Tables 4.2–4.4 make very clear the broad pattern of discrimination as practiced by the telephone companies against blacks of both sexes and white women. Black men have been excluded from white collar and crafts jobs. White and black women have been generally excluded from blue collar jobs. They have also been grossly underrepresented in most companies from sales jobs, both of the management and nonmanagement catagories. Our figures show that in the Officials and Managers category, white women were represented overall to a degree corresponding to their availability. However, this category ranges from people in low-level supervisory jobs to the upper echelons of management, and interpretation of performance in this category is impossible without a finer breakdown than was available to us.

The material we have prepared indicates that there is not a single company in the Bell System which has not discriminated significantly against black men, black women, and white women. Not one company can be rated as performing in even a remotely nondiscriminatory way. Nevertheless, there are a number of companies which deserve to be singled out for performance even poorer than the poor average of these companies: Southern Bell, South Central Bell, and Cincinnati Bell have particularly egregious records, especially with respect to black men and women.

What evidence is there of improvement in the performance of the companies of the Bell system? The roster of employees at any time will contain substantial numbers of employees hired one or more decades ago, as well as more recently hired employees. What is most germane to the evaluation of a company's current performance is the current hiring practices. Those hires currently being made are to fill vacancies which occur in the natural course of events—to replace those employees who leave and to expand the labor force of a company (if such expansion is occurring). It is these current hires and the future hires which will determine the speed with which the company advances from its current position toward the target percentages of minority and female representation.

We have developed a method of analyzing current hiring performance in terms of the implications of that current performance for the future.[4] If a firm currently falls short of a targeted share of employment in a particular job for a particular group, the

3 Where the target or share of eligibles was less than two percent, we have used 50 percent rather than 75 percent as the cutoff.
4 The details of the methodology are given in a paper by Barbara R. Bergmann and William R. Krause, "Evaluating and Forecasting Progress in Racial Integration of Employment," *Industrial and Labor Relations Review* 25 (April 1972) : 399–409.

Table 4.3 Summary of Employment Pattern of Black Females by Occupation and Company (1970)*

	Offls & Mgrs	Accnt Audit	Engin-eers	Staff Specians	Techni-cians	Sales Mgt	Sales Nonmgt	Secry Mgt	Cler & Steno	Tel Oper-S.A.	Super Oper-S.A.	Service Reps	Bldg & MtrVh	Tel Craft	Opera-tives
New England Tel & Tel	d	d	d			d		d					d	d	d
Southern New England		d		d		d		d,t					d	d	d
New York Tel	d,t	d	d			d		d,t					d	d	d
New Jersey Bell		d		d		d	d	d,t					d	d	d
Bell of Pennsylvania	d,t	d	d			d	d	d					d	d	d
Chesapeake and Potomac	d,l	d		d	d	d	d,l	d,l					d	d	d
Southern Bell	d	d		d	d	d	d	d	d	d,t	d,t	d,t	d	d	d
South Central Bell	d	d		d	d,l	d	d	d	d	d,t	d,l	d,t	d	d	d
Ohio Bell	d,t	d	d			d	d	d,t					d	d	d
Cincinnati Bell	d	d		d,t	d	d	d	d					d	d	d
Michigan Bell	d		d			d		d,l					d	d	d
Indiana Bell	d	d		d,t	d			d					d	d	d
Wisconsin Bell	d		d			d	d	d					d	d	d
Illinois Bell	d		d					d					d	d	d
Northwestern Bell	d	d		d		d							d	d,l	d
Southwestern Bell	d,l	d		d		d	d	d	d,t	d,t	d,t	d,t	d	d	d
Mountain States Tel	d		d	d		d	d	d,t			d,t	d,t	d	d	d
Pacific Northwest Bell	d	d				d							d	d,l	d
Pacific Tel and Tel	d,t	d		d,t				d,t					d	d	d

*"d" indicates evidence of discrimination, "d,l" indicates evidence of discrimination but also of improvement, "d,t" indicates that although the targets in Appendix A were substantially met, racial discrimination is evidenced. (See text for details.)

Table 4.4 Summary of Employment Pattern of White Females by Occupation and Company (1970)*

	Offls & Mgrs	Accnt Audit	Engin-eers	Staff Speclcians	Techni-cians	Sales Mgt	Sales Nonmgt	Secry Mgt	Cler & Steno	Tel Oper	Super S.A.	Service Reps	Bldg & Tel MtrVh	Tel Craft	Opera-tives
New England Tel & Tel	d		d										d,i	d	d
Southern New England	d		d	d		d	d						d	d	d
New York Tel	d		d			d							d	d	d
New Jersey Bell	d		d			d	d						d	d	d
Bell of Pennsylvania	d		d			d	d,i						d	d	d
Chesapeake and Potomac	d		d			d	d						d	d	d
Southern Bell	d		d			d	d						d	d	d
South Central Bell	d		d			d	d						d	d	d
Ohio Bell	d		d			d,i	d,i						d	d	d
Cincinnati Bell	d	d	d			d							d	d	d
Michigan Bell	d		d			d							d	d	d
Indiana Bell	d		d			d	d,i						d	d	d
Wisconsin Bell	d		d	d		d							d	d	d
Illinois Bell	d		d			d	d,i						d	d	d
Northwestern Bell	d		d			d	d						d	d	d
Southwestern Bell	d		d			d							d	d	d
Mountain States Tel	d,i		d			d	d,i						d	d	d
Pacific Northwest Bell	d		d		d,i	d							d	d	d
Pacific Tel and Tel	d		d			d							d	d	d

*"d" indicates evidence of discrimination, "d,i" indicates evidence of discrimination but also of improvement, "d,t" indicates that although the targets in Appendix A were substantially met, racial discrimination is evidenced. (See text for details.)

speed with which the firm will move towards that targeted share will depend on the share of that group in hiring, and on the speed with which vacancies open up. The speed with which vancancies open up depends, of course, on the labor turnover the company experiences and on the rate of growth or shrinkage in total employment in that job category. We have incorporated all of these considerations into our projection formula.

In Table 4.6 we show (on the third line for each group) for each of three race-sex groups our projection of the share of employment that group will have in 1980 of each company. The projections are in turn based on our estimates of hiring shares by race-sex group during 1970 (the estimate of hiring shares is shown on the first line for each group) and also on our estimates of separation rates. A description of the procedures we used to estimate the separation rates and the hiring rates is included in Appendix B. The projection to 1980 is based on the assumption that hiring rates and separation rates for each race-sex group in each job in each company would not change. Some of these separation and hiring rates are based on extremely small numbers of personnel actions, and small numbers have a tendency to move erratically. For these reasons, the 1980 employment share projection should be viewed, not as a categorical prediction of what will actually occur, but as a gauge of whether the general drift of hiring practices in the companies was in the right direction in 1970.

We have defined "substantial improvement" of current over past performance as involving a projected move from 1970 employment share to projected employment share in 1980 at least equal to 75 percent of the difference between the 1970 employment share and the target share, as shown in Appendix A. Where this criterion for substantial improvement has been met, we have placed the letter "i" in the corresponding place in Tables 4.2–4.4.[5] Thus Tables 4.2–4.4 present a convenient summary both of discriminatory past practices and of efforts to improve on past performance.

The overall impression one can draw from this material is that there has been some movement towards less discriminatory hiring practices, particularly with respect to black men in the Officials and Managers category, but that there are many areas where progress has appeared small or nonexistent. For black and white women, progress has been only very spotty. In some of the companies where past discrimination seems to have been strongest, such as Southern Bell, there seems to be a general lack of progress also. Just as none of the companies has anything approximating a clean record, so not a single one is making progress across the board.

In Table 4.7 (see Appendix A), we have computed hiring rates which we estimate would be sufficient to get the shares of employment to the targets shown in Table 4.6 by 1980. These "needed hiring rates" are valuable in judging the adequacy of af-

5 Where the targets of Appendix A to this chapter were substantially met, yet the citation of discrimination was made on the basis of racial discrimination as documented in Table 4.1, we have inserted the notation "t" instead of "i."

firmative action plans the companies submit, which should include numerical commitments on hiring.

A word deserves to be said concerning conflicts of interest between blacks and white women. As noted above, allowing the claims of white (and black) women to jobs up to now monopolized by white men means that the share of black men in the eligible group so defined is smaller than that share would be if the eligible group continued to be defined in a way that excluded women. When viewed in its proper light, this problem appears to lose much of its punch. We have computed white male targets in a manner similar to those in Appendix A, and present them, together with 1970 shares of white males in actual employment, in Table 4.5. In many of the occupations, the excess of white male employment over target levels is very large, with the crafts jobs being the outstanding example.[6] In these jobs, the room available for entrants who are not white males is so large that black males would constitute a relatively small percentage of those filling that "room" almost regardless of how the black male target was figured. There is room for substantial progress for all groups now discriminated against.

Those whose business it is to monitor progress in compliance with the laws against discrimination should therefore insist on progress for all groups. The overconcentration of white males in certain jobs and their almost complete absence in others is a key indicator of discriminatory performance and should be remedied. We may note in passing that when jobs are filled without discrimination due to race or sex there is good reason to believe that pay differentials between jobs requiring more or less similar qualifications will tend to disappear.[7] Thus the white males who will populate the jobs they now shun will not be making as great a financial sacrifice as might now appear.

Finally, we believe that the companies should be asked to make computations for themselves of the sort presented here. Undoubtedly, they could do so on a better basis than we have done since they would have better access to data on their own experience with rates of labor turnover, expected growth, hiring shares, and the like. They would also be able to make reports for groups we have been forced to omit from our calculations—Spanish-surnamed Americans, Indians, Orientals. On the basis of these computations they should be asked to show far greater and faster progress than we have been able to detect. Discrimination on the basis of race and sex is outlawed throughout the economy; the scandal of its continuing existence in companies shielded from the competitive market through federal regulation should be ended rapidly.

6 The approximate balance of white male employment with targets in the Officials and Managers category is most probably the balancing of an excess of women in the bottom ranks and a shortage in the top ranks.
7 See Barbara R. Bergmann, "The Effect on White Incomes of Discrimination in Employment," *Journal of Political Economy* 27 : 294–313.

Table 4.5 1970 Share of Total Employment and Target for White Males by Occupation for Bell Companies (percent)

	Offis & Mgrs	Accnt Audit	Engineers	Staff Specl	Technicians	Sales Mgt	Sales Nonmgt	Secry Mgt
New England Tel & Tel								
70 white male emp share	62.9	71.2	92.9	69.4	58.7	76.1	83.7	.0
Target	64.9	73.9	73.9	73.9	62.3	58.8	58.8	62.3
Southern New England Tel								
70 white male emp share	60.5	76.0	99.2	69.6	90.7	96.4	79.8	.0
Target	65.5	74.5	74.5	74.5	61.1	59.5	59.5	61.1
New York Tel								
70 white male emp share	55.8	60.7	91.2	65.5	51.0	88.0	49.7	.2
Target	63.9	72.5	72.5	72.5	58.0	58.2	58.2	58.0
New Jersey Bell								
70 white male emp share	54.1	54.2	88.0	71.6	56.3	95.5	91.6	.0
Target	66.5	76.6	76.6	76.6	58.4	59.8	59.8	58.4
Bell of Pennsylvania								
70 white male emp share	60.1	59.7	85.1	64.4	1.5	92.5	67.6	.0
Target	64.9	74.6	74.6	74.6	58.6	58.5	58.5	58.6
Chesapeake & Potomac Tel								
70 white male emp share	57.8	59.2	88.9	68.0	59.2	98.2	91.6	.3
Target	65.3	66.4	66.4	66.4	51.9	64.6	64.6	51.9
Southern Bell								
70 white male emp share	59.1	62.3	91.9	72.5	.9	93.5	77.4	.0
Target	59.9	65.7	65.7	65.7	48.1	56.1	56.1	48.1
South Central Bell								
70 white male emp share	55.7	75.5	91.1	73.7	.0	98.5	89.6	.0
Target	60.2	66.2	66.2	66.2	48.5	56.1	56.1	48.5
Ohio Bell								
70 white male emp share	57.1	57.1	90.4	56.1	49.0	93.0	73.9	.0
Target	64.4	73.3	73.3	73.3	99.9	58.5	58.5	99.9
Cincinnati Bell, Inc								
79 white male emp share	64.4	85.3	97.8	70.1	70.3	95.4	15.4	.0
Target	64.4	73.3	73.3	73.3	58.7	58.5	58.5	58.7

Table 4.5 Continued

	Cler & Steno	Tel Oper	Super S.A.	Service Reps	Bldg & Mtrvh	Tel Craft	Opera-tives	Service Workers
New England Tel & Tel								
70 white male emp share	6.1	.0	.1	.1	92.2	98.0	96.8	47.5
Target	62.3	62.3	62.3	58.8	62.3	62.3	62.3	62.3
Southern New England Tel								
70 white male emp share	13.3	.0	.0	.3	95.9	95.6	92.1	40.7
Target	61.1	61.1	61.1	59.5	61.1	61.1	61.1	61.1
New York Tel								
70 white male emp share	6.8	.0	.0	4.7	89.9	91.0	74.3	35.8
Target	58.0	58.0	58.0	58.2	58.0	58.0	58.0	58.0
New Jersey Bell								
70 white male emp share	6.6	.0	.0	.1	94.8	95.5	76.6	41.3
Target	58.4	58.4	58.4	59.8	58.4	58.4	58.4	58.4
Bell of Pennsylvania								
70 white male emp share	5.0	.0	.0	.0	94.7	95.2	83.7	34.7
Target	58.6	58.6	58.6	58.5	58.6	58.6	58.6	58.6
Chesapeake & Potomac Tel								
70 white male emp share	2.1	.0	.0	1.0	70.0	94.3	51.6	14.9
Target	51.9	51.9	51.9	64.6	51.9	51.9	51.9	51.9
Southern Bell								
70 white male emp share	3.5	.0	.0	.4	81.3	93.8	61.1	2.0
Target	48.1	48.1	48.1	56.1	48.1	48.1	48.1	48.1
South Central Bell								
70 white male emp share	4.3	.0	.0	.0	75.9	96.3	47.3	2.8
Target	48.5	48.5	48.5	56.1	48.5	48.5	48.5	48.5
Ohio Bell								
70 white male emp share	10.7	.0	.0	.3	87.0	93.8	58.5	15.4
Target	99.9	99.9	99.9	58.5	99.9	99.9	99.9	99.9
Cincinnati Bell, Inc								
70 white male emp share	13.3	.0	.0	.4	95.8	95.6	76.9	45.7
Target	58.7	58.7	58.7	58.5	58.7	58.7	58.7	58.7

Table 4.5 Continued

	Offls & Mgrs	Accnt Audit	Engineers	Staff Specl	Technicians	Sales Mgt	Sales Nonmgt	Secry Mgt
Michigan Bell								
70 white male emp share	66.1	78.4	90.4	67.5	35.5	91.1	11.4	.0
Target	63.6	72.0	72.0	72.0	58.5	58.1	58.1	58.5
Indiana Bell								
70 white male emp share	53.5	78.4	93.5	68.4	33.3	90.7	70.0	.0
Target	65.2	72.7	72.7	72.7	60.4	60.1	60.1	60.4
Wisconsin Tel								
70 white male emp share	63.8	73.6	97.1	78.6	60.5	96.5	68.0	.0
Target	65.1	72.8	72.8	72.8	63.2	59.9	59.9	63.2
Illinois Bell								
70 white male emp share	50.2	70.3	89.1	64.0	34.4	82.3	63.7	.0
Target	64.3	72.5	72.5	72.5	57.4	58.9	58.9	57.4
Northwestern Bell								
70 white male emp share	62.9	77.4	91.3	75.6	29.7	94.7	71.4	.0
Target	64.2	72.8	72.8	72.8	63.8	58.4	58.4	63.8
Southwestern Bell								
70 white male emp share	57.8	73.4	93.8	77.1	.2	93.5	67.9	.0
Target	63.0	69.9	69.9	69.9	57.1	58.3	58.3	57.1
Mountain States Tel & Tel								
70 white male emp share	67.9	87.9	98.2	84.6	70.5	96.4	74.5	.0
Target	65.5	72.6	72.6	72.6	63.8	60.8	60.8	63.8
Pacific Northwest Bell								
70 white male emp share	60.1	60.5	93.7	75.6	72.6	92.8	61.5	.0
Target	64.8	72.0	72.0	72.0	63.8	60.1	60.1	63.8
Pacific Tel & Tel								
70 white male emp share	57.4	72.9	88.8	66.5	20.8	77.6	20.3	.3
Target	63.9	71.3	71.3	71.3	60.8	59.0	59.0	60.8

Table 4.5 Continued

	Cler & Steno	Tel Oper	Super S.A.	Service Reps	Bldg & Mtrvh	Tel Craft	Opera-tives	Service Workers
Michigan Bell								
70 white male emp share	7.3	.0	.0	.0	88.4	89.0	78.8	28.6
Target	58.5	58.5	58.5	58.1	58.5	58.5	58.5	58.5
Indiana Bell								
70 white male emp share	5.9	.0	.0	.0	90.6	94.5	46.9	28.1
Target	60.4	60.4	60.4	60.1	60.4	60.4	60.4	60.4
Wisconsin Tel								
70 white male emp share	5.3	.0	.0	.0	94.5	97.5	90.9	26.5
Target	63.2	63.2	63.2	59.9	63.2	63.2	63.2	63.2
Illinois Bell								
70 white male emp share	15.0	.0	.0	.0	92.4	91.7	72.9	15.0
Target	57.4	57.4	57.4	58.9	57.4	57.4	57.4	57.4
Northwestern Bell								
70 white male emp share	5.9	.0	.0	.1	95.8	98.5	93.9	45.8
Target	63.8	63.8	63.8	58.4	63.8	63.8	63.8	63.8
Southwestern Bell								
70 white male emp share	3.6	.0	.0	.1	63.6	95.0	55.1	18.4
Target	57.1	57.1	57.1	58.3	57.1	57.1	57.1	57.1
Mountain States Tel & Tel								
70 white male emp share	10.3	.2	.0	.2	93.5	97.7	91.6	43.6
Target	63.8	63.8	63.8	60.8	63.8	63.8	63.8	63.8
Pacific Northwest Bell								
70 white male emp share	7.3	.1	.0	.1	97.4	96.8	89.9	41.2
Target	63.8	63.8	63.8	60.1	63.8	63.8	63.8	63.8
Pacific Tel & Tel								
70 white male emp share	6.2	.8	.1	.5	93.7	93.8	80.2	23.2
Target	60.8	60.8	60.8	59.0	60.8	60.8	60.8	60.8

Appendix A to Chapter 4

Employment and Hiring Share by Occupation for Bell Companies,
1970 and 1980

Table 4.6 Employment Share and Hiring Share in 1970, Estimated 1980 Employment Share, and Target for White Females, Black Males, and Black Females by Occupation for Bell Companies (Percent)

	Offls & Mgrs	Accnt Audit	Engin- eers	Staff Specl	Techni- cians	Sales Mgt	Sales Nonmgt	Secry Mgt
New England Tel & Tel								
White Females								
70 hire share	89.2	13.2	35.5	93.3	18.8	62.9	58.2	99.3
70 emp share	36.3	27.9	6.6	29.2	39.1	22.7	15.6	99.4
80 est emp share	66.8	10.0	18.8	67.5	18.7	27.9	24.4	99.3
Target	33.8	24.8	24.8	24.8	35.9	39.8	39.8	35.9
Black Males								
70 hire share	2.8	.0	64.5	6.7	.0	.3	.0	.0
70 emp share	.2	.4	.3	.6	.0	.9	.0	.0
80 est emp share	2.8	.2	46.8	6.7	.0	.7	.0	.0
Target	.8	.3	.9	.9	1.1	.3	.8	1.1
Black Females								
70 hire share	3.1	.0	.0	.0	5.4	.0	1.3	.3
70 emp share	.6	.0	.0	.6	2.2	.0	.6	.3
80 est emp share	2.1	.0	.0	.1	3.1	.0	.5	.3
Target	.5	.4	.4	.4	.7	.6	.6	.7
Southern New England Tel								
White Females								
70 hire share	37.7	92.7	.0	94.9	2.9	8.3	42.5	98.0
70 emp share	38.0	21.6	.3	27.9	6.1	2.7	15.2	98.1
80 est emp share	31.4	69.6	.0	72.3	3.5	2.9	20.3	98.1
Target	32.6	24.3	24.3	24.3	34.6	38.2	38.2	34.6
Black Males								
70 hire share	.2	.0	.5	5.1	1.0	.8	21.9	.0
70 emp share	.2	.0	.5	1.2	3.2	.9	3.9	.0
80 est emp share	.2	.0	.5	4.7	2.0	.9	22.3	.0
Target	1.1	.8	.8	.8	2.6	1.3	1.3	2.6
Black Females								
70 hire share	1.9	6.3	.0	.0	.0	.0	3.2	1.9
70 emp share	1.3	1.6	.0	1.2	.0	.0	1.1	1.9
80 est emp share	1.4	5.0	.0	.2	.0	.0	1.4	1.8
Target	.8	.4	.4	.4	1.7	1.0	1.0	1.7

Table 4.6 Continued

	Cler & Steno	Tel Oper	Super S.A.	Service Reps	Bldg & Mtrvh	Tel Craft	Opera-tives	Service Workers
New England Tel & Tel								
White Females								
70 hire share	93.3	91.2	93.7	97.6	99.5	.0	.0	65.3
70 emp share	90.7	95.0	96.3	97.8	5.8	.2	.4	48.8
80 est emp share	91.7	91.6	94.0	97.1	56.7	.0	.0	42.2
Target	35.9	35.9	35.9	39.8	35.9	35.9	35.9	35.9
Black Males								
70 hire share	.1	.0	.0	.0	.5	1.4	22.2	.0
70 emp share	.2	.0	.0	.0	1.7	1.6	2.8	2.2
80 est emp share	.2	.0	.0	.0	1.1	1.4	16.7	.2
Target	1.1	1.1	1.1	.8	1.1	1.1	1.1	1.1
Black Females								
70 hire share	5.1	7.5	6.3	1.4	.0	.0	.0	1.9
70 emp share	2.7	4.6	3.4	2.0	.0	.0	.0	1.2
80 est emp share	4.7	7.1	5.9	1.4	.0	.0	.0	1.2
Target	.7	.7	.7	.6	.7	.7	.7	.7
Southern New England Tel								
White Females								
70 hire share	83.1	100.0	76.4	89.9	.0	1.7	.0	76.1
70 emp share	74.3	80.3	89.9	94.4	.0	.2	.0	47.1
80 est emp share	81.8	99.8	77.5	89.7	.0	1.0	.0	64.4
Target	34.6	34.6	34.6	38.2	34.6	34.6	34.6	34.6
Black Males								
70 hire share	.0	.0	.0	.0	2.2	.0	.0	.0
70 emp share	.8	.0	.0	.0	4.1	4.2	7.9	8.6
80 est emp share	.1	.0	.0	.0	2.7	1.4	1.3	.5
Target	2.6	2.6	2.6	1.3	2.6	2.6	2.6	2.6
Black Females								
70 hire share	9.1	.0	23.0	4.4	.0	.0	.0	5.6
70 emp share	11.5	19.7	10.1	5.1	.0	.0	.0	3.6
80 est emp share	8.7	.2	21.9	4.2	.0	.0	.0	4.5
Target	1.7	1.7	1.7	1.0	1.7	1.7	1.7	1.7

Table 4.6 Continued

	Offls & Mgrs	Accnt Audit	Engineers	Staff Specl	Techni- cians	Sales Mgt	Sales Nonmgt	Secry Mgt
New York Tel								
White Females								
70 hire share	40.8	65.4	15.9	33.0	18.6	24.4	75.1	89.0
70 emp share	37.8	37.9	7.3	29.9	36.5	9.6	40.7	93.5
80 est emp share	32.4	51.0	10.0	24.7	17.6	15.7	70.6	88.3
Target	31.1	24.0	24.0	24.0	33.5	35.8	35.8	33.5
Black Males								
70 hire share	1.4	.2	1.0	3.6	16.1	.0	.0	.0
70 emp share	.8	.3	1.2	.9	7.5	1.8	2.8	.1
80 est emp share	1.5	.2	1.1	3.3	14.9	.2	.3	.1
Target	2.8	2.2	2.2	2.2	4.9	3.2	3.2	4.9
Black Females								
70 hire share	11.8	1.1	1.0	4.8	7.2	1.8	24.0	11.6
70 emp share	5.6	1.1	.1	3.4	5.1	.6	6.8	6.0
80 est emp share	8.4	.8	.6	3.3	5.2	1.1	21.3	10.9
Target	2.2	1.3	1.3	1.3	3.6	2.7	2.7	3.6
New Jersey Bell								
White Females								
70 hire share	28.4	97.4	11.5	39.1	55.6	5.2	.0	79.0
70 emp share	42.9	44.1	10.8	25.3	30.6	2.5	3.6	95.7
80 est emp share	26.5	84.0	9.2	31.2	45.7	1.4	.1	80.3
Target	29.7	20.8	20.8	20.8	33.0	35.7	35.7	33.0
Black Males								
70 hire share	1.0	.0	6.6	.0	12.3	.9	6.1	.0
70 emp share	.6	.0	1.1	1.5	10.0	2.0	4.7	.0
80 est emp share	.9	.0	5.3	.3	13.6	1.3	5.5	.0
Target	2.1	1.6	1.6	1.6	5.1	2.5	2.5	5.1
Black Females								
70 hire share	3.2	.0	.1	.0	24.6	.0	.0	20.7
70 emp share	2.3	1.7	.1	1.5	3.1	.0	.0	4.3
80 est emp share	2.5	.2	.1	.2	18.0	.0	.0	19.4
Target	1.6	1.0	1.0	1.0	3.5	2.1	2.1	3.5

Table 4.6 Continued

	Cler & Steno	Tel Oper	Super S.A.	Service Reps	Bldg & Mtrvh	Tel Craft	Opera-tives	Service Workers
New York Tel								
White Females								
70 hire share	60.3	56.7	52.4	72.3	.0	.4	2.7	30.4
70 emp share	65.5	55.9	59.6	78.6	.0	.1	2.0	31.6
80 est emp share	60.3	58.1	53.8	75.2	.0	.3	2.8	24.0
Target	33.5	33.5	33.5	35.8	33.5	33.5	33.5	33.5
Black Males								
70 hire share	3.4	.0	.0	2.0	15.3	12.5	32.0	38.8
70 emp share	2.7	.0	.0	1.2	9.9	8.7	23.3	25.0
80 est emp share	3.8	.0	.0	1.4	13.5	11.2	30.3	43.2
Target	4.9	4.9	4.9	3.2	4.9	4.9	4.9	4.9
Black Females								
70 hire share	30.1	42.1	46.3	18.2	.0	.0	.3	9.3
70 emp share	24.8	44.1	40.4	15.4	.0	.0	.5	7.5
80 est emp share	28.3	40.7	44.9	17.8	.0	.0	.3	6.9
Target	3.6	3.6	3.6	2.7	3.6	3.6	3.6	3.6
New Jersey Bell								
White Females								
70 hire share	74.8	71.7	87.7	95.3	.0	.2	.3	49.8
70 emp share	77.2	73.5	80.4	94.3	.0	.0	.3	46.4
80 est emp share	73.6	72.8	88.0	95.1	.0	.2	.2	45.0
Target	33.0	33.0	33.0	35.7	33.0	33.0	33.0	33.0
Black Males								
70 hire share	.?	.0	.0	.0	2.5	5.6	34.0	11.0
70 emp share	.8	.0	.0	.1	5.2	4.4	22.4	10.6
80 est emp share	.2	.0	.0	.1	2.8	5.2	32.0	11.5
Target	5.1	5.1	5.1	2.5	5.1	5.1	5.1	5.1
Black Females								
70 hire share	14.2	26.5	10.6	3.5	.0	.0	.0	.4
70 emp share	15.2	26.4	19.6	5.6	.0	.0	.0	1.7
80 est emp share	13.3	25.4	10.3	3.3	.0	.0	.0	.4
Target	3.5	3.5	3.5	2.1	3.5	3.5	3.5	3.5

Table 4.6 Continued

	Offls & Mgrs	Accnt Audit	Engineers	Staff Specl	Technicians	Sales Mgt	Sales Nonmgt	Secry Mgt
Bell of Pennsylvania								
White Females								
70 hire share	44.8	32.0	22.5	17.0	.0	5.2	97.3	100.0
70 emp share	37.9	39.5	14.0	32.8	91.2	5.7	27.0	100.0
80 est emp share	35.2	28.3	15.2	17.4	33.1	1.8	71.6	100.0
Target	31.3	22.6	22.6	22.6	33.6	37.1	37.1	33.6
Black Males								
70 hire share	.5	.0	6.0	29.1	.0	1.2	2.7	.0
70 emp share	.6	.0	.5	1.4	.0	1.8	5.4	.0
80 est emp share	.6	.0	3.9	20.1	.0	1.4	5.8	.0
Target	2.1	1.8	1.8	1.8	4.6	2.4	2.4	4.6
Black Females								
70 hire share	.0	13.5	1.2	9.1	.0	.0	.0	.0
70 emp share	1.4	.8	.4	1.3	7.4	.0	.0	.0
80 est emp share	.3	7.8	.7	5.2	2.5	.0	.0	.0
Target	1.6	1.1	1.1	1.1	3.2	2.0	2.0	3.2
Chesapeake & Potomac Tel								
White Females								
70 hire share	34.9	59.5	27.6	43.6	34.0	.0	1.7	84.1
70 emp share	38.8	39.8	10.2	28.7	36.8	1.4	5.1	94.2
80 est emp share	27.7	45.1	16.9	31.1	26.5	.0	.8	85.1
Target	26.5	24.7	24.7	24.7	28.9	27.6	27.6	28.9
Black Males								
70 hire share	3.5	.2	.0	14.1	.0	14.9	.0	.1
70 emp share	1.0	.5	.8	1.4	.1	.5	3.0	.2
80 est emp share	3.2	.3	.2	11.7	.1	12.1	.4	.1
Target	4.4	.3	.9	4.9	11.5	4.1	4.1	11.5
Black Females								
70 hire share	7.4	.3	.1	.0	.0	.0	10.3	15.3
70 emp share	2.4	.5	.1	1.8	3.8	.0	.4	5.3
80 est emp share	4.8	.3	.1	.2	.7	.0	4.5	14.2
Target	3.8	4.0	4.0	4.0	7.7	3.7	3.7	7.7

Table 4.6 Continued

	Cler & Steno	Tel Oper	Super S.A.	Service Reps	Bldg & Mtrvh	Tel Craft	Opera-tives	Service Workers
Bell of Pennsylvania								
White Females								
70 hire share	85.7	97.5	89.6	95.8	.0	1.1	.0	51.5
70 emp share	85.6	81.7	89.3	91.8	.0	.2	.0	32.7
80 est emp share	85.0	96.9	90.0	95.8	.0	.4	.0	44.1
Target	33.6	33.6	33.6	37.1	33.6	33.6	33.6	33.6
Black Males								
70 hire share	.9	.0	.0	.0	37.9	10.2	.0	.0
70 emp share	.3	.0	.0	.0	5.3	4.6	16.3	20.7
80 est emp share	1.0	.0	.0	.0	17.6	6.6	4.2	5.6
Target	4.6	4.6	4.6	2.4	4.6	4.6	4.6	4.6
Black Females								
70 hire share	12.9	.1	9.8	3.5	.0	.0	.0	45.5
70 emp share	9.1	18.2	10.7	8.1	.0	.0	.0	12.0
80 est emp share	11.8	.8	9.3	3.4	.0	.0	.0	36.2
Target	3.2	3.2	3.2	2.0	3.2	3.2	3.2	3.2
Chesapeake & Potomac Tel								
White Females								
70 hire share	75.7	73.4	77.2	93.1	.0	.5	.0	5.1
70 emp share	78.5	70.8	83.3	86.2	.0	.1	.0	3.1
80 est emp share	76.7	74.4	78.2	92.5	.0	.3	.0	3.8
Target	28.9	28.3	28.9	27.6	28.9	28.3	28.9	28.9
Black Males								
70 hire share	1.7	.0	.0	.0	27.3	14.0	6.6	33.7
70 emp share	.7	.0	.0	.3	30.0	5.5	48.1	56.6
80 est emp share	1.6	.0	.0	.0	27.5	10.7	11.0	43.4
Target	11.5	11.5	11.5	4.1	11.5	11.5	11.5	11.5
Black Females								
70 hire share	20.0	24.2	21.7	3.8	.0	.0	.2	44.2
70 emp share	18.6	29.1	16.7	12.3	.0	.0	.2	25.4
80 est emp share	19.1	23.3	20.7	3.8	.0	.0	.1	30.7
Target	7.7	7.7	7.7	3.7	7.7	7.7	7.7	7.7

Table 4.6 Continued

	Offls & Mgrs	Accnt Audit	Engineers	Staff Specl	Technicians	Sales Mgt	Sales Nonmgt	Secry Mgt
Southern Bell								
White Females								
70 hire share	51.5	74.0	21.3	70.0	94.3	13.4	19.4	100.0
70 emp share	40.6	37.7	7.7	27.0	95.7	6.5	22.0	100.0
80 est emp share	32.9	50.1	9.9	44.7	94.4	7.3	11.3	100.0
Target	32.2	26.0	26.0	26.0	26.8	36.3	36.3	26.8
Black Males								
70 hire share	.3	.0	.2	1.4	.0	.0	.1	.0
70 emp share	.0	.0	.3	.3	.0	.0	.1	.0
80 est emp share	.3	.0	.3	.4	.0	.0	.1	.0
Target	3.9	3.3	3.9	3.9	14.9	3.9	3.9	14.9
Black Females								
70 hire share	.9	.0	.1	2.9	5.3	.0	.0	.0
70 emp share	.3	.0	.1	.2	3.3	.0	.4	.0
80 est emp share	.5	.0	.1	1.7	4.7	.0	.0	.0
Target	4.0	4.4	4.4	4.4	10.3	3.7	3.7	10.3
South Central Bell								
White Females								
70 hire share	61.0	99.5	19.5	69.6	87.5	.0	25.7	99.6
70 emp share	44.0	23.6	8.5	25.3	99.2	1.5	10.4	99.6
80 est emp share	40.4	62.8	8.9	40.5	90.5	.0	10.5	99.7
Target	31.5	25.1	25.1	25.1	27.1	35.7	35.7	27.1
Black Males								
70 hire share	1.3	.5	2.9	.0	.0	.0	.0	.0
70 emp share	.1	.9	.3	.6	.0	.0	.0	.0
80 est emp share	1.1	.9	1.8	.3	.0	.0	.0	.0
Target	4.1	4.1	4.1	4.1	14.3	4.1	4.1	14.3
Black Females								
70 hire share	.3	.0	.2	1.5	12.5	.0	.0	.3
70 emp share	.2	.0	.1	.4	.8	.0	.0	.4
80 est emp share	.2	.0	.1	.8	9.4	.0	.0	.3
Target	4.3	4.6	4.6	4.6	10.1	4.0	4.0	10.1

Table 4.6 Continued

	Cler & Steno	Tel Oper	Super S.A.	Service Reps	Bldg & Mtrvh	Tel Craft	Opera-tives	Service Workers
Southern Bell								
White Females								
70 hire share	92.2	76.4	93.5	95.1	.0	8.7	.8	9.6
70 emp share	91.4	80.4	91.9	95.3	.0	3.6	.3	4.2
80 est emp share	90.3	77.3	93.8	95.2	.0	5.2	.6	7.5
Target	26.8	26.8	26.8	36.3	26.8	26.8	26.8	26.8
Black Males								
70 hire share	.1	.0	.0	.0	41.5	1.0	39.8	15.6
70 emp share	.2	.0	.0	.0	18.7	2.5	38.6	52.4
80 est emp share	.2	.0	.0	.0	32.8	1.5	38.6	34.5
Target	14.9	14.9	14.9	3.9	14.9	14.9	14.9	14.9
Black Females								
70 hire share	4.9	22.5	5.6	4.3	.0	.3	.0	72.7
70 emp share	4.8	19.6	8.1	4.4	.0	.1	.0	41.4
80 est emp share	4.6	21.5	5.3	4.1	.0	.2	.0	53.7
Target	10.3	10.3	10.3	3.7	10.3	10.3	10.3	10.3
South Central Bell								
White Females								
70 hire share	90.1	77.2	87.1	95.6	.0	11.4	.0	.0
70 emp share	91.2	84.4	95.3	96.4	.0	1.1	.0	.6
80 est emp share	68.3	78.3	87.8	95.8	.0	4.2	.0	.0
Target	27.1	27.1	27.1	35.7	27.1	27.1	27.1	27.1
Black Males								
70 hire share	.3	.0	.0	.0	100.0	9.8	51.6	20.0
70 emp share	.2	.0	.0	.0	24.1	2.5	52.7	53.8
80 est emp share	.5	.0	.0	.0	55.8	5.6	51.1	48.4
Target	14.3	14.3	14.3	4.1	14.3	14.3	14.3	14.3
Black Females								
70 hire share	7.2	21.2	12.5	4.2	.0	.0	.0	80.0
70 emp share	4.3	15.6	4.7	3.6	.0	.0	.0	42.7
80 est emp share	6.6	20.2	11.8	4.0	.0	.0	.0	50.8
Target	10.1	10.1	10.1	4.0	10.1	10.1	10.1	10.1

Table 4.6 Continued

	Offls & Mgrs	Acnt Audit	Engineers	Staff Specl	Technicians	Sales Mgt	Sales Nonmgt	Secry Mgt
Ohio Bell								
White Females								
70 hire share	32.7	95.2	28.6	54.8	100.0	50.0	43.7	86.0
70 emp share	37.6	39.5	8.2	39.2	44.3	3.5	18.8	97.4
80 est emp share	24.8	71.5	15.0	40.1	71.9	42.1	37.4	87.5
Target	31.5	23.4	23.4	23.4	33.1	36.9	36.9	33.1
Black Males								
70 hire share	2.5	3.1	.0	2.5	.0	50.0	7.5	.0
70 emp share	1.6	2.7	1.1	1.9	.9	3.5	6.1	.0
80 est emp share	2.6	4.0	.4	2.9	.5	47.0	7.6	.0
Target	2.3	2.1	2.1	2.1	4.9	2.5	2.5	4.9
Black Females								
70 hire share	10.5	1.6	.0	10.7	.0	.0	1.9	13.9
70 emp share	3.5	.7	.3	2.5	5.9	.0	1.2	2.6
80 est emp share	6.2	1.2	.0	6.7	.9	.0	1.5	12.4
Target	1.7	1.2	1.2	1.2	3.3	2.1	2.1	3.3
Cincinnati Bell, Inc								
White Females								
70 hire share	75.0	26.4	3.1	47.3	41.2	2.4	97.8	100.0
70 emp share	34.3	14.7	2.2	27.3	25.8	1.5	84.6	100.0
80 est emp share	52.6	15.3	1.7	30.7	30.8	.9	92.1	100.0
Target	31.5	23.4	23.4	23.4	33.1	36.9	36.9	33.1
Black Males								
70 hire share	.3	.0	.0	2.9	1.7	1.6	.0	.0
70 emp share	.5	.0	.0	1.8	3.9	3.1	.0	.0
80 est emp share	.5	.0	.0	2.9	2.9	1.9	.0	.0
Target	2.3	2.1	2.1	2.1	4.9	2.5	2.5	4.9
Black Females								
70 hire share	.0	.0	.0	2.0	.0	.0	.0	.0
70 emp share	.7	.0	.0	.6	.0	.0	.0	.0
80 est emp share	.1	.0	.0	1.2	.0	.0	.0	.0
Target	1.7	1.2	1.2	1.2	3.3	2.1	2.1	3.3

Table 4.6 Continued

	Cler & Steno	Tel Oper	Super S.A.	Service Reps	Bldg & Mtrvh	Tel Craft	Opera-tives	Service Workers
Ohio Bell								
White Females								
70 hire share	91.6	89.5	97.5	97.3	.0	5.4	.7	52.4
70 emp share	70.5	78.2	84.1	91.1	.0	.4	.4	35.7
80 est emp share	86.4	89.2	97.2	97.0	.0	2.0	.3	50.4
Target	33.1	33.1	33.1	36.9	33.1	33.1	33.1	33.1
Black Males								
70 hire share	.0	.0	.0	.0	15.2	.0	26.1	.0
70 emp share	1.9	.0	.0	.0	12.6	5.7	40.7	18.9
80 est emp share	.4	.0	.0	.0	13.6	2.6	29.0	2.5
Target	4.9	4.9	4.9	2.5	4.9	4.9	4.9	4.9
Black Females								
70 hire share	4.2	6.5	1.3	2.1	.0	1.8	.7	46.4
70 emp share	16.7	21.8	15.9	8.5	.0	.0	.4	30.1
80 est emp share	4.5	6.6	1.7	2.1	.0	.6	.3	42.1
Target	3.3	3.3	3.3	2.1	3.3	3.3	3.3	3.3
Cincinnati Bell, Inc								
White Females								
70 hire share	86.0	56.9	77.2	87.2	.0	2.3	.0	56.8
70 emp share	78.9	75.4	83.1	94.2	.0	.9	.0	30.9
80 est emp share	85.5	58.7	78.1	88.9	.0	1.5	.0	41.2
Target	33.1	33.1	33.1	36.9	33.1	33.1	33.1	33.1
Black Males								
70 hire share	.0	.0	.0	.0	4.2	.0	4.9	.0
70 emp share	1.0	.0	.0	.0	4.2	3.4	23.1	18.5
80 est emp share	.1	.0	.0	.0	4.1	1.5	5.3	2.2
Target	4.9	4.9	4.9	2.5	4.9	4.9	4.9	4.9
Black Females								
70 hire share	13.1	38.8	17.8	11.2	.0	.4	.0	9.2
70 emp share	6.9	24.6	16.3	5.4	.0	.1	.0	4.9
80 est emp share	12.1	37.1	17.0	10.7	.0	.2	.0	6.3
Target	3.3	3.3	3.3	2.1	3.3	3.3	3.3	3.3

Table 4.6 Continued

	Offls & Mgrs	Accnt Audit	Engineers	Staff Specl	Technicians	Sales Mgt	Sales Nonmgt	Secry Mgt
Michigan Bell								
White Females								
70 hire share	39.1	21.9	13.7	46.2	100.0	42.1	79.9	62.7
70 emp share	29.0	18.4	8.0	28.3	56.6	3.6	75.0	37.4
80 est emp share	29.0	16.2	8.7	33.7	89.3	6.8	66.6	64.4
Target	31.7	24.5	24.5	24.5	32.3	36.5	36.5	32.3
Black Males								
70 hire share	2.4	.0	8.4	.0	.0	.0	.0	.0
70 emp share	1.2	.0	1.3	2.0	2.6	4.6	.0	.0
80 est emp share	2.4	.0	6.7	.5	.6	.7	.0	.0
Target	2.7	2.2	2.2	2.2	5.6	3.0	3.0	5.6
Black Females								
70 hire share	6.8	21.8	.0	1.9	.0	8.5	17.9	37.1
70 emp share	3.5	3.2	.0	2.2	5.3	.7	13.6	2.6
80 est emp share	4.6	13.9	.0	1.4	1.0	1.3	14.1	35.4
Target	2.0	1.4	1.4	1.4	3.7	2.5	2.5	3.7
Indiana Bell								
White Females								
70 hire share	.0	45.8	13.4	100.0	69.2	.0	79.5	100.0
70 emp share	43.9	19.6	3.9	30.0	66.7	6.2	23.3	100.0
80 est emp share	10.7	25.0	5.8	62.6	66.8	.3	69.5	100.0
Target	31.9	24.8	24.8	24.8	33.8	36.7	36.7	33.8
Black Males								
70 hire share	10.3	.0	9.4	.0	.0	.0	3.3	.0
70 emp share	.7	.0	2.6	1.0	.0	2.1	1.7	.0
80 est emp share	6.4	.0	5.9	.5	.0	.3	4.2	.0
Target	1.6	1.5	1.5	1.5	3.5	1.7	1.7	3.5
Black Females								
70 hire share	.0	1.1	.0	.0	.0	.0	17.2	.0
70 emp share	1.8	2.0	.0	.6	.0	1.0	5.0	.0
80 est emp share	.4	.3	.0	.1	.0	.0	14.3	.0
Target	1.3	1.0	1.0	1.0	2.4	1.5	1.5	2.4

Table 4.6 Continued

	Cler & Steno	Tel Oper	Super S.A.	Service Reps	Bldg & Mtrvh	Tel Craft	Opera-tives	Service Workers
Michigan Bell								
White Females								
70 hire share	74.1	100.0	41.2	79.9	.0	7.9	.3	48.2
70 emp share	75.0	76.4	76.2	86.2	.0	4.5	.3	39.6
80 est emp share	70.6	99.6	43.3	80.9	.0	5.9	.3	42.1
Target	32.3	32.3	32.3	36.5	32.3	32.3	32.3	32.3
Black Males								
70 hire share	.0	.0	.0	.0	10.0	.0	4.9	4.7
70 emp share	.8	.0	.0	.0	11.6	4.9	20.2	9.7
80 est emp share	.1	.0	.0	.0	10.0	1.3	6.7	6.3
Target	5.6	5.6	5.6	3.0	5.6	5.6	5.6	5.6
Black Females								
70 hire share	17.0	.0	54.5	19.5	.0	.6	.3	23.4
70 emp share	16.7	23.3	23.5	13.8	.0	1.6	.3	21.8
80 est emp share	15.3	.4	52.4	18.5	.0	.7	.2	19.3
Target	3.7	3.7	3.7	2.5	3.7	3.7	3.7	3.7
Indiana Bell								
White Females								
70 hire share	86.8	.0	.0	96.8	.0	.3	.0	45.5
70 emp share	84.6	89.3	94.6	94.8	.0	.1	.0	23.0
80 est emp share	84.2	7.7	8.1	96.9	.0	.2	.0	32.0
Target	33.8	33.8	33.8	36.7	33.8	33.8	33.8	33.8
Black Males								
70 hire share	.0	.0	.0	.0	.0	.0	.0	22.0
70 emp share	.3	.0	.0	.0	9.4	5.4	53.1	28.1
80 est emp share	.1	.0	.0	.0	5.0	2.9	17.6	35.1
Target	3.5	3.5	3.5	1.7	3.5	3.5	3.5	3.5
Black Females								
70 hire share	8.7	.0	.0	2.9	.0	.0	.0	25.7
70 emp share	9.1	10.7	5.4	5.2	.0	.0	.0	20.7
80 est emp share	8.1	.8	.4	2.8	.0	.0	.0	17.2
Target	2.4	2.4	2.4	1.5	2.4	2.4	2.4	2.4

Table 4.6 Continued

	Offls & Mgrs	Accnt Audit	Engineers	Staff Specl	Technicians	Sales Mgt	Sales Nonmgt	Secry Mgt
Wisconsin Tel								
White Females								
70 hire share	39.7	93.9	5.6	14.0	.0	15.7	83.4	100.0
70 emp share	35.4	23.1	2.9	20.0	25.6	2.6	30.0	100.0
80 est emp share	29.2	58.8	3.0	11.1	6.8	11.6	72.6	100.0
Target	33.7	76.0	26.0	26.0	34.9	38.9	38.9	34.9
Black Males								
70 hire share	2.0	.6	.0	.4	50.0	4.0	.0	.0
70 emp share	.3	1.1	.0	.6	11.6	.9	.0	.0
80 est emp share	1.4	.3	.0	.5	36.2	3.5	.0	.0
Target	.8	.9	.9	.9	1.2	.7	.7	1.2
Black Females								
70 hire share	6.0	.0	.0	.8	50.0	.0	.0	.0
70 emp share	.5	.0	.0	.6	2.3	.0	.0	.0
80 est emp share	3.2	.0	.0	.5	21.8	.0	.0	.0
Target	.4	.3	.3	.3	.8	.5	.5	.8
Illinois Bell								
White Females								
70 hire share	42.8	66.0	14.5	47.4	15.8	23.5	79.6	100.0
70 emp share	44.5	28.6	9.7	31.7	25.6	13.1	24.9	100.0
80 est emp share	37.7	50.9	10.6	38.8	18.9	15.5	72.4	100.0
Target	30.2	23.2	23.2	23.2	32.2	34.8	34.8	32.2
Black Males								
70 hire share	3.9	.6	.9	.0	23.7	1.0	.4	.0
70 emp share	1.2	.4	.9	1.4	32.2	1.0	4.8	.0
80 est emp share	3.5	.6	.9	.4	23.0	1.1	1.1	.0
Target	3.2	2.7	2.7	2.7	6.1	3.5	3.5	6.1
Black Females								
70 hire share	6.4	.8	.3	16.4	4.9	6.3	19.0	.0
70 emp share	4.0	.4	.2	2.6	7.8	3.4	6.6	.0
80 est emp share	4.9	.6	.2	11.5	5.5	3.9	16.4	.0
Target	2.3	1.6	1.6	1.6	4.3	2.8	2.8	4.3

Table 4.6 Continued

	Cler & Steno	Tel Oper	Super S.A.	Service Reps	Bldg & Mtrvh	Tel Craft	Opera-tives	Service Workers
Wisconsin Tel								
White Females								
70 hire share	87.4	15.7	100.0	97.4	.0	2.2	.0	66.7
70 emp share	89.5	93.4	94.6	97.3	.0	.5	.0	65.5
80 est emp share	86.6	20.3	99.8	97.4	.0	1.0	.0	50.4
Target	34.9	34.9	34.9	38.9	34.9	34.9	34.9	34.9
Black Males								
70 hire share	.0	.0	.0	.0	1.3	2.5	2.8	6.8
70 emp share	.0	.0	.0	.0	5.5	1.7	9.1	3.1
80 est emp share	.0	.0	.0	.0	3.5	2.0	3.7	10.1
Target	1.2	1.2	1.2	.7	1.2	1.2	1.2	1.2
Black Females								
70 hire share	8.2	64.1	.0	.0	.0	.0	.0	6.1
70 emp share	4.9	6.2	5.0	2.0	.0	.0	.0	4.2
80 est emp share	7.4	60.0	.2	.1	.0	.0	.0	4.3
Target	.8	.8	.8	.5	.8	.8	.8	.8
Illinois Bell								
White Females								
70 hire share	75.5	73.2	100.0	81.4	.0	3.7	5.2	21.8
70 emp share	67.9	76.4	87.2	81.6	.0	.8	5.7	27.0
80 est emp share	72.2	73.6	99.7	82.3	.0	2.5	4.9	30.4
Target	32.2	32.2	32.2	34.8	32.2	32.2	32.2	32.2
Black Males								
70 hire share	.0	.0	.0	.1	4.1	8.6	25.4	32.8
70 emp share	2.3	.0	.0	.1	7.3	7.1	21.3	27.9
80 est emp share	.2	.0	.0	.1	4.9	8.0	24.1	24.3
Target	6.1	6.1	6.1	3.5	6.1	6.1	6.1	6.1
Black Females								
70 hire share	7.3	25.2	.0	17.5	.0	2.4	.0	18.3
70 emp share	14.6	23.5	12.7	18.2	.0	.3	.0	30.1
80 est emp share	7.0	23.9	.3	16.7	.0	1.5	.0	24.1
Target	4.3	4.3	4.3	2.8	4.3	4.3	4.3	4.3

Table 4.6 Continued

	Offls & Mgrs	Accnt Audit	Engineers	Staff Specl	Technicians	Sales Mgt	Sales Nonmgt	Secry Mgt
Northwestern Bell								
White Females								
70 hire share	58.0	44.0	10.7	32.8	100.0	1.5	36.3	98.8
70 emp share	36.5	21.9	8.5	23.1	68.9	2.6	24.8	98.9
80 est emp share	38.5	25.6	5.9	20.2	84.3	.7	19.8	98.8
Target	34.8	26.1	26.1	26.1	35.2	40.7	40.7	35.2
Black Males								
70 hire share	.9	.0	.1	1.3	.0	.0	4.8	.0
70 emp share	.2	.0	.1	.7	.0	.0	2.4	.0
80 est emp share	.9	.0	.1	1.2	.0	.0	5.4	.0
Target	.6	.0	.8	.8	.6	.5	.5	.6
Black Females								
70 hire share	.4	.0	5.4	9.8	.0	.0	1.4	1.1
70 emp share	.3	.0	.2	.5	1.4	.0	1.1	1.1
80 est emp share	.3	.0	2.3	4.9	.2	.0	.7	1.1
Target	.4	.3	.3	.3	.4	.4	.4	.4
Southwestern Bell								
White Females								
70 hire share	54.9	18.7	14.0	9.5	93.2	15.9	52.5	96.8
70 emp share	40.7	26.6	5.5	21.7	96.4	6.5	29.5	98.9
80 est emp share	41.8	15.1	8.0	9.1	93.1	8.7	36.3	97.0
Target	32.0	25.4	25.4	25.4	31.8	36.3	36.3	31.8
Black Males								
70 hire share	1.0	.0	1.5	.0	.0	.0	.8	.0
70 emp share	.2	.0	.4	.3	.0	.0	1.3	.0
80 est emp share	.9	.0	1.1	.1	.0	.0	1.1	.0
Target	2.7	2.4	2.4	2.4	6.6	2.8	2.8	6.6
Black Females								
70 hire share	4.5	.0	.0	.9	2.1	.0	3.0	.5
70 emp share	.6	.0	.0	.5	3.2	.0	1.2	.5
80 est emp share	2.8	.0	.0	.5	2.3	.0	2.0	.5
Target	2.4	2.2	2.2	2.2	4.5	2.5	2.5	4.5

Table 4.6 Continued

	Cler & Steno	Tel Oper	Super S.A.	Service Reps	Bldg & Mtrvh	Tel Craft	Opera- tives	Service Workers
Northwestern Bell								
White Females								
70 hire share	91.6	98.4	95.3	99.5	.0	2.6	.5	68.4
70 emp share	91.1	97.7	98.1	98.7	.0	.2	.8	44.2
80 est emp share	89.2	98.4	95.4	99.1	.0	1.1	.4	48.0
Target	35.2	35.2	35.2	40.7	35.2	35.2	35.2	35.2
Black Males								
70 hire share	.0	.0	.0	.0	.0	.0	1.9	.0
70 emp share	.1	.0	.0	.0	.2	1.1	4.9	6.4
80 est emp share	.0	.0	.0	.0	1.9	.5	2.6	.8
Target	.6	.6	.6	.5	.6	.6	.6	.6
Black Females								
70 hire share	3.4	1.5	1.7	.0	.0	1.1	.0	4.0
70 emp share	2.6	2.1	1.5	1.2	.0	.0	.0	2.4
80 est emp share	3.1	1.4	1.6	.0	.0	.4	.0	2.7
Target	.4	.4	.4	.4	.4	.4	.4	.4
Southwestern Bell								
White Females								
70 hire share	86.6	81.1	.0	94.6	.0	3.9	.0	19.3
70 emp share	90.3	82.8	93.9	95.7	.0	1.7	.0	14.4
80 est emp share	86.2	81.9	3.9	95.0	.0	1.9	.0	14.5
Target	31.8	31.9	31.8	36.3	31.8	31.8	31.8	31.8
Black Males								
70 hire share	.9	.0	.0	.0	40.5	3.1	19.2	2.0
70 emp share	.2	.0	.0	.0	35.4	3.0	44.5	45.1
80 est emp share	1.0	.0	.0	.0	37.4	3.0	26.6	9.8
Target	6.6	6.6	6.6	2.8	6.6	6.6	6.6	6.6
Black Females								
70 hire share	10.0	15.3	.0	4.8	.0	.0	.0	52.0
70 emp share	5.6	16.6	5.0	3.5	.0	.0	.0	21.6
80 est emp share	9.2	14.6	.2	4.5	.0	.0	.0	36.8
Target	4.5	4.5	4.5	2.5	4.5	4.5	4.5	4.5

Table 4.6 Continued

	Ofls & Mgrs	Accnt Audit	Engineers	Staff Specl	Technicians	Sales Mgt	Sales Nonmgt	Secry Mgt
Mountain States Tel & Tel								
White Females								
70 hire share	39.8	43.1	.0	29.3	29.5	.0	99.7	99.3
70 emp share	31.3	12.1	1.6	14.8	28.3	2.6	25.0	93.1
80 est emp share	26.7	25.2	.2	17.3	21.8	.1	77.1	99.3
Target	32.7	25.9	25.9	25.9	34.4	37.2	37.2	34.4
Black Males								
70 hire share	1.1	.0	.1	.0	.2	.3	.3	.0
70 emp share	.4	.0	.1	.0	.5	1.0	.5	.0
80 est emp share	1.0	.0	.1	.0	.3	.5	.6	.0
Target	1.1	1.0	1.0	1.0	1.1	1.2	1.2	1.1
Black Females								
70 hire share	.0	.0	.0	.1	.3	.0	.0	.4
70 emp share	.2	.0	.0	.1	.5	.0	.0	.4
80 est emp share	.0	.0	.0	.1	.3	.0	.0	.3
Target	.7	.5	.5	.5	.7	.8	.8	.7
Pacific Northwest Bell								
White Females								
70 hire share	84.8	50.8	10.1	87.9	60.4	16.1	95.4	94.4
70 emp share	38.4	37.8	5.9	22.7	25.8	5.2	35.6	97.1
80 est emp share	63.5	37.3	6.0	60.9	35.4	5.4	76.5	94.8
Target	33.1	26.0	26.0	26.0	34.7	37.8	37.8	34.7
Black Males								
70 hire share	.4	.0	.0	.0	.3	.0	.6	.0
70 emp share	.4	.0	.1	.5	1.6	2.1	1.0	.0
80 est emp share	.5	.0	.1	.2	1.1	.6	1.3	.0
Target	1.4	1.5	1.5	1.5	1.0	1.3	1.3	1.0
Black Females								
70 hire share	6.2	.0	.0	11.4	.0	.0	4.0	5.3
70 emp share	1.0	.0	.0	.8	.0	.0	1.9	2.9
80 est emp share	4.1	.0	.0	7.2	.0	.0	3.1	4.9
Target	.7	.5	.5	.5	.6	.8	.8	.6

Table 4.6 Continued

	Cler & Steno	Tel Oper	Super S.A.	Service Reps	Bldg & Mtrvh	Tel Craft	Opera-tives	Service Workers
Mountain States Tel & Tel								
White Females								
70 hire share	91.2	92.0	100.0	97.1	.0	.0	.0	51.1
70 emp share	86.5	95.5	97.4	98.6	.0	.9	.0	36.3
80 est emp share	87.7	92.0	100.0	96.5	.0	.1	.0	35.0
Target	34.4	34.4	34.4	37.2	34.4	34.4	34.4	34.4
Black Males								
70 hire share	.8	.0	.0	.0	1.6	1.9	9.1	2.1
70 emp share	.3	.0	.0	.0	6.5	1.1	7.8	8.4
80 est emp share	1.1	.0	.0	.0	3.2	1.6	8.5	3.7
Target	1.1	1.1	1.1	1.2	1.1	1.1	1.1	1.1
Black Females								
70 hire share	3.0	6.3	.0	1.4	.0	.0	.0	15.5
70 emp share	2.4	3.7	1.9	1.1	.0	.0	.0	10.8
80 est emp share	2.8	5.9	.0	1.3	.0	.0	.0	10.0
Target	.7	.7	.7	.8	.7	.7	.7	.7
Pacific Northwest Bell								
White Females								
70 hire share	87.7	96.7	100.0	93.3	.0	7.0	.6	71.0
70 emp share	86.5	95.0	97.1	97.7	.0	.6	.7	45.9
80 est emp share	86.1	96.4	93.9	94.1	.0	2.7	.5	63.4
Target	34.7	34.7	34.7	37.8	34.7	34.7	34.7	34.7
Black Males								
70 hire share	.9	.0	.0	.0	1.3	.0	.0	.0
70 emp share	.4	.0	.0	.0	1.3	2.1	8.6	3.9
80 est emp share	1.0	.0	.0	.0	1.3	1.2	1.9	.9
Target	1.0	1.0	1.0	1.3	1.0	1.0	1.0	1.0
Black Females								
70 hire share	6.5	.0	.0	4.0	.0	18.5	.0	27.6
70 emp share	4.9	4.1	2.5	1.7	.0	.1	.0	8.2
80 est emp share	6.0	.1	.1	3.8	.0	6.6	.0	23.3
Target	.6	.6	.6	.8	.6	.6	.6	.6

Table 4.6 Continued

	Offls & Mgrs	Accnt Audit	Engineers	Staff Specl	Technicians	Sales Mgt	Sales Nonmgt	Secry Mgt
Pacific Tel & Tel								
White Females								
70 hire share	51.0	38.5	15.5	35.6	35.1	32.8	83.9	95.2
70 emp share	39.1	23.7	9.8	30.5	69.7	20.0	72.6	93.6
80 est emp share	39.6	27.4	10.2	26.3	35.4	20.5	74.9	94.4
Target	31.0	24.5	24.5	24.5	33.4	35.3	35.3	33.4
Black Males								
70 hire share	2.4	.2	.3	.5	3.0	.6	.3	.1
70 emp share	.8	.3	.3	.9	1.3	1.1	1.0	.2
80 est emp share	2.4	.2	.3	.7	3.0	.8	.6	.1
Target	3.2	2.3	2.9	2.9	3.5	3.4	3.4	3.5
Black Females								
70 hire share	2.5	.9	.8	1.2	.8	1.6	3.0	1.9
70 emp share	1.9	.8	.1	1.1	3.9	.7	4.7	1.8
80 est emp share	1.8	.7	.4	.9	1.1	.9	2.6	1.8
Target	1.9	1.3	1.3	1.3	2.3	2.3	2.3	2.3

Table 4.6 Continued

	Cler & Steno	Tel Oper	Super S.A.	Service Reps	Bldg & Mtrvh	Tel Craft	Opera-tives	Service Workers
Pacific Tel & Tel								
White Females								
70 hire share	76.0	62.1	.0	88.4	.0	5.7	14.0	47.4
70 emp share	76.6	85.1	88.4	91.6	.0	.6	3.6	39.0
80 est emp share	71.8	83.3	.9	89.1	.0	3.0	8.1	35.3
Target	33.4	33.4	33.4	35.3	33.4	33.4	33.4	33.4
Black Males								
70 hire share	.8	.2	.0	.1	.0	1.8	5.7	6.4
70 emp share	.7	.1	.0	.1	3.5	4.0	11.3	11.1
80 est emp share	1.8	.2	.0	.1	1.1	2.5	6.8	10.5
Target	3.5	3.5	3.5	3.4	3.5	3.5	3.5	3.5
Black Females								
70 hire share	10.4	10.8	.0	9.3	.0	.0	.4	25.2
70 emp share	11.6	12.1	10.1	6.8	.0	.0	.3	16.3
80 est emp share	9.3	10.3	.1	8.8	.0	.0	.2	17.8
Target	2.3	2.3	2.3	2.3	2.3	2.3	2.3	2.3

Source: EEOC Request For Statistics.

Table 4.7 1970 Share of New Hires and Share of New Hires Needed to Reach Target by 1980 for White Females, Black Males, and Black Females by Occupation for Bell Companies (Percent)

	Offls & Mgrs	Accnt Audit	Engineers	Staff Specl	Technicians	Sales Mgt	Sales Nonmgt	Secry Mgt
New England Tel & Tel								
White Females								
70 hire share	63.2	13.2	35.5	93.3	18.8	62.9	58.2	99.3
Needed hire share	50.1	39.3	46.2	38.8	49.0	75.7	76.6	34.2
Black Males								
70 hire share	2.9	.0	64.5	6.7	.0	.3	.0	.0
Needed hire share	.9	.3	1.0	.8	1.5	.4	.6	1.1
Black Females								
70 hire share	3.1	.0	.0	.0	5.4	.0	1.3	.3
Needed hire share	.8	.7	.8	.6	.4	1.2	1.2	.7
Southern New England Tel								
White Females								
70 hire share	37.7	92.7	.0	94.9	2.9	8.3	42.5	98.0
Needed hire share	39.6	32.8	40.6	30.7	61.9	69.4	67.3	27.5
Black Males								
70 hire share	.2	.0	.5	5.1	1.0	.8	21.9	.0
Needed hire share	1.4	1.1	1.0	.6	2.0	1.0	.2	3.0
Black Females								
70 hire share	1.9	6.9	.0	.0	.0	.0	3.2	1.9
Needed hire share	.9	.2	.7	.3	3.4	1.9	1.8	1.8
New York Tel								
White Females								
70 hire share	40.8	65.4	15.9	33.0	18.6	24.4	75.1	88.0
Needed hire share	40.2	31.0	37.2	32.4	41.2	49.9	47.4	42.6
Black Males								
70 hire share	1.4	.2	1.0	3.6	16.1	.0	.0	.0
Needed hire share	3.0	2.5	2.3	2.3	3.5	2.9	2.7	4.2
Black Females								
70 hire share	11.8	1.1	1.0	4.8	7.2	1.8	24.0	11.6
Needed hire share	2.6	1.9	2.1	1.6	4.5	4.0	3.7	5.1

Table 4.7 Continued

	Cler & Steno	Tel Oper	Super S.A.	Service Reps	Bldg & Mtrvh	Tel Craft	Opera-tives	Service Workers
New England Tel & Tel								
White Females								
70 hire share	93.3	91.2	93.7	97.6	99.5	.0	.0	65.3
Needed hire share	46.6	35.4	51.5	48.8	68.1	71.4	56.7	59.4
Black Males								
70 hire share	.1	.0	.0	.0	.5	1.4	22.2	.0
Needed hire share	.9	1.1	.8	.7	.5	.5	.4	.6
Black Females								
70 hire share	5.1	7.5	6.3	1.4	.0	.0	.0	1.9
Needed hire share	.9	.7	1.0	.8	1.4	1.4	1.1	1.2
Southern New England Tel								
White Females								
70 hire share	83.1	100.0	76.4	89.9	52.0	1.7	.0	76.1
Needed hire share	34.2	33.7	33.8	38.7	52.4	56.3	42.1	49.8
Black Males								
70 hire share	.0	.0	.0	.0	2.2	.0	.0	.0
Needed hire share	2.7	2.7	2.7	1.3	1.9	1.7	1.6	1.7
Black Females								
70 hire share	9.1	.0	23.0	4.4	.0	.0	.0	5.6
Needed hire share	1.3	1.7	1.7	1.0	2.7	2.9	2.2	2.6
New York Tel								
White Females								
70 hire share	60.3	56.7	52.4	72.3	.0	.4	2.7	30.4
Needed hire share	36.0	32.7	32.8	28.2	44.1	46.2	34.8	42.3
Black Males								
70 hire share	3.4	.0	.0	2.0	15.3	12.5	32.0	38.8
Needed hire share	4.8	5.2	5.2	3.8	3.6	3.8	4.0	4.0
Black Females								
70 hire share	30.1	42.1	46.3	18.2	.0	.0	.3	9.3
Needed hire share	3.6	3.7	3.7	2.2	4.9	5.2	3.9	4.8

Table 4.7 Continued

	Offls & Mgrs	Accnt Audit	Engin-eers	Staff Specl	Techni-cians	Sales Mgt	Sales Nonmgt	Secry Mgt
New Jersey Bell								
White Females								
70 hire share	28.4	97.4	11.5	39.1	55.6	5.2	.0	79.0
Needed hire share	32.7	20.3	28.3	24.7	42.0	72.9	72.7	30.7
Black Males								
70 hire share	1.0	.0	6.6	.0	12.3	.9	6.1	.0
Needed hire share	2.4	2.0	1.8	1.6	3.0	1.6	.7	5.5
Black Females								
70 hire share	3.2	.0	.1	.0	24.6	.0	.0	20.7
Needed hire share	2.0	1.1	1.5	1.2	4.7	4.5	4.4	3.7
Bell of Pennsylvania								
White Females								
70 hire share	44.8	32.0	22.5	17.0	.0	5.2	97.3	100.0
Needed hire share	30.4	23.3	35.7	26.4	.8	69.6	66.0	28.4
Black Males								
70 hire share	.5	.0	6.0	29.1	.0	1.2	2.7	.0
Needed hire share	2.7	2.6	2.5	1.9	7.4	1.6	.6	5.2
Black Females								
70 hire share	.0	13.5	1.2	9.1	.0	.0	.0	.0
Needed hire share	2.4	1.7	1.9	1.4	1.2	4.0	3.8	3.6
Chesapeake & Potomac Tel								
White Females								
70 hire share	34.9	59.5	27.6	43.6	34.0	.0	1.7	84.1
Needed hire share	33.2	30.5	39.3	33.6	36.5	46.5	46.2	27.8
Black Males								
70 hire share	3.5	.2	.0	14.1	.0	14.9	.0	.1
Needed hire share	5.1	5.9	6.1	5.7	15.4	3.8	3.4	11.9
Black Females								
70 hire share	7.4	.3	.1	.0	.0	.0	10.3	15.3
Needed hire share	5.8	6.6	7.0	6.4	12.4	6.6	6.5	8.9

Table 4.7 Continued

	Cler & Steno	Tel Oper	Super S.A.	Service Reps	Bldg & Mtrvh	Tel Craft	Opera-tives	Service Workers
New Jersey Bell								
White Females								
70 hire share	74.8	71.7	87.7	95.3	.0	.2	.3	49.8
Needed hire share	35.4	31.0	30.8	41.2	40.6	42.6	38.5	37.2
Black Males								
70 hire share	.2	.0	.0	.0	2.5	5.6	34.0	11.0
Needed hire share	5.1	5.5	5.5	2.3	5.3	5.2	3.8	4.9
Black Females								
70 hire share	14.2	26.5	10.6	3.5	.0	.0	.0	.4
Needed hire share	3.8	2.9	3.1	2.6	4.5	4.7	4.3	4.2
Bell of Pennsylvania								
White Females								
70 hire share	85.7	97.5	83.6	95.8	.0	1.1	.0	51.5
Needed hire share	35.2	30.7	30.5	34.8	87.4	87.4	46.4	50.7
Black Males								
70 hire share	.8	.0	.0	.0	37.9	10.2	.0	.0
Needed hire share	4.6	5.1	5.1	2.6	3.8	4.0	.6	.0
Black Females								
70 hire share	12.9	.1	3.8	3.5	.0	.0	.0	45.5
Needed hire share	3.6	2.7	3.0	1.9	8.5	8.6	4.6	4.4
Chesapeake & Potomac Tel								
White Females								
70 hire share	75.7	73.4	77.2	93.1	.0	.5	.0	5.1
Needed hire share	26.3	27.6	27.6	29.2	44.5	49.2	35.9	40.3
Black Males								
70 hire share	1.7	.0	.0	.0	27.3	14.0	6.6	33.7
Needed hire share	12.4	12.2	12.2	4.2	2.1	12.8	6.6	7.0
Black Females								
70 hire share	20.0	24.2	21.7	3.8	.0	.0	.2	44.2
Needed hire share	7.6	7.7	7.9	4.2	12.1	13.5	10.0	11.2

Table 4.7 Continued

	Offls & Mgrs	Accnt Audit	Engineers	Staff Spcel	Technicians	Sales Mgt	Sales Nonmgt	Secry Mgt
Southern Bell								
White Females								
70 hire share	51.5	74.0	21.3	70.0	94.3	13.4	19.4	100.0
Needed hire share	49.1	40.8	48.7	43.5	17.6	52.7	51.9	24.4
Black Males								
70 hire share	.3	.0	.2	1.4	.0	.0	.1	.0
Needed hire share	4.1	4.4	4.6	4.4	16.2	3.4	3.3	15.9
Black Females								
70 hire share	.9	.0	.1	2.9	5.3	.0	.0	.0
Needed hire share	7.2	8.3	8.9	8.5	15.3	5.7	5.7	11.0
South Central Bell								
White Females								
70 hire share	61.0	99.5	19.5	69.6	87.5	.0	25.7	99.6
Needed hire share	46.0	44.3	51.5	43.5	4.3	62.5	61.6	21.4
Black Males								
70 hire share	1.3	.5	2.9	.0	.0	.0	.0	.0
Needed hire share	5.0	5.1	5.9	5.3	13.2	3.4	3.4	15.9
Black Females								
70 hire share	.3	.0	.2	1.5	12.5	.0	.0	.3
Needed hire share	8.2	9.8	10.2	9.7	13.4	7.4	7.4	11.2
Ohio Bell								
White Females								
70 hire share	32.7	95.2	28.6	54.8	100.0	50.0	43.7	86.0
Needed hire share	44.2	31.1	43.5	31.0	50.5	44.8	43.2	26.7
Black Males								
70 hire share	2.5	3.1	.0	2.5	.0	50.0	7.5	.0
Needed hire share	2.2	1.3	2.3	1.7	5.5	2.4	2.1	5.6
Black Females								
70 hire share	10.5	1.6	.0	10.7	.0	.0	1.9	13.9
Needed hire share	2.2	2.2	2.4	1.6	4.9	2.7	2.5	3.5

Table 4.7 Continued

	Cler & Steno	Tel Oper	Super S.A.	Service Reps	Bldg & Mtrvh	Tel Craft	Opera-tives	Service Workers
Southern Bell								
White Females								
70 hire share	92.2	76.4	93.5	95.1	.0	8.7	.8	9.6
Needed hire share	33.4	26.0	26.0	35.1	41.3	43.7	34.9	44.7
Black Males								
70 hire share	.1	.0	.0	.0	41.5	1.0	39.8	15.6
Needed hire share	12.7	15.6	15.6	4.1	13.4	19.0	10.4	7.2
Black Females								
70 hire share	4.9	22.5	5.6	4.3	.0	.3	.0	72.7
Needed hire share	14.8	10.6	10.7	4.0	16.2	17.7	14.0	18.2
South Central Bell								
White Females								
70 hire share	90.1	77.2	87.1	95.6	.0	11.4	.0	.0
Needed hire share	30.7	25.5	25.5	30.8	64.1	56.5	41.4	49.1
Black Males								
70 hire share	.3	.0	.0	.0	100.0	9.8	51.6	20.0
Needed hire share	12.9	15.2	15.2	4.6	1.6	21.6	.0	.0
Black Females								
70 hire share	7.2	21.2	12.5	4.2	.0	.0	.0	80.0
Needed hire share	15.0	10.4	10.6	4.3	24.2	21.9	15.8	18.9
Ohio Bell								
White Females								
70 hire share	91.6	89.5	97.5	97.3	.0	5.4	.7	52.4
Needed hire share	42.1	32.7	30.8	45.3	61.5	68.7	54.8	53.8
Black Males								
70 hire share	.0	.0	.0	.0	15.2	.0	26.1	.0
Needed hire share	4.1	5.2	5.3	2.2	.0	3.2	.0	1.7
Black Females								
70 hire share	4.2	6.5	1.3	2.1	.0	1.8	.7	46.4
Needed hire share	3.8	3.0	3.0	2.7	6.3	7.1	5.7	5.5

Table 4.7 Continued

	Offls & Mgrs	Accnt Audit	Engineers	Staff Specl	Technicians	Sales Mgt	Sales Nonmgt	Secry Mgt
Cincinnati Bell, Inc								
White Females								
70 hire share	75.0	26.4	3.1	47.3	41.2	2.4	97.8	100.0
Needed hire share	45.8	40.3	45.1	35.8	45.8	63.9	57.1	32.0
Black Males								
70 hire share	.3	.0	.0	2.9	1.7	1.6	.0	.0
Needed hire share	2.7	2.8	2.9	1.9	5.7	1.6	1.8	5.2
Black Females								
70 hire share	.0	.0	.0	2.0	.0	.0	.0	.0
Needed hire share	3.0	2.4	2.5	2.2	7.1	3.9	3.5	3.5
Michigan Bell								
White Females								
70 hire share	39.1	21.9	13.7	46.2	100.0	42.1	79.9	62.7
Needed hire share	43.1	35.5	38.0	33.6	28.7	82.3	81.8	31.3
Black Males								
70 hire share	2.4	.0	8.4	.0	.0	.0	.0	.0
Needed hire share	2.7	2.6	2.3	2.1	6.3	.6	.6	5.9
Black Females								
70 hire share	6.8	21.8	.0	1.9	.0	8.5	17.9	37.1
Needed hire share	2.7	1.7	2.3	1.9	3.9	6.0	5.9	3.9
Indiana Bell								
White Females								
70 hire share	.0	45.8	13.4	100.0	69.2	.0	79.5	100.0
Needed hire share	42.3	45.4	57.4	38.7	23.8	52.3	50.2	27.5
Black Males								
70 hire share	10.3	.0	9.4	.0	.0	.0	3.3	.0
Needed hire share	1.9	2.6	.3	1.6	4.8	1.4	1.5	3.9
Black Females								
70 hire share	.0	1.1	.0	.0	.0	.0	17.2	.0
Needed hire share	1.8	1.2	2.4	1.9	3.5	2.2	1.9	2.7

Table 4.7 Continued

	Cler & Steno	Tel Oper	Super S.A.	Service Reps	Bldg & Mtrvh	Tel Craft	Opera-tives	Service Workers
Cincinnati Bell, Inc								
White Females								
70 hire share	86.0	56.9	77.2	87.2	.0	2.3	.0	56.8
Needed hire share	33.7	31.3	31.1	13.1	60.0	60.8	34.7	49.1
Black Males								
70 hire share	.0	.0	.0	.0	4.2	.0	4.9	.0
Needed hire share	5.0	5.3	5.3	3.7	5.7	6.0	4.4	2.3
Black Females								
70 hire share	13.1	38.8	17.8	11.2	.0	.4	.0	9.2
Needed hire share	3.7	2.8	3.1	.8	6.1	6.2	3.6	5.2
Michigan Bell								
White Females								
70 hire share	74.1	100.0	41.2	79.9	.0	7.9	.3	48.2
Needed hire share	42.3	30.8	30.8	34.7	45.2	46.7	41.4	41.6
Black Males								
70 hire share	.0	.0	.0	.0	10.0	.0	4.9	4.7
Needed hire share	4.8	6.0	6.0	3.2	3.5	5.7	3.3	4.7
Black Females								
70 hire share	17.0	.0	54.5	19.5	.0	.6	.3	23.4
Needed hire share	5.1	3.5	3.5	2.3	5.3	5.3	5.0	5.0
Indiana Bell								
White Females								
70 hire share	86.8	.0	.0	96.8	.0	.3	.0	45.5
Needed hire share	38.8	28.3	27.9	34.3	74.8	77.3	51.5	54.5
Black Males								
70 hire share	.0	.0	.0	.0	.0	.0	.0	22.0
Needed hire share	3.3	4.0	3.9	1.9	.0	1.1	.0	.0
Black Females								
70 hire share	8.7	.0	.0	2.9	.0	.0	.0	25.7
Needed hire share	2.6	1.8	2.2	1.4	5.3	5.5	3.7	3.4

Table 4.7 Continued

	Offls & Mgrs	Accnt Audit	Engineers	Staff Specl	Technicians	Sales Mgt	Sales Nonmgt	Secry Mgt
Wisconsin Tel								
White Females								
70 hire share	39.7	93.9	5.6	14.0	.0	15.7	83.4	100.0
Needed hire share	48.1	41.8	54.2	43.5	62.7	50.0	46.3	25.0
Black Males								
70 hire share	2.0	.6	.0	.4	50.0	4.0	.0	.0
Needed hire share	1.0	.5	1.4	.9	.0	.7	.8	1.4
Black Females								
70 hire share	6.0	.0	.0	.8	50.0	.0	.0	.0
Needed hire share	.6	.6	.7	.4	.4	.7	.7	.9
Illinois Bell								
White Females								
70 hire share	42.8	66.0	14.5	47.4	15.8	23.5	79.6	100.0
Needed hire share	32.9	28.0	33.8	26.9	30.2	48.5	47.6	30.4
Black Males								
70 hire share	3.9	.6	.9	.0	23.7	1.0	.4	.0
Needed hire share	3.6	3.4	3.3	3.0	3.8	3.3	2.8	6.6
Black Females								
70 hire share	6.4	.8	.3	16.4	4.9	6.3	19.0	.0
Needed hire share	2.5	2.4	2.5	1.8	3.6	4.0	3.9	4.6
Northwestern Bell								
White Females								
70 hire share	58.0	44.0	10.7	32.8	100.0	1.5	36.3	98.8
Needed hire share	52.8	44.8	50.2	44.2	41.8	64.3	62.6	32.1
Black Males								
70 hire share	.9	.0	.1	1.3	.0	.0	4.8	.0
Needed hire share	.7	1.0	1.0	.7	.7	.5	.1	.6
Black Females								
70 hire share	.4	.0	5.4	9.8	.0	.0	1.4	1.1
Needed hire share	.6	.6	.6	.5	.3	.7	.6	.3

Table 4.7 Continued

	Cler & Steno	Tel Oper	Super S.A.	Service Reps	Bldg & Mtrvh	Tel Craft	Opera-tives	Service Workers
Wisconsin Tel								
White Females								
70 hire share	87.4	15.7	100.0	97.4	.0	2.2	.0	66.7
Needed hire share	33.9	31.5	31.5	35.9	77.6	79.4	42.8	53.0
Black Males								
70 hire share	.0	.0	.0	.0	1.3	2.5	2.8	6.8
Needed hire share	1.2	1.3	1.3	.8	.0	.5	.0	.4
Black Females								
70 hire share	8.2	64.1	.0	.0	.0	.0	.0	6.1
Needed hire share	.5	.5	.6	.5	1.7	1.7	1.0	1.1
Illinois Bell								
White Females								
70 hire share	75.5	73.2	100.0	81.4	.0	3.7	5.2	21.8
Needed hire share	34.4	39.9	30.2	29.1	46.3	48.5	37.2	21.5
Black Males								
70 hire share	.0	.0	.0	.1	4.1	8.6	25.4	32.8
Needed hire share	6.1	5.5	6.6	4.1	5.9	5.6	4.4	7.7
Black Females								
70 hire share	7.3	25.2	.0	17.5	.0	2.4	.0	10.3
Needed hire share	4.6	5.2	4.2	2.2	6.3	6.6	5.2	2.9
Northwestern Bell								
White Females								
70 hire share	91.6	98.4	95.3	99.5	.0	2.6	.5	68.4
Needed hire share	42.5	34.3	34.3	51.6	67.3	72.3	55.9	57.3
Black Males								
70 hire share	.0	.0	.0	.0	.0	.0	1.9	.0
Needed hire share	.5	.6	.6	.5	.0	.1	.0	.0
Black Females								
70 hire share	3.4	1.5	1.7	.0	.0	1.1	.0	4.0
Needed hire share	.4	.4	.4	.5	.7	.7	.6	.6

Table 4.7 Continued

	Offls & Mgrs	Accnt Audit	Enginers	Staff Specl	Technicians	Sales Mgt	Sales Nonmgt	Secry Mgt
Southwestern Bell								
White Females								
70 hire share	54.9	18.7	14.0	9.5	93.2	15.9	52.5	96.8
Needed hire share	40.6	36.1	44.9	39.0	9.2	54.4	52.3	27.7
Black Males								
70 hire share	1.0	.0	1.5	.0	.0	.0	.8	.0
Needed hire share	3.4	3.4	3.3	3.2	8.8	2.7	2.4	7.2
Black Females								
70 hire share	4.5	.0	.0	.9	2.1	.0	3.0	.5
Needed hire share	4.0	4.1	4.2	3.9	6.7	3.9	3.8	4.9
Mountain States Tel & Tel								
White Females								
70 hire share	39.8	43.1	.0	29.3	29.5	.0	99.7	99.3
Needed hire share	48.3	44.0	47.2	43.2	51.1	68.7	65.3	32.1
Black Males								
70 hire share	1.1	.0	.1	.0	.2	.3	.3	.0
Needed hire share	1.2	1.2	1.2	1.2	1.3	.9	1.0	1.2
Black Females								
70 hire share	.0	.0	.0	.1	.3	.0	.0	.4
Needed hire share	1.1	.9	.9	.9	1.1	1.6	1.5	.7
Pacific Northwest Bell								
White Females								
70 hire share	84.8	50.8	10.1	87.9	60.4	16.1	95.4	94.4
Needed hire share	43.8	32.9	47.4	39.5	58.9	71.0	66.3	30.5
Black Males								
70 hire share	.4	.0	.0	.0	.3	.0	.6	.0
Needed hire share	1.7	2.1	2.2	1.9	.1	.6	.8	1.1
Black Females								
70 hire share	6.2	.0	.0	11.4	.0	.0	4.0	5.3
Needed hire share	.9	.9	1.0	.7	1.2	1.6	1.4	.4

Table 4.7 Continued

	Cler & Steno	Tel Oper	Super S.A.	Service Reps	Bldg & Mtrvh	Tel Craft	Opera-tives	Service Workers
Southwestern Bell								
White Females								
70 hire share	86.6	81.1	.0	94.6	.0	3.9	.0	19.3
Needed hire share	33.0	29.2	28.9	29.7	62.6	65.9	47.0	48.5
Black Males								
70 hire share	.3	.0	.0	.0	40.5	3.1	19.2	2.0
Needed hire share	6.6	7.2	7.2	3.3	.0	8.2	.0	.0
Black Females								
70 hire share	10.0	15.3	.0	4.8	.0	.0	.0	52.0
Needed hire share	5.6	4.3	4.7	2.4	9.0	9.7	6.8	6.7
Mountain States Tel & Tel								
White Females								
70 hire share	91.2	92.0	100.0	97.1	.0	.0	.0	51.1
Needed hire share	43.1	37.4	33.8	45.9	53.5	61.1	42.4	55.3
Black Males								
70 hire share	.8	.0	.0	.0	1.6	1.9	9.1	2.1
Needed hire share	1.0	1.1	1.2	1.1	.0	.9	.0	.4
Black Females								
70 hire share	3.0	6.3	.0	1.4	.0	.0	.0	15.5
Needed hire share	.9	.8	.7	1.1	1.1	1.2	.8	1.1
Pacific Northwest Bell								
White Females								
70 hire share	87.7	96.7	100.0	93.3	.0	7.0	.6	71.0
Needed hire share	35.9	34.1	32.0	31.0	82.5	84.3	47.3	57.7
Black Males								
70 hire share	.9	.0	.0	.0	1.3	.0	.0	.0
Needed hire share	.9	1.0	1.0	1.6	.5	.0	.0	.1
Black Females								
70 hire share	6.5	.0	.0	4.0	.0	18.5	.0	27.6
Needed hire share	.3	.5	.5	.7	1.3	1.3	.8	.8

Table 4.7 Continued

	Offls & Mgrs	Accnt Audit	Engin-eers	Staff Specl	Techni-cians	Sales Mgt	Sales Nonmgt	Secry Mgt
Pacific Tel & Tel								
White Females								
70 hire share	51.0	38.5	15.5	35.6	35.1	32.8	83.9	95.2
Needed hire share	40.0	34.3	37.0	33.0	32.2	50.9	48.6	37.1
Black Males								
70 hire share	2.4	.2	.3	.5	3.0	.6	.3	.1
Needed hire share	3.4	3.3	3.3	3.1	3.7	2.9	2.8	3.4
Black Females								
70 hire share	2.5	.9	.8	1.2	.8	1.6	3.0	1.9
Needed hire share	2.6	2.0	2.1	1.9	2.6	3.5	3.3	2.8

	Cler & Steno	Tel Oper	Super S.A.	Service Reps	Bldg & Mtrvh	Tel Craft	Opera-tives	Service Workers
Pacific Tel & Tel								
White Females								
70 hire share	76.0	82.1	.0	88.4	.0	5.7	14.0	47.4
Needed hire share	40.4	30.5	30.4	32.1	50.4	56.4	50.4	52.5
Black Males								
70 hire share	.8	.2	.0	.1	.0	1.8	5.7	6.4
Needed hire share	3.2	3.3	3.9	3.8	3.6	2.9	1.4	2.2
Black Females								
70 hire share	10.4	10.8	.0	9.3	.0	.0	.4	25.2
Needed hire share	2.8	2.2	2.2	2.2	3.5	4.0	3.6	3.8

Appendix B to Chapter 4

Statistical Methodology for Computing Separation Rates, Current Hiring Rates, and Targets

The quarterly status reports for 1970 for each company, submitted to EEOC as item #38 of the "Requests for Documents," were used as the basic data source for employment by race and sex in different occupations. Each company's position as reported in its December 31, 1970, status report was used as the base from which the projections were made. The eighteen occupations listed on the status report were collapsed to sixteen: Laborers (if any) were added to Operatives, and Other Business Office Employees were added to Clerical and Stenographic. The other basic ingredients of the model, occupational growth rates and separation rates by race, sex, and occupation for each company, were estimated.

Since employment in the telephone company is related to the amount of services provided, and the latter is a function of population, the growth rate of employment in the telephone industry can be expected to be correlated with the growth rate of population. In the Affirmative Action Program submitted by Pacific Telephone and Telegraph Company, total employment of that company is projected to 1975. The implied compound growth rate of its employment from 1970 to 1975 was compared to the compound growth rate of population in California and Nevada over the same period.[1] The ratio of the employment growth rate to the population growth rate for Pacific Telephone and Telegraph was 0.9892. Therefore, the growth rate of employment to 1980 in each company was approximated by multiplying the compound growth rate of population in the states[2] in which the company is operating by this same ratio. All occupations in a company were assumed to grow at the same rate.[3]

Although separation rates by race, sex, and occupation for each company are required for the model, information was available only for separations by sex and department. Each Bell company files annually with the FCC a monthly personnel report for December and a quarterly supplement for the fourth quarter, on which total separations by sex, department, and cause are indicated. For each company, a separation rate could therefore be calculated by sex for each of the seven departments. (Diamond State figures were added to Bell of Pennsylvania and the four Chesapeake and

1 The 1975 population projections for California and Nevada were taken from US Bureau of the Census, *Statistical Abstract of the United States, 1970* (Washington, D.C., 1970), Table 12, p. 13.
2 Cincinnati Bell was assumed to grow at the same rate as Ohio; El Paso was not subtracted from Southwestern Bell nor added to Mountain States; all of Idaho was included in Mountain States. The population projections to 1985 for each state were obtained from the *Statistical Abstract of the United States, 1970,* Table 12 (Series I, D), p. 13.
3 Expansion in employment contributes an extremely small proportion of job openings relative to turnover. Therefore, the ten-year projections are insensitive to our particular assumptions about company growth rates.

Potomac companies were added together to conform to the unit of reporting of the quarterly status reports.) In calculating these separation rates, separations from a department included all separations of regular employees, transfers of regular employees to other departments, transfers of temporary employees to other departments, and all separations of temporary employees except those for the reason "Work Completed." Transfers were included as a proxy for promotions, since a promotion from an occupation creates a vacancy just as much as a quit, dismissal, death, retirement, or layoff. Admittedly, some promotions occur within the same department, and some interdepartmental transfers do not involve promotions, so that transfers are, at best, a crude approximation to promotions. Separations for both regular and temporary employees were used to ensure comparability between the status reports and the personnel reports.

The next stage in the estimation of the occupational separation rates was the distribution of employment in each occupation by department. Only indirect evidence on these distributions by company was available. From the EEOC Request for Statistics ("for the thirty SMSA's [Standard Metropolitan Statistical Areas] designated by EEOC, the sex and race composition as of December 31, 1970, by EEO-1 job categories, job titles, and departments"), it was possible to extract these distributions by sex for each of thirty SMSA's. The Office and Clerical job category was further broken down by job title to separate out Telephone Operators, Supervisors / Service Assistants, Secretaries (Mgt.), and Service Representatives from all other Stenographic and Clerical jobs. The two EEO-1 categories Officials and Managers and Professionals were added together for this part of the analysis. The distribution thus obtained for each SMSA was imputed as the distribution of the company of which that SMSA is a part (see Table 4.8). Where several SMSA's were located in a single company, the occupation-department distribution for total employment in those SMSA's was imputed to the company. Distributions were obtained in this manner for thirteen of the nineteen Bell companies; the remaining six companies were assigned the average of the distributions for the thirteen companies. These distributions were applied to employment by occupation reported in the December 31, 1970 quarterly status report of each company to generate, for each company and each sex, a matrix of employment by occupation and department. To ensure that the departments summed to the known totals reported in the personnel reports, the RAS method[4] of balancing rows and columns was applied to each matrix.

No data are published on separation rates by occupation, either for the telephone industry or for the nation as a whole. However, as described in the article by Bergmann and Krause,[5] the Bureau of Labor Statistics unpublished gross flow data are

4 See Richard Stone, *Programme for Economic Growth*, Vol. I of A Computable Model of Economic Growth (London: Chapman and Hall, 1962), pp. 69–72.
5 Bergmann and Krause, "Evaluating and Forecasting," pp. 405-406.

Table 4.8   SMSA's Used for Imputing Company Distributions, by Company

Company	SMSA
New York	New York
New Jersey Bell	Newark
Bell of Pennsylvania	Philadelphia
Chesapeake and Potomac	Washington, Baltimore, Richmond, Norfolk
Southern Bell	Miami, Greensboro-Winston-Salem, Atlanta, Jacksonville
South Central Bell	New Orleans, Mobile, Birmingham, Memphis
Ohio Bell	Cleveland
Michigan Bell	Detroit
Indiana Bell	Indianapolis
Illinois Bell	Chicago
Southwestern Bell	Dallas, Kansas City, San Antonio, Houston, St. Louis
Mountain States	Denver, El Paso, Phoenix
Pacific Telephone & Telegraph	Los Angeles, San Diego, San Francisco

valuable in gauging the size of occupational flows relative to one another. Therefore, a matrix of department-occupation separation rates for each sex and each company was computed on the assumption that the ratio of the rate for one occupation to the rate for another was the same as in the gross flow data, but that the absolute level was such as to produce a weighted average equal to the departmental separation rates calculated from the personnel reports. The eight gross flow occupation categories were matched to the sixteen telephone company occupation categories in the following way:

Officials and Managers	Officials and Managers
Accountants Engineers Staff Specialists	Professional & Technical
Technicians	Professional & Technical
Sales Mgt & Non-Mgt	Sales
Secretaries Stenographic & Other Clerical Telephone Operators Supervisors/Service Assistants Service Representatives	Clerical
Building & Motor Vehicle Craftsmen Telephone Craftsmen	Craftsmen

Operatives   Operatives

Service Workers   Service Workers

Finally, the separation rate for each occupation was computed as the weighted average of its separation rate in each department.

These same gross flow data suggest that differences in the distribution of blacks and whites by occupation account for almost all of the differences in black and white turnover rates.[6] For each occupation in each company, we have therefore assumed a ratio of black-to-white separation rates of 1.06, which is consistent with the gross flows observed by race and by occupation and the occupational distribution of whites and blacks in 1967.

Gross hires by race, sex, and occupation in the final quarter of 1970 were estimated as the sum of separations for the group during the quarter, calculated on the basis of the separation rate estimated for the group, plus the net change in employment of the group over the quarter as reported in the quarterly status reports. Gross hires of each group were taken as a proportion of total gross hires for each occupation to compute the current hiring proportion. This is reported as line 1 for each group in Table 4.6.

The 1980 employment composition with respect to white females, black males, and black females by occupation was projected for each company on the basis of the estimated separation rates and growth rates under the assumption that the companies continue their current hiring practices.

In the computations of targets we make for individual Bell companies, we have adopted a very simple definition of qualification based on information supplied by the EEOC Task Force on AT&T. A high school diploma is a requirement for only three jobs, Sales (Mgt), Sales (Non-Mgt), and Service Representatives. Therefore, the qualified group for these jobs is the labor force with an educational attainment of at least a high school diploma. Most jobs in the three Professional categories (Accountants, Auditors, Finance; Engineers; and Staff Specialists) require a college degree; the qualified group for these categories is consequently the labor force with educational attainment of at least a college degree. This is a conservative estimate since specifying a college degree requirement for all these jobs is overstating the average educational requirements. Lacking information on the exact breakdown of degree holders versus non–degree holders, we have erred on the conservative side by assuming that all these jobs require a college degree. Officials and Managers is the most difficult group for which to delimit the qualified group, and again we have tried to err on the conservative side. Some of this occupational group are recruited from college graduates in a management training program; the rest are promoted from other jobs within the company. The latter includes those promoted from Professionals, who will have a college

---

6 Bergmann and Krause, "Evaluating and Forecasting," p. 406.

degree, and those promoted from the non-Professional jobs, who may or may not have a high school diploma. Since the EEOC Task Force on AT&T suggested that 40 percent of Officials and Managers have a college degree, we computed the target for this occupation category on the assumption that 40 percent will have a college degree and 60 percent will have a high school diploma. Since no allowance is made for Officials and Managers without a high school diploma, we are overestimating the educational requirements of the occupation. The qualified group for all other occupation categories is the whole labor force. For most jobs in which no high school diploma is required, the companies have the practice of preferring high school graduates over nongraduates. The extent to which they are able to fill these jobs with high school graduates depends, of course, on how attractive these jobs are as compared with other jobs that high school graduates have access to. Since we have no information concerning the legitimacy of the preference, we have used requirements alone in figuring targets. For each group examined in this study—black males, black females, and white females—the proportion that it comprised of the total qualified group for each occupation was computed as the target for that group in that occupation.

The targets were computed for each company, by using state information and aggregating states to the area of the company's operations. As with the population projections, El Paso, Texas, was included in Southwestern and was not added to Mountain States; all of Idaho was included in Mountain States territory and none was portioned to Pacific Northwest Bell; Cincinnati Bell, Inc., was assigned the same targets as Ohio Bell.

Information on educational attainment by race, sex, and state was not available from the 1970 *Census of Population* at the time this study was undertaken, so that we had to rely on the 1960 *Census of Population.* The choice from the 1960 *Census* was educational attainment of the population aged 25 years and older or educational attainment of the population aged 14 years and older. We chose the former[7] in order to exclude those still attending school. The 1960 educational data understate the educational attainment of blacks relative to whites in 1970, since the educational distribution of blacks has risen faster during the 1960s. Also, from the aggregate figures released from the 1970 Census, it was evident that the black population grew faster than the white population in every company area except that of South Central Bell during the 1960s. For both these reasons, the 1960 figures are a very conservative estimate of the black share of each qualified group.

Since the relevant consideration for employment targets is the labor force, these population figures were converted to labor force by multiplying each race-sex group (including white males) by its labor force participation rate. The labor force participation rates used were national figures for December 1970, taken from *Employment*

---

7 US Bureau of the Census, *US Census of Population: 1960,* Vol. I, *Characteristics of the Population,* Parts 2-52 (Washington, D.C.: US Government Printing Office, 1963), Table 47.

and Earnings.[8] The 1960 labor force figures by state would seriously underestimate the black and white female labor force in 1970 because of the great increase in female labor force participation over the decade. Therefore, we compromised by using current labor force data on a national basis, and adjusted all the companies by the same labor force participation rates.

For each company, the sum of these labor force figures for each education group was used as the base on which the target proportions were calculated. Nonwhite males (25 years and over) with a high school diploma or better in the labor force were taken as a proportion of the total labor force (25 years and over) with a high school diploma or better; nonwhite females (25 years and over) with a college degree or better in the labor force were taken as a proportion of the total labor force (25 years and over) with a college degree or better; and so on. For the occupations with essentially no educational requirements, the total labor force for each race-sex group was calculated by multiplying the total population for each race-sex group[9] by its labor force participation rate; the target proportions were then calculated as described for the education groups.

The result was three different proportions for each race-sex group in each company: one for college degree or better; one for high school diploma or better; one for labor force. They were assigned to the occupations as described earlier. The Officials and Managers target was computed as .6 times the high school diploma proportion plus .4 times the college degree proportion. The target for each group in each occupation and company is shown in line 4 for each group of Table 4.6.

8 US Department of Labor, Bureau of Labor Statistics, *Employment and Earnings,* Vol. 17 (January 1971), Table A-4, "Labor Force by Sex, Age, and Color," pp. 27–28.
9 US Bureau of the Census, *US Census of Population,* Vol. I, *Characteristics of the Population,* Part 1, United States Summary (Washington, D.C.: US Government Printing Office, 1964), Table 57, "Race by Sex, by Regions, Divisions, and States: 1960." Since this table reports Negro as well as nonwhite, we used the Negro figures; the educational data were for all nonwhites.

5 Estimating the Effects on Cost and Price of the Elimination of Sex Discrimination: The Case of Telephone Rates

Orley Ashenfelter and John Pencavel

Employers may be said to discriminate in their hiring practices when, among workers of equal productive abilities, some workers have to offer their labor for hire at lower wages than others in order to gain employment. Firms are thus faced with the choice of employing the less favored workers at relatively lower wages or the more favored workers at higher wages. Among the least discriminatory employers, this difference in offered wages more than compensates for the employer's reluctance to hire the less desired workers and these employers fill a particular job category with the less desired workers. On the other hand, the highly discriminatory employers hire the more favored workers, their higher wages notwithstanding. In this way, some firms will have some of their job classifications filled with those workers who suffer from wage discrimination while other firms employ individuals from that group who are paid the higher wages. Alternatively, among workers of different skills, a given firm will find the wage differential sufficiently large to overcome its discriminatory preferences in some job categories and employ the cheaper workers for these tasks; for other jobs, however, the wage differential does not fully overcome the employer's reluctance to hire the cheaper workers and the preferred, yet more expensive, workers are employed. Thus, within a firm, discriminatory employment policies tend to be revealed by some job categories being almost wholly filled with one group of workers and other jobs being performed entirely by another group.

This implies that the less discriminatory firms employ the cheaper labor and operate at lower pecuniary costs than more discriminatory firms. Put differently, where the extent of discriminatory practices differs among firms in a given market, production is inefficient with some resources being organized in firms with lower costs than in other firms. In such a market environment, a firm is able to reduce its costs and, therefore, the prices at which it sells its output by ceasing its discriminatory practices. The size of the cost reduction partly depends upon how other employers behave at the same time. If each and every employer ceases discriminating against one group of workers, the wages of this group will rise relative to others. The fall in costs in such a situation will be less than that in which one firm ceases its discriminatory practices while all other firms do not alter their behavior in this respect. For in this second case, when the firm has a large pool of workers from which to hire, it may replace the more favored and expensive workers with the less favored and inexpensive workers without finding that the wage rates of the latter group rise to any significant degree.

The comments in the preceding two paragraphs are nothing more than a thumbnail sketch of the basic theory of the economics of discrimination as advanced first by

Gary Becker.[1] The purpose of this paper is to trace out one of the main implications of this theory and ask, "By what amount would the firm's costs be lower in the absence of discriminatory employment decisions on the part of its management?" Since in answering this question we shall assume that other firms' discriminatory practices do not alter and that market wage rates do not change as one group of workers is substituted for another in this firm, the solution to this problem may be regarded as the lower limit to which costs fall in situations in which wage rates do respond to these employment changes.

We want to emphasize that this paper does not contain new evidence for resolving the issue of the degree to which the overall observed differences in wages between individuals may be attributed to factors associated with their market productivity as distinct from factors that can be classed as discriminatory views held by employers. For our empirical purposes, with the available data we make the best estimates of differences between the market wage rates of male and female workers who have the same employment or productivity potential. Some readers no doubt will find our estimates large, while others will find them small. In either case the reader may want to modify the predicted cost decline accordingly. Nevertheless, as we have already stated, so long as these male-female wage differentials are not zero, production costs must eventually decline after females replace males in employment. Put differently, by the very definition of discrimination, an end to discriminatory employment practices by one firm in the presence of continued discrimination in the remainder of the economy must reduce that firm's pecuniary costs of conducting business. Alternatively, if a prescribed change in a firm's employment practices does not eventually lead to a reduction in the firm's pecuniary costs, then that change cannot have been remedying discrimination.

Turning now to the particular case of the American Telephone and Telegraph Company (AT&T or Bell Telephone), their employment data reveal that, at least until the last year or two, there were a number of occupations in which women comprised a very small fraction of the work force. For instance, in the Bell companies in 1969, 99.9 percent of the job category titled "foreman of telephone craftsmen among construction, installation and maintenance employees" were male; while women constituted practically 100 percent of experienced switchboard operators.[2] Recall that this pattern for women and men to congregate in particular job categories is exactly what is predicted on the assumption that management discriminates against female employees. We now consider the effects upon Bell Telephone's operating costs if female workers replace male in some or all job categories.

1 Gary S. Becker, *The Economics of Discrimination,* 2nd ed. (Chicago: University of Chicago Press, 1971). See also Kenneth Arrow, "The Theory of Discrimination," in *Discrimination in Labor Markets,* Orley Ashenfelter and Albert Rees, eds. (Princeton: Princeton University Press, 1973).
2 These data are taken from *Statistics of Communications Common Carriers,* FCC, year ended December 31, 1969, Table 10 (1971).

To arrive at conclusions about the change in costs that follows when Bell ceases discrimination and females are substituted for male workers, we require some behavioral model that describes the company's production decisions. Suppose that, in the face of given input prices, the company acts to minimize the total costs of producing any given level of output. It is also useful to this analysis to discover if information is available on the technical relationship under which Bell combines different types of labor and services from physical capital to product output, that is, the form of the production function. To date, this evidence strongly suggests that there exists a very convenient form of the factor input-product output relationship for Bell Telephone, namely, that if each factor input is increased by a given proportion, then output will increase in the very same proportion (that is, constant returns to scale). Thus, Bert G. Hickman could not reject the hypothesis that, in the telephone communications industry, the production function is linearly homogeneous.[3] Jorgenson and Handel assume that a Cobb-Douglas function holds in communications and find that use of such an assumption describes the data well.[4] In their econometric model of AT&T, Davis, Caccappolo, and Chaudry report that, among a variety of functions, a homogeneous production function fits their data best. They also record slightly increasing returns to scale, namely, a returns to scale parameter of 1.09.[5] Finally, Sankar fits a nonconstant returns to scale CES production function to the telephone industry, but finds that the hypothesis of constant returns (that is, linear homogeneity) cannot be rejected.[6] In all these four studies, homogeneous production functions were selected to describe the input-output relationship in AT&T and, in the only case in which constant returns to scale were not estimated, the calculated parameter (1.09) was sufficiently close to unity to make the assumption of a linear homogeneous production function a good approximation.[7]

Under these assumptions—that Bell minimizes the costs of producing any given level of output and that proportional changes in all inputs yield the same proportionate change in output—the eventual change in average costs that follows when the company substitutes female workers for male takes the following form:

(1) $\Delta\ln(c/q) = w_1\Delta\ln p_2 + \ldots + w_n\Delta\ln p_n$

3 Bert G. Hickman, *Investment Demand and US Economic Growth* (Washington, D.C.: Brookings Institution, 1965), pp. 49-52.

4 D. W. Jorgenson and S. S. Handel, "Investment Behavior in US Regulated Industries," *Bell Journal of Economics and Management Science*, spring 1971 : 213–265.

5 B. E. Davis, G. J. Caccappolo, and M. A. Chaudry, "An Econometric Planning Model for American Telephone and Telegraph Company," *Bell Journal of Economics and Management Science* spring 1973 : 29–56.

6 U. Sankar, "Investment Behavior in the US Telephone Industry: 1949 to 1968," *Bell Journal of Economics and Management Science* autumn 1973 : 665–678.

7 See Appendix A to this chapter for the role of the assumption of constant returns to scale in the estimates that are to follow.

where $\Delta\ln(c/q)$ is the proportionate change in average costs, $\Delta\ln p_i$ is the proportionate difference between male and female market wage rates in each job category, w_i is the fraction of total costs that are paid to workers in each job category, and the subscripts (1 to n) index the n different job classifications.[8] It is this equation (1) that constitutes the basis of our computations.

There are two types of estimates we have to make in order to arrive at a value for $\Delta\ln(c/q)$. First, there are estimates of male-female wage differentials in each job category. These were arrived at by making use of a sample of 13,085 working individuals from the Survey of Economic Opportunity for 1967. This sample of workers was classified into four groups: males living in large metropolitan areas (i.e., with populations of at least three-quarters of a million people); males in other metropolitan areas; females in large metropolitan areas; and females in other metroplitan areas. For each of these four groups, multiple regression equations were estimated relating the hourly earnings of each individual to sixty-two variables that measure characteristics of each of the individuals—such as years of schooling, years of market experience, their occupation, industry, and the region in which each lives and works.[9] In effect, after removing the effect of schooling, experience, unionism, marital status, and industrial class on wage differentials the wages in each of the four groups (male, female, large and small metropolitan areas) were cross-classified by occupation and by region (living in the South or not) within the communications industry. By this method, male-female wage differentials are estimated for each occupation and region in the United States in the communications industry and these provide our values for the $\Delta\ln p$'s in equation (1).

To evaluate (1) we also require estimates of w_i, the proportion of total costs paid to each class of workers. These data are available for each of the major metropolitan areas, and were submitted by AT&T to the Federal Communications Commission as of 1970. An overall estimate of $\sum_i w_i \Delta\ln p_i$ is obtained first by aggregating across job titles within a metropolitan area and second by aggregating across metropolitan areas.

In the calculation of equation (1), we take cognizance of adjustment costs and on-the-job training. The replacement of a large fraction of the work force cannot be effected immediately without substantial cost. If Bell adopted the strategy of hiring female workers on a nondiscriminatory basis as male workers voluntarily quit their employment, some job categories would be filled with women more quickly than others. For instance, Southern Bell Telephone and Telegraph Company reported in testimony submitted to the Federal Communciations Commission[10] that the overall

8 Equation (1) is the discrete approximation to equation (7b) of Appendix A to this chapter and the reader is referred to this Appendix for the theoretical justification of equation (1).
9 A summary of these estimated relationships given in Appendix B to this chapter.
10 See *South Florida Plant Force Loss Study*, Southern Bell Telegraph and Telephone Co., November 1971.

separation rate in 1970 was as high as 30.9 percent per year and that for installer-repairmen and framemen, in particular, the separation rates were 57.8 percent and 47.0 percent respectively. In this case, the replacement of quitting male installer-repairmen and framemen by females would probably be substantially accomplished within several years. However, job categories that normally result from internal promotions can be filled with females only over a longer period of time. For these reasons, we allow for differential adjustment rates to a largely female labor force. Three types of job classifications are distinguished:

(i)   entry-level jobs which consist of framemen and installer-repairmen, operatives, and service workers (except those with "head" or "senior" titles), and operators, service representatives, and all clerical jobs either with wage rates equal to or less than the operators' wage or which hired at least ten persons in 1970;

(ii)   all other nonmanagement jobs; and

(iii) management level jobs.

Clearly, we should expect a less rapid concentration of females as we move from the job titles classified from (i) to (iii). Hence, we distinguish in our calculations between the effects on average costs of women replacing men first in jobs categorized under (i), then under (i) and (ii), and finally under all three categories. The estimates of the decline in average costs obtained in this way using equation (1) are as shown in Table 5.1.

Thus, if the end of discriminatory employment practices resulted in females being substituted for males in all nonmanagement jobs, Bell Telephone's average costs would have fallen by approximately 2.3 percent of their level in 1970. This means that the average price of Bell Telephone's services could also fall by 2.3 percent without affecting Bell Telephone's profitability.

Table 5.1   Estimates of Percentage Decline in Average Costs

Type of Job Category in which Females Replace Males	Decline in Average Costs (%)
Entry-level jobs only	.77
All nonmanagement jobs	2.29
All jobs	3.91

Appendix A to Chapter 5

Model of Cost and Price Behavior

In order to quantify the impact of the wage rate changes that are implied by a decrease in discrimination on costs and price it is necessary to set out an approximate behavioral model of the cost and price behavior of the firm. The model that we draw on here is the conventional analysis of the behavior of the cost minimizing firm. Our goal is to construct a simple rule of thumb, useful where there is little opportunity to engage in substantial statistical analysis, that relates the firm's cost and price of output to the prices of the inputs it uses.

If we denote by p_i and x_i the prices and quantities of each of the factors used in production, then the firm's total costs, c, are

$$(2)\ c \equiv \Sigma p_i x_i.$$

If we suppose that the production of the firm's output, q, may be described by a function

$$(3)\ q = f(x_1, \ldots, x_m)$$

of the m inputs x_i, then the firm that chooses its inputs so as to minimize (2) subject to (3) will always operate where

$$(4)\ \lambda(\partial q / \partial x_i) = p_i \qquad (i = 1, \ldots, m)$$

That is, the marginal cost (λ) times the marginal product of each factor will equal its price.

Now the total differential of the cost identity (2) is

$$dc = \Sigma p_i dx_i + \Sigma x_i dp_i$$

or noting that $zd\ln z = dz$ for any variable z,

$$(5)\ cd\ln c = \Sigma\, p_i x_i\, d\ln x_i + \Sigma\, p_i x_i\, d\ln p_i,$$

where ln denotes the natural logarithm. Likewise, the total differential of the production function (3) is

$$qd\ln q = \Sigma(\partial q / \partial x_i)\, x_i\, d\ln x_i,$$

or, after substituting the equalities (4),

(6) $\lambda q \, d\ln q = \Sigma(p_i x_i) \, d\ln x_i$.

Substituting (6) into (5) and dividing both sides of the result by c then gives the proportionate change in total minimized costs as

(7) $d\ln c = [\lambda/(c/q)] \, d\ln q + \Sigma \, [(p_i x_i)/c] \, d\ln p_i = k \, d\ln q + \Sigma \, w_i \, d\ln p_i$,

where we set $k \equiv \lambda/(c/q)$, the ratio of marginal to average costs, and $(p_i x_i/c) = w_i$, the share of the ith factor's costs in total costs.

There are two special assumptions that we can use to make equation (7) useful in practice. First, if we assume that the production function (3) is homogeneous of degree η, then $k = \frac{1}{\eta}$, a constant, in equation (7)[1]. In this case $d\ln\lambda = d\ln(c/q) = d\ln c - d\ln q$, so that proportionate changes in marginal costs equal proportionate changes in average costs, and we may rewrite (7) as

(7a) $d\ln c - d\ln q = d\ln\lambda = (k-1)d\ln q + \Sigma w_i d\ln p_i$.

Second, if we assume that the production function possesses constant returns to scale, in which case equiproportionate increases in all factor inputs produce an equiproportionate increase in output, $k = 1/\eta = 1$, and (7) specializes to

(7b) $d\ln(c/q) = d\ln\lambda = \Sigma w_i d\ln p_i$.

Formula (7b) is extremely easy to use. It says that small proportionate changes in the cost minimizing firm's marginal (and average) costs are merely a weighted average of the small proportionate changes in the input prices the firm faces, with weights equal to the share of a factor's costs in total costs. The primary usefulness of (7a) is that it tells us by how much (7b) is amiss if some empirical information is available on the actual returns to scale in the firm. In practice, of course, the unobservable infinitesimal changes $d\ln p_i$ must be replaced by finite changes $\Delta\ln p_i$, in which case (7b) is an approximation only. In addition, if we define $\Delta\ln p_i = \ln p_{im} - \ln p_{if}$, w_i may be taken as either w_{im}, w_{if} or $(w_{im} + w_{if})/2$. Though the latter is perhaps preferred, it is unlikely that the results would differ appreciably no matter which procedure is used.

----

1 If the production function is homogeneous of degree η, then it is easy to show that $\eta q = \Sigma \, (\partial q/\partial x_i)x_i$. [See J. M. Henderson and R. E. Quandt, *Microeconomic Theory*, 2nd ed. (New York: McGraw-Hill Book Company 1971), p. 81.] Substituting the equalities (3), this is $\lambda \partial q = \Sigma p_i x_i$. But as an identity $c \equiv \Sigma p_i x_i$, so that dividing the former by the latter gives $\lambda/(c/q) - 1/\eta = k$.

Finally, we inquire after a rule of thumb to indicate how output price, R, will change. Since the firm we deal with is a regulated monopoly we may consider two extreme assumptions. First, suppose that the regulatory commission accomplishes its purpose and that, without disturbing the efficiency of the firm, it forces the firm to follow a rule of marginal cost pricing. In this case $d\ln R = d\ln\lambda$ and (7b) is directly applicable. Alternatively, suppose that the regulatory commission has no effect whatever and the firm acts as a profit-maximizing monopolist. Since total revenues are $M = R(q) \cdot q$, where $R(q)$ is the product-demand curve, marginal revenue is $dM/dq = (dR/dq)q + R = R[1 + (1/\epsilon)]$, where $\epsilon = (dq/dR)(R/q)$ is the price elasticity of product demand. Since the profit-maximizing monopolist sets marginal revenue equal to marginal cost we have

(7c) $d\ln R + d\ln[1 + (1/\epsilon)] = d\ln\lambda = \Sigma w_i d\ln p_i.$

So long as ϵ is (nearly) constant for small changes in output price, $d\ln[R(1 + 1/\epsilon)]$ $\approx d\ln R$, and proportionate changes in marginal revenue are equal to proportionate changes in output price, in which case (7b) is still a satisfactory approximation. The primary usefulness of (7c) is that it tells us by how much (7b) is amiss if some empirical information is available on how the elasticity of product demand varies.

Appendix B to Chapter 5

Estimate of Wage Differentials

The estimates of proportional male-female wage differentials ($\Delta \ln p$) were arrived at by making use of observations on the hourly earnings and other characteristics of individual workers (as compiled in the Survey of Economic Opportunity for 1967) to estimate multiple regression equations for males and females and for those living in small and in large metropolitan areas separately. These regression equations took the following general form within each group of workers (i.e., for males in large urban areas, for females in large urban areas, etc.):

$$\ln H = \text{constant} + \alpha Z + \beta_1 X + \beta_2 (XD) + \beta_3 (XDS) + \epsilon$$

where $\ln H$ is the natural logarithm of the hourly wage rate and where ϵ is a stochastic disturbance term. Z is a vector of variables that measure each individual's years of schooling (in quadratic form), years of subsequent labor force experience (in quadratic form), union membership status, seventeen dummy variables indicating the industry and type of employment in which each works, any health problems, information on any previous migration of the individual, marital status, and region of the country in which each lives and works. Our purpose in including so many righthand variables is not, of course, to conduct tests on particular determinants of the hourly earnings of workers, but simply to derive a prediction for the dependent variable that minimizes the residual variance (and thus also minimizes the variance of the prediction error). X is a set of occupational dummy variables that take the value of unity if the individual is classified in a given occupation and of zero otherwise. The occupations are categorized as professional workers, managers, clerical workers, craftsmen, operatives, private household workers, service workers, farm workers, and laborers. Finally, D and S are dichotomous variables: D takes the value of unity if the individual works in utilities, transportation, and communication; and S takes the value of unity if the individual lives in the South. The coefficients β_2 and β_3 permit estimates of occupational wage differentials specific to the communications industry that also vary between the South and the rest of the country.

Let Z_1 and Z_2 refer to the education and experience variables in the vector Z. Let us also write $\bar{Z}_m$ and $\bar{Z}_f$ for the mean values of each of the other variables in Z for males and females, respectively, and α_m and α_f for the estimated regression coefficients (including the constant terms) for males and females. Then, for any single occupational category (that is, where one of the elements of X takes the value of unity and all other variables in X are set equal to zero), the proportional male/

female wage differential in the communications and utilities industry outside the South is estimated as

$$\Delta \ln p = (\alpha_{1m} - \alpha_{1f}) 12 + \alpha_m \overline{Z}_m - \alpha_f \overline{Z}_f + \beta_{1m} - \beta_{1f} + \beta_{2m} - \beta_{2f},$$

where β_1 and β_2 are the estimated regression coefficients relevant to the communications and utilities industry for that particular occupation. In the South, we add β_{3m} and subtract β_{3f} from this expression. Our calculations of $\Delta \ln p$ explicitly assume a comparison of men and women who are high school graduates (that is, with 12 years of schooling) and have little or no labor market experience.

As an illustration of the order of magnitude of the estimates of $\Delta \ln p$, the Table 5.2 contains estimates, for the ten largest SMSA's, of the standardized proportionate male/female wage differentials in the occupations that underlie the calculations on the last page in the text.

Table 5.2   Estimates of Standardized Proportionate Male/Female Wage
Differentials

Occupation	Region			
	South	Northeast	North Central	West
Professional Workers	.296	.256	.330	.288
Managerial Workers	.171	.131	.205	.163
Clerical Workers	.411	.271	.346	.303
Craftpersons	.397	.357	.431	.389
Sales Workers	.444	.404	.478	.436
Operatives	.088	.221	.295	.253

II Socio-Psychological Perspectives

6 Psychological Dimensions of Labor Force Participation of Women

Judith Long Laws

Introduction

The question of the psychological dimensions of the labor-force participation of women is an issue of considerable complexity. Unfortunately, the typical analysis of women's occupational participation focuses narrowly on the individual woman worker to the exclusion of her job and its setting. When such an approach is taken, inequality in the occupational roles of women and men may appear to be justified by differing sex roles. If we are to seriously analyze the charges of discrimination against women in the occupational world, we must focus not only on the characteristics of the woman worker but also on the characteristics of the labor market, of the employer, and of the job itself.

Characteristics of the labor market include such structural factors as pay and promotion rates as well as social factors such as attitudes of supervisors, co-workers, and spouses. These factors strongly influence a worker's experience on the job which, in turn, affects work motivation and productivity. Thus, the psychological exploration of the work-force involvement of women must concern itself not only with women's psychology, but with men's; not only with characteristics of employees, but also with those of employers; not only with aspirations, but also with experience.

I will begin by examining the structural aspects of the problem: the work situation that a woman actually confronts. This analysis establishes the ways in which jobs, rewards, and prospects for women differ from those of male workers.

The second phase of the investigation examines the rationalizations commonly offered for the differential experience of women and men in the labor market. Although these rationalizations vary, they typically share an appeal to stereotyped sex-role concepts—i.e., to ideas about what is appropriate for women and for men. At the same time, the factual status of these rationalizations is examined.

In this context, I briefly address the issues of sex differences and work motivation. An attempt is made to correct for the superficial treatment often given to the issues of achievement motivation, aspiration and occupational choice, and job satisfaction and productivity.

Several recurring questions have arisen in the debate surrounding the question of women's rights in the work place: Do women and men differ in their orientation toward paid employment? And if so, are observed differences attributable to the characteristics of workers prior to their entry into the work force, or to their differential experience in the work force? To what extent is the work-force behavior of women and men attributable to deep-seated motivations, or to recent social factors which may affect behavior?

Some insights into these questions are provided by the study of the Bell Telephone System in the following chapter. The concluding sections of that chapter focus on recommendations for the changes needed to achieve equal employment opportunity.

Sex Segregation in Occupations

Perhaps the most basic fact of life in the occupational world is the extent of sex segregation of the work force. Women tend to be found in some occupations and not others, and the same is true of men. Many occupations are sex-typed as "female" or "male," and the workers in them are concentrated in one sex or the other. Sex segregation in occupations is more dramatic than racial segregation (Fuchs 1971).* This "balkanization" of occupations has prompted some writers to conclude that there are really two labor forces, one female and one male (Oppeheimer 1970).

Major Occupational Groupings: Extent of Sex Segregation

Sex segregation has long been a feature of the American occupational structure, although many other labor-force indicators show changes over time—e.g., the proportion of females entering the labor force or the relative sizes of the major occupational categories. Table 6.1 shows the trend toward increased sex segregation from 1940 to 1970. The proportion of occupations with a high female concentration, (70–90 percent) as well as those with a high male concentration, have steadily increased over the last thirty years. This means that the polarization of female and male labor forces has *increased*. The proportion of all occupations with a more nearly equal sex ratio has not increased. Sex segregation has decreased only in those occupations with the highest male concentration, and there only slightly.

By looking at sex concentration across the major occupational categories used by the census, we can pinpoint where the changes have taken place. At one end of the occupational pyramid, the proportion of draftsmen, nonfarm laborers, and farm workers who are women (a small percentage) is less than half what it was in 1940. At the other end of the pyramid, the professional and technical workers groups show some gain. In between, the pattern is for occupations dominated by females to become even more heavily concentrated with women, and those which had few women to become even more heavily male.

Causes and Consequences of Sex Segregation in Occupations

The separation of women and men into two virtually separate labor forces is neither accidental nor arbitrary. We need to examine both the causes and the consequences of this pattern. The argument has been made that the occupations reserved for women are those which utilize the skills that women possessed in the productive

*References cited in this and the following chapter will be found listed on pp. 171–178–editor.

Table 6.1 Male Occupational Categories (1940-1970, Percentage Distribution)

Percent Male	Percent of All Occupations			
	1940	1950	1960	1970
10 and under	3.3	4.9	4.9	6.9
11-20	1.3	1.6	2.2	3.2
21-30	2.3	2.2	2.5	3.2
31-40	2.0	3.0	3.8	3.6
41-50	3.0	4.1	3.3	2.5
51-60	5.6	6.0	5.7	5.5
61-70	3.3	6.8	6.3	8.0
71-80	6.3	6.0	6.8	11.8
81-90	13.8	16.6	16.3	14.7
91-100	59.2	48.8	48.2	40.8
	N=304	N=367	N=367	N=476
% Male in Labor Force	75%	72%	67%	62%

Source: Rosenthal, Evelyn R. "Structural Patterns of Women's Occupational Choice." (Unpublished Ph.D. Dissertation, Cornell University, 1974), p. 33.

economy of preindustrial times (Oppenheimer 1970). To the extent that this pattern can be substantiated, it illustrates a very traditional view of women's work capabilities and the ways in which these should be utilized.

It would be much more difficult to make a case for the argument that the predominantly male occupations require the kinds of skills men possessed in the preindustrial economy. The primary industries (e.g., farming, mining) do require brawn, and are dominated by men. The proportion of the total labor force working in these occupations has, however, steadily declined over the decades, as other occupational categories have expanded. Technological advances have substituted mechanization for brawn in many jobs. Today, many occupations (e.g., managerial, technical and professional; industrial production) require skills which did not exist fifty years ago. These skills do not have roots in traditional sex roles, and are taught neither in the family nor in the age-graded social structure of a traditional community, but in specialized institutions or on the job. They can be taught to persons of either sex. However, the assumptions made about the capacities of female and male workers appear to be different. It is assumed that men are limited neither by their anatomy nor by traditional roles, but, on the contrary, are capable of learning the skills requisite to a broad range of occupations.

The appeal to history is an inadequate explanation of why females are found in the occupations they practice today. The answer lies in current conditions, most notably in aspects of social structure. A major consideration is the bearing that sex roles have on occupation. We will need to explore the content of sex roles, and how they affect the behavior of workers of both sexes. We must take a closer look at *how* women and men are channeled, what options they have, what restrictions they confront, and what motivations come into play.

The foregoing gives a broad-brushstroke picture of the work situation that confronts women. Many economists and sociologists have tried to fill in the details by disaggregating data and studying smaller units such as the individual company or industry. A number of researchers have sought to study all the factors which could account for the disparity in pay between female and male workers, and to estimate the effect of pure sex discrimination (Hamilton 1970). Hamilton (1970) and McNulty (1967) both found that the discrepancy between pay rates of women and men is less when persons of both sexes are employed in the same establishment. When jobs are sex segregated, the wage differential is higher.[1] Another finding is that women tend to be overeducated relative to the requirements of their jobs; their education does not "buy" them the same rate of return as it does for men.

---

1 Although these authors do not attempt to explain this finding, one possible reason is that, to the extent that individuals of different sexes work more closely together, they are likely to know more about each other, including perhaps salary data. This same proximity permits comparisons of the ratio of their inputs to rewards with those of their fellow workers because males and females, interacting on the job, have an opportunity to exchange information about qualifications and pay. Under these conditions, inequitable ratios of inputs to payoffs may not be tolerated.

Sex-labeling of Jobs

The various features of the labor market that I have discussed are underscored by the pervasive sex-labeling of jobs. Ideas about the "appropriateness" or "suitability" of particular jobs for one sex or the other are widespread (Oppenheimer 1972, p. 45 ff.). These come about in various ways. Some formulations refer to real or putative abilities which may be distributed unequally between the sexes. Others refer to the interpersonal consequences—in most cases, anticipated rather than actual—of "mixing up" the sexes. Another factor is the expectation that a job will continue to be filled by a succession of similar persons. (In this way, an informal tradition grows up that a job is a man's or a woman's job.) Finally, judgments about the "appropriateness" of a job for a given individual may have nothing to do with the specific features of either the job or the individual but be based instead on very general notions of "masculinity" and "femininity." These various social factors often influence the individual's occupational choice.

One consequence of the sex-labeling of occupations is that the choice of an occupation in which most practitioners are of a different sex may impugn the individual's femininity (or masculinity). It is widely assumed that individuals are not attracted to jobs which are staffed predominantly by the "opposite" sex. It is viewed as highly unusual for a man to be attracted to hairdressing, or a woman to engineering, because such a choice would be viewed as sex-role incongruent. Sex-role expectations play a major part in occupational choice. The effects of the sex-role factor are very pervasive in labor force behavior, so much so that any analysis which fails to take them into account is likely to be superficial and misdirected.[2]

A second consequence of sex-labeling is that sex-role expectations are attached not only to individuals, but to jobs as well. Because of their history and their numerical composition, occupations come to be perceived as "masculine" or "feminine." This remains true even when the technology or job requirements responsible for the original sex-typing change (Gubbels 1972).

When occupations become sex-typed, many consequences follow. Pay rates are different for women and men and for jobs sex-typed as "male" or "female." Even the same job, when assigned to females and males, will carry a different salary. An example of this is the Switchroom Helper or Frameman job within the Bell Telephone System. In Detroit, this was considered a female job, and was paid according to the clerical scale, whose ceiling was $7,000 annually. In other operating companies

---

2 Sex-role congruence is only one of the incentive features of a given occupation. The greater "willingness" of men to cross the barriers into female occupations, noted by Hartley (1970), can be accounted for by the higher rates of pay which they command. Men entering "women's" occupations tend to be paid more and promoted to higher ranks, as compared with either the women in these occupations or the women who are entering "men's" occupations. For men in "female" occupations, apparently, the positive incentives outweigh the negative effect of sex-role incongruence.

within the Bell System, it was considered a male job, and paid between $7,500 and $8,500 (EEOC 1972).

A third effect of the sex segregation of the labor force relates to career opportunities—that is, the expectation that rewards, responsibilities, and recognition will continue to be increased with years of labor-force participation. The occupations which meet the definition of "career" tend to be largely those which have high concentrations of men, and which are sex-typed "masculine." The characteristics of "feminine" occupations are quite different.

A fourth effect of the sex-typing of occupations directly affects the occupational aspirations and occupational choices of women. The absence of examples of women practitioners in many occupations gives rise to the expectation that women cannot do certain jobs, and consequently young persons do not consider these among their options. Research on various forms of media (including TV, movies, advertisements and textbooks) shows that the media exaggerate this sort of distorted perception in failing even to represent occupations in their true statistical sex compositions (Himmelweit 1960).

A fifth effect of the sex segregation of occupations is increased competition for jobs among women. As we have seen, women are heavily concentrated in a few occupations and virtually excluded from some. This concentration has been increasing in recent years. At the same time, more women have entered the labor force. Since 1947, the increase of women in the labor force has outstripped that of men (75 percent as compared with 16 percent for men). The female labor force is more heterogenous now than it was in 1940; more of the women workers are older, are married, and have children living at home than was the case in previous years. Table 6.2 shows the increase in labor-force participation rate for married women classified by the age of their children. The female labor force of today is made up of women of greater diversity than formerly, but this wider range is restricted by even tighter segregation than before. Although the largest category of labor-force growth in recent years has been that of married women, these new recruits have been entering occupations previously dominated by women, rather than crossing the line into "masculine" occupations.

A sixth consequence of the "balkanization" of the labor force into two distinct pools is that it virtually cuts off competition between the sexes for jobs. A variety of factors makes women and men not "eligible" for the same job. Competition for jobs is thus limited, in the main, to those of the same sex. Female and male jobs carry different salaries and different potential for advancement, as well as differing in numerous intrinsic qualities.

"Competition" means something different in a labor market where jobs are scarce than in one in which workers are scarce. In view of recent increases in the female labor force, some economists (Bergmann and Adleman 1973) have reexamined the "overcrowding" hypothesis. Because women are restricted to certain occupations,

Table 6.2 Married Women, Husband Present, in the Labor Force, by
Presence and Age of Children   (1950-1969)[a]

	1950	1955	1960	1965	1969
Total	23.8	27.7	30.5	34.7	39.6
No Children under 18	30.3	32.7	34.7	38.3	41.0
Children 6-17 only	28.3	34.7	39.0	42.7	48.6
Children under 6	11.9	16.2	18.6	23.3	28.5
Also with children 6-17	12.6	17.3	18.9	22.8	27.8

Source: U.S. Bureau of the Census, Statistical Abstract
of the United States. 1970. (91st edition) Washington,
D. C., 1970: p. 223, Table 331.

a   Married women in the labor force as percent of married
    women in the population

wages may be depressed by the oversupply of these workers. On the other hand, the
male labor market shows a demand in some jobs which exceeds the supply. Labor
shortages have been reported in some jobs requiring education (but not specialized or
postgraduate training). The labor scarcity artificially induced by sex segregation is
one cause of the higher wages men command.[3]

The analysis so far has emphasized the extent to which women and men operate in
essentially separate labor markets. Where the question of discrimination is raised, we
must consider an additional question.

Is Separate Necessarily Unequal? Characteristics of "Female" Occupations
Oppenheimer (1970) has brought together the characteristics common to occupations that are sex-typed "female."
These include:
1. Low pay.
2. Requiring skills which the worker possesses before taking the job (little on-the-job
   training).

3 However, sex discrimination alone accounts for part of this differential. Within the same
occupation and rank, women with credentials equal to their male peers are commonly paid less
(Simon et al. 1966).

3. Requiring no career continuity.

4. Requiring little specialization, such that employment opportunities can be found wherever the husband chooses to domicile.

Each of these fits in systematically with the arrangement of sex-segregated labor markets, and with the underlying ideology.

1. The observation that pay is low may be relative to the amount of education (or other employee inputs) that the worker possesses, or relative to the pay scale for men with comparable qualifications.

2. Little on-the-job training. This characteristic of "female" occupations has two advantages for the employer: (a) he can treat workers as interchangeable, and hence insulate himself both from force loss and from worker demands for improvement of work conditions; and (b) he does not invest time and training in the female worker, hence risks minimal loss if he loses her. By doing thus, he fails to increase her value, either to himself or to another employer. It is possible that he also creates thereby a minimal job, which affects both worker motivation and performance. These effects will be examined in greater detail in the section on work motivation (pp.000ff.)

3. The lack of career continuity is related to the minimal job, one in which worker quality makes little difference. The worker's contribution is not unique; the work does not cumulate over her working life; it is not progressively more demanding. Such work does not have distinct, marked-off stages or statuses within it; there is no increasing curve of competence, achievement, or reward. Thus, the term "career" is a misnomer when applied to the minimal job, no matter how long its time span.

4. The lack of specialization is seen as an advantage, but only in the context of very traditional sex-role specifications for women. It assumes (a) that all women workers are married; (b) that their work force participation will be interrupted rather than continuous; and (c) that they will of necessity arrange their work around their husband's career decisions, including those that involve geographic mobility.

These vicissitudes of women's occupational life are often justified by reference to traditional sex-role expectations for women, which give priority to marriage. Traditional sex-role expectations for women—however well or ill these fit the individual worker—appear to be a major factor in the process by which occupations historically became sex-typed. According to Oppenheimer (1970), women were more "expendable" in the early days of industrialization than men, who were reluctant to leave the land. Before mechanization of industry, women were placed in jobs which required the same skills that they had been taught at home, as part of their sex-role training. The early sex-typing of teaching, nursing, and some jobs in the textile industry is explained on this basis. Other factors entered in, as well: "female" jobs were not well enough paid to lure men away from "male" jobs (while these, of course, were closed to women). The acquisition of new skills was barred to women in many cases; universities and professional schools did not admit women, and apprenticeship programs in many of the skilled trades are still closed to women. In addition, the sex composition of an occupation affects recruitment.

The relative weight of these factors may be estimated by examining a case study offered by Oppenheimer. Her example is elementary school teaching, an occupation which exhibits many of the characteristics of the typical "female" occupations and one which requires competence with young children, a skill considered to be part of the traditional female role. The educational requirement is high for a job at this pay rate. Yet Oppenheimer shows that of jobs in the Professional, Technical, and Kindred Workers category, only those with a very high percent female, or a very low educational requirement, pay less than elementary school teaching.

However, with the upgrading of teachers' salaries, we observe an influx of men into the profession. These recruits differ from the ordinary elementary school teacher in ways other than gender. Their career expectations are not the same as those of their female peers; they do not anticipate 30–40 years' service as teachers, but rather see themselves as being groomed for the higher paid and more prestigious administrative ranks.

A similar transition appears to be occurring within librarianship, another "female" profession. Kronus and Grimm (1971) found that men are overrepresented in the high ranks and prestigious positions within this profession, in proportion to their numbers. These two cases suggest that, even in the occupations most dominated (numerically) by women, the bosses are still men.

Keeping Women in Their Place: The Functions of Myth and Myth-making

Our review of the distribution of women in the labor force has revealed that women are found in places where one would not expect to find workers of their qualifications. This is particularly evident when it comes to education; we find that women do not command the jobs for which their education qualifies them, nor do they command the rates of pay commensurate with their years of education. Some of their characteristics as workers are *discounted* by employers, and this produces the pattern of participation in "women's occupations" that we have summarized. It appears that women are *restricted* to certain locations in the occupational structure, on the basis of certain ideas which are assumed to hold true for all women workers. Thus, although the female labor force is heterogeneous, and increasingly so, a pervasive mythology treats it as a homogeneous category. These beliefs, held by employers and applied without distinction to all potential female employees, significantly affect the work opportunities made available to women. This set of beliefs runs contrary to established facts, and for this reason, the US Department of Labor refers to them as myths.[4] They include assertions that women are not full-time or fully motivated workers; that they shun advancement and responsibility; that women's place is in the

4 Publications of the US Department of Labor, Women's Bureau, provide detailed factual information in rebuttal of the prevalent myths about women workers. These publications include *Background Facts on Women Workers in the United States* (1970), *The Myth and the Reality* (1971), and *Absenteeism and Turnover* (1970).

home; that women workers have high absenteeism and turnover; that children of working mothers show ill effects; that women cannot supervise men; that women are taking jobs away from men who must support a family.

Recognizing the mythical nature of these ideas about women workers draws attention to several important characteristics of such beliefs: (1) they are contrary to fact, but (2) they are nonetheless believed; consequently, (3) they must serve some function for the culture which believes them. Myths of primitive peoples often serve the function of giving an acceptable (although inaccurate) explanation of something troublesome or puzzling—for example, the uncontrollable quirks of the weather, or the mystery of biological paternity. The myth is an "explanation" that fits in with the rest of the culture. So it is with myths about women workers, for these reflect the traditional sex-role expectations concerning women. A second function of myths is to justify or legitimate the manner in which things are done in a culture, often by reference to the authority of a supernatural being, or to natural law, or the like. Thirdly, myths may be thought of as a form of wishful thinking. In the case of women workers, if the myths were true, they would "justify" inequitable treatment of women in the labor market.

A number of these myths about women workers seem to serve the function of suppressing the competition of women with men for jobs. Beliefs which state that women are less desirable than men as workers (for example, "because" they quit, are out sick, or don't have what it takes to rise through the ranks) serve this function. Myths which imply that it is inappropriate for women to commit themselves to their work, because they "should" give priority to being wives and mothers, serve the same function, but less directly. The myth which asserts that women are financial dependents—and completely ignores those who support themselves and a family, wholly or in part—is of this type. The myth that women cannot supervise men, and the myth that women are not interested in advancement, are rationalizations for the unwillingness of men to permit women these opportunities.

Like the myths of primitive cultures, myths about women workers articulate well with other patterns in our society. We can see, for example, a set of relationships between the myths concerning women workers and the objective characteristics of "women's jobs." The former might best be viewed as role prescriptions: things a woman worker ought to do or be, qua woman. The latter might best be viewed as incentives, positive or negative, which reward or punish the labor-market behavior of women. The way they interlock would seem destined to produce a self-fulfilling prophecy.

The Self-fulfilling Prophecy

A self-fulfilling prophecy involves a vicious circle which begins with a prejudicial attitude toward the worker—for example, the expectation that she will quit the job. A problem is assumed to exist. Consequently, the employer "protects himself" from this "threat" by structuring the job in such a way that the responsibility and discretion of the individual worker is minimized, and she can readily be replaced by any other worker. Managers hope to minimize their potential losses by minimizing investment in women workers. In so doing, they create impoverished jobs, which do not satisfy or challenge or reward the workers. As a consequence of these arrangements—not as a consequence of the worker's assumed, a priori characteristics, on which the "prophecy" is based—the worker's motivation is negatively affected, and she may leave. This is called a self-fulfilling prophecy because the initial premise sets in motion a set of consequences which themselves produce the undesired effect. A self-fulfilling prophecy is by definition a false prediction, since it looks to the wrong set of factors to "explain" the ultimate effect. If the assumptions were correct, then, in our example, the woman worker would quit her job even if it offered *positive* incentives; that is, if she were paid the same as a man, and given responsibility and advancement commensurate with her training and past performance. However, the self-fulfilling prophecy shortcircuits the possibility of testing out the effects of different incentive situations, for it assumes in advance what the outcome will be.

The self-fulfilling prophecy has two important consequences; the first affects the employer, and the second the employee.

For the employer, the self-fulfilling prophecy is a fallacious belief. Because he believes it, and because he acts in such a way as to bring about the prophesied outcome, it is difficult for the "hypothesis" to receive a real test.[5]

The second consequence of the self-fulfilling prophecy is its effect on the work motivation of women workers. Consider again the characteristics of "female" occupations: (1) low pay; (2) little on-the-job training; (3) no career continuity; and (4) no specialization. Lack of pay and of opportunity for advancement are both negative work incentives, while failure to provide skills and lack of specialization both impede the worker from moving up in the organization. If women workers are subjected to these job conditions because they are women, and certain assumptions are being made about their motivation toward work, then what we have is a classic example of the self-fulfilling prophecy.

The same cycle can be seen when we compare the myths regarding women workers, and the objective conditions which seem to embody them. If women are paid "pin money" (as contrasted with the living wage paid men), then this ought to affect their motivation. If women are censured for taking jobs, this also constitutes a cost or penalty for them. If women are denied the opportunity to take on more

---

5 A rather comprehensive educative process is required in order for employers to become aware of the contribution made by their own attitudes and behavior to the "problems" they report with employees. A long tradition of human-relations training in industry exists (e.g., Likert 1967; Kay, Meyer, and French 1965; McGregor 1960). A recent contribution focusing specifically on women, and containing many concrete suggestions and analyses, is the work by Rosalind Loring and Theodora Wells, *Women: Breakthrough into Management* (1973).

responsibility, they can never prove themselves. If mothers are denied employment because other people assume the responsibility to decide what their family obligations are, they are cut off from work. If employers refuse to promote women to supervisory positions, the hypothesis that women cannot manage men will never be tested.

We have arrived at a major paradox in our analysis of the factors affecting women's labor force participation: On the one hand, we find a body of emphatically believed myths about the kind of workers women are; but, on the other hand, we discover a set of objectively measured conditions which are likely to dampen anyone's enthusiasm for her job. In order to resolve these complexities, we will need to define and examine the concept of work motivation.

Theories of Work Motivation

At the present time, one seldom hears forthright assertions about the inferiority of women as a justification for paying them less and restricting their opportunities. Instead, employers (and, for that matter, social science experts) very commonly claim that women are not motivated toward work as men are, and hence do not deserve the same consideration. This, of course, is the premise underlying the "pin money" myth, the female-turnover myth, and others. These myths, as we have seen, are specious. Yet the underlying concept of work motivation continues to be taken very seriously by psychologists, both those who study achievement motivation in the universities and those who study worker morale and productivity in factories and work organizations.

The term "work motivation" is sometimes used without the clarity we would desire. Some people use the term interchangeably with the term "achievement motivation." Others infer the individual's work motivation from occupational choice or from labor-force attachment, without attempting to measure motivation directly. Sometimes the individual's work motivation is discussed as though the context of that motivation—the positive and negative incentives we have been discussing—can be safely ignored. In yet other treatments, a given context is invented, or assumed, and is not studied directly (e.g., Psathas 1968).

A number of theorists invent a special context for women workers' motivation. They assume that women give top priority to family considerations, and that their commitment to a job is consequently less than men's.[6] In fact, the connection between the two is completely unproven. What is needed is empirical evidence on the relationship between priorities (both men's and women's) and performance on the job.

6 There is evidence that women who have undertaken both family and job responsibilities work very hard at their two jobs. However, they meet these demands not by slacking off, but by increasing their efficiency, thereby getting more done in a given period of time.

Studies of job motivation in the work force as a whole indicate that a pattern of low job interest is characteristic of many workers, men as well as women. Nevertheless, the assertion is often made that women differ from men in this respect.[7] Such comparisons of women's work motivation with men's rests on the implicit assumption that men are devoted to their jobs, that their motivation is undivided, and that this has measurable effect on their productivity. Kuhlen (1963) simply asserts that ". . . a career role tends to be primary for males and relatively secondary for females" (1963, p. 56), with no citation of supporting evidence. It would certainly be a straightforward research strategy to ask women and men about the relative importance of various areas of endeavor. In fact, however, importance was not one of the variables measured in Kuhlen's study. Kuhlen did not treat his proposition about sex differences in importance of job as a hypothesis to be tested, but left it an assumption. Failing to test this "career saliency" of men and women, Kuhlen then explains his observed findings in terms of the assumed difference. His often-quoted conclusion, a classic illustration of logical circularity, is completely invalid. Even more serious, perhaps, is the perpetuation of his error by other scholars who uncritically cite him.

A first step in assessing women's work motivation is to correct the assumptions commonly made about men's work motivation. The model of male work motivation that is used as a reference point when female work motivation is discussed is one of doubtful validity. Blauner (1960) has shown that a majority of jobs in our occupational structure are neither demanding nor intrinsically rewarding, and the job incumbents do not show a pattern of intense work involvement. Rather, the values they find in their work are often extrinsic ones—pay, benefits, congenial co-workers, seniority.

Dubin (1955) discovered that for 75 percent of industrial workers in a large-scale study, neither work nor the work place was numbered among central life interests. These data cast doubt on the assumption that work is central to most men (e.g., Kuhlen 1963) and the invidious comparison with women which is commonly based upon it. In this same study, the great majority (91 percent) of workers made family and friends, rather than co-workers, the focus of their social life.

Morse and Weiss (1955) studied a national sample of employed men. The most common reason men gave for persisting in employment was "to keep occupied." The authors note that 36 percent of those who report they want to keep working give

7 Miller and Reissman (1961) have criticized the tendency to compare observations made on the working class with those made on the middle class (1961, p. 27). This preoccupation reflects the class-centeredness of researchers and scholars who are exploring this topic and, Miller and Reissman feel, constitutes an obstacle to valid understanding of working-class life. A parallel critique perhaps can be made of the literature on women workers. In this literature, very often comparisons with assumed characteristics of male workers are invoked. These tend not to be systematic comparisons of empirically measured variables. A consequence of this practice is that we tend to think we know more about women workers than we do, and we think we know how they differ from what we think we know about men.

only negative reasons for it, seeming to view their jobs as a means of warding off isolation, idleness or "trouble" (1955, p. 192). When asked what they would miss most if they stopped working, the largest proportion (31 percent) said friends and contacts. Only 12 percent said they would miss "the kind of work I do." Among the positive reasons for working, enjoyment of the kind of work was mentioned by less than 7 percent of the men. These data do not lend much support to the assumed generality of the masculine model of work motivation.

To the extent that this model has any validity, it would seem to apply to those in middle class and particularly in professional occupations. Morse and Weiss (1955) found that the bases for job satisfaction varied by occupation: professionals and sales persons cite the content of the job itself, managers cite salary, and service workers mention contacts with co-workers and customers. Inkeles (1960), in reviewing multinational comparisons, reports that workers preferred incentives which assured security, while employers preferred riskier incentives. Again, professionals cite occupational values which include challenge and self-actualization about three times as frequently as unskilled workers. These findings strongly suggest that what we are observing is a class effect rather than a sex effect. Another study cited by Inkeles investigated the reasons for working of Dutch workers, and found them to be primarily instrumental in nature. Men worked for their families, and for money. No mention of intrinsic work motivation is reported.

Centers and Bugental (1966) failed to find overall sex differences when they interviewed 692 employed adults about the aspects of their jobs that they valued. Rather, like Dubin, they found class effects: at lower occupational levels, workers valued extrinsic factors more, while at high occupational levels workers valued intrinsic factors more. Significant sex differences were found on one of the intrinsic factors (with men higher than women in valuing "self-expression") and on one of the extrinsic factors (women higher than men in valuing "co-workers"). However, occupational level was not controlled in this analysis, so it is impossible to ascertain whether male respondents were disproportionately concentrated in the higher occupations and women in the lower, as is the case in the labor force as a whole (Peterson 1964). The study employed a stratified sampling technique, making it highly likely that the sex distribution parallels that of the total labor force. The elusive, perhaps mythical ideal of "career saliency," as shorthand for the kind of masculine career motivation model we have discussed, fails to appear in many studies. Kuhlen (1963), in attempting to explain the low incidence of significant correlations in his study, suggests that career is less salient for teachers than for some occupational groups—but does not say what these might be. There is a real possibility that this idea, too, is a myth.

If the model of the hardworking, intensely committed worker with a lifetime involvement with a career fits anyone, it fits the professional (Hall 1969)—and the research here shows that women professionals do not differ from men in what they put into their work, nor in their productivity. This tends to be true across the professions, whether we are considering law (White 1972), academia (Simon et al. 1966), medicine (Phelps 1968), or secondary school teaching (Kuhlen 1963).

The professions appear to represent the ideal situation, in terms of work motivation. Besides affording high pay and prestige, these occupations commonly allow the worker a high degree of control over her work, responsibility, and the opportunity to use and develop valued skills. In addition, they may offer a succession of ranks, with increasing pay and perquisites. These inducements seem to have the same effect on women's work motivation and performance as men's. Occupations offering these inducements are commonly called careers, and those who are fortunate enough to occupy them are often called career-oriented.

Some writers (e.g., Tyler 1972) state that the proportion of working women who exhibit "career orientation" is a minority, while implying that the majority of working men are career-oriented. A concern with the size of the group of women interested in the kind of work involvement associated with the professions is a red herring. The question is, rather, what are the factors which feed, and which dampen, work motivation?

Another source of distortion—the under-estimation of the proportion of women with substantial labor-force participation throughout the life cycle—may derive from the use of the term "career." This term invokes the image of intense, single-minded commitment—the masculine professional model we have already identified. In addition, the term "career woman" has the force of an epithet.[8] Very few women would voluntarily apply this label to themselves; and yet many have the expectation of continuous labor-force participation in their adult lives, and would undoubtedly report this to a researcher who asked about behavior rather than abstract labels.[9] For the researcher interested in validity and prediction, the preferable strategy is probably to focus on behavior. One should study labor-force participation and labor-force attachment, rather than motivational constructs. But in any case, the researcher should avoid becoming confused as to whether he is studying motivation or behavior.

8 Tenopyr (1970) studied the attitudes of college students toward the "career woman." Perceptions that emerged in this study included ones of frigidity, undependability, unattractiveness, as well as perceptions that working women were bad wives and mothers, man-haters, castrating, and sexually frustrated. These attitudes were shared by both women and men, but endorsed more emphatically by the latter.

9 This difficulty is apparent in the study reported by Oppenheimer (1972). College graduates shied away from the self-attribution of "career women." When we look at data on labor-force participation, it is clear that a much larger percentage of women have continuous work involvement than are willing to describe themselves in this way. The problem is one of "situated vocabularies of motive" (Mills 1940)—to what kinds of things it is acceptable for a person in a particular social niche to admit. We are dealing with women who expect to be married, and are well aware of the role prescriptions for that niche. Respondents in a study by Glenn (1959) endorsed a number of conditions under which they considered it acceptable for a mother to work. These included a variety of situations in which the woman's work facilitated the well-being of her family, but did not include the desire for self-actualization, fame, success, achievement, or recognition for the woman as an individual.

The most noticeable difference between women and men professionals at present is not in personality traits or desire for success, but simply in their relative numbers. Some of this disparity can be accounted for by structural barriers to equal participation by women (e.g., admissions quotas, lack of financial support, lack of childcare, restrictions against part-time study, employer prejudice). Some is accounted for in terms of motivation, and this in turn reflects the positive and negative incentives perceived by the individual. Thus far we have discussed the differences in incentives provided for women and men in the labor force. We now examine how these incentives affect motivation.

Aspiration, Achievement Motivation, and Expectancy × Value Theory

Achievement motivation was widely studied throughout the fifties and sixties. Performance on competitive tests, aspiration levels on games of skill and chance, and occupational aspiration all came under study as parts of the general motivational-research phenomenon. Social psychologists who have devoted themselves to the study of achievement motivation have found it necessary to distinguish two components of achievement motivation: the desire for a goal (called its *incentive value*) and the individual's expectation of attaining it (called *subjective probability* or *expectancy*). In order to predict how hard the individual will try (or what she will try for) the psychologist needs to know both components. The behavioral tendency cannot be predicted from knowing only the value of a goal. Conversely, neither the value nor the expectancy can be inferred from the observed behavior, since it is the outcome of an interaction between the two.

In general, the theory is expressed by

$$F = E \times V,$$

where F is the resultant motivational force (or effort), E is the subjective probability of success (usually expressed as a percentage—e.g., .50, .20, etc.), and V is the value the goal has for the individual. The outcome F is usually conceived in terms of the effort the person exerts to achieve the goal. However, we could use this model to predict occupational choice as well. The individual's occupational choice may be a compromise between that which is most preferred (high V) and that which is most attainable (high E).

Research on achievement motivation has revealed that, given a choice, persons high in the need for achievement prefer to work in situations where the probability of success or failure is about the same (Atkinson 1958). For these persons, a task having a very high probability of success is too easy to arouse the achievement motive—the sense of achievement at mastering an easy task is too low. Conversely, although a very difficult task may be challenging enough to arouse the motive, the threat of failure which accompanies a very low probability of success diminishes

Table 6.3   Illustration of Expectancy x Value Theory

	Value	Expectancy	(Effort)
Mrs. X	7	.1	.7
Ms. Y	7	.5	3.5
Mr. Z	5	.25	1.25

motivation. This theory predicts that individuals high in the need for achievement will shun both the very risky and the riskless, preferring odds approximating 50/50. This prediction would hold for both women and men. If women and men differ in terms of achievement motivation for occupational attainment, it may be due to differences in value, in expectancy, or both.

As an illustration, let us take three hypothetical individuals with different expectancies and values for occupational success. In this example Mrs. X and Ms. Y have the same degree of desire for the goal (value), but Ms. Y has a higher chance of attaining the goal (i.e., higher expectancy). Mr. Z represents a hypothetical individual who, though less motivated by the goal than either of the women, can expect a higher probability of success than Mrs. X. According to the theory, the resultant effort, given these combinations, would be as revealed in the last column of Table 6.3. The differences are in line with the theory: no matter how strong the motivation, if paths to goal attainment are blocked, the resultant force is drastically restricted.

The implications of this model should be borne in mind when we review the research on women's occupational "choice." When women lower their occupational aspirations, this may reflect a realistic assessment of their chances for success. Expectancy is thus conditioned by knowledge of the current labor market.[10]

The implications of the expectancy × value model are even more striking for predicting future labor-force behavior of women. If it is the expectancy factor, rather than the value factor, which is restricted by current conditions, then any improvement in the objective probability of success should be mirrored by an increase in the subjective probability of success. As barriers to women's equal participation in the

10 Many studies of occupational aspiration and occupational "choice" are naive with regard to achievement motivation theory. Some authors (e.g., Tyler 1972) attribute sex differences in occupations to the value factor in the equation, neglecting the expectancy factor. There are many studies which show, however, that women (and blacks) desire the same goals as white men. The difference comes in the expectation of attaining these goals. Insofar as expectancy reflects the real-life facts of the sex composition of occupations, we would not expect that the average women worker's expectancy term would equal that of the average male worker. When women and men are matched not only on value, but also on expectancy, however, their occupational preferences are equivalent (Gurin 1974, pp. 16–17). Similarly, when women believe they have a fair chance at promotion, their desire to work matches that of men.

labor market are removed, we can predict that the subjective probability of goal attainment will increase, and the resultant effort will also increase.

Determinants of Women's Occupational Choice

Earlier in this chapter I noted that the jobs which women hold are often far from an expression of choice. Often they represent what is left over after the range of possible occupations has been thinned by the simultaneous operation of many constraints: restriction of opportunities for women, family demands, sexist counseling, arduous demands of some occupations, considerations of transportation, hours, and pay. Many studies of women's occupational "choice" are really studies of occupational default.[11] They neglect to collect data on women workers' occupational preferences. We are particularly in need of studies of the process by which occupational aspirations are adjusted downward. Research is needed on the critical points at which this "adjustment" takes place, and on the agents which induce the individual to settle for her less preferred options. For the woman currently employed, we need to know what her occupational preferences *were* as well as what they *are*.

At present we know very little about the dynamic process by which women's work orientation is formed: the development of attraction to different types of work, the processes of exploration and mastery that underlie competence motivation, the desire for achievement, the perception of instrumentalities for goal attainment, the history of attempts and of successes and failures, the consequent differentiation of goals and changes in aspiration—and, of course, the competing or contradictory internal and external pressures on women.

At present our knowledge about these questions is both superficial and fragmentary. It would clearly be a misguided form of scholarship to tap into one point in this process and then offer conclusions about the whole. Similarly, if women's occupational behavior is a process, and if this process ebbs and flows in consonance with the life cycle, then it will be dangerous to generalize from studies based on one point in time. Thus if the individual's current occuaption is taken as the end point in a process of occupational "choice," the research will be unprepared to predict changes in that individual's occupational behavior. Yet aggregate data on the female labor force strongly indicate that such changes are now taking place, and will accelerate in the future (*Handbook of Women Workers* 1969).

An approach which traced the history of a woman worker's occupational choice from girlhood to adulthood would still be heavily oriented toward the status quo. It

11 It is worth noting, however, that some occupations are almost never chosen. In Harmon's (1971) list of occupations ever considered by a sample of college freshmen, Telephone Company Supervisor received *no* choices. In Davis's (1964) study, only 4 out of 925 young women mentioned Telephone Operator as a possible occupation. Yet the 30 operating companies of the Bell Telephone Company employ upwards of 165,000 women as operators, and an additional 13,000 as Group Chief Operators. It would probably be a mistake to infer that these individuals *chose* this occupation.

neglects the possible influence of perceived incentives on occupational "choice," and consequently ignores the possibility of change. The limited horizons of many women workers reflect conditions as they are. These may (partially in response to governmental pressure) change. Increasing the positive incentives—or even decreasing the negative ones—will affect women's aspirations. Indeed, critical research on women's aspiration, occupational choice, and job-relevant attributes shows clearly that removing barriers (negative incentives) brings about an immediate upward spurt in women's applications for "male" jobs (Bem and Bem 1972), expression of career aspiration (Farmer and Bohn 1970), and problem-solving performance (Carey 1955).

A look at the research on occupational aspirations of young girls gives us some insight into the influences which transform preferences into "choice." Long before they enter the world of work, young girls appear to weigh the attractions of various occupations against other factors, largely sex-role considerations. Davis (1964), in a study of junior high and high school women of blue collar background, found that 60 percent believed most women want a job as well as a family. Only 25 percent of this sample, however, *expected* to obtain their most perferred job. The other 75 percent most commonly listed marriage as the major obstacle to accomplishing their occupational aspiration.

Other findings from this study cast light on the considerations that influence the work orientation of women in its formative stages. (1) The girls, contrary to the stereotype that women are casual about employment, have given more thought to their future occupation than have the boys in this study. (2) Boys show less tolerant attitudes toward women's working than the girls do.[12] (3) Although girls are able to give ratings on the prestige of occupations, they do not choose the high prestige occupations for themselves. (4) The girls' choices pile up in certain traditional female occupations: secretary, teacher, nurse, and beautician account for more than half of their choices. (5) The incentive values they attribute to the jobs they chose seem to fall into three groups. The most frequent was intrinsic interest in "the work itself"; a second group includes people orientation (helping others plus congenial co-workers); and a third, economic considerations such as job security and pay. Opportunities for promotion ranked sixth.[13] (6) Considerations of sex-appropriateness appeared as a determinant in several ways. In addition to the anticipation of marriage, and concern about potential mates' attitudes, certain job-relevant self-attributions differed by sex. Davis found that only a third of the girls wanted to be known as ambitious, while 49 percent of the boys did.

Davis's study suggests that occupational planning by women involves a conscious weighing of many factors. Even as adolescents, girls see a conflict between their de-

12 Other studies which index males' disapproval of employment of women who are their future or actual partners include Hartley (1960), Fichter (1964), and Axelson (1963).
13 Economic issues are accorded more importance by adults who are actually working. In AT&T force-loss studies, pay and promotion were the most important factors for women as well as men when they quit.

sire to work and the desires of others; they give substantial consideration to the constraints stemming from the adult female sex role. They appear ready to accept the channeling of their work orientation into traditionally feminine occupations—though few of them seem willing to give it up altogether. Such findings raise the question of what aspirations and what pattern of labor-force participation we would see in women if the current traditional policies and values were changed.

The importance of the factors uncovered in Davis's study is underlined by the findings of other research. The apprehension that women feel about male reaction to their competence or desires for achievement and consequent male rejection has been found in studies of college women (Horner 1968; Schwenn 1970) and younger women (Matthews and Tiedeman 1964). Schwenn's research shows clearly that women *lower* their occupational aspirations in response to these pressures. A similar process may account for Hartley's (1960) finding that the proportion of girl children (5 to 11 in age) who express the intention to hold down a job when they grow up *decreases* in progressively older groups. Not coincidentally, boys' intolerance for their hypothetical future wives' working is very strong, and increases with age. Hartley suggests that this kind of intolerance is part of the acquisition of "masculinity."

A great deal of influence over women's work orientation is exerted by sex-role ideology—i.e., ideas of what is appropriately feminine. Ideas of what is masculine, of course, form the other side of the picture. Since roles work in tandem, a female sex-role of a certain style implies (and indeed requires) a male sex-role which complements it. The obverse is also true: to maintain a certain version of masculinity requires that the female adopt a certain version of femininity. It appears that the masculine male forbids his partner to demonstrate her skills, competence, or independence by working. The male must be dominant—economically, by virtue of being the sole breadwinner, and in other areas, by virtue of his economic dominance. Nor is this sex-role prescription limited to the elementary grades. The link between masculinity and occupational dominance appears repeatedly in the sociological literature, irrespective of the age group being studied.

Many sociologists have concerned themselves with potentially problematic consequences for the family when a wife is employed outside the home. One consideration is a norm that the husband shall exceed his wife in income and prestige (Nye and Hoffman 1963, p. 5). Oppenheimer (1972) has put forth the proposition that the wife has an obligation to do nothing that will detract from her husband's status.

The model consists of the following statements:

1. A wife derives a social status from her husband.
2. The significance of any status derived from her working has to be positive, has to add something to the family's social (rather than economic) status in order for her to work.
3. The wife has an obligation not to take an occupation that will reflect poorly on the family's standing in the community.

4. The wife is permitted to take a lower status occupation if it is only temporary.
5. The definition of what constitutes a good job opportunity for a given woman at a given socioeconomic level, and the prediction of whether she will seek employment, and which job she will take, are based on these considerations.

To the extent that this model is valid, it illuminates some of the constraints on the labor-force participation of married women.

The higher a woman's social status as derived from her husband, the higher her occupation must be if she is to work. In most American marriages the husband exceeds the wife in status-bearing characteristics (for example, age and education). Under Oppenheimer's model, the forces against employment for the ordinary college educated woman will be substantial. If she is married to a professional man, but does not herself have professional training, then by working she would add nothing to the family's status; in such a case, her work may be seen as detracting.[14]

Unless a woman is a professional, she will be restricted to the female sex-typed occupations. Very few of these are commensurate with the socioeconomic status that a college educated woman can expect to occupy by virtue of her husband's occupation. The wife's pay will not match that of her husband's occupation. With respect to the two incentives of prestige and income, therefore, the incentives for the college educated woman to work are slight.

The likeliest woman to seek employment will be a woman who has crossed the sex line and is in one of the masculine sex-typed professions. However, these professions require years of difficult preparation, deferred gratification, hard work, and competition. These demands occur at the period of the life cycle when most women are courting, marrying, and bearing children. If a woman gives priority to these sex-role concerns, she is unlikely to persist in professional training, or even complete college.[15]

These tests of Oppenheimer's model illustrate the validity of the concerns expressed by Davis' (1964) junior high school respondents. Marriage can, in quite a specific way, interfere with the attainment of occupational goals.

The Motive to Avoid Success
The research just cited directs our attention to a major set of determinants of women's orientation toward work and achievement. It is apparent that women are

14 This may be the explanation for a great deal of the resistance of men to having their wives work (Axelson 1963; Orden and Bradburn 1968).
15 Oppenheimer (1972) reports that the wives of men in the higher paying male professional and managerial occupations are much less likely to have completed college than their husbands. Fewer than half as many wives as husbands have completed college in this group.
  Oppenheimer's model would predict that the wives of professional men will be found in upper and middle level female occupations. She also found a significant minority in the male professions, but a smaller minority in blue collar or service occupations. As Oppenheimer would predict, the wives of professional and managerial men avoid these occupations.

profoundly affected (and from an early age) by the threatening responses of males to their achievement or ambition. That this is a realistic fear is attested by a number of studies of the negative attitudes men (and from an early age) hold toward women's working.[16] Even women who persist in high aspirations are dependent upon the good opinion of men, and there is evidence that these women selectively associate with, and gain support from, men who approve of their goals (Almquist and Angrist 1970; Schwenn 1970).

In the presence of such strong external pressures, it is easy to see that "success" has negative as well as positive incentive value for women. Such is the conclusion which emerges from Horner's research on the motive to avoid success in women. The motivational state to which this term refers is a complex one. Rather than being a simple tendency to avoid a negative incentive, the motive to avoid success is an approach-avoidance conflict. The motive is aroused only when the situation is achievement-relevant, and holds the promise of success. And it afflicts mainly the high-achievement -motivation, high-ability women. The avoidance motivation that is aroused by the possibility of success is based on the fear of social rejection, particularly by men. Horner found that women's test performance was decreased by this conflict, and that this effect was maximized when the woman was required to perform in the presence of, and in competition with, men (Horner 1968). In the fantasy stories invented by Horner's respondents, a very common way to disarm this conflict was for the woman to lower aspirations or otherwise "undo" the achievement which caused so much trouble. This fantasy behavior appears to have its parallel in the real-life tendency of women to lower or abandon career aims.

Much of the behavior of women in the labor force can, I believe, be related to this conflict. Almost no woman is immune to it. It seems likely that the means of reconciling the two forces vary a good deal with educational level and background.[17] However, as a factor in women's work orientation, it ought not to be overlooked.

Failure to take account of the conflict between success and rejection results in a number of predictable fallacies in formulations about women's work motivation. (1)

---

16 Attitudes toward "the" career woman are even more negative, for it is difficult to think of this individual as frivolous or incompetent. Consequently the attempt to discredit or neutralize her is aimed at her female identity, and she is dismissed as "unfeminine."

17 Watley and Kaplan's (1971) follow-up study of National Merit Finalists discovered that a conflict between career and marriage was most severe for those of highest ability. Those of lowest ability resolved the conflict most quickly, and in the traditional direction: marriage now. In research populations less highly selected on ability, the career option is repudiated earlier. In Harmon's (1971) study of occupational preference, she found most choices had achieved salience before the age of 10. These were the traditional female occupations (e.g., housewife, actress, elementary school teacher). The more technical and demanding occupations seemed to enter the girls' awareness later and drop out sooner. This suggests that there are specific influences relevant to females' consideration of nontraditional occupations. New research is needed to identify the agencies by which such options are made salient and attractive to women (see Harmon 1970; Rossi 1970; Almquist and Angrist 1970). Existing research can tell us much about the agencies by which women are discouraged from choosing these options.

Women are viewed as deficient because their enthusiasm for the occupational sphere does not appear as whole-hearted as men's. (This fallacy is, of course, based on a prior fallacy which we have examined: that all men's work motivation conforms to the professional model.) (2) The strength and validity of the Approach Success motive in women is denied. Insofar as this fallacy reflects a sincere error, it is based on the incorrect conclusion that the *resultant force* (in terms of the expectancy × value theory) is equivalent to the value factor. Yet as we recall, this is not so. Rather, the resultant force is produced thus:

$$F = E \times V.$$

Horner's research allows us to see something in the value factor of this equation which is unique to women. For many women, it appears that

$$V = (M + \text{success}) + (M - \text{success}),$$

or perhaps that

$$V = (M + \text{success}) + (M - \text{social rejection})$$

To the extent that the fear of rejection works against M, the motive to approach success, the resultant force F is diminished in magnitude.

In addition, the expectancy factor in the motivation equation may be different, on the average, for women and men. This reflects the unequal chances for success which are built into the occupational structure.

The achievement motive is an acquired or learned motive (Atkinson 1958). Both the expectancy and value factors reflect the individual's learning about relevant social conditions. These conditions confronting women are substantially different from those confronting men. Failure to take this into account leads to a final fallacy in assessing women's work motivation.

(3) There is a tendency to ignore or even deny the external pressures on women to hedge or relinquish their ambitions. Related to this is a tendency either to deny or to rationalize the lack of parity in rewards to working women and men. Men's self-interest in maintaining dominance and restricting occupational competition is rarely acknowledged in policy discussions or in the theoretical literature.[18]

---

18 An exception is the analysis of Hodge and Hodge (1965), who point out how the economic self-interest of white males is served by restricting the participation of women and blacks in occupations. They report that the higher the proportion of women and blacks in an occupation, the lower the wages of white males in that occupation.

A Misplaced Emphasis on "Sex Differences"

In an era of demands for change in the status of women, there appears to be a revival
of interest in sex differences. The idea of sex differences is appealed to as providing a
basis for categorical distinctions between the sexes. There is the additional implication that sex differences are innate and immutable; even perhaps, so much so as to be
classifiable as "natural law."[19] This in turn provides a justification for different opportunities, rewards and responsibilities, commensurate with the different "natures"
of women and men.

   Discussion of sex differences ranges over the domains of abilities, personality
traits, and interests. In general, the distribution of abilities between the sexes is not
sharply polarized. Variability within each sex is great, and overlap between the two is
substantial (Maccoby 1966). The same tends to be true of personality variables. There
are relatively few traits or abilities in which observable differences are reliable or significant. Even more to the point, the relevance of such sex differences as can be documented to occupations, in specific or in general, has not been demonstrated.

   The complexity of existing sex differences (such as those discussed in the preceding section) cannot be explanied by sweeping generalizations such as Tyler's (1972)
assertion that there are "well-known patterns of occupational interests, preferences,
and preparations of women" (1972, p. 2). In her discussion, Tyler fails to distinguish
among these, or to identify their antecedents and the relationships among them.
Certain characteristics (which, empirically, characterize professionals) are imputed to
all male workers, and a quite different set to all females. The differences (probably
exaggerated by Tyler's analysis) are linked to the undefined concept of "cultural sex
roles" (1972, p. 3). No specific dimensions of sex roles—whether masculine or feminine—are analyzed. Consequently, no telling link between occupational roles and sex
roles is established.

"Masculinity" and "Femininity"

One way of attempting to give substance to the vague, umbrella concept of sex role
is the construction of "masculinity/femininity" scales. These tend to be attitude
scales, with little power in predicting behavior. They are constructed in such a way
that "masculine" items are endorsed by most males and few females, and "feminine"
items are endorsed by most females and few males. They are validated, not against
measures of personality or behavior, but against membership in biological categories
(i.e., female and male). This has a number of troublesome consequences: (1) measures
of "masculinity"/"femininity" are composed of only the most exaggerated and stereotyped statements; (2) partly as a result of this, they are easy to fake (Bieliauskas
et al. 1965); and (3) as an artifact of the method of test construction, "masculinity"

---

19 Pierce (1971) and Hoffman (1968) have analyzed the ideological utility of "natural law"
arguments in justifying inequitable treatment of women and homosexuals, respectively.

and "femininity" appear to be uncorrelated, or even negatively correlated. Current research which does not have this methodological constraint, however, finds that individuals can score high on both scales (Bem 1973) and that the scales are correlated (Jenking and Vroegh 1969). Finally , the conventional approach emphasizes the minority of items on which females and males differ, and ignores the very large overlaps and similarities between the sexes.

A serious problem in placing any reliance on masculinity/femininity scores has been noted by many researchers: the various measures of "femininity" or "masculinity" show correlations so low that the reader is forced to conclude that they are measuring different entities (Shepler 1951; Barrows and Zuckerman 1960). Finally, the relevance of masculinity/femininity to occupational choice or success has not been demonstrated.

For many reasons, then, psychologists have become disenchanted in recent years with the conventional measures of "masculinity"/"femininity" (Edwards and Abbott 1973; Pleck 1973a; Vincent 1966). Attention has shifted toward more serious analysis of the content and enactment of sex roles (Laws 1970; Laws 1974; Pleck 1973b).

"Vocational Interests" as a Proxy for Sex Discrimination

At variance with the new approaches emphasized in this report is the tradition of research on vocational interests. The conceptual framework for the development of this tradition is that of sex roles, vague and undefined. Interest in outdoor pursuits, exploit and adventure, was considered appropriately masculine; and sedentary, indoor, and "ministrative" interests appropriately feminine. Perhaps because of the stereotypic approach, there was little concern with ascertaining the ways in which such preferences are formed, or under what conditions they change.

It was a short step to identifying certain occupations appropriate to highly sextyped interests. The next step was, however, more questionable. Strong (1943), building upon the work of Terman and Miles (1936), constructed two forms of the Strong Vocational Interest Blank (SVIB), which have been in use for thirty years. Females are tested with one, and males with the other. For thirty years, it was consequently impossible to ascertain the degree and kind of similarity of vocational interests between the sexes, or to see the change in these over time.

This strategy for test construction can be criticized because it blocks the possibility of obtaining empirical answers to questions of differences or similarities between the sexes. Unfortunately, however, invidious comparisons between the sexes have frequently been made with reference to the SVIB, although its customary use does not support such an enterprise. An incorrect conclusion has commonly been drawn that females are unsuited to certain occupations, since their profile does not match that of successful practitioners of the occupation. As long as women are tested with a different instrument, however, it is impossible to judge whether they do or do not have the qualities of the criterion group.

A further shortcoming of the approach embodied in the SVIB is that it does not measure abilities which relate directly to successful task performance. The characteristics which emerged as predictors (in a correlational rather than in a causal sense) may well have been correlated, not with the criterion, but with some other variable which was correlated with the criterion. Gender may well be such a variable. We have seen that sex is correlated with expectancy of success, and, with the anticipation of social approval or disapproval, of striving for success. Opportunities are correlated with gender, and the opportunity variable mediates between the individual and the successful outcome. It would be embarrassing to discover that for thirty years testing specialists have been confusing phenotype with genotype. The law of parsimony would urge that we simply use biological gender as a basis for selection, rather than a proliferation of derivative traits.

A further reservation about the selection strategy inherent in the SVIB is the likelihood of change in the relationship between the epiphenomena and the criterion. Thirty years has seen some change in the interests, avocations, and sentiments which are considered to be appropriately masculine. Failure to restandardize the test may well result in a decline of predictive power over the decades. Restandardizing the test, however, would not correct the basic flaw. The test-construction strategy itself guarantees the perpetuation of the status quo, including the sex-composition of the occupation.

The "vocational interests" approach appears to have little to offer regarding current issues in employment of women. It leads the practitioner (e.g., Tyler 1972) to cast too wide a net in attempting to deal with sex differences in personality, attitudes, or abilities which have no demonstrated relevance to job performance. It is conservative, and will not be useful in selecting the individual who can perform outstandingly in a job, but differs in major ways (e.g., sex, race) from the majority of those currently in the occupation. It is an approach, based not upon the components of the task itself, but upon similarity to characteristics of job incumbents. At best, it can only perpeturate the status quo. At worst, it is a test for compatibility rather than ability.

A more useful approach would be based upon the tasks and skills required for effective practice of a given occupation. With job performance as the criterion, training procedures designed to produce the requisite skills and based upon job analysis could be developed. However, the profile of requisite abilities has not been broken down and analyzed for most occupations at present.

To recapitulate: for most discovered sex differences, two things may be said. First, the differences are not clearcut, they are not of great magnitude, and the overlap between the sexes is substantial. Second, very few sex differences have demonstrated occupational relevance. An exception to this generalization appears to be some aspect of spatial ability.

Sex Differences in Spatial Ability

The realm of spatial abilities is both broad and various. Within this realm, there are many specific abilities, and these are not highly correlated. However, there is currently a great deal of interest in sex differences in spatial abilities. By and large, women exceed men in perceptual speed, and men exceed women in ability to visualize and manipulate objects in space mentally (Schmidt 1973). As with other sex-linked differences, there is some controversy about the origin of spatial abilities. Some authors hypothesize that they are inherited (Stafford 1961), some that they are the result of environmental influences (Sherman 1967) and still others demonstrate that these abilities are modifiable by learning (Blade and Watson 1955; Brinkman 1966). These experiments suggest that how well the sexes do on tests of these spatial abilities is affected by their view of the task as sex-appropriate or inappropriate. This raises the possibility that individuals' performance on such tests reflects, not their native ability, but their desire to appear appropriately "feminine" or "masculine."[20] The sex-labeling of such tasks could, of course, be manipulated experimentally. Given the present situation, we would predict that males would not be motivated to perform well on tests of perceptual speed (sometimes referred to as "clerical ability").[21] Conversely, females will probably not be motivated to excel at tasks they perceive as masculine.

The concern with sex-appropriateness is a factor in the image which a given occupation has, and perhaps affects individuals' willingness to enter it. It appears that although sex-role congruency is an important factor in individual motivation (Pleck 1973a), the perception of sex-role appropriateness is easily modified.

The occupational relevance of spatial abilities remains somewhat ambiguous. Schmidt (1973) reports that the US Employment Service lists 84 occupations (of the 4,000 in the *Dictionary of Occupational Titles*) which "require" spatial abilities available only in 10 percent of the US population. No detail is offered, however, on the tests or cutoff points used to ascertain spatial ability.

---

20 Nichols (1962) suggests that defensiveness enters into self-ratings on masculinity/femininity scales in a major way (1962, p. 458). In this study, female respondents who showed behavioral similarities of males made haste to score high on Nichols' scale of stereotyped femininity, based on fictitious but widely "known" sex differences.

An even more generalized source of distortion is "conventionalization" discovered by Edmonds (1967) as a major component in self-ratings of marital happiness. This should not be surprising, since this, too, is an area where sex-role ideology carries heavy weight. Self-report data should be interpreted with caution.

21 Longstaff (1954) reported training effects for both females and males on perceptual speed. This suggests that initial sex differences are not fixed, but modifiable. Another aspect of the question of sex differences in "clerical ability" is illustrated by Schneidler and Patterson's (1942) finding that men actually employed in clerical occupations do better than the average men, and 30 percent equal or exceed the average woman clerk. These two studies illustrate the effects of learning and incentive on performance, if not ability.

Mechanical comprehension (Bennett and Cruikshank 1942) appears to be relevant to some occupations, and in Bennett's original research, few (5 percent) high school girls exceed the average high school boy on the test. The major component of mechanical comprehension, however, appears to be spatial ability, and here the females' performance is much closer to the boys'. This finding leads one to focus on the characteristics of the tasks or examples in the test. These employ pulleys, gears, and similar artifacts with which girls and boys have differential familiarity. In a sense, this means that females and males taking the same test are confronting different tasks. In much the same way, current attempts to develop a "culture fair" test of intelligence grow out of the realization that a reading test in English is not the same task for those who are native speakers and those for whom English is a second language. The way in which abilities are tested, and the test materials used, remains a neglected but important problem. The finding that girls perform better on logically identical problems, when feminine content in examples is substituted for masculine content, deserves careful consideration.

Another variable, sometimes considered as a kind of spatial ability and sometimes as a "cognitive style," has received a great deal of attention from psychologists. Field dependence/independence shows fairly consistent differences in favor of males, and the argument has been made (following Stafford) that these are inborn. Other studies, however, show that the sex differences do not appear before the age of eight (Witkin 1962), that they are sometimes reversed and sometimes nonexistent in cross-cultural comparisons (Berry 1966), and that training can alter performance. Further, there are a number of tests of field dependence/independence, and these fail to show high correlations. A further consideration, commonly neglected in studies of abilities, is the social context of the testing situation. Sex of experimenter, sex of subject, and sex-typing of the task affect performance. In the case of field dependence/independence, there is evidence that subjects construe the test as an achievement situation (Crandall and Sinkeldam 1964). Given the motive to avoid success, we can predict an inhibiting effect on performance if the subjects are female, irrespective of their native ability.

Our examination of sex differences in spatial abilities and field dependence suggests caution in overgeneralizing the existing findings. Against a baseline of sex differences, we must consider (1) evidence for modifiability of tested performance, as an effect of (*a*) training or (*b*) incentives; (2) entraining effects due to sex-typing of testing materials, sites, or personnel; and (3) a moot connection with occupational performance. We may be permitted the following conclusions: (1) to the extent that validly measured abilities predict to occupational success, they may be used to select individuals for jobs; (2) the pool of job aspirants possessing the requisite ability can be expanded via training procedures; and (3) the pool of eligibles is unlikely to be overwhelmingly of one sex or the other. There is little possibliity that gender can be used as a proxy for occupationally relevant abilities.

Psathas' Theory

Neither sex differences in interests nor in abilities seems to provide an explanation powerful enough to account for the discrepant experiences of women and men in the labor force. There is, however, a third line of argument which is invoked to explain and justify the inequalities in work experience. This approach emphasizes differences in motivation (sometimes called career orientation or labor-force attachment) between the sexes. Women are presumed to differ from men in giving first priority to family concerns, and peripheral emphasis to career concerns. Psathas' work, which I will summarize here, is an often-quoted and influential theory.

Psathas' (1968) theory of female occupational choice relies heavily on a traditional view of the female sex role. Psathas sees the young woman's occupational orientations as determined in part by her father's social class (which controls her access to education and advanced occupational training), and partly by her estimation of the matrimonial pool in which the fishing will be best (1968, p. 258). Psathas attributes this expectation to the young woman without acknowledging the extent to which his assumption puts blinders on his own analysis. Thus, for example, Psathas is so accustomed to regarding a woman—at whatever age—as a financial dependent that he calculates the probability of her entering an occupation requiring costly training on the basis of her husband's income. He ignores the substantial proportion of women who finance their own training; those who remain unmarried and support themselves; and those who support a family. Psathas tends to lump all women together, even though some of the studies on which he relies (e.g., Weil 1961) provide the basis for a differentiated typology of women's labor-force participation. He fails to discriminate the conditions under which one or another pattern will be observed. Rather, he falls back upon sex-role considerations (e.g., intention to marry, time of marriage, husband's attitudes toward wife's working) as the major determinants of women's occupational behavior. The effect of this line of reasoning is to discount any intrinsic work motivation in the woman, and to view her occupational behavior as interstitial to her marital status.

However, Psathas does not deal with the issue of compatibility between the occupational and sex roles (1968, p. 257), and thus disregards a major set of determinants of the occupational behavior of women. Little in the way of empirical evidence is presented, and the analysis may well be dated as well as class-biased.

Nevertheless, Psathas' work—and its continued popularity—illustrates a kind of wishful thinking that justifies the treatment women receive in the labor market in terms of their "preferences," and the appropriateness of these preferences.

The interest in sex differences—whether in goals, abilities, or motivation—is allied with the desire to find justifications for different outcomes for women and men in the society at large. The paradigm for this attempt is the following:

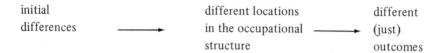

| initial differences | ⟶ | different locations in the occupational structure | ⟶ | different (just) outcomes |

In this line of argument, it is as though the outcomes for the individual faithfully mirror his abilities with no distortion. To explain—much less to justify—the different statuses of women and men in the occupational structure in terms of such differences is probably untenable. It seems much more likely that the fate of each sex in the labor market reflects its status in the society. Turning the conventional argument around, we should focus on the way in which experiences on the job affect the individual.

Effects of Work on Workers

There are many possible outcomes of the individual's work experience on which we could choose to focus. In their research, industrial psychologists study work satisfaction and work productivity. Related to the first is the phenomenon of job-leaving, or quitting, and this can be particularly important as an index of negative job satisfaction. Although the relationship between the individual's satisfaction with his job and the quality of his output is not perfect, research has repeatedly shown a strong relationship between the two (Brayfield and Crockett 1955; Likert 1967; Blauner 1960). Consequently employers have attempted many different strategies to increase workers' job satisfaction, expecting a payoff in terms of work productivity. Among the organizational variables which have been manipulated are worker participation in decisions affecting his work conditions (e.g., the Scanlon Plan; Coch and French 1948), strengthening the work group (Cartwright 1951), supervisory style (Bowers and Seashore 1966; Fiedler 1961; Patchen 1962), job enlargement (Killbridge 1960), and communication (Katz and Kahn 1966). All of these practices are designed to increase the worker's motivation to fulfill company goals (Katz 1964).

The outcome of these programmatic efforts is individual productivity, whether conceived in terms of quality or quantity, gross or net. These organizational causes are assumed to act upon the individual worker and, by affecting his motivation, to affect his productivity. A number of theories focus specifically on the worker's motivation, not as a result of prior conditions or inner personality traits but of what she actually experiences in the work situation.

Equity Theory

What are the considerations that affect a worker's satisfaction and productivity on the job? A major approach to this question is provided by recent research on the individual's perception of the fairness, or equity, of his treatment compared to the perceived treatment of other workers. According to Equity Theory (Adams 1963; Lawler 1968), the individual compares the ratio of his inputs (including skill, education, etc.) to outcomes (or reward) with that of his neighbor. The work motivation (and consequent work output) of the individual is affected by his (her) judgment of the fairness of his rewards relative to other workers. To take an example from the Bell Telephone System, if the requirements for entry-level jobs are the same in the Craft and Traffic divisions, but the pay is different, we would expect a negative effect on the work motivation of the underpaid worker. The most common way that the worker adjusts the input : output ratio to an equitable state is to reduce output. Another way to achieve an equitable exchange might be to seek a better bargain in another job, if the worker feels she has a choice.[22] In a recent study in the computer industry, Shuster and Atchison (1973) found that workers with lower education (consequently in a less competitive position in the labor market) emphasized work factors internal to the organization, while those with higher education emphasized external labor market factors in judging whether they were fairly paid. Thus the degree to which a worker is a member of a "captive population" may affect the manner in which conflicts about inequity are acted out. This may be of particular relevance to the operator position in the Bell Telephone System.

In the Shuster and Atchison study, these workers, when equitably paid, were loyal and hardworking employees. Moreover, their data indicate that perception that the company rewards its workers equitably increases with length of employment. Thus, it is to the employer's benefit to make sure his workers feel they are being treated fairly. However, in this study it was the younger, more educated and less well paid who felt they were being paid inequitably.

Early research on equity highlighted the importance of workers' comparing their input : outcome ratio for feelings of equity or inequity to arise (Adams 1963). This is similar to the theory of relative deprivation (Stouffer et al. 1949; Laws 1972a). In this theory, discontent arises not in proportion to the absolute unfavorability of one's situation, but rather its relative unfavorability when compared with the treatment accorded to others who are similar.

Both relative and absolute deprivation are relevant to the question of effects of inequity on job performance. As data on the inequitable rates of pay and promotion which are women's lot in the labor force become well known, we can predict that feelings of inequity will arise.

However, to the extent that sex segregation in the labor market, and in particular establishments, persists, it will be more difficult for workers to compare their ratios of inputs to outcomes. The existing sex segregation may act to "keep the lid on" feelings of inequity.

Equity theory sensitizes us to consequences of the individual's perception of how (s)he is treated in the work place. In this theory, individual characteristics—especially

---

22 Penner (1967), in a study of General Electric, found that the annual quit rate for those who perceived their salary as inequitable was 200 percent.

job-relevant ones such as age, education, and skill—are not irrelevant, but have an effect only in the context of the rewards or outcomes they "buy" in the exchange with the employer. Feelings of equity or inequity (and the job-relevant activity they motivate) arise only in comparison with the bargain the worker observes that comparable others are getting.

Equity theory seems particularly applicable to the motivation of working women. The "going price" of certain worker characteristics (notably education) is well known and accepted; it is expected that workers having these charactertistics will qualify for certain jobs, whose features can be considered as outcomes in equity theory. Outcomes are any conditions which are regarded as rewards: not only pay, but also fringe benefits, responsibility, autonomy, control over one's work. The discriminatory practices which are widespread in the labor force, however, make it inevitable that the inputs and outcomes of workers will not be similar as long as they are of different sexes. However, a number of factors enter into the question of whether feelings of inequity will arise, and what their effects on labor-force participation will be. I have mentioned that the sex-segregation of the labor force would militate toward inhibiting comparison. Here I point to lack of information as a factor. In addition, "false consciousness" may operate to inhibit feelings of unfairness. The idea of false consciousness applies only to the beliefs of women in this situation. False consciousness would be indicated by knowledge of the inequities coupled with the tendency to justify them. I would anticipate that the "justification" would be in terms of traditional sex-role ideology. The myths about women in the labor force will be invoked; the idea of women as a reserve labor force will be highlighted and, in the more popular versions of false consciousness, we can expect to hear a lot about sex differences and about women's different work motivation.

Many of the issues discussed here are evident in the AT&T case, as will be seen in the following chapter. The public hearings on employment practices of AT&T made available a great deal of specific data. The largest private employer in the world discriminated against women.

In this case study we can find, in microcosm, the structural features that women workers confront; the myths promulgated about them; and the outcomes and resulting behavior. In addition, we can acquire a detailed understanding of the specific procedures and policies which produced these outcomes. In so doing, we can identify the kinds and the scope of change that would be needed to achieve equality in employment.

7 The Bell Telephone System: A Case Study

Judith Long Laws

Among the voluminous findings of fact and extensive expert testimony marshaled
by the Equal Employment Opportunity Commission in the AT&T case were:
(1) extreme sex segregation of jobs; (2) pay differentials by sex; (3) characteristically
"female" occupations; (4) sex differential in opportunities for promotion; (5) monopolistic hiring and promotion policies; (6) the frustration of women's work motivation; and (7) many myths and ideological justifications for practices which discriminated against women.

Structural Discrimination against Women in the Bell System: Practices and Policies

At the time of the study made by the EEOC, racial and ethnic discrimination existed
within the Bell System. However, these occurred within parallel structures which
were sex-segregated from the outset. Sex discrimination was the primary organizational arrangement; upon this, racial, ethnic, and age discrimination were superimposed. In many of the specific jobs within AT&T sex segregation was even more
extensive than that observed in society at large. The concentration of women was
higher in "female" jobs, and the concentration of men higher in "male" jobs. For
example, as of 1960, 78 percent of cashiers in the United States were female, compared to 95 percent in the Bell System. Indeed, 90 percent of the female workers
at Bell were in occupations where more than 80 percent of the workers were female
(Oppenheimer 1972).

Sex segregation at Bell was not of a piecemeal variety, however. Men and women
worked in quite separate divisions. The major divisions which we will contrast were
Plant and Traffic. Jobs in the Plant Department included craft jobs such as frameman (an inside the plant job), lineman, cable splicer's helper, and installer-repairman
(outside jobs). Jobs in the Traffic Department included operator and clerical worker.
Every aspect of employment, from recruitment through pay and promotion, was
managed within sex-segregated limits.

Recruitment Procedures: The Entry-Level Position
AT&T traditionally maintained a rather elaborate set of recruitment materials, among
which were included newspaper advertisements, pictorial materials, and visits to high
schools. All formal recruiting was sex-specific, as were materials filtered down into
schools and other agencies with which the Bell companies maintained contacts.
Females were shown one set of materials and males another. Thus it was impossible
for a prospective employee to express interest in a job that the company had decided
was sex-inappropriate. A restricted set of options was presented to each sex.

Bell had traditionally relied heavily on employee referrals for recruiting new hires. In some of the operating companies, almost all new hires were obtained in this way. Given the sex segregation within each company, it was to be expected that employees recruited others like themselves for jobs like their own. As a consequence, sex segregation was perpetuated and perhaps even intensified.

Potential employees were recruited for either the Plant or the Traffic Department. Women who wished to be considered for craft jobs were discouraged from doing so, as were men who expressed an interest in traffic. The tests used for selection among new recruits also differed by division (or sex), so that it was difficult for a woman to substantiate her claim that she had the appropriate background or aptitude for a craft job. Indeed, sex-segregated procedures made it impossible to prove or disprove that women or men were unqualified for jobs that were "sex-inappropriate." Many Bell System managers were recruited from within the craft jobs—from which women were categorically excluded by the initial recruitment procedures.

A second consequence of the testing policy was to protect the myth of female inadequacy. Bell management asserted that women were unsuited for the jobs from which they were excluded. This assertion could be tested (and disconfirmed) only if women's test scores and performance measures could be compared with men's. The use of different forms of the SVIB for females and males served to maintain the status quo. Procedures for selection and procedures for employment thus dovetailed in such a way as to maintain sex-segregated labor markets, and the associated inhibition of competition.

Since women were not allowed to take the tests, they could not qualify for craft jobs in the Plant Department. When openings arose in the Plant Department, women employees with seniority were not permitted to bid on them. In 1971 Lorena Weeks challenged this policy in the courts and won her case, (*Weeks vs. Southern Bell,* 1971) but only subsequent to the signing of the consent decree did AT&T establish goals for integrating the craft jobs in the Plant Department and Traffic Department.

Operator: The Entry-Level Female Job
The principal entry-level job for women was that of operator. It is a classic dead-end job; in many locales it had become a revolving-door job as well. Some Bell companies reported 100 percent turnover in this position. From the employee's point of view, this means that she was offered a job which was good for a year or less, and which had no long-term opportunities for advancement. We have already seen (Harmon 1971)* how phone company jobs rank in terms of preference. This rating is probably an accurate reflection of the incentive value of the operator job. Table 7.1 shows one major incentive—salary—offered women and men at different levels in the Bell System.

*See pp. 171–178 for references cited—editor.

Table 7.1   Mean Salary by Sex, All Companies

	Women	Men
Entry Level	$ 6,114	$ 8,613
Management Level I	$11,194	$14,220
All Levels	$ 7,003	$11,655

Source: Data made available to author by EEOC.

Turnover in the Traffic Department (i.e., among operators) had long been recognized by AT&T as a problem, and the company had undertaken a number of research studies. The operator turnover was viewed as a matter of "problem girls" rather than a problem position. Indeed, recommendations from a study made for Southwestern Bell suggested changes in personnel, not in the structure of the job (e.g., EEOC 1970b). When male force loss was the subject of the research, recommendations included changing elements of organizational structure (EEOC 1969a). In a study of Illinois Bell, the male workers' complaints were identical to those made by terminating women in other studies: progression from one grade to another was too slow, pay was too low, the jobs did not utilize the workers' particular skills. However, the recommendations based on the Illinois study included speeding up promotion, increasing wages, and tailoring jobs to skills. The recommendations based on the Houston study (EEOC 1970b) were to hire only those women who could be counted on not to complain. In another study of terminating service representatives in the Chesapeake System (EEOC 1970c), the authors recommended that the system stop recruiting ambitious, educated young women and take older employees who were "more realistic about [her] goals within the Company." They recommended hiring "someone who isn't looking for a glamorous *career*" (italics mine).

Women in Management: Recruitment and Prospects

The sex discrimination seen at the entry level in nonmanagement positions had its parallel at management levels as well. Managerial status within the Bell System is defined in terms of levels. Level One management is the equivalent of foreman and includes the Group Chief Operator, who supervises a group of operators. Only attaining Level Three or above, however, represents a management career in the Bell System.

Table 7.2   Management Positions in Bell System by Sex and Rank (Dec. 31, 1969)

	Total Employed	1st Level	2nd Level	3rd Level and above
Men	330,392	58,524	33,385	14,412
Women	390,494	50,508	2,782	154
Total	720,886	109,032	36,167	14,566
Women as % of Total	54.2%	46.3%	7.6%	1.1%

Source: EEOC 1289, p. 4.

Table 7.2 shows the distribution of management personnel across the different levels, by sex. Although the majority of employees were women, their percentage declined dramatically as rank increased. Women comprised about 1 percent of career management personnel in the Bell System. There was a sharp cutoff after Level One. One study of the utilization of women in management in the Bell System showed that the chances of a male Level One manager's reaching the District Superintendent (Level Three) were 1 : 4, while the women Level One manager's chances were 1 : 300 (EEOC 1970d, p. 20).

Most managers of Level Two and above came from two sources: they were selected from within the craft jobs in the Plant Department, or they were recruited from outside, beginning with persons holding a college degree. Prior to the 1973 consent decree, women were almost excluded from craft jobs, and hence were denied the opportunity to be promoted into the ranks of upper management.

A second route into management was via recruitment of college graduates, usually into Level Two and above. Women were excluded from the management training programs that men with the same credentials entered (EEOC 1970d, p. 17) by company policy. The official justification of this policy of exclusion was based on some of the familiar myths—that women are not committed to careers, do not want management responsibility, and so forth. It is interesting to note that management, at the time of the public hearing, clung to these myths even though disconfirming data were available on the female labor force as a whole (see Chapter 6, Note 4)and on Bell's female labor force in particular (EEOC 1969b, 1970b, c).

There was another difference between the opportunities provided men and women, even at the same level of management. Bell tended to place (and to keep) women in staff or specialist roles, removing them from the mainstream of line authority. In this way qualified women were utilized (although in very small numbers), while at the same time men were protected from being supervised by a woman.

Table 7.2 shows that most of the women in management at Bell (95 percent) are at Level One (EEOC 1970d, p. 4). Like the entry-level nonmanagement job for women (operator), this too was a dead end. The study just cited reveals that the career expectations of Level One managers were determined by their sex: for women this was regarded as a terminal appointment while men were expected to move through these positions (EEOC 1970d, p. 20) on their way up.

One position in management (Group Chief Operator) was reserved for women, and the rest, by and large, for men. Few women escaped upward from this position. Only those at Level One had line authority, and they supervised only women. Above Level One, women tended to be limited to staff functions and consequently had advisory, rather than supervisory, responsibility. This, of course, meant that the Bell System provided little opportunity for women to learn to supervise men or for men to learn to work under the supervision of a woman. These very traditional arrangements had two further consequences. First, an opportunity to test the factual basis of the myth that women's supervising men is a "problem" was wasted, and with it the opportunity to find solutions if, indeed, a problem emerged. Second, it meant that women who qualified for and entered management positions were denied the further training that their male peers received. This was, of course, consistent with the observations of researchers who have studied women in the professions (Simon et al. 1966; Epstein 1970; Wells 1973) that women are deprived of some aspects of professional socialization, even after being credentialed. It was also consistent with one of the features of "female" jobs noted by Oppenheimer, namely, that employers do not invest further training in their female employees. If we observe this occurring with female incumbents even of "male" jobs (e.g., management), we are forced to realize that it is the fate of female workers rather than of "female" jobs. Furthermore, it suggests that the women professional and the "ordinary" working woman have more in common than many authors have supposed.

Effects of Discrimination on Work Motivation

Substantial research was conducted within the Bell System on employee turnover, or "force loss." Quitting a job may legitimately be construed to mean extreme job dissatisfaction, and it is instructive to examine the reasons which women who quit the Bell System gave for their decision. Forty-eight percent of service representatives terminating in the Chesapeake System (EEOC 1970c) gave dissatisfaction with salary as the major reason, as compared with 41 percent of craftsmen in a Chicago study (EEOC 1970d) who gave pay as a reason for quitting. In the Chesapeake study, 69 percent of terminating operators gave the lack of opportunity for advancement as a major reason for leaving. Dissatisfaction with opportunities for advancement was the second most frequent cause of termination among Houston operators (EEOC 1970b), salary being the first. In another study (EEOC 1969b), 50 percent of terminating women said that they had career goals in mind, and had been disappointed by the company. These data show that women workers were interested in the long-term economic issues of pay and promotion, and evaluated the job rationally, in terms of means and ends.

The study of terminating operators in the Houston company suggests a further dimension to the problem of motivation. These data suggest that it was the most promising women who were lost to the Bell System. A comparison of terminating operators with a control group of employees with at least one year's tenure showed that the former were more able and more independent than the latter. The authors of the study blamed the loss of these employees on the authoritarian style of supervision prevailing in the company. In particular, they noted that an overemphasis on punctuality produced many incidents of friction which reduced the attractiveness of the job. The authors pointed out that many of the "resignations" reported in these turnover statistics were forced resignations of persons whose task performance had been adequate but whose attendance was unsatisfactory (EEOC 1970b, pp. 6 ff.). It seems likely that the more able and independent women were affected to a greater negative degree by this rigidity and that it contributed to the loss of those employees who were the best candidates for promotion into management.

These data suggest a parallel to the dynamics of the motive to avoid success. Just as that conflict—and its detrimental effects on performance—is more likely to affect the more able and achievement-oriented woman, so the frustrating organizational environment of the telephone company was likely to have had a greater negative effect on the employee with the greatest potential.

Whether we look at management women or the rank and file, it appears that the Bell System presented its women employees with an integrated system of negative incentives for work performance and satisfaction.

The Problem of Male Attitudes

The management study to which we have referred (EEOC 1970d) offers a detailed look at the kinds of attitudes I have in the preceding chapter referred to as myths, and evidence concerning the real-world effects they have on women's careers. In this company-sponsored study of the utilization of women in management, extensive data on the attitudes of men high in management were revealed.

The AT&T study differentiated between structural obstacles to women's careers in management (e.g., exclusion from training programs) and attitudinal obstacles. The study (EEOC 1970d, pp. 16–17), details many attitudes held by managers surveyed which are detrimental to women's chances in management. Some are beliefs about characteristics of women that "disqualify" them from positions of managerial

Table 7.3 Prediction from Expectancy x Value Theory, Given Promotion Rates in the Bell System (See EEOC 1970d for Data)

	Value	Expectancy	Effort
Ms. X	50	.003	.15
Ms. Y	70	.003	.21
Mr. W.	50	.25	12.50
Mr. Z	30	.25	7.50

responsibility (e.g., "Women are not as mobile as men"). (The authors pointed out that research shows that single women are as willing to move as men, as are married women when the incentive is made attractive enough.) Moreover, no connection between these attributes and managerial productivity has been demonstrated. This criticism can be made of many objections to women in management. In the absence of proof of such connection, these objections must be understood to be prejudice.

Other objections stem from the anticipated negative consequences of placing women in management (e.g., other men suspect favoritism when a woman is promoted) or even more direct expressions of the shortcomings of the *male* management group (e.g., "Women in management are a threat to men," or "Men cannot consider women as equals"). It is apparent, in short, that the study uncovered areas where there is a need for management-development training procedures.

Still other objections quoted in this study illustrate the "Catch 22" nature of opposition to women in management. We have seen, from the force-loss studies, that lack of opportunities to progress caused some of the ablest women to withdraw from the Bell System. We have seen too, what the odds were against a woman's succeeding in management. See Table 7.3 for effects of these odds as predicted by expectancy × value theory. In the public hearing a Bell spokesman noted that "the best women leave before a management job is available to them." It might equally well be said that if a woman waits patiently for a management job, with 300 : 1 odds, Bell would not be interested in her anyway.

A similar logic is apparent in the objection, "in order to manage men, a woman must have 'masculine' characteristics," or "women think differently than men—those who get into management think more like a man." Although the evidence seems to indicate that in the past, being male was the best qualification for a managerial position, there is a tinge of disapproval in these quotes. It seems, then, that a woman who isn't "masculine" isn't suitable for management, but a woman who is "masculine" (whatever that means) is not desirable.

This last objection illustrates the "double whammy" to which working woman is subjected. We have become familiar with the motive to avoid success, and the fear of social rejection (of being labeled "unfeminine") which underlies it. This study illustrates why this fear is justified, and how the punishment is administered. It is a "double whammy"—the characterization is inelegant, but apt—because the individual put into this position cannot win either way. If she is competent, and successful at the task (which, in the work situation, is defined as the appropriate and top-priority concern), she will be judged deficient as a female. Conversely, if she satisfies these self-appointed judges as to her femininity, she will not be doing the job.

This evidence from the Bell System is a strong argument for the serious deleterious effect of sex-role stereotyping on occupational life, and gives some indication of the changes required to end sex discrimination. (See Chapter 13 and the Appendices for a discussion of the AT&T consent decree and its implementation.)

Recommendations for Change

In the foregoing, I have tried to separate the counterfactual from reliable research evidence. We are now able to pinpoint problems in need of change and questions in need of research. Although the issues we have considered are many, they seem to group themselves into a few major areas.

Skills and Qualifications
If we accept the premise that being female is not in itself a disqualification, then our attention is directed to the following:

a. It will be necessary to establish explicitly and objectively what skills are requisite for any given job, and what level of proficiency is required. It would probably be desirable to have tests machine scored, and to approximate "blind" reviewing as nearly as is practical.

b. Whatever selection measures are used, these should be validated against actual (not simulated) task performance. Data should be collected over a period sufficient to give confidence in performance levels and decisions.

By paying careful attention to job requirements, we are led to consider both training procedures and talent-finding or promotion.

Training
Most jobs require some on-the-job training. This may be done casually or carefully, and its efficacy recorded or not. With respect to women, it is important to:

a. include women in any training offered;

b. be sensitive to particular problems women trainees have with materials (e.g., "masculine culture" problems) or personnel;

c. feed back this learning into the training program; and

d. evaluate and follow up the effects of training.

Wells (1973) has noted that training opportunities also include education outside the organization, which the employer usually supports financially; participation in conferences and professional meetings; sponsorship by "higher-ups"; and training programs offered by the organization, other than on-the-job training. The employer should be sure that he does not exclude women from any of these opportunities.

A very promising method of training is suggested by the work of Brinkman (1966) and Suppes (1968), who used programmed instruction in the teaching and evaluation of, respectively, spatial and mathematical skills. We might predict, arguing by analogy from Suppes's finding with black school children, that a nonpersonal teacher and noncompetitive learning situation might maximize the learning of women.

Promotion and Talent-Finding

Most organizations have some procedures for talent-finding, but these have tended to exclude or to overlook women. It is likely that conscientiously using the standard procedures in a search for women will produce candidates. However, it is possible that this is one area where new learning or sensitization on the part of management would facilitate the goal. A number of mechanisms are available for this, including the use of outside consultants and task forces within the organization.

An important part of talent-finding will be the monitoring of the choices made. A good choice should continue to advance in the hierarchy. If she fails to do so, the employer may be alerted to the problem of tokenism (Laws 1972b), of bad faith, or of inadequacies in the talent-finding procedures.

Responses to Female Competence

This category subsumes two major sorts of problems: difficulties that women have in connection with their actual or aspired competence, and difficulties that men have. The latter problem, of course, is not limited to employers and co-workers, for we have seen that negative attitudes toward working women are prevalent across the society. However, within the work place there are many things the employer and co-workers can do to reward or to punish competence in the female worker. Here we will limit ourselves to pointing out specific behavior patterns that help and hinder women's task performance.

Men's problems with female competence. The potential conflict between competence and femininity can be aroused—with negative effects on performance—in any situation where women work under the surveillance of men. The appropriate behavior for men in the work situation is to respond to and take seriously the task performance of the women workers. It is inappropriate to invoke other roles—particularly aspects of the sex role, e.g., by being too personal, by flirting, by forms of address which involve diminutives, too much familiarity, and so forth. It is inappropriate for an executive to have his wife invite a woman executive to lunch, as she might do with his secretary. Employers (and male co-workers) may want to consult the book by Loring and Wells (1972) for many specifics. A reliable guideline, however, is to treat a worker in terms of her status and her job, rather than her sex.

Also to be avoided are disrespectful behaviors to which women in general are subjected, but which are especially counterproductive in a setting where work is to be done. Here I refer to practices such as ignoring the inputs of a woman to a discussion; her contribution is treated as an interruption and a distraction, and the discussion simply detours around it. This is a wasteful practice, if the employer is in fact paying for the expertise that the worker brings to the job.

These behavior patterns are profoundly habitual, and may be unconsciously practiced. Women, however, are sensitive to them; particularly women who have earned the right to participate as equals in the work setting. When they are not treated as equals, it is a reminder of their "proper place," and conflict is aroused.

For the same reason, constant references—no matter how benevolent— to the personal appearance, social life, and potential marriage and family plans of women have the same effect. They convey the message that a woman's work, and a woman as a worker, are not being taken seriously. The failure to be appreciated, as every worker knows, undermines motivation.

Women's problems with female competence. We have seen that the effect of the avoid success motive is to inhibit striving behavior. The conditions for the arousal of this conflict are ubiquitous. Although some efforts can be made to avoid arousing this conflict in the workplace, another direction for effort is the reduction or neutralization of the conflict itself.

Promising leads are found in the research of Bem and Bem (1972), Farmer and Bohn (1970), I. Katz (1969), and Carey (1955). The research of Farmer and Bohn and of Carey involves verbal behavior. Both demonstrate that a simple and explicit verbal intervention is efficacious in reducing the detrimental effects of a perceived conflict between femininity and competence. In the Farmer and Bohn study, when subjects were told that there was no necessary conflict between career and marriage, they permitted themselves to score much higher on the career-orientation scale of the Strong Vocational Interest Blank. In Carey's study, the problem-solving scores of women college students improved after they had participated in a group discussion aimed at improving attitudes toward problem-solving. No changes occurred in the male subjects. These studies suggest that talking through the fears of rejection that are aroused by situations of achievement and competition helps to remove the inhibiting effects.

The Bem and Bem study showed that, contrary to the conventional wisdom, women can be recruited for "men's" jobs, and vice versa, simply by rewording the advertising copy. "Translating" tasks or instructions from "masculine" language to "feminine" can eliminate some of the difficulties which women have traditionally had in some areas (e.g., spatial perception). Many instances of instruction quite unconsciously rely on examples or vocabulary that are familiar to males via a cultural context that differs from that to which females are exposed. This differential history constitutes an advantage for the male learner, but is really extraneous to the task being taught, or to the adequacy of the learning which is taking place. Those responsible for training and development may want to experiment with alternative teaching methods, and assess any differences in effectiveness which they may produce.

Katz's (1969) study has a complex lesson to offer us. Katz was interested in giving assertion training to black subjects and examining the results. After running baseline trials of mixed-race groups in a competitive task, he gave the black subjects separate sessions in which they were highly rewarded for taking a risk on the task, but not penalized for wrong answers. When they returned to the mixed group, after this "assertion training," their task behavior was more effective than in the baseline trials. We can see a possible analogy to women in mixed-sex work groups. An unanticipated finding in Katz's study is probably also relevant to women. Although the objective performance of "assertion-trained" blacks improved, their white peers did not perceive it, and rated the blacks, in postexperimental evaluations, as inferior (just as they had initially). This suggests that, however we improve the objective performance of women workers, the lifelong blinders of some co-workers may prevent these from recognizing female achievement. Clearly, it is not enough to change the behavior or attitudes of women alone. We can train the members of a minority group, but we must retrain the majority, as well.

Attitudes of Men

The classic theories point out that attitudes serve a number of functions for the individual (Katz 1960). The functional basis of an attitude—i.e., what it does for the individual—is important in any attempt at attitude change. Where an attitude is no more than a factual belief, introducing objective information will correct the attitude. Often, however, attitudes serve the self-interest of the individual: racist or sexist attitudes boost the sense of superiority of the white male; stereotyping is "efficient," in permitting faster information processing and decisions, etc. We have reason to believe that prejudicial attitudes toward women go deep, and will require nonsuperficial efforts to change them.

Many of the techniques currently in use by industry will be effective in developing sensitivity to sex-relevant attitudes and practices. Sensitivity training has long been a tool of management development, and could be a worthwhile activity in this context. Workshops in which actual co-workers discuss issues that arise in their common history, and gain practice at equal-status patterns of interaction, can be very effective.

Same-sex groups, meeting on a regular basis to explore the personal ramifications of sex-role issues that arise in the work place, could be an important source of insight and of support for change. No matter how electrifying a special workshop or one-shot training experience may be, the changes gained will gradually ebb away without continuing (and visible) support. This sad fact of organizational life suggests an important point.

Monitoring, Maintenance, and Good Faith

Changes in legislation and judicial precedent have served as a gentle prod to work organizations to initiate new structures which will be helpful in maintaining change. Reporting practices and affirmative action guidelines and goals have given employers some help in bringing about equitable sex ratios in their organizations and obtaining an idea of their progress. Some organizations have created new staff functions with the responsibility of initiating and monitoring programs aimed at these concerns.

While these efforts are all to the good, they are no substitute for organized groups composed of the constituency such offices are charged with "looking out for." Affirmative action is not a static concept, nor a program to be "administered." Rather, the process of defining goals and optimizing goal attainment is a dynamic one, benefitting from an ongoing sensitization which can only come from those who are "on the firing line" daily. Many such groups have organized spontaneously. These can be a valuable source of input or a thorn in the side of management, depending—as 20 years of research in formal organizations has repeatedly shown—on the workers' estimate of whether management is for or against them. Natural groups organized around working women's concerns will be the best ally the employer has, *if* his attempt to develop sensitivity toward inequities and to correct them is sincere.

It is unfortunately necessary to deal explicitly with the issue of retaliation against women who are active in their own behalf. Wells (1973) reports research showing a drop in the performance evaluations of women who were active in such groups as I am advocating here, when the evaluations were compared pre- and post-activism. When pay and promotion-eligibility are tied to these evaluations, they provide a cruel means of resisting change and punishing those who would foster it.

Clearly, a topic for future research is the backlash against attempts to thwart equal employment. Such research will be useful in informing the legislation which will surely be a necessary backup for good will. Within a given organization, once again, the female employees will be an invaluable source of information about what the trouble spots are, and of suggestions for improving them. It is essential, however, that if such employees are to work for the company in this way, they must be protected from retaliation. This is a moral as well as a legal obligation of high levels of management.

Leadership for Change

Many informal reports from work organizations attest to the impact of highly visible leadership in equal rights issues. Leadership might be exercised in numerous ways, but of these, two stand out: (*a*) the explicit commitment, by word and deed, of high level individuals to goals and programs of equality; and (*b*) highly visible and strategic appointments of women. The proportion of such appointments must be larger than mere tokenism. Similarly, the filling of quotas without regard to qualifications, training, or selection will be unconvincing. If employers hire or promote women unsuited to the task requirements, it is likely that the objectives of equal employment opportunity will not be achieved.

Bibliography for Chapters 6 and 7

Adams, J. S. 1963. "Toward an Understanding of Inequity." *Journal of Applied Social Psychology* 47 : 422–436.

Almquist, E. and Angrist, S. 1970. "Role Model Influences on College Women's Career Aspirations." Paper read at the meeting of the American Sociological Association.

Amundsen, Kirsten. 1971. *The Silenced Majority.* Englewood Cliffs, New Jersey: Prentice-Hall.

Atkinson, J. W. 1958. "Towards Experimental Analysis of Human Motivation in Terms of Motives, Expectancies and Incentives." In *Motives in Fantasy, Action and Society,* J. W. Atkinson, ed., pp. 288–306. Princeton: D. Van Nostrand Company.

Axelson, L. J. 1963. "The Marital Adjustment and Marital Role Definitions of Husbands of Working and Nonworking Wives." *Marriage and Family Living* 25 : 189–195.

Barrows, G. A., and Zuckerman, M. 1960. "Construct Validity of Three Masculinity-Femininity Tests." *Journal of Consulting and Clinical Psychology* 24 : 441–445.

Bem, S. L. 1974. "The Measurement of Psychological Androgyny." *Journal of Consulting and Clinical Psychology* 42: 155–162.

Bem, S. L. and Bem, D. J. 1972. "Do Sex-Biased Job Advertisements Discourage Applicants of the Opposite Sex?" Testimony before the Federal Communications Commission.

Bennett, G. K. and Cruikshank, R. M. 1942. "Sex Differences in the Understanding of Mechanical Problems." *Journal of Applied Psychology* 26 : 121–127.

Bergmann, B. and Adelman, I. 1973. "The 1973 Report of the President's Council of Economic Advisors: The Economic Role of Women." *American Economic Review* 63 : 509–514.

Bernard, J. 1971. *Women and the Public Interest: An Essay on Public Policy and Protest.* Chicago: Aldine Atherton.

Berry, J. W. 1966. "Temne and Eskimo Perceptual Skills." *International Journal of Psychology* 1 : 207–230.

Bieliauskas, V. J. 1965. "Recent Advances in the Psychology of Masculinity and Femininity." *Journal of Psychology* 60 : 255–263.

Blade, M., and Watson, W. S. 1955. "Increase in Spatial Visualization Test Scores During Engineering Study." *Psychological Monographs* 69 : 12.

Blauner, R. 1960. "Work Satisfaction and Industrial Trends in Modern Society." In *Labor and Trade Unionism,* W. Galenson and S. M. Lipset, eds. New York: Wiley.

Blumberg, R. L., and Winch, R. F. 1972. "Societal Complexity and Familial Complexity: Evidence for the Curvilinear Hypothesis." *American Journal of Sociology* 77 : 898–920.

Bowers, D. G. and Seashore, S. E. 1966. "Predicting Organizational Effectiveness with a Four-Factor Theory of Leadership." *Administrative Science Quarterly* 11 : 238–263.

Brayfield, A. H., and Crockett, W. H. 1955. "Employee Attitudes and Employee Performance." *Psychological Bulletin* 52 : 396–424.

Brinkmann, E. H. 1966. "Programmed Instruction as a Technique for Improving Spatial Visualization." *Journal of Applied Psychology* 50 : 179–184.

Caplow, T. 1954. *The Sociology of Work.* Minneapolis: University of Minnesota Press.

Carey, G. L. 1955. "Reduction of Sex Differences in Problem-Solving by Improvement of Attitude Through Group Discussion." Ph.D. dissertation, Stanford University. Cited in Maccoby (1966).

Cartwright, D. 1951. "Achieving Change in People: Some Applications of Group Dynamics Theory." *Human Relations* 4 : 381–392.

Centers, R. and Bugental, D. E. 1966. "Intrinsic and Extrinsic Job Motivations Among Different Segments of the Working Population." *Journal of Applied Psychology* 50 : 193–197.

Coch, L, and French, J. R. P., Jr. 1948. "Overcoming Resistance to Change." *Human Relations* 1 : 512–532.

Conant, E. H., and Kilbridge, M. D. 1965. "An Interdisciplinary Analysis of Job Enlargement: Technology, Costs, and Behavioral Implications." *Industrial and Labor Relations Review* 18 : 377–395.

Crandall, V. C., and Battle, E. S. 1970. "The Antecedents and Adult Correlates of Academic and Intellectual Achievement Effort." *Minnesota Symposium on Child Psychology,* J. P. Hill, ed., Vol. 4. Minneapolis: University of Minnesota Press.

Crandall, V. J., and Sinkeldam, C. 1964. "Children's Dependent and Achievement Behavior in Social Situations and their Perceptual Field Dependence." *Journal of Personality* 32 : 1–22.

Davis, E. "Careers as Concerns of Blue-Collar Girls." In *Blue-Collar World: Studies of the American Worker,* A. Shostak and W. Gomberg, eds., pp. 154–164. New York: Prentice-Hall.

Dubin, R. 1955. "Industrial Workers' Worlds: A Study of the Central Life Interests of Industrial Workers." *Social Problems* 3 : 131–142.

Duncan, O. D., and Duncan, B. 1955. "A Methodological Analysis of Segregation Indexes." *American Sociological Review* 20 : 210–217.

Edmonds, V. H. 1967. "Marital Conventionalization: Definition and Measurement." *Journal of Marriage and the Family* 29 : 681–688.

Edwards, A. L., and Abbott, R. D. 1973. "Measurement of Personality Traits: Theory and Technique." *Am. Rev. Psychol.* 24 : 241–78.

EEOC (Equal Employment Opportunity Commission). 1969a. *Report on Special Industrial Relations Investigation for Illinois Bell.* (C-571) Washington, D.C.

    1969b. *I Quit: A Study of Short Tenure Losses in the Plant Departments.* (R-791) Washington, D.C.

1970a. *Plant Force Retention Project Interviewing Summary*. (Z–728) Washington, D.C.

1970b. *Psychological Factors Affecting Operator Turnover*. (R–798) Washington, D.C.

1970c. *The Service Representative: Her Story*. (Z–727) Washington Commercial Personnel: Washington, D.C.

1970d. *The Utilization of Women in the Management of the Bell System*. (#1289) Washington, D.C.

1972. *"A Unique Competence": A Study of Equal Employment Opportunity in the Bell System*. Washington, D.C.

Epstein, C. F. 1969. "Women Lawyers and their Profession: Inconsistency of Social Controls and their Consequences for Professional Performance." Paper read at the meetings of the American Sociological Association.

1970. "Encountering The Male Establishment: Sex-Status Limits on Women's Careers in the Professions." *American Journal of Sociology* 75, No. 6 : 965–82.

1971. *Women's Place: Options and Limits in Professional Careers*. Berkeley: University of California Press.

1972. "Sex Role Stereotyping, Occupations and Social Exchange" Paper at the Radcliffe Institute Conference, April.

Farmer, H. S., and Bohn, M. J. 1970. "Home-Career Conflict Reduction and the Level of Career Interest in Women." *Journal of Counseling Psychology* 17 : 228–232.

Fichter, J. H. 1964. *Young Negro Talent: Survey of the Experiences and Expectations of Negro Americans who Graduated from College in 1961*. Chicago: (National Opinion Research Center).

1965. *Negro Women Bachelors: A Comparative Exploration of the Experiences and Expectations of College Graduates of the Class of June, 1961*. Chicago: NORC.

Fidell, L. S., and DeLamater, J. 1971. "Women in the Professions: What's All the Fuss About?" *American Behavioral Scientist* 15, No. 2 : 163–171.

Fiedler, F. E. 1961. "Leadership and Leadership Effectiveness Traits: A Reconceptualization of the Leadership Trait Problem." In *Leadership & Interpersonal Behavior*, L. Petrullo and B. M. Bass, eds., pp. 179–186. New York: Holt, Rinehart, and Winston.

Fuchs, V. R. 1971. "Differences in Hourly Earnings Between Men and Women." *Monthly Labor Review* 94 : 9–15.

Glenn, H. M. 1959. "Attitudes of Women Regarding Gainful Employment of Married Women." *Journal of Home Economics* 51 : 247–252.

Glueck, S., and Glueck, E. 1957. "Working Mothers and Delinquency." *Mental Hygiene* 41 : 327–352.

Goodman, P., and Friedman, A. 1971. An examination of Adams' theory of inequity. *Admin. Sci. Quart.* 16, 271–286.

Gubbels, R. 1972. "The Supply and Demand for Female Workers." In *Woman in a Man-made World,* Nona Glazar-Malbin and Helen Youngelson Waehrer, eds., pp. 208–218. Chicago: Rand McNally.

Gurin, P. 1974. *Psychological Issues in the Study of Employment Discrimination.* Paper presented at the Research Workshop on Equal Employment Opportunity, M.I.T., January.

Hall, R. H. 1969. *Occupations and the Social Structure.* Englewood Cliffs, N.J.: Prentice-Hall.

Hamilton, M. T. 1970. "Woman Power and Discrimination in the Labor Market." Unpublished paper, University of Chicago.

Handbook of Women Workers. 1969. Women's Bureau Bulletin 294. Washington, D.C.: US Department of Labor.

Harmon, L. W. 1969. "Predictive Power Over Ten Years of Measured Social Service and Scientific Interests Among College Women." *Journal of Applied Psychology* 53 : 193– 98.

        1970. "Anatomy of Career Commitment in Women." *Journal of Counseling Psychology* 17 : 77–80.

        1971. "The Childhood and Adolescent Career Plans of College Women." *Journal of Vocational Behavior* 1 : 45–56.

Hartley, R. E. 1970. "American Core Culture: Changes and Continuities." In *Sex Roles in a Changing Society,* G. H. Seward and R. C. Williamson, eds. New York: Random House.

        1960. "Children's Concepts of Male and Female Roles." *Merrill-Palmer Quarterly* 6 : 84–91.

Hedges, J. N. 1970. "Women Workers and Manpower Demands in the 1970's." *Monthly Labor Review,* June, pp. 19–29.

Himmelweit, H. 1958. *Television and the Child.* New York: Oxford University Press.

Hodge, R. W., and Hodge, P. 1965. "Occupational Assimilation as a Competitive Process," *American Journal of Sociology* 71 : 249–264.

Hoffman, M. 1968. *The Gay World,* Ch. 6. New York: Basic Books.

Hornaday, J. A., and Kuder, G. F. 1961. "A Study of Male Occupational Scales Applied to Women." *Educational and Psychological Measurement* 21 : 859–864.

Horner, M. 1968. "The Motive to Avoid Success in Women." Paper read at the meeting of the American Psychological Association.

        1969. "Women's Will to Fail." *Psychology Today,* November, pp. 36–39.

        1970. "Femininity and Successful Achievement: A Basic Inconsistency." In *Feminine Personality and Conflict,* Bardwick, J., Douvan, E., Horner, M., and Gutmann, D., eds. Belmont, Calif.: Brooks-Cole.

Horner, M., Tresmer, D.W., Bereus, A. E., and Watson, R. I. 1973. "Scoring manual for an emprically derived scoring system for Motive to Avoid Success." Unpublished Paper, Harvard University.

Hulin, C. L., and Blood, M. R. 1968. "Job Enlargement, Individual Differences, and Worker Responses." *Psychological Bulletin* 69 : 41–55.

Inkeles, A. 1960. "Industrial Man: The Relation of Status to Experience, Perception and Value." *American Journal of Sociology* 66 : 1–31.

Jenkin, N., and Vroegh, K. 1969. "Contemporary Concepts of Masculinity and Femininity." *Psychological Reports* 25 : 679–697.

Joseph, J. 1961. "Attitudes to Work and Marriage of 600 Adolescent Girls." *British Journal of Sociology* 12 : 176–183.

Katz, D. 1960. "The Functional Approach to the Study of Attitudes." *Public Opinion Quarterly* 24 : 163–204.

———. 1964. "The Motivational Basis of Organizational Behavior." *Behavioral Science* 9 : 131–146.

Katz, D., and Kahn, R. L. 1966. *The Social Psychology of Organizations.* New York: Wiley.

Katz, I. 1969. "A Critique of Personality Approaches to Negro Performance, With Research Suggestions." *Journal of Social Issues* 25 : 13–29.

Kay, E., Meyer, H. H., and French, J. R. P., Jr. 1965. "Effects of Threat in a Performance Appraisal Interview." *Journal of Applied Psychology* 49 : 311–317.

Kilbridge, M. 1960. "Reduced Costs Through Job Enlargement." *Journal of Business* 33 : 357–362.

Kronus, Carol, and Grimm, J. 1971. "Women in Librarianship: The Majority Rules?" *Protean,* December.

Kuhlen, R. G. 1963. "Needs, Perceived Need Satisfaction Opportunities, and Satisfaction with Occupation." *Journal of Applied Psychology* 47 : 56–64.

Lawler, E. E. 1968. "Equity Theory as a Predictor of Productivity and Work Quality." *Psychological Bulletin* 70 : 596–610.

Laws, J. L. 1970. "Toward a Model of Female Sexual Identity." *Midway,* summer, pp. 39–75.

———. 1972a. "A Feminist Analysis of Relative Deprivation in Academic Women." *The Review of Radical Political Economics* 4 : 107–119.

———. 1972b. The Psychology of Tokenism. Unpublished paper, Cornell University.

———. 1974. *The Second XX: Studies in the Social Roles of Women.* In preparation, 1974.

Levitin, T., Quinn, R. P., and Staines, G. L. 1971. "Sex Discrimination Against the American Working Woman." *American Behavioral Scientist* 15 : 237–254.

Likert, R. 1967. *The Human Organization.* New York: McGraw-Hill.

Longstaff, H. P. 1954. "Practice Effects on the Minnesota Vocational Test for Clerical Workers." *Journal of Applied Psychology* 38 : 18–20.

Loring, R., and Wells, T. 1972. *Breakthrough: Women into Management.* New York: Van Nostrand Reinhold.

Maccoby, E., ed. 1966. *The Development of Sex Differences.* Stanford University Press.

McGregor, D. 1960. *The Human Side of Enterprise.* New York: McGraw-Hill.

McNulty, D. 1967. "Differences in Pay Between Men and Women Workers." *Monthly Labor Review* 90 : 40–43.

Matthews, E., and Tiedeman, D. V. 1964. "Attitudes Toward Career and Marriage and the Development of Life Style in Young Women." *Journal of Counseling Psychology* 11 : 375–384.

Miller, S. M., and Riessman, R. 1961. "The Working Class Sub-culture: A New View." *Social Problems* 9 : 86–97.

Mills, C. W. 1940. "Situated Actions and Vocabularies of Motive." *American Sociological Review* 5 : 904–913.

Morse, N. C., and Weiss, R. S. 1955. "The Function and Meaning of Work and the Job." *American Sociological Review* 20 : 191–198.

Naditch, S. F. 1972. "Sex Differences in Field Dependence: Fact or Artifact?" Unpublished paper, Cornell University.

National Manpower Council. 1957. *Womanpower.* New York: Columbia University Press.

Nichols, R. C. 1962. "Subtle, Obvious and Stereotype Measures of Masculinity-Femininity." *Educational and Psychological Measurement* 22 : 449–461.

Nye, F. I., and Hoffman, L. W. 1963. *The Employed Mother in America.* Chicago: Rand McNally.

Oppenheimer, V. K. 1970. "The Female Labor Force in the United States: Demographic and Economic Factors Governing Its Growth and Changing Composition." University of California at Berkeley: Population Monograph Series, no. 5.

——— 1972. Testimony before the Federal Communications Commission, August.

Orden, S. R., and Bradburn, N. M. 1968. "Dimensions of Marriage Happiness." *American Journal of Sociology* 73 : 715–731.

Patchen, M. 1962. "Supervisory Methods and Group Performance Norms." *Administrative Science Quarterly* 7 : 275–294.

Penner, D. 1967. A Study of Causes and Consequences of Salary Satisfaction. Crotonville, N.Y.: General Electric Behavioral Research Service.

Peterson, E. 1964. "Working Women." In *The Woman in America,* 1968. R. F. Lifton, ed. Boston: Beacon Press.

Phelps, C. E. 1968. "Women in American Medicine." *Journal of Medical Education* 43 : 916–924.

Pierce, C. 1971. "Natural Law Language and Women." In *Women in Sexist Society,* V. Gornick and B. Moran, eds., pp. 160–173. New York: Basic Books.

Pleck, J. H. 1973a. "New Concepts of Sex Role Identity." Paper read at the Society for the Scientific Study of Sex.

        1973b. "Social Science and Sex Role Change." Unpublished paper, Harvard University.

Psathas, G. 1968. "Toward a Theory of Occupational Choice for Women." *Sociology and Social Research* 52 : 253–268.

Rossi, A. 1964. "Equality Between the Sexes: An Immodest Proposal." In *The Woman in America,* R. J. Lifton, ed. Boston: Beacon Press.

        1965. "Who Wants Women In The Scientific Professions?" In *Women in the Scientific Professions,* J. Mattfeld and C. G. Van Aken, eds. Cambridge: M.I.T. Press.

        1970. "Status of Women in Graduate Departments of Sociology, 1968-69." American Sociologist 5 : 1–12.

Safilios-Rothschild, Constantina. 1971. "A Cross-cultural Examination of Women's Marital, Educational and Occupational Options" *Acta Sociologica* 14 : 96–113.

Schmidt, F. 1973. "Sex Differences in Some Occupationally Relevant Traits." Unpublished paper, Michigan State University.

Schneidler, G., and Paterson, D. 1942. "Sex Differences in Clerical Aptitude." *Journal of Educational Psychology* 3 : 303–309.

Schwenn, M. 1970. "Arousal of the Motive to Avoid Success." Junior Honors Thesis, Harvard University.

Shepler, B. 1951. "A Comparison of Masculinity-Femininity Measures." *Journal of Consulting Psychology* 15 : 484–486.

Sherman, J. A. 1967. "Problems of Sex Differences in Space Perception and Aspects of Intellectual Functioning." *Psychological Review* 74 : 290–299

        1971. *On the Psychology of Women,* Springfield, Ill.: Charles C Thomas.

Simon, R. J., Clark, S. M., and Tifft, L. L. 1966. "Of Nepotism, Marriage and the Pursuit of an Academic Career." *Sociology of Education* 39, No. 4 : 344–358.

Shuster, J. R., and Atchison, T. J. 1973. "Examining Feelings of Pay Equity." *Business Perspectives* 9 : 14–19.

Simpson, L. 1970. "A Myth is Better than a Miss: Men Get the Edge in Academic Employment." *College and University Business* : 72–73.

Stafford, R. E. 1961. "Sex Differences in Spatial Visualization as Evidence of Sex-linked Inheritance." *Perceptual and Motor Skills* 13 : 428.

Stein, A., and Bailey, M. 1973. "The Socialization of Achievement Orientation in Females." *Psychological Bulletin* 80 : 345–366.

Stouffer, S. A., Suchman, E. A., DeVinney, L. C., Star, S. A., and Williams, R. M., Jr. 1949. *The American Soldier: Adjustment During Army Life.* Princeton: Princeton University Press.

Strong, E. K., Jr. 1943. *Vocational Interests of Men and Women.* Stanford: Stanford University Press.

Suppes, P. 1968. "Computer Technology and the Future of Education." *Phi Delta Kappa,* 49 : 420–423.

Tenopyr, M. L. 1970. "Dimensions of the Now Generation's Attitudes Toward Working Women." Paper read at the meetings of the American Psychological Association, September.

Terman, L. M., and Miles, C. C. 1936. *Sex and Personality: Studies in Masculinity and Femininity.* New York: McGraw-Hill.

Thompson, B., and Finlayson, A. 1963. "Married Women Who Work in Early Motherhood." *British Journal of Sociology* 14 : 150–168.

Tyler, L. 1972. "Sex Differences in Vocational Interests and Motivation Related to Occupations." Testimony before the Federal Communications Commission, August.

US Department of Labor. 1970. *Absenteeism and Turnover,* Washington, D.C.

US Department of Labor, Women's Bureau. 1970. *Background Facts On Women Workers in the United States.* Washington, D.C.

    1971. *The Myth and the Reality,* Washington, D.C., 1971.

Vincent, C. E. 1966. "Implications of Changes in Male-Female Role Expectations for Interpreting M-F Scores." *Journal of Marriage and the Family* 28 : 196–199.

Waldman, E. 1970. "Changes in the Labor Force Activity of Women." *Monthly Labor Review* 93 : 10–18.

Watley, D. J., and Kaplan, R. 1971. "Career or Marriage? Aspirations and Achievements of Able Young Women." *Journal of Vocational Behavior* 1 : 29–43.

Weil, M. W. 1961. "An Analysis of the Factors Influencing Married Women's Actual or Planned Work Participation." *American Sociological Review* 26 : 91–95.

Wells, T. 1973. "Equalizing Advancement Between Women and Men." *Training and Development Journal,* August, pp. 1–4.

White, J. J. 1972. "Women in the Law." In *Toward a Sociology of Women,* C. Safilios-Rothschild, ed., pp. 277–300. Lexington, Mass.: Xerox College Publishing, 1972.

Witkin, H. A., et al. 1962. *Psychological Differentiation.* New York: Wiley.

Zytowski, D. G. 1969. "Toward a Theory of Career Development for Women." *Personnel and Guidance Journal* 47 : 660–664.

8 Equal Opportunity and Black Employment in the Telephone Industry

Bernard E. Anderson

I. Introduction

The Equal Employment Opportunity Commission (EEOC) challenge to the American Telephone and Telegraph Company (AT&T) called national attention to the employment practices of the nation's public utility industry.[1] Despite the fact that utilities operate in every section of the nation, and exert a profound influence on the nation's economic progress, standard of living, and economic development, the racial employment policies and practices of public utilities escaped close examination prior to the late 1960s. Studies since that time have revealed a long history of discriminatory employment practices more severe in the utilities than in the economy as a whole.[2] As the nation's largest privately owned utility, and one having a marked impact on almost every sector of society, AT&T and the Bell operating companies have attracted special attention in the assessment of equal job opportunity in American industry.

Management officials of AT&T and its affiliated Bell operating companies have long expressed pride in their commitment to fair employment practices. In testimony presented to the Federal Communications Commission, for example, John Kingsbury, Assistant Vice-President of AT&T for Human Resources Development, recalled that while a district traffic manager in Southern Indiana shortly after World War II, he broke the color bar and hired black women as telephone operators despite expected opposition from both the public and the company's white employees.[3] As it turned out, the expected opposition failed to materialize and the black women performed effectively on the job.

The corporation's commitment to fair employment was also expressed in the early 1960s when H. I. Romnes, President of the Western Electric Company, and later Chairman of the Board of AT&T declared:

Equal opportunity is a fine phrase. Making it come true is an arduous, sometimes painful process. But there are many good reasons why management needs to demonstrate not merely good faith but practical initiative in support of this basic American tenet. The good opinion of the world is only one of them . . . in the final analysis there is one reason above all others for giving our best management attention to making equal opportunity come true—and that is because it is right.[4]

1 Petition for Intervention Before the FCC, *Equal Employment Opportunity Commission vs. American Telephone and Telegraph Company* (December 10, 1970).
2 Bernard E. Anderson, *Negro Employment in Public Utilities* (Philadelphia, University of Pennsylvania Press, 1970), and Equal Employment Opportunity Commission, *Promise vs. Performance: Public Hearings on Equal Opportunity in the Nation's Electric Power and Gas Utilities* (Washington, EEOC, June 1972).
3 Testimony of John W. Kingsbury, FCC Docket No. 19143 (August 1, 1972), p. 5.
4 *Ibid.,* p. 12.

More recently, Board Chairman John deButts reemphasized the company's commitment in the following words—which represents, perhaps, the most unequivocal public statement on equal opportunity ever issued by a major AT&T official:

But one thing should be clear: it is the policy of the Bell System—North, South, East and West—to assure that every employee has a fair and equal chance to realize his full potential along any career path he or she may choose. That's the way I read the law of the land. More fundamentally, that's the way I read our country's purpose, a purpose we have a responsibility to help fulfill. And furthermore, that's what I *personally* believe is the right course for us. In short affirmative action to achieve equal opportunity is a major factor in every Bell System manager's job—a factor on which he can expect to be measured on the basis of the *results* he achieves.[5]

Despite the avowed commitment to fair employment reflected in the public statements of management officers, the performance of the Bell System in hiring and upgrading minority group workers was, until very recently, far less than satisfactory by any reasonable standard of equal opportunity. The record shows that black workers have been employed by Bell and other telephone companies for many years. Before the 1960s, however, the number of blacks employed was markedly low in relation to the total industry work force, and among those hired, very few black workers held skilled, professional, technical, and supervisory jobs. Until very recently, the Bell System commitment to equal employment seemed confined to black women, and then, only in the job of telephone operator. The underutilization of black workers was not unique to the Bell System, however, and was not confined to any state or region. Instead, the restriction on opportunities for minority group workers was a pervasive feature of the telephone industry's operations throughout the nation.

Telephone industry employment practices are the result of many forces, including labor market conditions, company policy, union policy, and community attitudes. Government intervention against race and sex discrimination has been a major factor affecting company employment practices during the past few years. Under the combined effects of labor market conditions and government pressure, the industry has shown an increase in black employment since 1968 that exceeds in number and occupational scope any gains registered by blacks in the telephone industry at any comparable period in the past. Most of the gains were registered by the Bell System and their magnitude promises to exert a major influence on the status of blacks throughout the telephone industry and may represent a bellwether for minority group employment progress throughout the economy in the years ahead.

In the following sections of this paper, evidence will be presented in support of these statements. Section II sketches the trend of black employment in the telephone industry from the turn of the century through 1960. In Section III, the

5 *Ibid.*, p. 11.

trend in black employment in the telephone industry during the 1960s will be discussed. Section IV identifies several major factors which have influenced the pace and direction of change in black employment over time, and especially during the decade of the sixties. Section V summarizes the most important implications of past trends for the future of the black worker in the telephone industry.

II. Past Trends in Black Employment

The telephone industry is a post–Civil War industry developed on a new technology. When the early telephone companies were organized, few members of the labor force possessed the skills necessary to produce telephone service. Consequently, from its earliest experience, the industry developed the practice of training almost all its employees on the job—a practice which continues to the present day.

Although black artisans in significant numbers had worked in the mechanical trades in the antebellum South, the competition from white workers, the inability to obtain skills training, and racial discrimination within the trade unions after the Civil War prevented most blacks from acquiring a foothold in the emerging electrical industries.[6]

Few blacks were among those hired and trained by the telephone industry during its formative years. Employment statistics by race are incomplete for the public utilities before 1920, but the limited data available show 529 blacks employed as telephone and telegraph linemen, and 69 employed as telephone operators among the 89,912 workers employed in those occupations in 1900.[7] Because the census classification includes helpers and laborers in the "lineman" category, the skill level of blacks is uncertain. The evidence on the characteristics of the black labor force through the 1920s, however, suggests that most black linemen were employed in unskilled jobs. Perhaps the most skilled, and certainly the most prominent black man associated with the early telephone industry was Granville T. Woods, an inventor whose experiments led to the development of a voice receiver that gained widespread use in commercial telephones.[8]

1920 to 1930

The 1920 to 1930 period was one of rapid growth and consolidation in public utilities—especially in the North, where the nation's industrial production and commercial trade were concentrated. Native-born whites provided most of the labor supply for the expanding utilities, but foreign-born whites also held a prominent place in some occupations. For example, almost one-fourth of the machinists

6 Herbert R. Northrup, *Organized Labor and the Negro* (New York: Harper & Brothers, 1944), pp. 17–47.
7 *US Census of Population: 1900, Special Reports, Occupations*, Table 2.
8 John P. Davis, *American Negro Reference Book* (Englewood Cliffs: Prentice-Hall, 1966), p. 53.

Table 8.1   Telephone Industry Employment by Race and Sex (1930–1970)

	1970	1960	1950	1940	1930
All Employees	899,997	692,480	594,120	316,600	578,602
Black	71,469	17,127	7,920	2,320	3,995
Percent	7.9	2.5	1.3	0.7	0.7
Male	427,463	303,884	220,380	126,920	267,354
Black	18,096	6,121	4,290	1,940	3,478
Percent	4.2	2.0	1.9	1.5	1.3
Female	472,534	388,596	373,740	189,680	311,248
Black	53,373	11,006	3,630	380	517
Percent	11.3	2.8	1.0	0.2	0.2

Source: U.S. Census of Population:
          1930: Vol. V, General Report on Occupations, Chapter VII,
                 Table 2 (Gainful workers, 10 years old and over.)
          1940: Sample Statistics, The Labor Force, Industrial
                 Characteristics, Table 1.
          1950: Special Report P-E No. 1D, Characteristics of the
                 Population, U.S. Summary, Table 2.
          1960: PC(2) 7F, Industrial Characteristics, Table 3.
          1970: PC(1)-D1, U.S. Summary, Detailed Characteristics, Table
                 236.

[a] Includes telegraph employment in 1930.

(24.6 percent), and slightly more than one-fifth of the carpenters (22.4 percent) in the electric power industry in 1930 were foreign-born whites.[9] It is interesting to note that at that time, the foreign-born also accounted for a sizeable proportion of the unskilled laborers (22.8 percent) and janitors and porters (27.7 percent). Such unskilled jobs in other industries were often reserved for black workers.

The telephone industry employed fewer blacks and foreign-born whites than the other utilities during the 1920 decade. Among the blacks who did have jobs in telephone firms, however, almost all were employed as laborers, janitors, and porters. In contrast, the small number of foreign-born whites in the industry could be found occasionally holding jobs as telephone operators, linemen, foremen, and inspectors. Thus, during the first four decades of the telephone industry's existence, the hiring pattern clearly marked the industry as the preserve of white employees. The industry's early hiring practices set the pattern for many subsequent years, and generated a negative image among black workers.

9 Anderson, *Negro Employment,* p. 68–71.

1930 to 1950

Beginning in 1930, the Census of Population provides a continuous series of employment by race in the telephone industry (Table 8.1). The evidence documents the historic exclusion of black workers from the telephone industry at least until the 1960 decade. Despite the fact that the industry had more than one-half million workers in 1930, fewer than 4,000 blacks were employed. Of course, during this period, black workers were not prominent in the work force of most nonagricultural industries.[10] Still, even in an environment of generally restricted opportunities for blacks in the industrial world, the telephone utilities were notable for their racial exclusionist practices.[11]

From 1930 to 1940, the industry experienced a 45.3 percent decline in manpower as a result of depressed business conditions and numerous company mergers. The industry's small black work force also declined, and at the end of the decade it was only slightly more than half its size in 1930.

During the 1940 decade, employment in the telephone industry recovered strongly in response to labor demand generated by the war effort. Between 1940 and 1945, employment rose by 92,000—a growth of 29 percent. By the end of the decade there were almost 600,000 employees in the industry, yet blacks continued to represent little more than one percent of the work force. The failure of the industry to hire black women in nonservice jobs produced further evidence of racial disparity: while women outnumbered men in the total industry work force, black men outnumbered black women by a sizeable proportion at least until 1960.

The disparate sex composition of employment between blacks and other workers largely reflected the unwillingness of the telephone industry to hire blacks on a basis of equality with others at a time when the total industry work force was expanding rapidly. Between 1940 and 1950, for example, the industry's male workforce increased by almost 100,000 and the female workforce by almost 200,000 employees. Black men accounted for 2.5 percent of the increase among males and black women comprised 1.8 percent of the net addition to female employment. The bulk of the increase in the industry's female work force occurred among telephone operators, but black women gained relatively few of such jobs. During the decade the number of black telephone operators rose to 2,481 while the total number of operators expanded by over 100,000. Because black women did not enjoy equal hiring opportunity with whites in operator jobs, the industry's most rapidly expanding occupation, the number of black women relative to black men was reduced markedly below the level that might be expected from the industry's job

10 Charles H. Wesley, *Negro Labor in the United States* (New York: Vanguard Press, 1927), pp. 20–40.
11 An account of racial discrimination against hiring black women in the Chicago Telephone Company may be found in Chicago Commission on Race Relations, *The Negro in Chicago* (Chicago: University of Chicago Press, 1922), pp. 391–392.

composition. As will be discussed below, the 1950 to 1960 decade brought visible changes in this pattern, but movement away from the industry's exclusion of black workers was uneven and was concentrated in relatively few localities.

1950 to 1960

The uneven progress of blacks in obtaining telephone industry jobs during the 1950s is shown in the trend in black employment in the states shown in Table 8.2. The twenty-six selected states and the District of Columbia accounted for the bulk of the nation's black population in 1950. Together the selected states had 83.2 percent of the telephone industry work force and 96.5 percent of all blacks employed by the industry in 1950.

Employment in the telecommunications industry increased by 140,919, or 26.5 percent, in the selected states during the 1950 decade. Blacks gained 10,115, or 7.2 percent, of the industry's total employment growth. Black women, however, gained 7,236 jobs, or almost one and one-half times the 2,899 jobs gained by black men in the industry during the decade.

Five states (New York, Pennsylvania, Illinois, Michigan, and Ohio) accounted for 5,049, or 69.8 percent, of the increase in black women employed by the industry during the 1950s. In comparison with the gains of black women, the employment of all women rose by only 1,833 in the five states combined, and actually declined in Pennsylvania and Illinois. Similarly, the states showing the greatest employment gains for black women also accounted for almost one-half the growth of employment among black men in the telecommunications industry.

The narrow range and limited magnitude of employment gains among blacks are reflected in the almost imperceptible change in black participation rates in the industry during the decade (Table 8.3).[12] Only one state, New York, and the District of Columbia had a black female participation rate as high as 5.0 percent in 1960. Further, the participation rates for black telephone workers in the twenty-seven selected states, and in the nation as a whole, remained below one-third the proportion of blacks in the labor force during the decade.

Metropolitan Area Trends

Further examination of the employment data show that black gains in the telephone industry during the 1950s were concentrated not only in a small number of states, but also in a small number of metropolitan areas within the states. Especially significant were the gains registered by blacks in the seventeen SMSA's (Standard Metropolitan Statistical Areas) to which substantial numbers of blacks migrated during and after World War II. Total industry employment increased by 32,427

12 The participation rate equals the number of blacks in the employment sector divided by the total number of employees.

Table 8.2   Change in Employment in the Telecommunications Industry, by Race and Sex (1950-1970)

| | Male | | | | Female | | | |
| | All | | Black | | All | | Black | |
State	1960-1970	1950-1960	1960-1970	1950-1960	1960-1970	1950-1960	1960-1970	1950-1960
Alabama	819	2,253	28	72	1,591	1,125	573	64
Arkansas	268	635	8	6	265	-245	123	5
California	7,152	20,159	922	364	17,846	10,459	4,770	827
Connecticut	1,105	2,407	214	19	958	1,055	598	129
Delaware	77	507	5	3	89	168	46	1
District of Columbia	-297	-394	406	34	843	831	2,062	178
Florida	5,743	7,306	177	216	8,074	5,590	1,775	14
Georgia	2,200	2,839	145	50	4,264	825	1,532	-10
Illinois	815	5,342	1,059	266	-1,896	-2,829	2,662	870
Indiana	2,079	2,116	199	66	332	700	592	127
Kentucky	62	2,058	-13	98	600	150	195	13
Louisiana	-721	2,214	-4	-6	796	1,449	816	0
Maryland	2,836	2,915	247	124	3,489	1,007	1,356	36
Massachussetts	1,040	4,761	170	2	2,286	-492	538	62
Michigan	679	4,089	324	158	515	1,380	2,119	597
Mississippi	614	785	35	46	140	509	66	16
Missouri	-506	2,375	62	87	113	138	1,095	33
New Jersey	2,307	3,640	612	54	1,446	-455	1,873	503
New York	-176	15,568	2,622	665	987	3,002	8,017	2,658
North Carolina	2,620	3,229	247	45	3,621	1,530	1,020	60
Ohio	2,782	6,020	600	136	2,795	1,644	2,433	400
Pennsylvania	-1,059	7,345	348	154	-3,211	-1,249	1,235	523
South Carolina	763	1,400	70	24	1,140	743	324	25
Tennessee	-373	2,980	-87	70	633	400	799	-35
Texas	343	5,163	179	126	2,930	751	1,980	44
Virginia	2,315	3,257	204	6	2,317	1,754	803	89
West Virginia	-44	1,185	-45	70	-949	553	61	7
27 State Total	34,189	112,155	8,757	2,899	50,042	28,764	39,447	7,236
Total, United States	33,053	139,565	9,369	2,933	46,298	35,651	27,496	8,069

Source: U.S. Census of Population:
1950: Vol. II, Characteristics of the Population, Part 1, U.S. Summary, Table 133 and State Volumes, Table 83.
1960: PC(1) D, Detailed Characteristics, State Volumes, Table 129, and PC(2) 7F, Industrial Characteristics, Table 3.
1970: PC(1) D, Detailed Characteristics, State Volumes, Table 236, and PC(1)-D1, U.S. Summary.

Table 8.3 Black Participation Rate in the Telecommunications Industry in
Selected States (1950-1970)

State	Male			Female		
	1970	1960	1950	1970	1960	1950
Alabama	5.1	5.4	7.4	10.5	2.4	1.4
Arkansas	3.7	3.8	5.0	5.1	1.0	0.8
California	2.9	1.4	1.1	9.1	2.1	0.4
Connecticut	3.4	0.6	0.4	10.1	2.2	0.2
Delaware	1.4	1.0	1.5	5.8	0.5	0.5
Dist. of Columbia	73.7	23.9	16.1	84.6	14.9	4.0
Florida	4.0	4.4	7.1	9.5	0.8	1.4
Georgia	5.6	5.3	7.3	13.9	1.2	1.5
Illinois	6.7	2.6	1.9	15.3	4.6	1.3
Indiana	3.7	2.6	2.4	7.2	1.6	0.4
Kentucky	2.5	2.8	3.3	4.6	1.1	0.9
Louisiana	5.5	4.7	8.1	12.5	1.5	1.9
Maryland	5.8	4.7	5.0	14.4	2.2	2.0
Massachusetts	1.4	0.2	0.3	3.6	0.6	0.2
Michigan	4.4	2.5	2.0	16.7	4.6	1.1
Mississippi	7.6	8.1	9.3	4.5	2.6	2.5
Missouri	3.5	2.7	2.3	11.0	0.7	0.4
New Jersey	3.5	0.7	0.5	12.9	3.8	1.1
New York	7.8	2.4	1.6	22.0	7.1	2.5
North Carolina	6.2	4.8	8.4	10.9	1.5	0.8
Ohio	4.8	2.2	2.2	14.1	3.2	1.1
Pennsylvania	3.2	1.4	1.1	8.6	2.6	0.5
So. Carolina	6.8	6.2	10.3	8.8	1.8	1.4
Tennessee	3.3	4.4	6.3	12.2	0.8	1.5
Texas	4.4	3.6	4.0	9.2	0.9	0.7
Virginia	4.2	2.7	4.7	9.4	2.0	1.1
West Virginia	2.6	4.1	2.8	3.8	1.2	1.1
27 State Total		2.6	2.6		3.1	1.2
Total, U.S.	4.2	2.2	2.3	11.3	2.8	1.0

Source: U.S. Census of Population:
    1950: Vol. II, Characteristics of the Population, Part I, U.S.
        Summary, Table 133 and State Volumes, Table 83.
    1960: PC(1) D, Detailed Characteristics, State Volumes, Table
        129, and PC(2) 7F, Industrial Characteristics, Table 3.
    1970: PC(1) D, Detailed Characteristics, State Volumes, Table
        236, and PC(1)-D1, U.S. Summary.

in the 17 areas between 1950 and 1960, with blacks accounting for 7,488, or 23.1 percent, of the total employment growth. Among all blacks, the largest gain in jobs was registered by black women, whose employment rose by 5,853, while total female employment in the selected areas declined by 2,319, or 1.5 percent.

The employment of black women in the industry grew significantly in several SMSA's. In New York, black women gained 2,540 jobs and rose from 3.3 to 9.6 percent of all female employees in the industry. In Philadelphia, the increase was 532, raising the relative number of blacks among all female telephone workers from 0.6 to 5.1 percent. Chicago, Detroit, and Los Angeles each showed increases of 400 or more black women; and in 1960, each of these areas had three or more times as many black women as were employed by the industry in 1950.

These gains, while small, signaled a change in company hiring practices that represented an observable departure from the past. Still, progress was not universal, and black men had more difficulty than black women in obtaining jobs in the telephone industry during the 1950s. The number of black men increased at a significant rate in several areas, including New York City, Chicago, and Los Angeles, but the numerical gains were much smaller, on the average, than the employment increases registered by black women. In the seventeen SMSA's combined, the black male participation rate in the industry rose from 2.3 to 2.9 percent during the decade, while that for black women rose from 1.7 to 5.5 percent of the industry's female work force.

Gains Among Telephone Operators

The limited gains registered by blacks in the telephone industry during the 1950s were almost entirely confined to the employment of black women as telephone operators. In the twenty-seven states shown in Table 8.2, the number of blacks employed as operators rose to 7,791 in 1960—more than three times the number of black telephone operators employed in 1950. The rapid growth of employment for blacks exceeded the net increase in all operators in the selected states (4,200) and raised the relative number of blacks among all telephone operators from 0.9 to 2.8 percent.

The largest gains for black telephone operators were recorded in five states: New York, Pennsylvania, Illinois, Michigan, and California. Together these states accounted for almost 82.1 percent of the increase in the number of black telephone operators throughout the nation. In three of the five states, black employment gains occurred while the total employment of telephone operators declined. These gains are especially notable in comparison with the near exclusion of black women from employment as telephone operators prior to World War II.

The gains recorded by black telephone operators were confined to the North and West; few blacks broke the color bar against their employment as operators in the

South during the 1950 decade. In twelve southern states,[13] the number of telephone operators increased by 6,611 between 1950 and 1960. Blacks, however, gained less than one percent of the additional jobs. Throughout the southern region the proportion of blacks among all telephone operators failed to reach one percent by 1960, in marked contrast to the slow but perceptible gains recorded in other regions.

Within the states where blacks registered some progress in obtaining jobs as telephone operators, the employment growth was almost entirely concentrated in the large cities. The largest numerical gains between 1950 and 1960 were recorded in New York, Chicago, Detroit, Los Angeles, and Philadelphia. Each of these metropolitan areas showed increases of 350 or more in the number of blacks employed as telephone operators. Moreover, in each of the five cities, the relative growth rate of black employment greatly exceeded that of all employees. In fact, there is some evidence to suggest that in several metropolitan areas, blacks actually replaced whites previously employed as telephone operators.[14]

The occupational gains of black men in the telephone industry cannot be traced as clearly as that of black women because the census data do not provide separate occupational detail by race for the telephone industry. Employment in the male-dominated industry jobs such as linemen, installers, and other crafts are combined with similar jobs in other utilities in the census publications. Still, the combined occupational data on utility industries lends support to the conclusion that few gains were registered by black men in skilled jobs in the telephone industry.

For example, in the nation at large, the number of public utility linemen and servicemen increased by 66,069 between 1950 and 1960. Black men, however, gained only 1,477 of the jobs, increasing their participation rate among linemen and servicemen from 0.9 to 1.2 percent. Even if the gain recorded by black men in such jobs occurred entirely within the telephone industry—an unlikely event—the rate of increase still would have been insignificant in comparison with the total jobs available, and would have fallen far short of the limited, but measurable, gains registered by black women in telephone operator jobs.

For black men, as for black women, most occupational gains were concentrated in a small number of states. California, leading all states, showed an increase of 202 black linemen and servicemen. Other states, including Illinois, Michigan, New York, Pennsylvania, and Texas each showed increases of 90 or more blacks in similar jobs. It is interesting to note that excluding Texas, the six states of significant black penetration into lineman and serviceman jobs were also the states where black women registered their largest numerical gains as telephone operators. The fact that almost 63 percent of the net increase in black employment occurred in six

13 The states were: Alabama, Arkansas, Florida, Georgia, Louisiana, Mississippi, North Carolina, South Carolina, Tennessee, Texas, Virginia, and West Virginia.
14 Anderson, *Negro Employment,* pp. 92–101.

states and the small magnitude of the gains in such states demonstrate the continuing failure of most telephone companies to improve the occupational status of black men during the decade of the 1950s.

III. Black Employment Gains from 1960 to 1970

The 1960 decade brought black employment gains of dramatic proportions in the telephone industry. Four dimensions of the employment progress deserve attention. First, the numerical and proportionate increase in black employment between 1960 and 1970 greatly exceeded the gains registered in any previous decade. Slightly more than 54,000 blacks obtained employment in the telephone industry during the decade. The 18,096 black men employed in 1970 represented three times the number, and the 53,373 black women, almost five times the number employed in the industry in 1960. The magnitude of the growth in black employment raised the industry's black participation rate from 2.5 to 7.9 percent, and the black female participation rate from 2.0 to 11.3 percent during the decade.

Secondly, the employment gains registered by blacks during the decade were more widely distributed across geographic areas than in previous years. In 1960, for example, only the state of New York and the District of Columbia showed female participation rates of 5.0 percent or more. By 1970, however, twenty-four states had black female participation rates in excess of 5.0 percent and most states doubled their proportion of black female employees during the decade. The gains were especially notable in such states as Alabama, Georgia, Louisiana, North Carolina, and Tennessee, where black women failed to register any measurable gains between 1950 and 1960.

Thirdly, although notable for their size and geographic distribution, the black employment gains continued to be heavily concentrated among women. Of the 54,432 blacks newly hired during the decade, 42,367, or about three of every four (77.9 percent) were women. In contrast, among all employees fewer women (83,965) than men (123,579) gained job opportunities during the decade. Largely because of the uneven sex distribution of employment progress, black female participation rates in 1970 were double the comparable rates for black men in twenty of the twenty-seven selected states shown in Table 8.3. In almost one-half the selected states, including some states in the South, black women accounted for 10 percent or more of the telephone industry work force in 1970.

Finally, there is some evidence that the black employment gains were not distributed evenly throughout the decade, but were concentrated in the years after 1965. For example, according to the Census of Population, black employment in the telephone industry grew by slightly more than 54,000 between 1960 and 1970. In comparison, available data show for the Bell System alone an increase in black

employment of 53,903 during the years 1965 –1971. The net addition of blacks in
the industry during the decade is a joint product of gross hiring and labor turnover.
Because the Bell System is by far the industry's largest employer, it is reasonable
to conclude that Bell's volume of hiring influenced significantly the industry-wide
pattern. This suggests that while many independent telephone companies might
have registered gains in black employment during the 1960 decade, the strong up-
surge of black hiring in Bell companies after 1965 accounted in large part for the
rate of growth of black employment observed in the industry at large.

Recent Black Employment
An examination of the occupational status of blacks in the Bell System reveals both
the dimensions of black progress registered during the 1960 decade, and the distance
blacks have yet to go in acquiring parity with other employees in the System
(Table 8.4). Blacks accounted for 10.0 percent of the Bell System work force in
1971, but were most prominent among service workers (35.8 percent) and semiskilled
operatives (25.4 percent)–two occupational groups which together comprise less
than one of every ten telephone workers.

The two dominant occupational groups in the Bell System are craftsmen, 27.5
percent of the work force, and office and clerical employees (a large proportion of
whom are telephone operators), 46.4 percent of the work force. In these dominant
industry occupations, the black participation rate varied sharply from the black
participation rate among all employees. Blacks were underrepresented among craftsmen (5.0 percent) and overrepresented among office and clerical workers (15.5 percent), reflecting, in large part, the continued disparity between black male and female employment in the Bell System.

For example, blacks accounted for 4.9 percent of all male employees compared
with 14.5 percent of all females in the System. Because the occupational mix in the
System continues to reflect a heavy concentration of men among craftsmen and
women among office and clerical workers, the disparity between the aggregate participation rates for black men and women is revealed as a disparity in their participation
in the two dominant industry occupations. The continuation of the disparity may be
expected from recent hiring rates for black men compared with black women. Between 1968 and 1971, for example, newly hired black craftsmen comprised 14.0 percent of the net gain in all employees in that occupation, while black women accounted for 60.5 percent of the newly hired office and clerical workers.

Additional evidence on disparities in black employment may be seen in the low
participation rates of black workers in such high paying jobs as managers and officials,
professionals, and technicians in the Bell System. Both black men and black women
accounted for significantly less than 5.0 percent of all employees in such occupations
in 1971. Moreover, blacks within the ranks of management were heavily concentrated

at the lowest levels, reflecting their very recent entry into the executive suite.[15]

Thus, although the Bell System demonstrated significant growth in black employment during the late 1960s, the hiring patterns remained largely consistent with practices established at least as early as the 1950s. Black women received the bulk of expanding opportunities, and even among women, a disproportionate number were telephone operators. The uneven progress of black men compared with black women demonstrates the difficulty of achieving racial parity in employment opportunities when present attempts to accelerate minority employment are heavily burdened by a legacy of unequal opportunity in the past.

The Bell System and the Independents

A comparison of the Bell System and independent telephone companies shows that racial employment patterns do not differ markedly throughout the industry (Table 8.5). The number of blacks employed by independent companies in 1968 was markedly below that in Bell companies, mainly because the independents tend to be relatively small companies and are heavily concentrated in small communities in which few blacks reside. When adjustments are made for the difference in location and in the level of employment in the Bell System compared with the independents, differences in the utilization of blacks in each sector of the industry become insignificant. In both there is a heavy concentration of blacks in the lower-classified blue- and white-collar jobs, and a disproportionate number of black female compared with black male employees—a pattern which differs markedly from that among other groups.

IV. Factors Determining Black Employment

The review of the statistical data discussed above is useful in documenting past trends and the recent status of black employment in the telephone industry. It is equally important, however, to identify and explain the forces which determine the magnitude and direction of the observed patterns. The employment trends suggest the following questions: What accounts for the dramatic rise and geographic scope of black female employment in the telephone industry during the 1960s? Why did black men fail to experience gains similar in scope to those of black women? What role does the industry job composition, market structure, labor demand, and labor supply play in determining racial employment patterns? To what extent did government equal employment policy provide a stimulus to employment gains of blacks in the telephone industry?

15 Testimony of John W. Kingsbury, Appendix Table 5A. (See n. 3.)

192   Anderson

Table 8.4 Bell System Employment by Race, Sex, and Occupational Group (1971)

Occupational Group	All Employees			Male			Female		
	Total	Black	Percent Black	Total	Black	Percent Black	Total	Black	Percent Black
Officials and managers	97,712	3,274	3.4	58,829	767	0.8	38,883	2,507	2.6
Professionals	70,098	1,383	2.0	55,379	707	1.0	14,179	676	1.0
Technicians	7,838	463	5.9	4,141	185	2.4	3,697	278	3.5
Sales workers	13,760	564	4.1	10,281	286	2.1	3,479	278	2.0
Office and clerical	369,542	57,373	15.5	12,419	1,393	0.4	357,123	55,982	15.1
Total white collar	558,950	63,057	11.3	141,049	3,338	2.4	417,361	59,721	14.3
Craftsmen	218,812	11,050	5.0	215,841	10,801	4.9	2,971	249	0.1
Operatives	7,921	2,009	25.4	7,773	1,985	25.1	148	24	0.3
Service workers	10,308	3,695	35.8	5,398	2,158	20.9	4,910	1,537	14.9
Total blue collar[1]	237,041	16,754	7.1	229,012	14,944	6.5	8,029	1,810	22.5
Total	795,991	79,811	10.1	370,061	18,282	4.9	425,390	61,531	14.5

Source: Federal Communications Commission Docket No. 19143, Bell Exhibit, August 1, 1972, Testimony of John W. Kingsbury, Appendix tables 6-13.

[1]The Bell System does not classify employees as laborers; all blue collar employees are included within the three designated occupational groups.

Table 8.5 Employment by Race and Occupational Group in Thirty-seven Telecommunications Companies (1968)

Occupational Group	All Companies			Bell System			Independent Companies		
	Total	Negro	Percent Negro	Total	Negro	Percent Negro	Total	Negro	Percent Negro
Officials and managers	83,148	981	1.2	73,401	963	1.3	9,747	18	0.2
Professionals	49,104	355	0.7	47,308	346	0.7	1,796	9	0.5
Technicians	5,614	89	1.6	4,102	82	2.0	1,512	7	0.5
Sales workers	8,172	178	2.2	7,667	177	2.3	505	1	0.2
Office and clerical	326,169	31,375	9.6	296,958	30,722	10.3	29,211	653	2.2
Total white collar	472,207	32,978	7.0	429,436	32,290	7.5	42,771	688	1.6
Craftsmen	177,173	3,142	1.8	153,774	2,891	1.9	23,399	251	1.1
Operatives	8,570	1,325	15.5	5,715	1,137	19.9	2,855	188	6.6
Laborers	115	17	14.8	4	4	100.0	111	13	11.7
Service workers	10,977	3,950	36.0	9,790	3,577	36.5	1,187	373	31.4
Total blue collar	196,835	8,434	4.3	169,283	7,609	4.5	27,552	825	3.0
Total	669,042	41,412	6.2	598,719	39,899	6.7	70,323	1,513	2.2

Source: Data in author's possession.

Answers to these and similar questions are important for what they reveal about the dynamics of change in a large, complex, monopolistic corporation with high visibility in American society. Unfortunately, definitive answers to such questions can rarely be found. At best the observer must draw inferences from limited empirical evidence sifted through a set of hypotheses regarding the nature of change in large economic organizations.

The two basic determinants of change in the employment status of black workers are (1) market forces, characterized by shifts in the demand for and supply of labor in response to the profit-maximizing behavior of firms and the income-maximizing behavior of individuals; and (2) the institutional environment, which consists of discretionary power exercised by management and public policy developed and implemented by government. In most cases, the level and rate of change in racial employment patterns will reflect the influence of both market forces and the institutional environment although one set of forces may be relatively more important than the other at any given time. Some insight into the process of change might be gained by looking at each set of forces separately with a view toward assessing the degree to which the observed changes in black employment confirm the expectations drawn from economic theory and some basic notions of organization behavior.

Labor Demand and Supply in the Telephone Industry
Labor demand in the telephone industry is determined by the technological characteristics of service production, and the demand for telephone services. The industry is characterized by a heavy investment in plant and equipment, much of which operates through automatic controls and sophisticated electronic devices. Productivity per employee is high in the telephone industry, and fluctuations in the level of service production may occur within wide boundaries in the short run with little or no change in the level of employment.

Because of the nature of telephone technology, new employees are typically hired into lower level occupations, and are given on-the-job training. The two most numerous entry-level jobs have been telephone operator and telephone craftsman, the most common of which is the job of telephone installer. For telephone operators, few qualifications other than general aptitude are imposed in the hiring process. For telephone installers, however, mechanical and electrical aptitude are required in addition to general intelligence.

With the exception of management, professional, and technical jobs requiring college training, most occupations above the entry level in telephone companies are filled through promotion from within. Many of the supervisory jobs are filled by upgrading installers and central station craftsmen who, through personnel assessment techniques, have shown potential for management positions. The practice of promotion from within operated for many years to limit employment in entry-level jobs to men who displayed potential for upgrading. Because of the restricted oc-

cupational scope of women and the expectation that many women would not remain in the work force for an extended period of time, fewer conditions for pro-
motability were imposed in the hiring process for women in the industry.

The nature of the demand for telephone workers influences the supply of
workers available to the industry. In the past, young, inexperienced high school
graduates were preferred by telephone companies for entry-level craft and operator
jobs. Although not required by technological considerations, almost all craft jobs
were filled by men, and all operator jobs, by women. This pattern of job assignment
based on sex has been changed dramatically by the EEOC/AT&T Consent Decree,[16]
but for the period of time covered in this discussion, the sex allocation of jobs represented the prevailing industry practice.

Manpower Requirements and Black Employment
The labor demand and supply characteristics of the telephone industry help explain
several features of its changing utilization of blacks. First, the telephone company
work force is typically drawn directly from the local labor market in which the
firm's operations are located. For many years, and especially before 1960, telephone
companies found a more than adequate labor supply among young white male and
female members of the labor force. Few blacks voluntarily applied for employment,
and when they did, they were often hired into service jobs outside the mainstream
of the industry's occupational hierarchy. As the racial composition of the labor
force in the operating areas changed, however, it was necessary for the industry to
use more black labor, especially women, in order to meet normal staffing requirements. The evidence on black employment gains during the 1960s in comparison
with earlier periods lends strong support to this interpretation.

For example, between 1950 and 1960 whites accelerated their exodus from the
inner city to suburban communities. This trend contributed significantly to the
rising proportion of blacks within the inner city work force of the major cities,
especially in the northeastern and midwestern states. The changing composition of
labor supply generated by shifting population growth probably accounts for the
modest breakthrough experienced by blacks in telephone industry employment
during the 1950s.

Between 1960 and 1970, inner city population trends continued to move in a
direction favorable to black employment. The number of blacks aged 14–24 in the
central cities increased by 78.0 percent compared to an increase of 22.8 percent
among whites in the same age group.[17] In addition to the rapidly increasing numbers

16 *Equal Employment Opportunity Commission and US vs. American Telephone and Telegraph
Company,* Consent Decree (US District Court, Eastern District of Pennsylvania, January 18,
1973).
17 Jack Nelson, "The Changing Economic Position of Black Urban Workers," *The Review of
Black Political Economy* 4 (winter 1974) : 37–38.

of blacks in the young adult age group relevant to telephone industry hiring needs, there was an improvement in the educational quality of the black work force. Between 1962 and 1970, for example, black women raised their median years of schooling to 12.1 years compared to 12.5 years for white women. Although black men also made gains in educational attainment, their 11.1 median years of school continued to lag significantly behind the 12.4 years displayed by white men.[18] The expansion of the number and productivity of blacks relative to whites in the cities during the 1960s was met by the telephone industry's strong demand for labor arising from increased demand for telephone services, and by labor replacement needs. The result is that telephone companies turned increasingly to the black work force during the 1960s, and did so in all regions of the nation.

This interpretation gains strength from the observation that much telephone exchange equipment and many central station operations have remained in the inner city despite the population shifts and the exodus of many nonutility firms to suburban areas. There is some evidence, however, that some telephone operations have been moved to suburban communities in recent years.[19] The consequence of this development for black employment has not escaped the attention of equal employment advocates who argue that plant location decisions should be challenged when they promise to affect adversely the employment of minorites.

Labor Turnover and Black Employment

The second major factor influencing black employment in the telephone industry is the high rate of turnover in entry-level jobs, especially that of telephone operators. The resignation rates of telephone operators in seventeen Bell operating companies ranged from 8.6 per 100 employees in Indiana to 31.7 per 100 in New York in 1971.[20] These resignation rates in 1971 were registered at a time when the unemployment rate of adult women was 5.7 percent—a level of unemployment that probably reduced the quit rate of women below the level associated with a more vibrant economy.

As a result of the high turnover among telephone operators, the number of workers who must be hired each year is several times the number observed in the work force at any time during the year. In 1969, for example, the Bell System hired 125,000 employees but ended the year with a net gain of only 15,000 over the level of employment in 1968.[21] During the sixties, operators were quitting at twice the rate experienced during the previous decade, and male craftsmen were quitting four times as fast. As a result of such turnover, Bell operating companies

18 *Ibid*, p. 44.
19 David Andelman, "555-1212 Has Moved Out of the City," *New York Times,* August 1, 1973, p. 79.
20 Testimony of John W. Kingsbury, Appendix Table 27. (See n. 3.)
21 Allan T. Demaree, "The Age of Anxiety at AT&T," *Fortune* 81 (May 1970) : 266,269.

had a large number of job openings for new employees during the late 1960s compared with earlier periods. The volume of job opportunities created the base for accelerating the hiring of black employees.

The volume of turnover generated numerous job openings conducive to increased employment of blacks, but because the bulk of the new jobs were oriented toward females, black women experienced the greatest relative gain from the expanding employment opportunities. Evidence on economic gains of blacks in the economy at large during the 1960s reveals the greater occupational and income progress of black women relative to black men.[22] Much of the disparity between the two groups has been attributed to the concentration of female employment in occupations where on-the-job training and cumulated experience are less important and where gross turnover of the work force is rapid. This interpretation finds much support in the empirical evidence on the telephone industry where women have for many years been confined to entry-level operator and clerical jobs. Black women were better able to compete with white women for such jobs than were black men able to compete with white men for entry-level jobs as telephone installers and craftsmen. Thus, although telephone companies had numerous job opportunities for both men and women during the last decade, the characteristics of the jobs were more favorable to the employment of black women than black men, both because of the nature of the black labor force and the different expectations for long-term employment and on-the-job training for the industry's male and female employees.

Some Institutional Determinants of Black Employment

The following factors in the institutional environment surrounding the telephone industry might be discussed in relation to trends in black employment: (1) public utility regulation, (2) company personnel practices, and (3) public policy on fair employment enforcement.

Because of their monopoly status telephone companies enjoy special privileges including, but not limited to, a guaranteed market or operating area, the use of public property, and a limited authority to exercise the power of eminent domain. In return, telephone companies are subject to public regulation. Such regulation has important implications for the industry's racial employment composition.

Economic theory suggests that firms with regulated profit rates will tend to practice discrimination more than competitive firms. The evidence discussed above showed very clearly the exclusionist practices of the telephone industry prior to the 1960s. Although there are few economic constraints on the proclivity of regulated firms to discriminate, there are substantial political constraints. As a result, regulated companies might show rapid change in racial employment practices when political

---

22 Richard B. Freeman, *Change in the Labor Market for Black Americans, 1948–72*, Brookings Papers on Economic Activity, No. 1 (1973), pp. 95–98.

realities make such changes necessary. Clear evidence supporting these expectations may be found in the telephone industry during the 1950s and the 1960s.

In the 1950 decade blacks registered few employment gains except in several telephone companies in the Northeast and the Midwest. There was almost no change in black employment in the South despite the rapid growth of total industry employment in the region.

During the 1960s, however, blacks showed marked increases in telephone industry employment in both regions, and in fact, appeared to replace some whites employed in the industry. The major difference between the two decades, of course, was the civil rights revolution of the 1960s and the greatly increased pressures applied by federal enforcement agencies, civil rights groups, and others to break down the barriers of discrimination in employment. In the face of such pressures, the telephone industry in general and the Bell System in particular showed a reversal of past trends in black hiring practices which far exceeded in both size and scope the gains experienced by blacks in the electric power and gas utilities, and in most other industries.

Company Personnel Practices

For many years the Bell System pursued personnel practices that, although inherently neutral, were in practice biased against the employment of black workers. Among these practices were the heavy reliance on employee referrals and walk-ins for new employees, the requirement that all successful job applicants pass a formidable battery of tests and interviews, and the assignment of new employees to job classifications based upon management's assessment of the employee's potential for upgrading. Such practices tended to restrict telephone companies to a very narrow pool of potential black employees, and within that group, a disproportionate number of black job applicants were rejected.[23]

Many of the gains in black employment in the Bell System during the 1960s were due in large part to a relaxation of rigid, and often unrealistic, hiring standards. The movement toward modifying traditional hiring standards in an effort to increase black employment was slow and uncertain within the Bell System at least as late as 1967, but the changing trend in employee selection procedures was irrevocable.[24] The phalanx of hiring standards that had been used for many years and which tended to discriminate against minorities had for the most part been declared unlawful by EEOC guidelines and federal court decisions before they were finally dropped by Bell operating companies. At the same time some company personnel policies injurious to the interest of blacks were being dropped; however, other practices potentially injurious to blacks were being contemplated. Among these were a labor-

23 Petition for Intervention, *EEOC vs. AT&T,* pp. 23–25.
24 Anderson, *Negro Employment,* pp. 185–189.

market survey designed to select the best locations for new Bell installations.[25] Because the survey methodology is biased toward duplicating the current profile of the Company's work force, the use of such surveys for management decisions in plant location may restrict the job opportunities for minorities.

Evolving Equal Employment Enforcement Policy

One of the most important factors affecting the status of blacks in the telephone industry in recent years has been government equal-employment enforcement activities. During the 1960 decade, enforcement objectives moved from a concern with nondiscrimination in employment to the requirement for affirmative action as evidence of compliance with the equal employment edicts. The litigation under Title VII of the Civil Rights Act of 1964 shows that the federal courts have a proclivity toward looking at the record of performance in employment practices when deciding whether a violation of the Act has occurred. Judicial concern with performance, rather than with policy statements, also reveals itself in the remedies designed by the courts in Title VII cases. Most of the remedies are based upon a demonstration of underutilization of minority and female workers as revealed in the statistical record on the race and sex composition of the work force.

The increased interest by enforcement officials and the courts in the numbers of minorities employed no doubt increased the interest of telephone company management in greater hiring and retention of black workers during the 1960s. In the Bell System, for example, there is evidence that conscious efforts were made to broaden the range of minority and female participation in management-training programs, as well as in divisions of the corporation where no blacks or women were employed prior to 1965.[26] Such efforts represent a sharp break with the past tradition of race and sex awareness in the Bell System, and has been, without any doubt, a major factor responsible for many of the employment gains experienced by black telephone workers during the past few years.

V. Conclusion

This review of black employment in the telephone industry documents the transformation of a major sector of employment in the American economy from an exclusion of racial minorities to a fuller use of minority manpower. The change in the position of the industry on black employment occurred within the last two decades, and was greatly accelerated during the 1960s.

25 American Telephone and Telegraph Co., *Annual Report of the Department of Environmental Affairs*, 1970.
26 Letter of John W. Kingsbury, Assistant Vice President of AT&T to all Personnel Vice Presidents, dated May 23, 1972.

The factors responsible for the increasing racial integration of the telephone industry work force are numerous and interrelated, but the evidence suggests that both traditional market forces and institutional developments played a major role. Although it is difficult to assign causation to specific changes in black employment, both the relative level and the timing of black occupational gains support reasonable inferences concerning the factors primarily responsible for the observed progress. In the case of operators, for example, the volume, location, and timing of the increase in black female employment strongly suggests that the change was attributable, in large part, to forces at work in the labor market. With respect to blacks in professional, managerial, and technical positions, however, the recent increases have been more likely the result of government pressures exerted through the affirmative action requirements.

Indeed, one of the major issues confronting the industry prior to the recently adopted Consent Decree was the difference of view between corporate management and equal employment enforcement officials over the meaning of affirmative action. EEOC, for example, consistently looked to the statistical record for evidence that equal employment, in fact, existed in the telephone industry. Corporate managers, however, often emphasized company progress in changing the focus, direction, and energy devoted to equal employment issues within the firm. Such changes often did not result in significant numerical gains in the number of blacks employed or promoted to responsible positions in the firm. To management, changes in the employment process that might result in long term gains for black workers were often considered more important than short term gains in the numbers and status of blacks employed. One of the major results of the EEOC/AT&T Consent Decree is that by focusing on occupational goals and timetables, it will resolve the issue of acceptable criteria for measuring affirmative action, at least as far as the telephone industry is concerned.

III Personnel Assessment

9 The Testing Issue

Philip Ash

The use of psychological tests to select potential employees from among applicants, and to upgrade employees to higher-level positions, has been widespread in the Bell System. The operating companies had enjoyed a high degree of autonomy with respect to personnel practices, including selection testing, but the issuance of federal guidelines on selection procedures pursuant to Title VII of the Civil Rights Act of 1964 led to systemwide policy procedures and supervision, exercised by a personnel research unit located at AT&T headquarters and manned by professional psychologists.

This personnel research organization functioned to develop and validate tests and to thus ensure a reasonable degree of system-wide compliance with EEOC guidelines and OFCC (Office of Federal Contract Compliance) rules and regulations. The unit has concentrated in three areas: management selection and evaluation, maintenance worker selection, and nonmanagerial white-collar selection (operators, clerical personnel, service representatives).

In the first area, AT&T has been an acknowledged leader in American industry. The top psychologists of the personnel research unit developed a managerial assessment procedure widely imitated throughout the industry.[1]

In the second and third areas, more traditional approaches led to the development and dissemination of conventional test batteries of aptitudes deemed relevant to job success.

Studies by EEOC[2] led to the conclusion that

... these [latter] test batteries reject a vastly disproportionate number of black applicants and hence give white applicants an appreciably better chance of getting a job in the Bell System.

... the specific tests which compose the craft battery have changed periodically, but the impact on blacks has remained essentially the same, irrespective of the name of the test given. In 1964, the two primary tests in the craft battery were the Wonderlic Personnel Test and the Bennett Test of Mechanical Comprehension. This particular combination of tests has been widely used in industry and was the same set of tests which the Supreme Court rejected as being unrelated to job performance in the seminal case of *Griggs vs. Duke Power Co.*

... in the Fall of 1964, AT&T dropped the ... Wonderlic Personnel Test from the craft battery and substituted another general intelligence test published by the Educational Testing Service [School and College Ability Test, Level 2]. This test is now known throughout the Bell System as BSQT I (Bell System Qualification Test I). The Bennett Test was retained until 1967 and became known as BSQT II.

1 D. W. Bray, "The Assessment Center Method of Appraising Management Potential." In J. W. Blood, ed., *The Personnel Job in a Changing World* (New York: American Management Association, 1964), pp. 225–234. See Bibliography to this chapter for further references.
2 Equal Employment Opportunity Commission, *"A Unique Competence": A Study of Equal Employment Opportunity in the Bell System passim* (Washington, D.C.: EEOC, 1971).

. . .both the BSQT I and BSQT II rejected a very lop-sided proportion of black applicants. In one study conducted by AT&T at five Bell companies in 1965, 40 percent of white applicants but only 15 percent of black applicants scored high enough on BSQT I to qualify for craft jobs. Thus, a white applicant had more than two-and-one-half times better chance of getting a craft job than did a black. In a study of the BSQT II, 58 percent of all white applicants qualified but only 20 percent of all black applicants passed. In other words, a black had only 1/3 the chance of passing the BSQT II as did a white. These same disparities in qualifying rates for black and whites on BSQT I and BSQT II are constantly reported.

In 1968 the craft battery was changed again; BSQT II was eliminated and replaced by a test of abstract reasoning [non-verbal reasoning subtest of the Psychological Corporation's Differential Aptitude Tests] . . . known as BSQT IV. This new combination of tests, BSQT I and BSQT II and BSQT IV, has the same disproportionate impact on blacks, and whites continue to obtain a substantial advantage in qualifying for craft jobs solely on the basis of test scores. The disadvantage blacks suffer because of low "intelligence test" scores far outweighs the disadvantage inflicted by the System's educational prerequisites.

The EEOC decided to focus its attack upon the craft battery for at least two reasons: first, the impact of the battery primarily resulted in the exclusion of blacks from the system; and second, the justification for the validity of the battery was extensively defended by publication in a professional journal.[3] The research was acclaimed by some professionals as highly innovative and criticized by others as irrelevant. However, the hearings themselves were diverted from the central question, "Are the tests any good?" to a subsidiary question, "Is the work-simulation job performance test criterion (the innovation) any good?"

The craft battery was intended to select entry workers for a variety of occupations involving electrical assembling, installing, and repairing. Typical among them are specific occupations such as central office repairman, installer repairman, station repairman, lineman, PBX installer, station installer, test deskman, transmission man, frameman, and cable splicer.[4]

These jobs share a variety of tasks such as tracing circuits and using hand tools (screwdrivers, pliers, side-cutters, soldering irons) to make and unmake connections between wires and binding posts. Some of them involve following circuit diagrams. The descriptions collected in the *Dictionary of Occupational Titles*, emphasize finger and hand dexterity, spatial perceptual ability, mechanical (including electrical circuitry) insight, and, in some cases, physical agility. The jobs involve only an occasional use of arithmetic, and verbal communication skills demands are minimal.

The principal study designed to validate the selection tests for entry into this sequence of craft occupations, however, focussed not on *job* behaviors for prediction, but on the "aptitude to learn." The trial test battery was made up of five tests of "aptitude":

3 D. L. Grant and D. W. Bray. "Validation of Employment Tests for Telephone Company Installation and Repair Occupations." *Journal of Applied Psychology* 54 (1970) : 7–14.
4 *Ibid.*

1. The Educational Testing Service School and College Ability Test, designed and widely used in school systems to select college entrants, and measuring verbal facility and numerical reasoning within the Bell System, referred to as BSQT I)[5]
2. The Bennett Test of Mechanical Comprehension
3. BSQT III, an internally developed test of memory
4. The Psychological Corporation Differential Aptitude Test series nonverbal *Abstract Reasoning* test
5. The Psychological Corporation *Crawford Small Parts Dexterity Test.*

The process of test validation is essentially one of relating scores on a test with some organizational measure(s) of job proficiency, called a *criterion,* or, collectively, *criteria.* Two major categories of criteria have been used to validate the usefulness of job aptitude tests:

a. Training criteria—used primarily to establish that particular selection devices will predict who has the aptitude to succeed in a training program.

b. Job proficiency criteria—used primarily to establish that particular selection devices will predict who has the aptitude to succeed on the job itself.

Training criteria are generally easier to predict than job performance criteria,[6] mainly because training course measurements which are frequently tests themselves, obviously share the same characteristics, such as reading skill, that are major components of the original aptitude tests.[7]

Job performance criteria[8] include four major subcategories:

5 The "BSQT" ("Bell System Qualification Test"), followed by an appropriate roman numeral, designates a test or test combination almost always wholly bought or borrowed. The implied claim to proprietorship, or even development, lends an aura of relevance that may be only questionably justifiable. Psychologists may want to compare the Bell System nomenclatural embrace of published tests with the practices of other large corporations that have sophisticated test programs using purchased tests.

6 P. Ash, "Validity of the Bennett Mechanical Comprehension Test." Sixty-six studies of the validity of the Bennett were reviewed. Fifty-two test-job performance criterion coefficients were reported and seventy-one test-training criterion coefficients were reported. The median test-performance correlation was .17; the median test-training correlation was .30. Another study is P. Ash, "Validity of the Wonderlic Personnel Test." Forty-seven published validity studies on the Wonderlic were reviewed. Fifty-seven test-job correlations and twenty-three test-training correlations were reported. The median validity for job performance criteria was .08. The median validity for training criteria was .11. See also C. W. Brown and E. E. Ghiselli, "The Relationship Between Predictive Power of Aptitude Tests for Trainability and for Job Proficiency," *Journal of Applied Psychology,* 36 (1952) : 370–392; and E. E. Ghiselli, *The Validity of Occupational Aptitude Tests* (New York: John Wiley & Sons, 1966).

7 Brown and Ghiselli, "The Relationship Between Predictive Power"; Ghiselli, *The Validity of Occupational Aptitude Tests.*

8 J. Smith, E. Neidzwiedz, M. Davis, and C. Knieser, *Handbook of Job Proficiency Criteria* (Columbus, Ohio: Ohio Department of State Personnel, 1973).

1. Measures of on-the-job productivity such as number of pages typed, number of typing errors made, quality of work, earnings, sales, scrap, waste, and so forth. Positive or negative, they tend to be very specific to the job.
2. Measures of systematically observed job performance, and production of standardized work samples.
3. Administrative indices such as absenteeism, turnover, accident history, reprimands and disciplines, awards and commendations, customer complaints, grievances filed.
4. Judgmental estimates of performance, primarily supervisory ratings.

In the AT&T validity study, a somewhat different, and novel, criterion was used to validate the selection tests: a work-simulation programmed instruction test originally designed *to select employees for admission to training programs.* This work sample was called the Learning Assessment Program (LAP).[9]

The LAP. . .was developed by a team of six plant craft training specialists. . . The design and development of the program required approximately eight months.

The LAP is essentially a *performance test* [emphasis added]. It is a direct measure of a person's ability to learn to perform key tasks required in plant craft work (e.g., installing a telephone, locating trouble in a complex circuitry). Its rationale evolves from the fact that there are certain basic tasks craftsmen must learn before they can enter the job, and that in any training course there are certain fundamental skills which must be mastered before continuing with the more complex portions of the course. Because training exists at various levels, the samples of training in the LAP represent the fundamental skills required at each level of training. The LAP used in the test validation study covered station (installer and repairman) and top craft level jobs (switchman, PBX installer, PBX repairman). Levels 1-4 of LAP were designed for the station jobs (installation and maintenance of telephone equipment), while Levels 5-7 were designed for jobs requiring the installation and maintenance of complex circuitry. [The sequence of levels is shown in Figure 9.1.]

From the results of the trials. . .standards of performance on the tests appropriate to station and "top craft" jobs and time limits for each of the training sequences were established. The time limits were set to allow persons going through the program more than enough time to complete each sequence. The objective was to screen people in, rather than to screen them out. Only those who were clearly deficient in ability or motivation were expected to fail.

In addition, a generous time limit for completing each level of the program was allowed (up to 21 days for all 7 levels).

The total validity study implied a five-step design:
1. Test a sample of applicants on the proposed selection tests (listed above).
2. Select from among examinees a sample of white and black applicants matched to ensure a broad distribution of test scores. This selection washed out any possibility of estimating, for the unrestricted applicant sample, any differential effect of the tests on selection.

Five companies agreed to participate inthe study: Pennsylvania, Chesapeake and Potomac, Michigan, Illinois, and Pacific. Five urban locations were involved: Philadelphia, Washington, D.C., Detroit, Chicago, and San Francisco. Each participating company agreed to employ 100 people:

---

9 Grant and Bray, "Validation of Employment Tests."

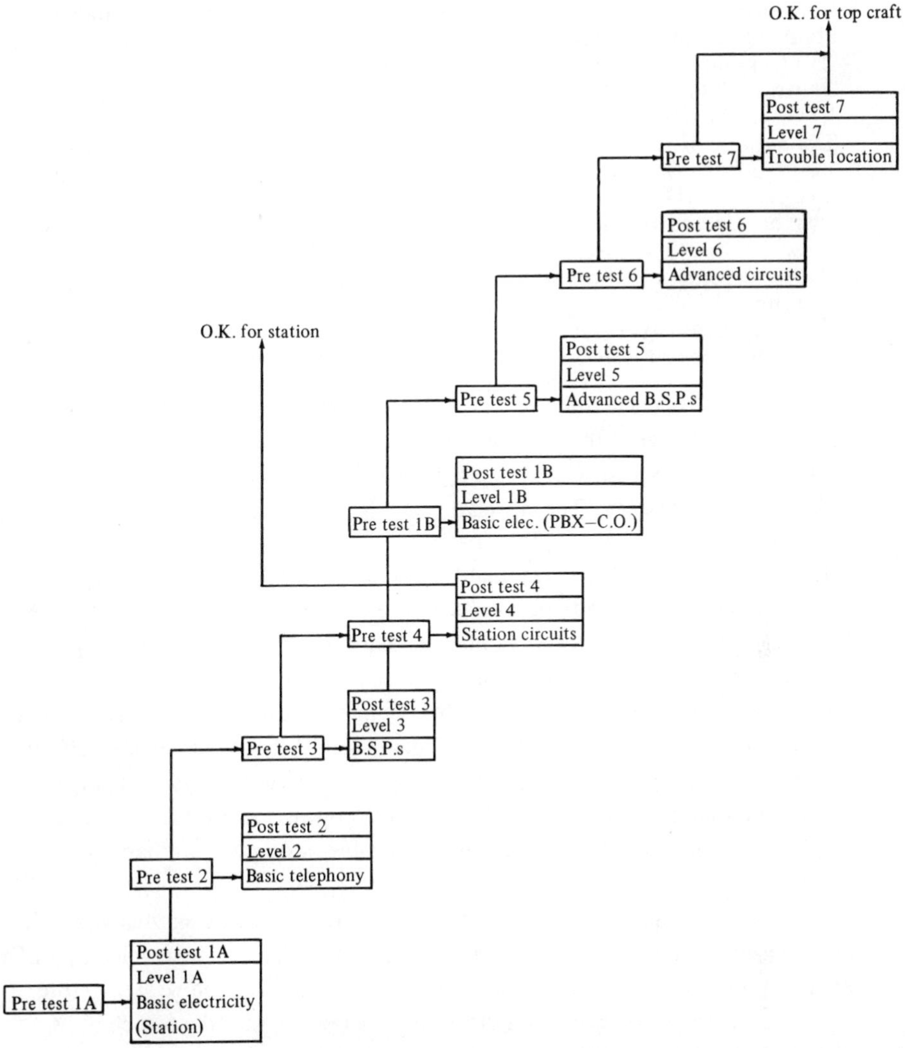

Figure 9.1 Sequence of LAP (Learning Assessment Program) levels.
Source: S. Gael and D. L. Grant, "Validation of a General Learning
Ability Test for Selecting Telephone Operators," Experimental
Publication System, Feb. 1971, 10, Ms. No. 351-2.

- 25 whites meeting employment test standards recommended at the time [the study was initiated in 1966] ;
- 25 blacks meeting the employment test standards;
- 25 whites falling below recommended employment test standards.
- 25 blacks falling below the test standards.

The purpose of selecting the sample in accord with the above prescriptions were to insure (*a*) a broad range of test scores for both the minority and nonminority samples, (*b*) a sufficiently large sample, and (*c*) adequate representation of minorities.

3. Put the selected sample, immediately after hire, through the LAP, performance on which was to be used as a criterion of the validity of the selection tests.
4. Put *some* hires (i.e., those who passed LAP at an acceptable level) into craft jobs and through job training programs.
5. After actual job experience, collect job performance measures and relate these to both the selection tests and the LAP criterion.[10]

When the case opened, data were available, through the published study, only on the relationship between the selection tests and the LAP criterion. These data showed that the selection tests correlated to a significant degree with ability to get through the LAP performance test. The correlations with the LAP criterion were as shown in Table 9.1.

Multiple correlations were computed between the LAP criterion (highest level passed) and all possible combinations of the foregoing tests. The combination of the SCAT Total and Abstract Reasoning yielded a multiple R of .48; this combination was selected for administrative use.

A comparison of the regression lines for the minority and nonminority samples indicated that the slopes were practically identical, but that the intercepts differed: nonminority group means on both the criterion and the test arrays were slightly higher than minority group means. The authors proposed to use the combined sample regression line, which would tend to *overpredict* minority group criterion scores.

Although the data in the published study does not point to a significant ethnic difference *in prediction of the LAP criterion,* other AT&T data assembled by EEOC tended to show an adverse impact against blacks.[11] The situation was, therefore, that the company was claiming on the basis of the study, that the test composite score was psychometrically "fair" and valid against a legitimate job-related criterion. The LAP was never used to train a single plant craft worker.

The thrust of the EEOC critique was addressed to two separate but related issues: (1) the degree to which job performance on telephone maintenance jobs can be predicted from scholastic tests of verbal and numerical ability and abstract reasoning, and (2) the degree to which job performance and success in training can be predicted from performance on a preemployment, pretraining work simulation exercise. The published validity study made the *assumption* that this latter relationship was positive and probably high. The literature, however, contains little evidence to support this assumption.

10 *Ibid.*
11 EEOC, *"A Unique Competence."*

Table 9.1   Correlations of Selection Tests and the LAP Criterion

	Minority	Non-Minority	Total
SCAT total	.41	.36	.39
SCAT Quantitative	.41	.37	.40
SCAT Verbal	.32	.24	.27
Bennett Mechnical Comprehension	.31	.32	.34
BSQT III (Memory)	.38	.38	.38
Abstract Reasoning	.38	.50	.44
Crawford Small Parts (I)	.25	.19	.24
Crawford Small Parts (II)	.16	.17	.19

First, it has been consistently noted that substantially higher correlations are obtained between aptitude test scores and training outcomes, than between such scores and job proficiency measures. For example, Ghiselli[12] gives the data reproduced in Table 9.2.

The difference in predictability shown in Table 9.2 is probably due to a wide variety of factors, but a central element is undoubtedly the verbal and academic nature that training programs share with objective-type tests of the BSQT I variety, even though the job itself may not impose significant verbal demands. A foreign (e.g., Spanish speaking) individual could do very poorly on a test of electrical knowledge while, at the same time, he could be an excellent electrician. Thorndike's[13] study of the post–World War II occupational histories of air crewman in relation to their aptitude-test performance suggests that neither general intellectual ability nor numerical ability is especially required of telephone installers or linemen and cablemen.

Gulliksen[14] discusses the tendency in test development to accept validity coefficients without questioning whether they should be high or low in a given situation. Gulliksen and Frederiksen investigated validity coefficients while working on aptitude and achievement test development for the Navy during World War II. At the gunners' mates school they found that the validity pattern for the reading test was high while the mechanical knowledge and comprehension tests had low validity.

12 Ghiselli, *Validity of Occupational Aptitude Tests.*
13 R. L. Thorndike and E. Hagen, *Ten Thousand Careers* (New York: John Wiley & Sons, 1959).
14 Harold Gulliksen. "Looking Back and Ahead in Psychometrics." *American Psychologist* (April 1974) : 251–261.

Table 9.2 Aptitude Test Scores and Training Outcome

| Criteria: | Mechanical Repairmen | |
	Training	Proficiency
Intellectual		
Abilities:		
Intelligence	.40	.17
Arithmetic	.42	.24

| Criteria: | Electrical Repairmen | |
	Training	Proficiency
Intellectual		
Abilities:		
Intelligence	.48	.24
Arithmetic	.53	.18

Source: E. E. Ghiselli, The Validity of Occupational Aptitude Tests (New York: Wiley, 1966).

The pattern was not reasonable in view of the stated course objectives which were the ability to disassemble and assemble the guns and to detect and correct malfunctioning. Checking on the tests originally used in measuring training progress revealed that the course, as initially taught and graded, had placed great emphasis on verbal memorizing and repeating of material from the manuals and did not require that the students know how to disassemble and assemble the guns, or how to detect and correct malfunctioning. New training course tests were developed which ensured that the students were being tested on their ability derived from the objectives stated by the instructors. The validity pattern after the introduction of the new testing system, as a measure of training success, indicated that the students were coming much closer to learning what the instructors wanted them to learn. On the basis of the grades on the new achievement testing program, the validity of the reading test plunged downward, and the mechanical comprehension and mechanical knowledge went up. The original arithmetic test was replaced by other aptitude tests based on the school objectives as stated by the instructors. The validity pattern of the new tests indicated that the students were approximating the objectives stated by the instructors. The point that the new performance-testing system demonstrated is that the pattern of validity coefficients over a set of aptitude tests can indicate, by its disagreement or agreement with course objectives, whether or not the teaching, testing, and grading procedures match the objectives of the instructor. Thus, tests which have low validity in predicting performance—given the stated course objectives and relevant training methods and learning-assessment techniques—can be eliminated.

The second point advanced concerning correlations between test scores and job proficiency was that success in training is not a good predictor of on-the-job success. In some areas—for example, the relationship of school performance to job performance—the observed correlations are usually low and frequently zero. The relation of trainability to eventual job proficiency has not been studied extensively, but the studies that are available clearly indicate that this correlation is less than perfect. Ghiselli and Haire[15] in a study of taxicab drivers, found that rate of improvement during an 18-week period in which learning took place, was best predicted by a test of mechanical principles and degree of interest in active occupations. Neither of these predictors, however, were correlated appreciably with total production, which was predictable from different tests. The possibility that a measure like LAP might correlate with eventual job performance certainly exists; but the data are sufficiently mixed to preclude the *assumption* that the two are related, *without appropriate study.*

Furthermore, the relationships among aptitude test scores, learning success scores, and job performance include backward effects that must be taken into account. Training and experience on the job may affect not only subsequent work performance but also scores on the aptitude test predictors. A good training program may be particularly beneficial for the disadvantaged, whose educational and cultural background results in poor test performance. It could present their first opportunity to profit from systematic instruction, and significantly alter not only their job performance but also (if it were remeasured) their test performance. This generalized remediation for minority group applicants cannot be ignored.

In testimony before the FCC (Docket No. 19143, 1972), I concluded the following:

1. Although in the study minority and nonminority test score means and pass rates were about equal, this was an artifact brought about by deliberate sampling. In the actual employment market, if SCAT and Abstract Reasoning were used for selection, the pass rates of minority group applicants would be much less than those of majority group applicants.

2. The use of SCAT for selection of plant craft workers was itself challenged as questionable: the test was designed for quite different purposes, and its use in

---

15 E. E. Ghiselli and M. Haire. "The Validation of Selection Tests in the Light of the Dynamic Character of Criteria." *Personnel Psychology* 13 (1960) : 225–232.

personnel selection depends *critically* upon validation against an appropriate job performance criterion.[16]

3. Although the correlation between the combined SCAT and Abstract Reasoning scores and the LAP scores was significant, this fact was alleged to provide no information about *either* (*a*) the correlation of LAP scores with job performance (JP), or (*b*) the correlation of SCAT and Abstract Reasoning with job performance. Available research gave no cause for believing that *either* of these relationships was significant.[17]

4. Whatever the relationship, the probability that predictor test scores would, for disadvantaged minority group applicants, be improved significantly as a result of the years-long training and experience on the job, could not be ignored. For the disadvantaged, therefore, the predictor SCAT and Abstract Reasoning, at point of application, could not be taken seriously as a measure of future performance potential.

5. The Bell System's Plant Craft Study was of some academic interest, but did not answer the questions that are critical to use of SCAT and Abstract Reasoning as an operational selection device. Without a demonstration of a relationship with job performance, its use was deemed unjustified by plaintiff witnesses.

During the course of the proceedings, AT&T submitted a follow-up study which addressed itself, though discreetly, to the issues raised by the plaintiffs[18] and completely confirmed the plaintiffs' contention that the composite test score was uncorrelated with *either* success in training or with *any* posttraining measure of job success. Furthermore, the correlation of the test predictor with the LAP criterion shrank to zero in the surviving sample on whom follow-up data became available. It must be pointed out that, although the *data* bearing on the validity of the test selection battery were included in the follow-up study, not one line of the text refers to the validity of the test battery, or, indeed, to the test battery at all. The focus is placed on the LAP criterion as a device for ". . .identifying persons with high career potential in telephone company installation and repair occupations." Under usual selection procedures, however, applicants are initially screened by the test battery, and they do not get a chance to demonstrate their potential on LAP *or* their ability in training or on the job if they fail that first screen. If the screen itself has no validity, the LAP would seem to be irrelevant.

Of 491 applicants who were tested, hired, and put through the LAP procedure, 348 were included in the test validation study and 169 survived all the way through

16 S. Gael and D. L. Grant. "Validation of a General Learning Ability Test for Selecting Telephone Operators." *Experimental Publication System* 10 (February 1971) : 351–352.
17 R. M. Guion. *Personnel Testing* (New York: McGraw-Hill, 1965). See Bibliography to this chapter for further references.
18 D. L. Grant, *Plant Craft Study Follow-up,* Attachment C, FCC Docket No. 19143, Testimony of Donald L. Grant, August 1, 1972.

data collection in December 1971. Sample reduction resulted initially from termination due to failure to pass levels 1-4 of LAP, and then because of termination, mostly by resignation. An interesting and important characteristic of the sample attrition is that the distribution of test scores remained essentially unchanged—there was no restriction in range. There was a restriction in range on the LAP criterion, apparently due largely to company termination of applicants who failed levels 1-4 of LAP. There were no significant differences in such variables as age, education, length of service, etc., between the original sample and the 1971 survivor sample.

From the point of view of the validity of the composite test score, which was the original target of the plaintiff's case, the data are clear: its predictive validity was about zero. Furthermore, the LAP "criterion" failed to correlate with any after-placement measures, although these correlations are explained on the basis of restriction in range due to termination before placement of those applicants who failed to pass LAP levels 1-4.

These conclusions are based on results shown in Tables 14-15 of the follow-up report, from which the pattern is overwhelmingly clear: the composite score of SCAT plus Abstract Reasoning is useless as a predictor of success in training or performance on telephone repair and maintenance jobs, and the LAP performance test is equally useless. See Table 9.3.

LAP was an ingenious approach to synthetic criterion measurement, but in fact it was not a good surrogate of performance either in training or on the job. These results are similar to those in automobile driving performance prediction: performance on the various simulators such as the Link trainer is essentially uncorrelated with on-the-road performance.

This review of the test issue does not directly address the question of adverse impact of the test composite. The two studies, by their sample design, eliminated any possibility of such an analysis. To the extent to which EEOC otherwise established that the result of using the test composite has adverse impact against minority-group applicants, the use of a nonvalid test was inevitably discriminatory.

Table 9.3 Correlations of the Test Composite and the LAP Performance Test
(Pass Levels 1-4) with Various Demographic and Performance Criterion Measures

Variable	(Table 14) Minority Sample		(Table 15) Non-Minority Sample	
	Test	LAP	Test	LAP
Age	-00	00	-24*	-05
Education	-05	02	27*	05
Test	--	05	--	-01
LAP	05	--	-01	--
1968 Data				
Plant Schools (# Days)	04	00	-05	12
Plant Courses (# Completed)	21	-02	-12	09
Performance-Schools	21	16	-01	-18
Supervisor Ratings-Overall	29*	-11	-00	-11
Supervisor Ratings-Tech. Competence	28	03	-07	-05
Times Absent	01	09	14	06
No. Accidents	-14	-13	-12	-12
No. Disciplinary Actions	03	07	06	04
1969 Data				
Plant Schools (# Days)	-20	-04	26*	10
Plant Courses (# Completed)	-25	-15	09	10
Performance-Schools	-17	18	13	07
Supervisor Ratings-Overall	-29*	02	13	-14
Supervisor Ratings-Tech. Competence	-29*	07	23	-19
Times Absent	-01	-11	08	05
No. Accidents	-03	-02	04	-28*
No. Disciplinary Actions	02	-01	10	-12
Actions-Length of Service	-02	-30*	-09	-19
Occupational Classification 1969	-09	13	-21	10
Occupational Classification 1968	02	11	-16	-02

*Significant at the .05 level

Bibliography for Chapter 9

This bibliography contains further references for the footnotes cited.

Note 1
D. W. Bray and D. L. Grant. "The Assessment Center in the Measurement of Potential for Business Management." *Psychological Monographs* 80 (1966) : 17.

"Situational Tests in Assessments of Managers." In *Management Games in Selection and Development,* The Executive Study Conference, May 5–6, 1964 (Princeton, N.J.: Educational Testing Service, 1964), pp. 121–138.

R. J. Campbell and D. W. Bray. "Assessment Centers: An Aid in Management Selection." *Personnel Administration* 30 (1967) : 6–13.

D. L. Grant. "Influence of Motivation on Progress in Management: Retention and Development." In *Motivation of Managers,* The Executive Study Conference, November 15–16, 1966 (Princeton, N.J.: Educational Testing Service, 1967) pp. 61–73.

D. L. Grant and D. W. Bray. "Contributions of the Interview to Assessment of Management Potential." *Journal of Applied Psychology* 53 (1969) : 24–34.

D. L. Grant, W. Katkovsky, and D. W. Bray, "Contributions of Projective Techniques to Assessment of Management Potential," *Journal of Applied Psychology* 51 (1967) : 226–232.

Note 17
Personnel Research Branch. "Adjutant General's Office Department of the Army. Validity information exchange. No. 10–54, DOT code 1–38.04. Ordinance Supply Specialist." *Personnel Psychology*, 10 (1957) : 513–515.

"Adjutant General's Office Department of the Army. Validity information exchange. No. 11–13, DOT code 4–97.420. Wireman." Reprinted in *Personnel Psychology* 11 (1958) : 242–244.

"Adjutant General's Office Department of the Army. Validity information exchange. No. 11–14, DOT code 5–53. Carrier Equipment Repairman." Reprinted in *Personnel Psychology*, 11 (1958) : 245–247.

"Adjutant General's Office Department of the Army. Validity information exchange. No. 11–15, DOT code 5–53.270." Teletypewriter Repairman. Reprinted in *Personnel Psychology* 11 (1958) : 248–250.

"The Adjutant General's Office Department of the Army. Validity information exchange. No. 11–16, DOT code 5–72.010. Powerman." Reprinted in *Personnel Psychology* 11 (1958) : 251–253.

"The Adjutant General's Office Department of the Army. Validity information exchange. No. 11–17, DOT code 5–83, Fire Control Equipment Repairman." Reprinted in *Personnel Psychology* 11 (1958) : 254–256.

"The Adjutant General's Office Department of the Army. Validity information exchange. No. 11–18, DOT code 5–83. Fixed Station Receiver Repairman. Fixed Station Transmitter Repairman." Reprinted in *Personnel Psychology* 11 (1958) : 257–259.

10 The Bell System's Non-Management Personnel Selection Strategy

Felix M. Lopez

Since the passage of the Civil Rights Act of 1964, American employers have been confronted with two new but critical questions. Is it possible for an employer to discriminate unfairly against specific subgroups of an applicant population simply by the selection strategy adopted to recruit and select people for positions in his labor force? Can the selection standards and procedures effectively bar eligible females and members of minority groups from the better-paying jobs no matter how impartial and objective the strategy nor how unintentional the bias?

Affirmative answers to these questions appear to apply to the operating companies of the Bell System during the period 1965 –1971. The same answers would have to be given regarding many other employers in the public and private sectors of the American economy even today. What was unique about the Bell System, however, was that while the architects of their strategy knew about its adverse impact upon women and minority groups they resolutely maintained that it was fair and economically necessary.[1]

Briefly, the situation was this: At the end of 1970, six years after the passage of the Civil Rights Act of 1964 and almost thirty years after the passage of the first fair employment laws, the Bell operating companies employed 165,000 persons in the low paying operator classifications, 99.9 percent of whom were female. Of 190,000 higher paying craft workers, 99 percent were male.[2]

Nationwide, 9.8 percent of all Bell System employees were black. In the low-paying service worker categories, 37 percent were black. Over 34 percent of its telephone operators were black; but less than 5 percent of its craft workers were black.[3]

Since people in our society are not recruited, selected, and placed in occupations randomly, the distribution of workers by sex and race in this labor force is a direct outcome of the employer's selection strategy and the structure of his labor market. There are, therefore, two possible explanations for the uneven and inequitable distribution of women and minority groups on the company payroll: (a) The labor market does not contain a sufficient number of females and/or minority group members qualified to perform effectively in the positions where the underrepresentation has been observed, (b) The firm's selection strategy operates, deliberately or not, to create a pattern of sexual and ethnic segregation and discrimination.

In the light of the job census data cited above, the burden of proof was on the Bell System to support the first explanation. This proof had to consist of a demon-

1 Testimony of John W. Kingsbury, FCC Docket No. 19143 (August 1, 1972), p. 4.
2 EEOC W-459.
3 *Ibid.*

stration that its operating companies were vigorously pursuing a recruitment and selection program that was based on the concept of business necessity as specified by the Supreme Court in the *Griggs*[4] decision.

It is apparent from the outcome of the EEOC hearing before the Federal Communications Commission that the Bell System could not marshal sufficient evidence to support the first explanation. The focus of this paper then centers on the second explanation and on those elements of Bell's selection strategy for non-management personnel that contributed to the disproportionate distribution of women and minority groups in the better-paying jobs.

Elements of a Selection Strategy

To understand the following evaluation of Bell's selection strategy it will be helpful first, to consider certain issues on which psychologists may differ: differential validity, models of test fairness, and the criterion problem.

Differential Validity

It has been observed that a selection instrument may be valid for one group in an applicant population but not for another. Studies have shown that a test may be valid for white but not for minority-group applicants.[5] Such a result is thus unfair because, as Guion has defined it, "unfair discrimination exists when persons with equal probabilities of success on the job have unequal probabilities of being hired for the job."[6]

When differences between minority and nonminority groups in the relationship of their test scores to job performance were first reported in the psychological literature, efforts were made to explain them by the notion of moderator variables. Certain selection instruments predict job performance more accurately for persons who are preselected by another standard. The trait measured by the latter test is referred to as a "moderator variable" because it determines how well the instruments predict job performance. It was suggested that race might be a moderator variable because the predictive efficiency of a test seemed in some studies to be enhanced or attenuated by the racial factor. But this theory did not explain sufficiently why race and ethnic membership should affect the relationship between a predictor score and a criterion variable such as performance rating or sales volume. Psychologists were forced, therefore, to examine more closely the notion of differential validity.

4 *Griggs vs. Duke Power Company,* 401 U.S. 424 (1971).

5 J. J. Kirkpatrick et al., *Testing and Fair Employment* (New York: New York University Press, 1968); F. M. Lopez, "Evaluating the Whole Man," *Long Island University Magazine* 2 (1968): 17–22.

6 R. M. Guion. "Employment Tests and Discriminatory Hiring." *Industrial Relations* 5 (1966) : 20–37.

This question was particularly relevant in the EEOC/AT&T hearings. In the Bell System Craft Selection Battery, for example, 50 percent of the white applicants were able to qualify while only 20 percent of the blacks could do so. For the Service Representative Selection Battery, 60 percent of the white applicants qualified as against 33 percent of the minority-group applicants.

Yet, for many psychologists, the evidence for race as a moderator variable and the concept of differential validity was not conclusive. In 1967, Bray, AT&T's Director of Management Selection and Development Research, stated, "I have yet to see adequate proof that disproportionate numbers of minority candidates should not be rejected."[7]

An American Psychological Association statement entitled "Job Testing and the Disadvantaged," prepared by a Committee chaired by Brent Baxter, one of AT&T's principal witnesses in the EEOC hearings, concluded that "existing evidence is inadequate to determine whether aptitude tests actually discriminate unfairly because of different validities from one subgroup to another."[8] Various researchers present different tabulations of the number of studies showing differential validity. Ruch, in fact, concluded that "following OFCC [Office of Federal Contract Compliance] and EEOC Guidelines will reduce, not increase, the employment opportunities for blacks."[9]

It appears that most industrial psychologists favor the position that psychological tests do not discriminate unfairly against minority-group applicants when they are administered correctly; thus psychologists doubt the existence of differential validity. All point out, however, that most of the studies reported show the need to pay more attention to the criterion problem.

Selection Bias

An important corollary of the differential validity controversy is the question of what constitutes selection bias and how to offset it. Cole examined the implications of six different definitions of selection bias to show their probable effect on the employment opportunity of minority groups. She referred to Guion's definition of

7 M. D. Dunnette. "President's Message." *The Industrial Psychologist Newsletter* 4 (1967) : 1–3.
8 American Psychological Association." Job Testing and The Disadvantaged." *American Psychologist* 24 (1969) : 637–650.
9 V. R. Boehm. "Negro-White Differences in Validity of Employment and Training Selection Procedures: Summary of Research Evidence." *Journal of Applied Psychology* 56 (1972) : 33–39.
    J. J. Kirkpatrick. "Differential Validation. What Is It? Why Is It Necessary?" Paper presented at the meeting of the American Psychological Association, Honolulu, September 1972.
    D. B. Rosen. *Employment Testing and Minority Groups,* New York State School of Industrial and Labor Relations Issue Series No. 6 (Ithaca: Cornell University Press, 1970).
    W. W. Ruch. "A Reanalysis of Published Differential Validity Studies." In *Differential Validation Under EEOC and OFCC Testing and Selection Regulations.* Symposium presented at the meeting of the American Psychological Association, Honolulu, September 1972.

test bias as the "employer's model" because, as she demonstrated, it is especially advantageous to the employer.[10]

Of particular interest is the fact that each model is based on a multiple regression equation between selection variables and a single criterion of job performance. In multiple regression analysis an equation is computed from the correlations of each variable with the criterion and their intercorrelations. Each predictive score in the equation is weighted according to how much it contributes to the prediction of the criterion score. Cole showed the inadequacy of each model and presented her own model, which she termed an equal employment opportunity model and viewed it as "intuitively appealing and socially desirable."[11] While in many respects a distinct improvement over the others, her model still depends upon a single index of job performance. This dependency is the Achilles' heel of all multiple regression models and, it is contended in this essay, is the source of the differential validity controversy and the criterion problem.

The Criterion Problem

The differential validity issue evolved out of a rather naive notion of a stable, measurable, and unitary index of job performance. To begin with, it is imprecise to speak of "job performance" because this term represents only one aspect of what the employer really seeks, job effectiveness. The other and equally important aspect is job satisfaction. Basically, job performance refers to the value of an employee's efforts to a company; job satisfaction refers to the extent to which an employee's efforts meet his or her personal needs. Job performance criteria measure how well persons are doing their jobs; job satisfaction criteria measure how long they will continue to do them well.

These aspects strongly imply that job effectiveness has many dimensions. Some will refer to the quantity and quality of output; some will refer to adherence to organizational policy on such matters as attendance, neatness, punctuality and honesty; some will refer to relations with superiors, co-workers, subordinates, and customers; some will refer to ability to progress to higher levels of responsibility; and some will refer to willingness to put up with hazardous, uncomfortable, or trying working conditions.[12]

It is also apparent from even a cursory review of published criterion research that these effectiveness dimensions relate to each other in varied ways; some correlate positively with other dimensions; some are independent of all of the other dimensions; and some correlate negatively with other dimensions. It is impossible, there-

10 N. S. Cole. *Bias in selection. ACT Research Report No. 51* (Iowa City: Research and Development Division of the American College Testing Program, 1972).
11 *Ibid.*
12 F. M. Lopez. *Evaluating Employee Performance.* (Chicago: Public Personnel Association, 1968).

fore, to combine them all into a global index of effectiveness. As Dunnette points out:

There has also been a tendency to ignore that any given level of job "success," defined globally, can be the consequence of any number of interacting factors. For example, two salesmen selling exactly the same amount of life insurance . . . may have achieved their goals by widely different patterns of job behavior . . . Certainly the two would differ sharply from one another in personal characteristics; yet the classic model, for purposes of analysis, would lump them together in the same "success" group.[13]

In his employment strategy the employer must therefore specify the various configurations of job effectiveness he can accept to meet the demands of his business. He may accept a lower task performance level to maintain job stability; or he may accept a high turnover rate in exchange for low training costs and wage rates. He can rarely acquire high task performance, job stability, and low training costs and wages with a uniform set of selection standards—simply because the personal attributes necessary to achieve these three effects do not occur often in the same person. The configuration of employee effectiveness the employer adopts, implicitly or explicitly, will be intensified or attenuated by the applicant-processing model he adopts.

Applicant-Processing Models

The idea that an applicant should undergo a screening process to save both him and the employer time and money is accepted unquestioningly by the majority of American employers, including AT&T. This strategy, known as the "successive hurdle approach," requires an applicant to hurdle a series of progressively more difficult obstacles in the form of application blanks, tests, and interviews on the way to job selection. An applicant is automatically eliminated upon failure of a hurdle even though it measures only a minor portion of his or her total job qualifications.

The varied and multidimensional nature of job effectiveness, however, makes it essential to abandon this traditional selection strategy based on the principles of multiple regression analysis and successive hurdles. Various authorities have pointed out that the traditional model by no means constitutes the only one and is, in fact, subject to serious limitations.[14] They suggest that, since the purpose of any selection procedure is to help make an accurate selection decision, its utility must be evaluated on the basis of the particular decision to be made, the cost, and the level of accuracy of the information necessary to make that decision.

13 M. D. Dunnette. Personnel Selection and Placement (Belmont, California: Wadsworth Publishing, 1966), p. 105.
14 L. J. Cronbach and G. C. Gleser. Psychological Tests and Personnel Decisions (Urbana: University of Illinois Press, 1965).
    C. Fincher. "Testing & Title VII." *Atlantic Economic Review* 15 (1965) : 15–19.

In a selection validity study, consequently, the researcher must not only present regression equations between predictors and criterion, but also demonstrate what percent of total job effectiveness is accounted for by the criterion chosen. He may show, for example, a high multiple correlation coefficient between a set of predictors and a criterion that accounts for only 10 percent of job effectiveness. If he adopts a naive empirical approach and incorporates his predictors into a successive hurdle strategy, he will disqualify a large number of applicants who could qualify if other equally applicable measures of job effectiveness had been evaluated.[15] A much more effective strategy requires an employer, through appropriate job analysis, to determine the personal traits relevant for clearly acceptable performance of the essential job functions. Then he must design the instruments to measure these traits and to define the threshold points that clearly indicate possession of them.

In effect, an employer must adopt a decision-making selection strategy that emphasizes those criteria of effectiveness that guarantee the most satisfactory achievement of business objectives. If he needs to increase job stability, he can select measures that emphasize this dimension of job effectiveness. If, however, he needs promotable employees because of an expanding operation or expected retirements, he can choose measures that predict this criterion. To adhere to the goals set forth in his affirmative action program, for example, he can emphasize those job performance criteria that will favor minority groups and women without reducing overall job effectiveness. This is not discrimination in reverse, but rather an example of effective managerial decision making. In essence, the employer evaluates the whole person for the total job and he does so on the same basis for each applicant.

A review of AT&T's employment strategy demonstrated that it was not designed along these lines. A complete review of an employer's selection strategy requires evaluation of his job analysis procedures, recruitment efforts, employment standards, selection sequence, instrument validation, the qualifications and attitudes of those involved in the selection process, as well as statistical data concerning recruitment, selection, and termination activities. Many of these elements are discussed elsewhere in this volume. The remainder of this chapter will deal only with job analysis, the selection sequence, the turnover data, the interview and testing procedures.

Job Analysis

The first step in the development of an effective selection strategy for a particular job is to analyze its major and critical functions to identify the personal traits necessary to perform the job effectively. The Bell System claimed that it had done so, but furnished little evidence to support this contention. In its General Employment

15 See F. M. Lopez, *Personnel Interviewing: Theory and Practice,* rev. ed. (New York: McGraw-Hill, 1975), Chapter 6.

Interview Training Workshop there were references to job specifications that contained minimum requirements for performance in various jobs. But there were no indications of how these standards were arrived at except the note that, "Usually someone in the department took a look at the better performers on each job and attempted to list those characteristics that appeared to be common to the group."[16]

As I shall indicate below, the Workshop Manual contained frequent references to the authors' doubts as to what traits predict job effectiveness. Several test validation studies to be described below report that job analyses were carried out to ascertain the critical requirements of an occupation. A variety of methods were used, singly or in combination, to obtain the necessary information.

Besides criterion development, job analyses were carried out for other purposes such as the formulation of relevant training programs. But Bell Company employment manuals, the Interview Training Workshop, and the test validation study reports failed to present clear-cut specifications of what was needed to perform various jobs effectively. One can only conclude that the job analyses completed by the company were inappropriate for selection purposes.

Job Analysis Techniques
American management has produced a number of techniques to enable it to analyze jobs for a variety of purposes.[17] The oldest approach consists of those traditional work requirement systems designed by industrial engineers. These techniques provide measures of work, time study, production standards, and other objective indicators of work results. Very closely related to these are the work flow techniques used in some manufacturing and process studies. Other methods vary from the minute task analysis approach used in human engineering to the very broad narrative descriptions developed by wage and salary analysts.

None of these techniques produces a format suitable for selection purposes. Work flow or process analysis cannot be applied to people. Task analysis, the technique apparently used most often by AT&T, provides data that are difficult to synthesize into a form that makes the development of measuring instruments practical. In addition, few of these measures provide any indication of the psychological and social demands of a job.

The resulting selection strategy may lead, as in AT&T's case, to an overemphasis on certain traits that may only partially predict job effectiveness. For example, in his description of various plant craft jobs, Joe H. Hunt, AT&T's Plant Department Assistant Vice President, indicated numerous aspects of job effectiveness that are not accounted for in the construct "ability to learn" which was, as we shall point

16 American Telephone & Telegraph Company. General Employment Interview Workshop (F. M. Lopez, unpublished ms., 1968).
17 E. P. Prien and W. W. Ronan. "Job Analysis: A Review of Research Findings." *Personnel Psychology* 24 (1971) : 371–396.

out below, the principal element in the hiring decision for these jobs. He said that an installer must have "a high degree of self-responsibility" and be able to "perform effectively with a minimum of personal attention." A frameman must be good at "record keeping," must develop good "work habits," and must be "flexible" to "numerous instantaneous demands" and emergencies. Finally, he must religiously practice "secrecy." A switchman "must react immediately and on his own to unusual or emergency conditions" and must have "a strong sense of responsibility."[18]

Overemphasis on specific traits to the exclusion of other critical traits normally leads not only to an adverse impact upon some classes of applicants but to high turnover among employees.

Force Losses in Nonmanagement Positions

Apparently by the end of 1970 most of the Bell operating companies were deeply concerned about the high turnover in plant, traffic, clerical, and other nonmanagement positions. A number of comprehensive, penetrating, and candid force loss studies were completed to identify possible remedies for this problem. The following reasons for leaving the telephone company were explored for solutions: pay, employment, training, the job, career planning, supervision, and communication.

Of immediate interest were the conclusions with respect to the selection process. Repeated complaints were made about the fact that operating company interviewers did not know the details and the demands of the jobs they were attempting to fill and that they did not explain these details adequately to applicants. Here are a few quotations from these reports:

Vague job descriptions, the run-around encountered in a few employment offices, and unfriendly interviewers detract from effective employment processing.

Working conditions unattractive—pole climbing, working in crawl spaces, high crime areas, working in inclement weather.

Better selection job by employment office. Pay particular attention to the over-qualified.

Above average test scores are no assurance of success on job. Fifteen percent with test scores well above average had below average job performance.

While a Bell System spokesman later belittled these remarks as coming from "a handful of turnover studies" the consistency of the comments, the breadth and scope of the studies, and the expense to the company cited as resulting from the reported force losses make it difficult to dismiss them lightly.[19]

The Selection Sequence

The inadequacies of the job analyses undertaken at Bell were then amplified by the selection sequence adopted, which was, as we have already described, based on

18 Testimony of Joe H. Hunt, FCC Docket No. 19143, August 1, 1972.
19 Testimony of John W. Kingsbury (see note 1), p. 89.

the multiple regression–successive hurdle approach. Such a system can have disastrous consequences for minority employment.

Operating Company Procedures

The typical applicant processing sequence in the operating companies began with a gross prescreening procedure that consisted of an initial interview on the premises or over the telephone. The "initial contact interview" was designed to identify applicants whom the company wished to process further, to encourage those applicants who really wanted to work for the phone company, and to save processing time for both the applicant and the office.

The interviewer asked questions about previous Bell System Service, date of birth, type of job desired, educational background, previous work experience, military work experience, marital status, home environment, availability for work, transportation, and, for male applicants, motor vehicle record.

The interview proceeded until sufficient information had been obtained to reach a decision or the applicant indicated lack of interest in the job the company had to offer. A qualified applicant was referred immediately for testing. If the recommended test score was met, the applicant then completed an application, an employment questionnaire, and a health questionnaire and then was directed to an interviewer for the selection interview. If the minimum test score was not met the applicant was directed immediately to an interviewer for a rejection interview.

Those applicants who were disqualified during the interview were rejected and those who passed were referred for security checks, reference checks, and physical examinations. The verification procedure was accomplished by telephone inquiries to schools and previous employers. An employment representative who made this call completed a form calling for information about dates of employment or attendance, quality of work, punctuality and attendance, and attitude towards work, supervision, and other employees.

Evaluation

It was quite difficult to evaluate this employment sequence because the statistical information necessary to determine the percentage of rejections by sex and race at each decision point in the employment process was unavailable. While it appeared that the principal hurdle in this sequence was the test, some applicants, according to a company spokesman, were disqualified in each of the various stages. The rationale for this policy, he said, involved the needs of applicants and the economics of employment. He felt that, from the applicant's point of view, any procedure that lessened the time commitment to an unsuccessful application was advantageous. And the stakes for the telephone companies were also high because the total cost of the employment process expanded or contracted in proportion to the amount of time applicants spent in the process.

There are indications from the force loss studies, however, that this selection procedure not only failed to produce enough qualified employees but also contributed to high turnover rates. The majority of the resigned or dismissed employees had less than six months of service.

To judge the effectiveness of this strategy, therefore, and to evaluate more accurately the Bell System's claim that it was fair and impartial, it is necessary to examine closely the two selection instruments that eliminated the bulk of the applicants from employment—the interview and the test battery.

The Employment Interview

In the light of the Civil Rights Act of 1964, the EEOC Testing Guidelines, the OFCC Testing Order, and current selection theory and research,[20] two characteristics of the Bell System interviewing program were quite striking:

First, the company offered no statistical data to determine whether there was a disparate rejection rate (*a*) by major job categories, (*b*) for each race, sex, or ethnic group, and (*c*) for both the gross prescreening interview or the selection interview.

Second, the Bell System presented no studies designed to establish a standardized interview format nor to validate interviewer judgments. Subsequent to the EEOC hearings, there have been indications that such research is in progress.

These omissions were surprising (1) in the light of the evidence suggested by some operating company reports that approximately 30 percent to 40 percent of their applicants were eliminated by the interview and (2) by virtue of the fact that other employers who, like the Bell System, employed full time industrial psychologists, had already developed weighted application and interview techniques to make these tools more objective and more effective.[21]

There is evidence, to be cited below, to suggest that the reason for this apparent apathy was based on the conviction held by some psychologists that the interview is a poor predictor of job effectiveness. But if this is the reason it did not coincide with the New Jersey Bell Employment Manual, which stated that the prediction of an applicant's probable adjustment to a job had to be based to a great extent on information secured in the interview.

This absence of data, however, was offered by a Bell System spokesman as grounds for the rejection of an expert witness's criticisms of the interview techniques used in the Bell System. Since the Bell System was unable to provide data to validate or in-

20 R. M. Guion. *Personnel Testing* (New York: McGraw-Hill, 1965).

E. C. Mayfield. "The Selection Interview—A Reevaluation of Published Research." *Personnel Psychology* 17 (1964) : 239–260.

21 H. Laurent. *Early Identification of Management Potential,* Social Science Research Report (New York: Standard Oil Co. of N.J., 1961).

G. W. England. *Development and Use of Weighted Application Blanks* (Dubuque, Iowa: Wm. C. Brown Co., 1961).

validate the interviewer's judgment or any data as to the disparate effect of this judgment on applicants rejected by the interviewer, this spokesman claimed that the expert's testimony was without foundation and, therefore, inadmissable.[22]

Evaluation of the Bell System Interview

At a minimum, a valid employment interview requires:

1. Adequate job analysis and occupational research to determine the traits necessary to perform a job effectively.
2. Selection of interviewers with the technical background, personality, and motivation to conduct the interview properly.
3. Intensive interviewer training.
4. An interview format that assures uniformity of information discussed in each interview and by different interviewers.
5. An adequate interview report form to facilitate the objective and uniform recording and interpretation of interview information.
6. A monitoring program to refine, modify, and validate interview techniques, the information obtained, and the standards of employment.

Based upon the information furnished, one can only conclude that the interview as conducted in the Bell System failed to meet most of the above requirements.

1. Job Analysis

We have already noted the limitations of the job analysis procedures used by the Bell System. Based on a typical operating company employment manual, each interviewer was given a "hiring information" sheet and an employment requisition. The hiring information sheet listed department, job title, job qualifications, job requirements, working conditions, training period, and promotional opportunities. This information was rather ambiguous. For example, the job qualifications for Service Representative were described as follows:

The Service Representative must possess maturity, the ability to learn quickly, verbal facility in sufficient quantity to be able to deal with customers on a variety of subjects under many conditions . . . Initiative, accuracy, organizational ability, resourcefulness, good judgment and self-confidence are also attributes essential for success.

Since the form listed no definition of such constructs as "maturity," "initiative," or "resourcefulness" the employment interviewer was left to his or her own devices to define and to set standards of acceptability for them.

The employment requisition was of little help since the listed "job requirements" referred to such skills as typing, stenography, or telephone answering.

2. Selection of Interviewers

Interviewers were drawn from the operating departments because, in the company's view, this practice had definite advantages. No guidelines were set down regarding

22 Testimony of John W. Kingsbury, p. 4

their qualifications although operating departments were cautioned to take care to obtain the best candidates available. This practice has definite disadvantages that normally offset its advantages, the principal one being that surplus, obsolete, or long-term employees are often selected. We have no way of knowing whether this was the case in the Bell System but at least one force loss report said that

Company interviewers who administer, score and interpret the test results as well as conduct interviews meet only minimum standards of competence.

It is interesting to note that the phrase "as well as conduct interviews" appears to be an afterthought with respect to interviewers.

3. Training

Presumably the interviewing situation throughout the Bell System in 1968 was deemed serious enough to generate action on the national level to "carefully reappraise interviewing techniques and the training of interviewers." Consequently the Personnel Relations Department developed a general interviewing workshop to train interviewers in a new interview pattern and format.

Originally, interviewers used such categories as male or female, high school diploma, age, and specific work experiences as minimum employment requirements. In addition, each department in each company specified the criteria for the job in the department. A review of these standards led one company researcher to conclude that the operating companies "have been using these criteria for many years without ever seriously questioning their validity in terms of either relevance to our needs or capability of measurement."

Because these standards were found to be "obsolete," "too high," "ill-defined," and "lacking validity" they were reduced to five: *ability to learn, physical condition, employability, motivation,* and finally, *gross negative disqualifiers.*

Ability to learn was defined as "basic intelligence and aptitudes" which the company felt could be measured by administering a battery of tests.

Physical condition was ascertained by means of medical examination and/or medical history.

Employability was defined as either the likelihood of the job candidate staying with the company long enough to provide a reasonable return on investment or the riskiness of his employment.

Motivation was defined as the degree to which the applicant obtained satisfaction from things that are intrinsic to the work itself, such as accomplishment, achievement, and responsibility. After some field testing the company dropped this category.

Gross negative disqualifiers referred to any obvious impairment in the applicant's ability to perform on the specific job for which he was being considered, such as fear of heights or inability to express himself.

While the amount of time—an average of 191 hours after appointment—devoted to training newly selected interviewers was ample, the training content was questionable. The following statements in the Leaders Guide are significant:

The interview is the weakest means we have for predicting how the applicant would do the job.
The interview is a social form of "combat."[23]

If these statements were accepted by an employment interviewer he would be likely to succumb to a widely noted hazard of seeking out the applicant's deficiencies and in emphasizing his unemployability rather than his employability.[24] In other words, he would be much more sensitive to "gross negative disqualifiers." Such an orientation is bound to be hard on minority group applicants, particularly on those who come from disadvantaged backgrounds.[25] It can also have a detrimental effect upon a situation where an applicant is seeking a position traditionally reserved for members of the opposite sex.

4. Interview patterns

The recommended interview pattern consisting of the five stages: establishing rapport, setting the stage, reviewing chronology, probing fertile areas, and closing the interview, is, on the surface, certainly adequate. The interviewer is given little guidance, however, as to which are the "fertile areas." Once again he is left to determine for himself what might or might not be a fitting topic to probe.

5. Evaluation criteria

Seven criteria were specified for making a decision about an applicant's qualifications for employment: ability (tests), physical condition (medical examination), permanence, employability, risks to company, gross negative disqualifiers, and reference checks. Permanence, risks to company, employability, and gross negative disqualifiers were left largely to individual interviewer interpretation. Nothing in the Training Manual, the Leaders Guide, the Employment Manual, the Position Specifications, or the Employment Requisition would give him much help in the way of solid information on which to base a judgment.

This employment strategy, therefore, created another opportunity for the interviewer to inject, consciously or unconsciously, his own personal biases into the decision.

6. Research

As previously mentioned, the Bell System offered no information to suggest either that the interview procedure did not reject a disproportionate number of women or

23 American Telephone & Telegraph Company. *General Employment.*
24 American Psychological Association, "Job Testing," and Mayfield, "The Selection Interview."
25 E. A. Shaw. "Differential Impact of Negative Stereotyping in Employment Selection." *Personnel Psychology* 25 (1972) : 333–338. See also M. E. Ace. "Psychological Testing: Unfair Discrimination?" *Journal of Economy and Society 1971* 10 (1971) : 301–313

minority groups or that it was in the process of validating this significant part of its selection strategy. Unlike other aspects of its defense, it offered no distinguished authorities to support its interview program. One can only conclude, therefore, that despite the number of hours devoted to interviewer training, the interview pattern and format not only failed to control cultural and social bias but actually invited it. It seemed fair to infer from this state of affairs that the critical factor in the Bell System selection strategy, the dominant "go–no go" element in the overall decision, was the test score. Here is where the company took its stand. Here is where it and some distinguished industrial psychologists—Baxter, Bray, Grant, Guion, and others—averred that its selection strategy stood on solid ground.

The Testing Program

Since the Bell System testing program is explored at length elsewhere in this volume it will be necessary here only to evaluate it in the light of the selection strategy and the basic principles presented earlier in this essay.

The Replacement of the Wonderlic

Selection tests have been administered in Bell System companies since at least 1942 for various occupations. Some tests were custom built by Bell System companies, and others were purchased from commercial test publishers. Until 1965 the Wonderlic Personnel Test, a commercially developed and widely used test of general mental ability was extensively administered throughout the system. In the early 1960s, the Wonderlic was seriously questioned—not because of its invalidity but because of its widespread use throughout metropolitan communities.

The Personnel Research Staff of AT&T, therefore, began the task of replacing the Wonderlic with another comparable test that correlated as closely as possible with it. At the end of 1965, the Bell System Qualification Test I (BSQT I), was chosen as a suitable substitute for the Wonderlic. This test, known commercially as the School and College Ability Test (SCAT) Level 2, published by the Educational Testing Service, was one of a series developed primarily to aid counselors in predicting success of students in appropriate grades in schools and in counseling students about appropriate courses of study. As might be expected, the SCAT is heavily oriented academically and correlates positively with any training or educational measure whose major variance is due to verbal comprehension.

Since the BSQT I, consisting of four separately timed parts, required over an hour to complete, the Personnel Research Staff recommended a shorter version, the BSQT I (Short Form). This short form consisted of Part 2, *Arithmetic,* and Part 3, *Word Understanding* of BSQT I, and was compared to the Wonderlic in a study that included both white and black applicants. The correlations between the Wonderlic and BSQT I were .74 for white applicants, .65 for Negro applicants, and for the combined groups, .80.

The study included a number of tests from the regular battery for operator, clerical, and service representative occupations—tests of arithmetic, number comparison, filing, number transcription, and spelling. As the mean scores for the white applicants were consistently higher on all of the tests than those for black applicants, and the differences statistically reliable, the researchers concluded that smaller percentages of black than white applicants met recommended system employment standards. On the Wonderlic and BSQT I approximately 70 percent of whites and 20 percent of black applicants met the recommended standards. They also concluded that general learning ability was a major influence on performance on these tests.

Consequently, directives were transmitted to all associated companies recommending that the Wonderlic be replaced by the BSQT I (Short Form) in all locations where trained test administrators were available and optimum test security could be observed.

Over the next five years nearly all companies complied with this directive, and in fact the Wonderlic was discontinued. Many other tests were utilized during this period, but the principal components of the prediction indexes for traffic, clerical and plant position was the BSQT I (Short Form), and it is no exaggeration to say that it had become the anchoring point of the Bell System's employment strategy.

Bell System Test Validation Studies
In the hearings held by the FCC, the Bell System submitted twenty-seven validation studies conducted from 1965 to 1971 as evidence of the fairness of its testing program for nonmanagement personnel.[26] Seven of these were conducted under the supervision of the Personnel Research Staff of the parent company, AT&T, and the remainder by local staff. For an itemized listing see Table 10.1.
General assertions. While the studies varied in professional competence and the data furnished were incomplete, sufficient information was obtained to determine whether the Bell System had a case for the validity of its testing program. Ten studies provided information about the ethnic composition of the applicant group studied, twenty-three involved the use of the BSQT I (Short Form) and four involved its college counterpart, SCAT I. In nearly every study resulting in positive findings, either the BSQT I or the SCAT I achieved the highest correlation with the criterion. Five key studies, four of which were complete at the time of the hearings, enabled the research staff to make the following assertions:
1. The correlations between the predictors and the criteria are about the same for minority and nonminority groups.
2. The mean scores on the predictors are significantly higher for whites than for blacks.

26 Thirty-one studies were reported in all. Four of these related to management personnel. See John B. Miner, "Psychological Testing and Fair Employment Practices: A Testing Program that Does Not Discriminate," *Personnel Psychology* 27 (1974).

Table 10.1 Bell System Validation Studies

	DATE	JOB TITLE (s)	LOCATION	NO. SUBJECTS	ETHNIC GROUPINGS
1	1966	Directory Assistance Operator	Pacific Tel.	202	70%W, 23%B, 7%S
*2	1969	Toll Operators	Southern Bell	348	70%W, 30%B
*3	1970-1	Toll, Direct. Assist., Traffic Serv.	12 locations	1100	43%W, 46%B, 11%S
4	1967	Toll Operators	Southern Bell	364	Not Given
5	1968	Traffic Operators	Pacific Tel.	41	100%S
6	1968	Toll Operators	So.Central B.	226	Not Given
7	1968	Toll Operators	So.Central B.	370	Not Given
8	1967	Telephone Oper. & clericals	Michigan Bell	373	57%W, 43%NW
9	1967	Traffic Operators	Pacific Tel.	143	Not Given
10	1967	Traffic Operators	Pacific Tel.	78	Not Given
11	1968	Traffic Operators	Pacific Tel.	170	Not Given
*12	1970-1	Clerical Occupations	12 locations	625	40%W, 40%B, 20%S
13	1967	Directory Clerks	Pacific Tel.	102	Not Given
14	1969	Directory Clerks	Pacific Tel.	52	Not Given
15	1971	Switchroom Helper	Michigan Bell	62	Not Given
*16	1969	Plant Craftsman	5 Companies	430	50%W, 50%B
17	1969	Plant Craftsman	Pacific Tel.	32	100%S
18	Undt'd	Directory Salesmen	3 Companies	202	Not Given
19	Undt'd	Directory Salesmen	Pacific Tel.	42	Not Given
20	1968	Communications Consultants	14 Companies	78	Not Given
21	Undt'd	Marketing Salesmen	Pacific Tel.	101	Not Given
22	Undt'd	Marketing Reps.	Pacific Tel.	43	Not Given
23	1968	Customer Serv. Reps. & Engrs.	Southern Bell	109	Not Given
24	Undt'd	Programming Positions	Six Companies	337	94%W, 6%B
25	1969	Computer Programmers	N. J. Bell	25	Not Given
*26	1969	Service Representatives	3 Companies	300	65%W, 35%B
27	1969	Service Representatives	Southern Bell	271	Not Given

*Key Studies

M-Minority   W-White
NM-Non-Minority   B-Black
NW-Non-White   S-Spanish-surnamed

Table 10.1 Continued

	PREDICTORS (TESTS)	CRITERIA
1	BSQT(SF) + RB + X	PTWX
*2	BSQT(SF) + BSQT AA	PT PX (Job Simulation)
*3	BSQT(SF) + RB + X	PT PX (Job Simulation)
4	BSQT(SF) + BSQT AA (PQT)	PTIR + PTO + PESR
5	BSQT I (SF)	PESR
6	BSQT I (SF)	PEO - % Load Carried
7	BSQT I (SF)	PEO - % Load Carried
8	BSQT I (SF) + RB	PESR - 3 - 5 months later
9	BSQT I (SF) + RB	PTIR
10	BSQT I (SF) + RB	PESR
11	BSQT I (SF) + RB	PTO - Leave - Stay
*12	BSQT I (SF) + RB + X	Post Employment Simulation
13	BSQT I (SF) + SCAT	PESR
14	BSQT I (SF)	PESR (6 Factors)
·15	BSQT I (SF) + BSQT IV + RB	PESR (8 Measures)
*16	BSQT I (SF) + BSQT II, III, IV + X	LAP
17	BSQT I (SF) + BSQT IV	PESR (2 Factors)
18	BSQT I (SF)	PTIR + PESR
19	BSQT I (SF)	PT PX (Programmed Learning Test)
20	SCAT I + X + Assessment Staff Judgments	PESR + Field Review Team Ratings
21	SCAT I + Crit. Thinking	PTWX
22	BSQT I + IV	PESR (2 Measures)
23	BSQT I + CSWS	PTO (Completed Training) PEO - (on Job 90 days)
24	SCAT I, BSQT III + X	PTIR
25	SCAT I	PESR (Composite)
*26	BSQT I (SF) + RB + SCAT	PTWX + PT PX
27	BSQT I (SF)	PTO - Completed Training

RB - Regular Battery   PTWX-Post Training Written Exercise   PESR-Perf.Eval. Suprv's Rating
X - Experimental   PTPX-Post Training Perf. Exercise   PEO-Perf.Eval.Suprv's Rating
                        PTIR-Post Training Instructor's Rating

Table 10.1 Continued

	RESULTS
1	W-Score Higher on most tests; most tests predictive; B-Few Predictive
*2	W-Score Higher on most tests; both test predictive of composite criteria for both groups
*3	Preliminary: Tests are Predictive-Study still in progress
4	BSQT I Predicts PTPK (load carried); PQT products PTIR + PTPK but not PESR
5	BSQT I not predictive of any of 6 perf. criteria
6	Overall BSQT I not predictive-in two locations it is predictive for W but not B
7	BSQT I Predictive (two locations) New Orleans data dropped
8	BSQT I + Filing + Number Transcription predictive for all job titles & ethnic groups
9	BSQT I + Transcription Predictive
10	BSQT I not predictive except "ability to learn," similar results for rest of battery
11	BSQT I, Filing, Number transcription predictive of completing training
*12	No results - Study in progress.
13	Neither test predictive
14	BSQT I Not predictive
15	BSQT I Predicts overall performance; no other measures predict
*16	All Test predictive for W & NW
17	Both Tests Predictive
18	Test not predictive of either criteria
19	Test Predictive
20	SCAT, critical thinking, contemp. affairs & ASJ predictive of FRT but not PESR
21	Both Tests Predictive
22	Neither test predictive of overall performance or ability to learn.
23	BSQT I Predictive of PTO but not PEO
24	All Tests Predictive
25	Not Predictive w/o Correction
*26	All but one test predictive of composite index
27	Test predictive

Table 10.1 Continued

STUDY NO.	EEOC DOCUMENT NO.
1.	EEOC C-1600
2.	EEOC C-1601
3.	EEOC C-1602
4.	EEOC C-1557
5.	
6.	EEOC C-1622
7.	EEOC C-1621
8.	EEOC C-1614
9.	EEOC C-1553
10.	EEOC C-1554
11.	EEOC C-1556
12.	EEOC C-1603
13.	EEOC C-1547
14.	EEOC C-1548
15.	EEOC C-1613
16.	EEOC C-1604
17.	EEOC C-1549
18.	EEOC C-1605
19.	EEOC C-1550
20.	EEOC C-1606
21.	EEOC C-1551
22.	EEOC C-1552
23.	EEOC C-1624
24.	EEOC C-1607
25.	EEOC C-1617
26.	EEOC C-1610
27.	EEOC C-1623

3. The recommended minimum scores result in over twice as many blacks as whites being excluded from employment.

4. The tests chosen for the Bell System test battery do not discriminate unfairly against black applicants.

Evaluation of the validation studies. Presumably, a test measures such personal traits as physical strength, mental ability, or verbal comprehension that produce such job-performance outcomes as production, sales, errors, or dissatisfaction. These personal traits are termed the independent or causal variables; the outcomes are dependent or end-result variables which are the ultimate criteria of job effectiveness. In the validation process it is essential to show a relationship between a measure of an independent variable such as a test score or an interviewer's rating and a measure of a dependent variable, consisting of some critical aspect of job effectiveness.

But as we have noted earlier, the multidimensionality of the criterion, job effectiveness, makes the development of an overall measure of job proficiency very difficult. As Fincher has pointed out, the specification of a meaningful criterion of job performance "is left entirely to the employer and becomes an inherent part of the burden of proof that he must bear."[27]

Faced with this difficulty and in the absence of appropriate job analysis, some researchers, particularly those with a psychometric orientation, choose such intermediate factors as successful completion of a training program or a job-knowledge test as the criterion. These criteria are not end-result variables. In the general sense of the term they can be construed at most as intervening variables provided they have a functional relationship to both an independent and a dependent variable. Likert, for example, refers to "organizational climate," as an intervening variable because it has a functional relationship to an independent variable, "leadership style," and to a dependent variable, "productivity."[28] Therefore, when such a variable as knowledge acquired in a training program is established as a criterion, the employer must demonstrate its functional relationship to both the predictor and the end-result variable. Without this complete evidence the criterion becomes highly suspect. If the "validated" predictor has a disparate effect upon a protected class its use in the selection strategy is unwarranted.

Over half (fifteen of twenty-seven) of the studies submitted by the Bell System adopted some type of posttraining or simulation exercise as the criterion to validate either the BSQT I or the SCAT I. In the four key studies conducted by the AT&T research staff the sole criterion was a posttraining exercise and the assertions previously referred to were based on this type of criterion.

27 C. Fincher. "Personnel Testing and Public Policy." *American Psychologist* 28 (1973) : 489–497.
28 R. Likert. *The Human Organization: Its Management and Value* (New York: McGraw-Hill, 1967), p. 76.

Only three of the fifteen studies using some type of end result variable, such as supervisors' rating or retention, showed clearly positive results. Three studies showed both positive and negative results, and nine studies yielded completely negative results. The Bell System's case for the validity and business necessity of its traffic, plant, and service-representative test batteries rested, therefore, on the functional relationship of a posttraining or simulation exercise to both the independent and dependent variable.

Posttraining exercises as criteria. The Bell System psychologists were well aware of possible objections to their choice of criteria to validate the BSQT I. In the final report of each study they pointed out that they were trying to validate tests which measure the applicant's capacity to acquire task proficiency. Day-to-day job performance, they said, was not usually a good measure of task proficiency because it was contaminated by the nature of supervision, peer pressures to control output, and individual motivation. A direct measure of task proficiency after training was, therefore, a much purer criterion of what the test measured.

This contention, of course, begs the question. If peer pressures, quality of supervision, and individual motivation are of such importance to job performance of what value is the unadulterated task proficiency? Might not a person with a high degree of innate skill and ability be frustrated completely by inadequate supervision and peer pressure? Of what use is an "instant criterion," to use AT&T witness Robert Guion's term, if it has little or no effect in the real world of work?

It is interesting to note that in each validation report the authors included a paragraph similar to the following:

The present study is to be extended longitudinally by the yearly collection of data on the participants. The data will include carefully controlled supervisory ratings, retentions and the plant craft occupations to which are assigned, promotions, performance in training programs, absences, tardiness, disciplinary actions, and so forth.[29]

This follow-up study was completed on one test battery with results which I shall now discuss.

Evaluation of the Bell System Test Program

Despite the support of their research during the public hearings by many distinguished psychologists and psychometricians, and more recently by Miner,[30] it appears that the Bell System program is vulnerable on the several counts reviewed in the following paragraphs.

1. The lack of job analysis

We have noted the apparent lack of adequate job analysis to identify the nature and relative importance of the personal traits necessary for job effectiveness. Even if we

29 D. L. Grant, and D. W. Bray. "Validation of Employment Tests for Telephone Company Installation and Repair Occupations." *Journal of Applied Psychology* 54 (1970) : 7–14.
30 J. B. Miner. "Psychological Testing."

were to accept the BSQT I as predictively valid, we have no way of knowing how critical whatever it measures is to overall job effectiveness. The force loss studies seemed to suggest that even if ability to learn was measured by this test it was not very important.

2. Misuse of the construct "ability to learn"

Current learning theory and research view the ability to learn not so much as a generalized construct but a very complex phenomenon that does not permit general application in the manner used by the Bell System.[31] And certainly a test such as the BSQT I cannot predict rate of learning but only gains in learning. This is a critical issue. Nowhere does the Bell System data indicate the effect of extending the training period for those scoring lower on the BSQT I. It is fair to ask whether the undoubtedly increased training costs would be more than offset by lower force losses.

3. The lack of evidence to show the relationship between the training exercises and job performance

The Bell System offered no data to show the functional relationship between the posttraining exercises and measures of job effectiveness. A follow-up study of the plant craft selection battery, using 19 performance measures, yielded only one significant relationship with test scores. Only 5 of the 19 end result variables correlated significantly with the intermediate criterion performance on a work simulation exercise that was originally designed as a predictor.[32] It is to be noted that the principal investigator refused to accept such measures as supervisors' ratings, absences, accidents, and disciplinary actions as performance measures but rather referred to them as "indicia of behavior."

This follow-up study clearly showed that the craft test battery was not predictive of behavior on the job. Rather it demonstrated that blacks who failed the test battery were just as likely to perform successfully on the job and in training as whites who passed the test battery. In other words, this follow-up study showed that the craft battery predicted the intermediate criterion but virtually nothing else. It did not support the propositon made by a Bell System spokesman that "unless we maintain relevant hiring standards our training costs would soar astronomically."

Conclusions

Judging from the evidence reviewed it is difficult to see how the Bell System could maintain its apparent equanimity when faced with the obvious impact its selection strategy was having on women and minority groups. It would be purely speculative to

31 E. A. Fleishman, and C. J. Bartlett. "Human Abilities." *Annual Review of Psychology* 20 (1969) : 355.
32 Testimony of Donald L. Grant, FCC Docket No. 19143, August 1, 1972, Attachment C. It is difficult to understand why Dr. Miner omitted reference to this study in his analysis of the Bell System Testing Program cited above.

enumerate the many organizational, social, and economic factors that prevented this great institution from taking more positive steps toward leadership in this vital management area. But we can enumerate three probable causes for this defensive posture with respect to the civil rights movement in the United States.

One of the problems was an evident lack of a unified, integrated employment strategy throughout the Bell System. Different units of the System seemed to be responsible for different aspects of the total strategy and apparently they did not communicate with one another.

A second problem stemmed from a rather limited view of the employment process that construed it in terms of short run economic considerations. Admittedly, the latter are measured rather easily by profit and loss statements but as Likert has pointed out, the long term disadvantages, while not as easily traceable or identifiable, can be economically and socially devastating to a company and to society.[33]

A third problem lay in the unquestioned acceptance of traditional psychological and personnel theory and practice as incontrovertible dogma. When the indications were clear that the rigid application of this dogma has a socially undesirable effect, the Bell System apparently was unable to respond imaginatively and responsibly to the challenge. The implementation of the affirmative action plans specified by the Consent Decree of January 1973 should provide such an opportunity.

33 Likert, *The Human Organization*, p. 115.

IV The Institutional Environment

11 Legal Processes and Strategies of Intervention

Phyllis A. Wallace and Jack E. Nelson

This chapter examines the events and processes that took place between December 1970, when the EEOC initiated its case against AT&T, and its settlement two years later in January 1973. The proceeding involved many meetings between the parties, nearly sixty days of public hearings, the testimony of 150 witnesses, the presentation of over 200 exhibits, and a record of some 8,000 pages of transcripts. Even prior to 1970, AT&T's employment practices had been reviewed on various occasions by the federal government, and it would be useful to discuss the background which provided the setting for the action by EEOC.

At the time the legal action against AT&T was undertaken more than 2,000 charges alleging employment discrimination had been filed against the company by individuals protected by Title VII of the Civil Rights Act of 1964. During the late 1960s, in-depth analyses of Southwestern Bell, Southern Bell, South Central Bell, and Pacific Bell had been prepared by the EEOC. Detailed studies of the entire Bell System were used as background material in discussions conducted between senior officials of the EEOC and of AT&T between 1967 and 1969. As a result of these meetings, AT&T had promised to hire more blacks and Hispanics. Although by December 1970 AT&T had made an effort to hire more workers from minority populations, the record of the company on utilization of women workers was less impressive.

The incident which precipitated the EEOC's action was the decision by AT&T to seek an increase in its federally-regulated rates for long distance telephone service. Under the proposed rate increase filed with the FCC on November 19, 1970, the Bell System requested permission to increase the guaranteed rate of return from 7.5 percent to 9.5 percent.[1] The EEOC petitioned to intervene in the FCC proceedings and expressed its opposition to the rate increase on the grounds that the company violated the Federal Communications Act and other federal statutes by its alleged discriminatory employment practices against women, blacks, and Spanish-surnamed Americans. The EEOC's petition asserted:

That because AT&T's operating companies engage in pervasive and unlawful discrimination in employment against women, blacks, Spanish-surnamed Americans, and other minorities, the rate increase proposed and filed by AT&T with the Commission is unjust and unreasonable, in violation of [the Federal Communications Act of 1934, Title VII of the Civil Rights Act of 1964, the Equal Pay Act of 1963, Executive Order 11246, the Civil Rights Act of 1866, the fair employment practice acts of approximately 30 states and ordinances of numerous large cities] . . .

1 The American Telephone and Telegraph Company's petition for a rate increase was docketed as "Tariff FCC No. 263." As of August 1974 the case was still pending.

Wherefore, petitioner, EEOC asks that the Commission grant the EEOC's Petition to Intervene, suspend the operation of AT&T's proposed rate increase, conduct a hearing, and declare the proposed increase illegal until AT&T's operating companies have ceased their unlawful discrimination against women, blacks, Spanish-surnamed Americans, and other minorities.[2]

The FCC did not accept the EEOC's argument that employment discrimination in violation of federal and state laws was proper grounds to deny AT&T's request for a rate increase. The Commission did, however, order that the employment practices of AT&T be reviewed as requested by the EEOC, but ruled that the matter would be handled in a proceeding separate from the rate case. On January 21, 1971 the employment discrimination issue was spun off as a separate case—FCC Docket No. 19143.

Providing a forum for the EEOC's charges against AT&T was compatible with the FCC's own equal employment opportunity regulations which require that "equal opportunity in employment shall be afforded by all common carrier licensees or permittees to all qualified persons, and no personnel shall be discriminated against in employment because of sex, race, color, religion or natural origin." In addition, there is specific reference in the regulations calling for cooperation with the EEOC: "The Commission will consult with the EEOC on all matters relating to the evaluation and determination of compliance by the common carrier licensees or permittees with the principles of equal employment as set forth herein."[3] The FCC was one of a very few federal regulatory agencies willing to include equal employment opportunity enforcement responsibilities as a valid aspect of its regulatory work.

Before Title VII was amended by the Congress in 1972, actions initiated under the statute could be investigated and conciliated by the EEOC, but it could neither offer redress nor initiate litigation on behalf of charging parties; Congress had vested that authority in the Department of Justice. The EEOC did, however, have the very limited authority to participate as an amicus curiae in cases in which the furtherance of the goals of Title VII were at issue. A careful reading of Title VII also led the EEOC to believe that the statute did not contain any language which prevented it from petitioning a government proceeding in which Title VII issues were at stake.[4]

2 Petition for Intervention, Before the FCC, Washington, D.C., Docket No. 19129, *Equal Employment Opportunity Commission v. American Telephone and Telegraph Company,* December 10, 1970, pp. 2–3.
3 FCC, Memorandum Opinion and Order, p. 5, Docket No. 18742, August 11, 1970.
4 As a protective strategy in the possible event the EEOC was prohibited from intervening in the proceedings of another government agency, several civil rights groups copetitioned the FCC. On December 11, 1970, the National Association for the Advancement of Colored People, the National Organization for Women, Legal Defense and Education Fund, the American Civil Liberties Union, the California Rural Legal Assistance, the Mexican-American Legal Defense Fund, and the American G.I. Forum joined the case as copetitioners. The appeal of the FCC's ruling spinning off the employment practices case from the rate case was made by the copeti-

The EEOC had participated in a somewhat similar utility rate case some months before it initiated its legal action against AT&T. In May 1969 the Washington, D.C., chapter of the Urban League requested that the Public Service Commission of the District of Columbia deny a rate increase to the Potomac Electric Power Company (PEPCO) on the grounds that it discriminated against minorities. The chairman of the D.C. Public Service Commission, Jeremiah C. Waterman, contacted the chairman of the EEOC, William H. Brown, III, for assistance in determining whether the Public Service Commission could take jurisdiction over the matter. David A. Copus, an attorney on the EEOC's General Counsel's staff, was assigned to assist the Public Service Commission in the matter.

With the aid of the EEOC the Public Service Commission issued an order on April 15, 1970, stating that it had jurisdiction over PEPCO's employment practices and outlined an affirmative action plan for the company to correct deficiencies in its treatment of minorities. PEPCO appealed the action in court, and the EEOC joined in as an amicus. The court ruled in 1971 that the Public Service Commission did in fact have the authority and power to examine PEPCO's employment practices, either as part of a rate proceeding or as an independent matter.[5] The court, however, did not uphold the affirmative action plan imposed by the Public Service Commission for procedural reasons.

While the PEPCO case was being litigated, AT&T's request for a rate increase came to the attention of Copus, who approached Chairman Brown with the idea of instituting an action by the EEOC, similar to the Urban League's. Brown approved the idea and assigned two other EEOC attorneys, Susan Ross and Lawrence Gartner, to work with Copus on the preparation of the petition to intervene in the case. The petition was filed with the FCC on December 10, 1970.

The Public Hearing

Early in 1971 the stage was set for a hearing on AT&T's employment practices. None of the parties was sure at that point whether the issue would ultimately be rejoined to the rate increase proceeding since a decision on the appeal of the ruling had not yet been reached. The FCC had two legally separate roles: representative of the public interest, and judge.

tioners. The civil rights groups were represented in the appeal by David Cashdan, a Washington-based lawyer and former EEOC attorney. The EEOC was allowed to intervene in the appeal which lasted for many months and was finally lost; a motion to reconsider was made and also subsequently lost. However, whatever the appellants may have lost in terms of establishing an important precedent by imposing fair employment practices as an element in the rate case, was probably more than offset by the expediency gained through a separate proceeding since the original rate case had not been completed as of early 1974.

5 *Potomac Electric Power Company vs. Public Service Commission of the District of Columbia* (D.D.C., Civil Action Nos. 2382-70 and 2384-70, February 23, 1971).

The FCC order establishing the adjudicatory hearings specified five broad areas of inquiry:

1. Whether the existing employment practices of AT&T tend to impede equal employment opportunities in AT&T and its operating companies contrary to other purposes and requirements of the Commission's Rules and the Civil Rights Act of 1964.

2. Whether AT&T has failed to inaugurate and maintain specific programs, pursuant to Commission Rules and Regulations, insuring against discriminatory practices in the recruiting, selection, hiring, placement, and promotion of its employees.

3. Whether AT&T has engaged in pervasive, system-wide discrimination against women, Negroes, Spanish-surnamed Americans, and other minorities in its employment practices.

4. Whether any of the employment practices of AT&T, if found to be discriminatory, affect the rates charged by that company for its services, and if so, in what ways is this reflected in the present rate structure.

5. To determine, in light of the evidence adduced pursuant to the foregoing issues, what order, or requirements, if any, should be adopted by the Commission.[6]

Government hearings are often rather complex and protracted legal encounters, but in most cases they follow the same general procedural format. After a Hearing Examiner is assigned to a case, the parties file pretrial briefs giving their preliminary interpretations of the law. Then, each party moves to *discover* facts from the other party to support its contentions. Third, each side presents witnesses who are cross-examined. Fourth, the parties move that exhibits, or documents of various kinds, be submitted into the record; there are challenges and some are admitted, others excluded. Fifth, each party submits a proposed finding of facts based upon the record and conclusions of law. Sixth, the hearing examiner writes a decision passing judgment on the facts, the law, and the law as applied to the facts. The recommended decision of the hearing examiner may be appealed to an appeal board. Seventh, a final decision in the case is made by the presiding authority of the agency (which at the FCC consists of a seven member board of presidentially appointed commissioners). These are the basic steps in a hearing procedure. The current case did not progress beyond step four, at which point a settlement was reached, over two years after the case had been opened.

From the outset the Administrative Law Judge, Frederick Denniston, instructed the parties to pursue informal negotiations to obtain information necessary for discovery. It is often tactically advantageous for parties in a litigation effort to fight discovery either by denying the opponent information vital to the case or by delaying the orderly progression of the proceeding. In the present case, however, dis-

6 FCC, Memorandum Opinion and Order, Docket No. 19143, January 21, 1971, p. 5.

covery was successfully obtained through informal negotiations completed in February 1971. It was agreed that, by June 1, AT&T would turn over a list of documents and respond to a set of interrogatories requested by the EEOC. Statistical data covering AT&T's workforce in thirty selected standard metropolitan statistical areas (SMSA's) detailing their employees' sex, race, job title, and department were also to be provided the EEOC by July 1. The EEOC, in turn, was to provide AT&T access to its case file consisting of the outstanding charges and all investigative and research reports on the Bell companies. In addition the EEOC was to prepare by June 1971 a preliminary finding of facts outlining the strength of the agency's evidence alleging Title VII violations on the part of AT&T.

In April 1971 the EEOC established a special task force to handle what was to become the largest, and perhaps the most important, case in the history of the agency. The special task force was headed by David Copus, along with Lawrence Gartner, from the EEOC's General Counsel's Office, Randall Speck from the Office of Compliance, and William Wallace from the Office of Research. Substantive support was provided the task force mainly by a small group of university social scientists who functioned as an advisory panel and appeared as witnesses. This group was established in July 1971. Primary responsibility for preparing AT&T's case was assumed by Bell System attorneys George Ashley and Harold Levy. Counsel for AT&T was also provided by attorney Thompson Powers, of the Washington law firm of Steptoe and Johnson, who had served briefly as the first executive director of the EEOC.

On April 15, 1971, the EEOC filed a "prehearing memorandum" in the case outlining its position on the law of employment discrimination.[7] The memorandum emphasized the importance of combatting institutionalized practices which result in systemic discrimination against minorities and women. It directed particular attention to practices within the Bell System which, although applied impartially, tended to have an adverse affect on minorities and women. The memorandum also emphasized then-current practices at Bell which perpetuated the effects of prior discriminatory policies. The two major thrusts in the EEOC's interpretation of Title VII law as applied to the case entered on: (1) employment practices which have a disparate affect on minorities and women and which cannot be defended on grounds of business necessity; and (2) practices which perpetuate the effect of past discriminatory conditions, irrespective of whether the previous acts of discrimination occurred before the passage of the Civil Rights Act of 1964.

The EEOC also held that the law provided whatever remedy the situation required "to effectively terminate the practice and to make the victims whole." The document listed examples of common, but allegedly illegal, employment practices in the area of recruitment, hiring standards, job assignment (including the notion of

7 EEOC, Prehearing Memorandum, Docket No. 19143, April 15, 1971.

the restrictive "bona fide occupational qualification"), promotion and transfer, and terms and conditions of employment. The EEOC concluded that in the course of the hearing it would attempt to evaluate AT&T's employment practices in the context of the legal interpretations presented in the memorandum.

AT&T's official response to the EEOC's prehearing memorandum stated, essentially, that the EEOC's interpretations went beyond established law and represented how it would like the law to read rather than its actual state. The company contended that the major issue to be resolved was whether the Bell System was making a good-faith effort to meet the requirements of the law.

While the hearings progressed through the spring and summer of 1971, an important development took place behind the scenes. In August the EEOC and AT&T began to negotiate privately in an attempt to initiate an out-of-court settlement of the case. Representatives of the two groups met on a weekly basis to present and discuss proposals and counterproposals on ways to resolve the dispute. AT&T's representatives at these meetings were Harold Levy and Lee Saterfield, both AT&T attorneys, and John Kingsbury, Vice President for Personnel. The EEOC was represented by David Copus, director of the special AT&T task force, Charles Wilson, Chief of the Office of Conciliations, and John Pemberton, Jr., Deputy General Counsel. The two parties thus initiated informal as well as formal proceedings to reach a settlement of their differences.

The formal hearings were scheduled to begin on December 1, 1971, with the presentation of evidence by the EEOC. Prior to the opening of the proceedings the EEOC released a report that summarized its case against AT&T. The title for the EEOC report, *"A Unique Competence": A Study of Equal Employment Opportunity in the Bell System*, was culled from a statement by AT&T Vice President Walter Straley in 1968, "We think our experience as an employer, hiring some 200,000 persons each year, provides us with a unique competence to play a leading role in the improvement of employment opportunity." (This report is summarized in Chapter 12, which deals with the perspective of the federal compliance agencies.) The primary thrust of the EEOC's case was based upon allegations of sex discrimination. However, because of the high correlation between sex and income, jobs, and departmental organization in the Bell System, an analysis of employment patterns by sex also produces important implications regarding the position of blacks and Hispanics since the vast majority of the company's minority employees are females.

December 1971 was important for another reason. The Office of Federal Contract Compliance (OFCC) of the US Department of Labor issued Revised Order No. 4, which for the first time required affirmative action plans to specify goals and timetables for the hiring and promotion of female as well as minority employees. Thus the AT&T now had to submit to the OFCC information on the utilization of its female workforce and plans for ways to correct any deficiencies.

This issue became a critical one in both the private negotiations and in the formal hearings on the AT&T case. By mid-January 1972, however, the negotiations were discontinued because of major differences between the parties over back pay to women and minority employees of AT&T. The EEOC had estimated nearly $175 million was necessary in back pay to fully rectify its allegations of discrimination.

Other issues raised in these private sessions included sex-stereotyping in AT&T's recruitment advertising, the level and timing of the hiring and promotion of minorities and women in each occupation (and also including the hiring of males into operator positions), and the terms and conditions under which minorities and women would be allowed to transfer to jobs with better career opportunities without jeopardizing their seniority rights.

Despite the discontinuation of the negotiations, the hearings continued, and on January 31, 1972, AT&T began its cross-examination of EEOC's witnesses.[8] The company challenged 3500 summaries presented as exhibits by EEOC of AT&T documents purporting to represent evidence of discriminatory behavior. The hearing examiner instructed the two parties to reach agreements on suitable summaries for each of the documents. This task was not completed before the case was settled.

Meanwhile in the late winter of 1972 the EEOC inadvertently discovered that AT&T had submitted an affirmative action plan to the General Services Administration (GSA) as required under OFCC's Revised Order No. 4. This agency served as the compliance agency for the telephone company under the regulations of the OFCC. GSA officials provided the EEOC a copy of the affirmative action plan and assured the latter that the plan would not be approved without further consultation with them.

Also during the spring of 1972, the Mexican American Legal Defense Fund (MALDF) and the California Rural Legal Assistance (CRLA) requested and were granted the opportunity to present witnesses in the case. Because of the difficulties of scheduling such witnesses for a Washington session, the hearings were transported to Los Angeles and San Francisco. From April 17 through April 21, grassroots

8 The following witnesses presented testimony on behalf of the EEOC. General background testimony on employment discrimination: Judith Long Laws, Assistant Professor of Sociology and Psychology, Cornell University; Bernard Anderson, Associate Professor of Economics, Wharton School, University of Pennsylvania. Testing: Felix M. Lopez, Jr., Managing Partner, Felix M. Lopez & Associates, and Adjunct Professor of Organizational Behavior, Long Island University; William H. Enneis, Staff Psychologist, Office of Research, EEOC; Philip Ash, Professor of Psychology, University of Illinois at Chicago Circle. Socio-economic issues: Ronald Oaxaca, Assistant Professor of Economics, University of Massachusetts at Amherst; Orley Ashenfelter, Professor of Economics, Princeton University. Recruitment: Sandra Bem, Assistant Professor of Psychology, and Daryl Bem, Associate Professor of Psychology, Stanford University; Suzan B. Leake, Placement Officer, Simmons College. Maternity leave: Robert H. Barter, M.D., Professor of Obstetrics and Gynecology, George Washington University School of Medicine; Andre E. Hellegers, M.D., Professor of Obstetrics and Gynecology, and Director of Population Research, Georgetown University. Employees: Lorena Weeks and Helen Roig.

testimony was obtained from witnesses who discussed their experiences as applicants or employees of the Bell System. Most of the testimony was concerned with the treatment of Chicanos and Asian-Americans by the Pacific Telephone and Telegraph Co.

The Center for United Labor Action requested that the hearings be held in New York City so that witnesses from that area could also be heard. From May 8 to 12, field hearings were held in New York. Testimony was taken from representatives of the black and Spanish communities, women's groups and other organizations, such as the Center for United Labor Action and the Suburban Action Institute. The Suburban Action Institute opposed the relocation of AT&T's headquarters from downtown New York to suburban Basking Ridge, New Jersey. Spokesmen for the nonprofit group presented evidence which showed that poor accessibility and restrictive zoning laws which severely limited the availability of low and moderate income housing at Basking Ridge adversely affected the opportunity for black and Hispanic workers to either retain or obtain jobs at the new suburban site.

Individual witnesses were also heard. In a move to protect witnesses it planned to present at the New York hearings, the FCC sought and obtained a protective order for witnesses who were current employees of AT&T. The Hearing Examiner directed the company to notify him fifteen days prior to either firing or suspending the pay of any of its employees who testified at the hearings. The directive protected AT&T employees from retaliation by the company for evidence volunteered in the case. One final set of field hearings was held in Washington, D.C., from June 5 to 9. Again testimony was taken from individuals and representatives from various interested groups. One of the more important organizations presenting evidence was the National Organization for Women (NOW).

Following a month and a half break, AT&T presented its case on August 1, 1972. The essential elements of AT&T's position were incorporated in the testimony of John W. Kingsbury, Assistant Vice President for Human Resources Development.[9] The company's witnesses presented testimony addressing issues such as the significance of the operator and craft jobs at Bell; a review of employee benefits and leaves of absence policy; a response to the Suburban Action Institute's testimony regarding the transfer of AT&T's headquarters out of New York City; relevant bases for comparing the participation rates of women and minority employees; employee testing; and AT&T's outreach efforts with hardcore unemployed workers.[10] Testimony was also presented by representatives of each of the twenty-four individual Bell operating companies.

9 Testimony of John W. Kingsbury, FCC Docket No. 19143 (August 1, 1972), p. 3.
10 The following witnesses presented testimony for AT&T. Affirmative action: John W. Kingsbury, Assistant Vice President, Human Resources Development; Robert W. Ferguson, Assistant Vice President, Operations-Traffic; Joe H. Hunt, Assistant Vice President, Operations-Plant; Therese F. Pick, Employee Benefits Secretary; Stanley L. King, Jr., Assistant Vice

Just prior to the cross-examination of AT&T's witnesses, in September 1972, the GSA informed the EEOC that it had approved AT&T's affirmative action plan and would officially announce its decision on the following day. The acceptance of AT&T's affirmative action plan had not been made with the concurrence of the EEOC. If the affirmative action plan were accepted as meeting the requirements of OFCC's revised Order No. 4, AT&T could then state that in the opinion of its federal contract overseeing agency it was in compliance with the law.

The EEOC had not been given advance notice that an agreement was pending. One of the signatories to the agreement for AT&T had only three days earlier contacted Chairman Brown of the EEOC on the possibility of reopening the negotiations but had failed to mention the pending agreement with GSA.[11]

The EEOC filed a list of twenty-two complaints against the agreement. Equally forceful opposition was voiced by the NAACP, NOW, MALDF, and other civil rights groups. Finally the EEOC complained to the Solicitor of the Department of Labor—the agency which has primary responsibility for the federal contract compliance program—about the agreement and the manner in which it was handled. Major objections were raised by the EEOC over the methodology used to calculate the goals and timetables used in the plan. The transfer procedures designed to provide opportunities for minorities and women to move into more desirable jobs were deemed inadequate in light of the existing discriminatory patterns. No attempt had been made to identify "affected classes," and thus the whole issue of back pay had been avoided. The agreement also did not deal with the issue of testing. After reviewing the case, the Office of the Solicitor concluded that GSA had not acted in the best interests of the program, and decided to assume jurisdiction in the matter.

Shortly after these actions, the negotiations were resumed, and the Department of Labor (parent organization of the OFCC) participated as a third party in the discussions. Negotiating teams from AT&T, EEOC, and the Labor Department met weekly;[12] at the same time that AT&T, EEOC, and the FCC pressed forward in the

President, Human Resources Development, AT&T. Evaluation of EEOC's case: Hugh Folk, Professor of Economics, University of Illinois at Urbana-Champaign; Nathan Glazer, Professor of Education and Social Structure, Harvard Graduate School; Lewis J. Perl, Assistant Professor of Economics, Cornell University. Employment testing: Robert M. Guion, Professor of Psychology, Bowling Green State University; Brent Baxter, Vice President, American Institutes for Research; Douglas W. Bray, Director, Management Selection and Development Research, AT&T; Donald L. Grant, Personnel Manager, AT&T. Employee training programs: Jules Cohn, Professor of Political Science, City University of New York; Louis K. O'Leary, Assistant Vice President, Human Resources Development, AT&T. Sex discrimination: Leona E. Tyler, Dean Emeritus, Graduate School, University of Oregon; Valerie Kincade Oppenheimer, Research Sociologist, Department of Sociology, University of California.

11 Interview with David Copus, February 20, 1973.

12 The following negotiators represented the three parties in the renewed round of discussions. EEOC: David Copus, Charles Wilson, and Jack Pemberton, Jr. AT&T: Thompson Powers, Clark Reddick, Daniel Davis, and Lee Satterfield. DOL: (OFCC) Solicitor Richard F. Schubert, William Kilberg, and Ronald Green; (Equal Pay Act) Carin Clauss and Karl Heckman.

hearings. On October 30, 1972, the government began its cross-examination of AT&T's witnesses.

The Settlement

On the negotiating front, the inclusion of the Labor Department in the discussions became a major turning point in the case. The outcry over the premature GSA accord with AT&T brought the government's forces together. The Labor Department negotiating team, therefore, represented the OFCC and the Wage and Hour Administration, with the latter responsible for the administration of the Equal Pay Act.

One charge of violation of Title VII, Executive Order 11246, and the Equal Pay Act was related to the job category "frameman," which was primarily a male job in all of Bell's operating companies except Michigan Bell. At that company the job was titled "switchroom helper," and was primarily a female job.

Another charge under the Equal Pay Act dealt with the method that the Bell System used to determine wage rates after an employee had been promoted. The promotion pay scales were calculated so that employees obtaining promotions to a particular position from "male jobs" received greater benefits than those transferred or promoted to the same position from "female jobs" at Bell.

As the case neared settlement, the cross-examination of AT&T's witnesses progressed and the negotiators attempted to resolve their differences. The hearing recessed for the Christmas holiday and was scheduled to resume on January 15, 1971. The negotiations were continued, and on January 14 the Hearing Examiner was requested to postpone the resumption of the hearings because it appeared that an agreement had been reached. Finally, on January 18, the historic settlement was announced. The agreement was carried before the US District Court for the Eastern District of Pennsylvania with Judge Leon A. Higginbotham, Jr., presiding. At that time charges had been filed against the company in three federal jurisdictions, New York City, Philadelphia, and Washington. The company selected Philadelphia as the court to file the Consent Decree. The Consent Decree was handed down by the court on January 18, 1973. The comprehensive agreement and consent decree are discussed in chapter 13.

12 Equal Employment Opportunity

Phyllis A. Wallace

At the beginning of the administrative proceedings in 1970, the EEOC and the AT&T held divergent views on the meaning of equal employment opportunity. The same records, materials, and information were available to both sides. The EEOC emphasized the consequences of past actions of exclusion, segregation, sex-stereotyping, and the adverse impact on minorities of tests and other personnel assessment techniques. The AT&T tended to highlight past achievements in reducing racial discrimination and the progress made by the company since 1965, with certain notable gains in 1968–1970. The two perspectives are reviewed in this chapter.

A primary reason for filing the charge with the FCC was that in 1970 the EEOC lacked enforcement powers, and as the FCC regulations were comparable to Title VII one could test employment discrimination laws in a new arena—administrative litigation before a regulatory agency. A second and sometimes overlooked reason was that the EEOC was overwhelmed with a large backlog of cases. Since AT&T accounted for five to six percent of all such charges pending before EEOC, the hearing may be viewed as a cost-effective technique of reducing the backlog. The consent decree model could be applied on a system-wide or national scale to other industries. Negotiations between the interested groups might prove far less costly for all parties.

The major differences in the AT&T case were resolved as a result of the public hearings and the private negotiations. In addition to the series of meetings at the working level, William H. Brown, III, Chairman of EEOC, and Robert Lilley, President of AT&T, met frequently to resolve problems that arose from the private negotiating sessions.[1]

Perspective of Federal Compliance Agencies

In December 1971, one year after the petition had been made to block granting of a rate increase to AT&T because of alleged unlawful employment practices, the EEOC released its analysis and summary of its investigation. This report, *"A Unique Competence": A Study of Equal Employment Opportunity in the Bell System*, presented the EEOC's case alleging nationwide patterns of employment discrimination by the Bell System on the basis of sex, race, and national origin.

The eleven chapters of *A Unique Competence* and an additional 500 pages of charts and tables relied heavily on the statistics and data provided by AT&T as evidentiary materials. A detailed analysis of the characteristics of the Bell System was made for thirty Standard Metropolitan Statistical Areas (SMSA's) with the largest

1 In an attempt to gain some perspective on the high level private negotiations I was able to talk with the senior EEOC official but not with the senior AT&T official.

number of minorities. These SMSA's accounted for half of the nation's work force, half of the total black population, and half of the Hispanic population. At the end of 1970, the Bell employment in these thirty areas totaled 374,190—or more than half of all persons employed by the operating companies (See Tables 12.1, 12.2).

Women Workers

A Unique Competence reported:

1. Sex segregation of jobs and departments was extensive. In the thirty SMSA's included in the study, 92.4 percent of all employees in major jobs were concentrated in classifications filled by 90 percent or more of the same sex. Almost every major low-paying job in the Bell System was a "female" job.

Operator, plant and Accounting Department clerical jobs, Service Representative, inside sales jobs in the Commercial and Marketing Departments, and first level management jobs in the Traffic and Commercial Departments [were identified as female jobs]. Craft jobs, outside sales jobs, and middle and upper level management jobs were always identified as male jobs.[2]

2. Whether or not the operating companies claimed a bona fide occupational qualification (BFOQ) as the reason for sex-segregation of jobs was not important. Females were consistently excluded from "male" jobs, and males were excluded from "female" jobs. (See discussion in Chapter 7 of this volume.)

3. Bell's employment practices (recruitment, hiring, and promotion) restricted opportunities for women. Sex-stereotyping of jobs was reinforced by the dual recruitment systems for females and males, sex-typing of advertisements, and the processing of males and females through separate employment channels with dual employment criteria.

4. Sex-stereotyping of jobs and departments inhibited equal opportunity between the sexes for promotion to better-paying positions in both nonmanagement and management ranks. (See Table 12.3 for summary of female participation in the Bell System).

There (were) five basic obstacles to female progress in Bell's promotion system: (1) obscure, informal procedures, (2) sex-segregated lines of progression, (3) departmental seniority, (4) restricted transfer to entry level jobs, and (5) unreachable standards for promotion to "male" jobs.[3]

Although one-third of all managers in the Bell System [were] females, the vast majority of them (94 percent) [were] in the lowest level of the managerial ranks. For male managers, half of whom are second level or above, the beginning management jobs [were] only stepping stones to better positions with greater responsibility. For women, the initial and ultimate positions [were] identical.[4] [See Chapter 7 of this volume.]

2 EEOC, *"A Unique Competence": A Study of Equal Employment Opportunity in the Bell System,* November 1971, p. 36.
3 *Ibid,* p. 128.
4 *Ibid,* p. 153.

Table 12.1   Bell Employment in 30 SMSA's (Dec. 31, 1970)

Standard Metropolitan Statistical Area	Bell Employment	Black	Hispanic
1. New York	82,380	19,904	2,645
2. Los Angeles	35,344	4,478	2,564
3. Chicago	34,380	5,227	324
4. San Francisco	26,903	2,262	1,118
5. Philadelphia	19,844	2,648	34
6. Detroit	18,946	3,391	59
7. Washington, D. C.	17,046	3,571	12
8. Newark	12,818	2,132	166
9. Cleveland	11,081	1,847	13
10. St. Louis	10,015	1,064	18
11. Atlanta	10,010	1,301	6
12. Miami	9,458	957	480
13. Baltimore	8,867	1,425	1
14. Houston	8,147	1,224	332
15. Denver	8,129	276	409
16. Dallas	7,795	874	108
17. San Diego	7,358	332	352
18. Indianapolis	6,007	613	2
19. Phoenix	5,792	193	237
20. New Orleans	5,133	664	7
21. Kansas City	4,988	537	60
22. Birmingham	4,409	513	1
23. Richmond	4,008	642	--
24. Jacksonville	3,678	319	2
25. San Antonio	3,249	135	678
26. Norfolk	2,261	159	--
27. Memphis	2,135	274	1
28. Greensboro-Winston-Salem	1,759	263	--
29. Mobile	1,192	72	--
30. El Paso	1,058	38	191
Total (30 SMSA's)	374,190	57,335	9,820

Source: EEOC C-661 - EEOC C-690

Table 12.2   Total Employment by Selected Bell Company (1970)

Company	Male Employment	Female Employment	Total
Bell Telephone Co. of Penna	15,492	18,801	34,293
Chesapeake and Potomac (D.C.)	4,001	5,024	9,025
Chesapeake and Potomac (Md.)	6,919	8,011	14,930
Chesapeake and Potomac (Va.)	6,276	7,774	14,050
Chesapeake and Potomac (W. Va.)	2,292	2,830	5,122
Diamond State (Pa.)	942	843	1,785
Illinois Bell Telephone Co.	20,064	21,843	41,907
Indiana Bell Telephone	5,009	5,661	10,670
Michigan Bell Telephone Co.	13,473	15,861	29,334
Mountain States Telephone & Telegraph	14,199	18,261	32,460
New England Telephone & Telegraph	20,746	22,700	43,446
New Jersey Bell Telephone Co.	13,662	16,096	29,758
New York Telephone Co.	47,614	54,322	101,936
Northwestern Bell Telephone Co.	11,757	14,864	26,621
Ohio Bell Telephone Co.	12,904	14,381	27,285
Pacific Telephone & Telegraph	40,980	57,709	98,689
Pacific Northwest Bell	8,416	9,999	18,415
South Central Bell Telephone Co.	18,320	26,399	44,719
Southern Bell Telephone & Telegraph	24,585	35,056	59,641
Southwestern Bell Telephone	29,439	40,602	70,041
Wisconsin Telephone Co.	5,252	6,183	11,435
Total	322,342	403,220	725,562

Source: Exhibit 1:   Charts and Tables, p. 456.   Excludes Cincinnati
Bell, The Southern New England Telephone Co. and Long Lines, and AT&T
administration.

Table 12.3 Summary of Female Participation in the Bell System (Dec. 31, 1970)

	Total Employment		Female Employment		Percent Female
Officials and Managers	88,301		36,295		41.1
Professionals	58,756		12,051		20.5
Technicians	4,791		3,052		63.7
Sales Workers	12,113		3,168		26.2
Mgmt.		5,814		661	11.4
Non-mgmt.		6,299		2,507	39.8
Office and Clerical	359,119		348,071		96.9
Secretaries (Mgmt.)		4,929		4,919	99.8
Clerical and Stenog.		141,394		131,677	93.1
Telephone Operators		165,372		165,148	99.9
Supvs./Serv. Assts.		13,440		13,437	100.0
Service Repres.		33,093		32,740	98.9
Other Bus. Off. Empls.		891		150	16.8
Craft Workers	192,328		2,120		1.1
Operatives	7,437		119		1.6
Service Workers	9,605		4,648		48.4
Total	732,450		409,524		55.9

Source: EEOC W-659

5. Even when women were promoted (changed wage schedules) their new wage rates were based on their lower previous wage. The sizeable difference between actual wages and expected wages had male wage criteria been applied to women, has been a source of difficulty with the pay-adjustments model during the first year of the affirmative action plan. (See Chapter 13.)

Black Employees

In addition, the EEOC report reviewed the historical exclusion and segregation of blacks in the Bell System. The research of Bernard Anderson was utilized for this analysis. (See Chapter 8 for recent research findings by Professor Anderson. See also Table 12.4.)

Since most blacks in the Bell System were females (mainly operators) they suffered a dual handicap of both race and sex.

Table 12.4　Summary of Black Participation in the Bell System (Dec. 31, 1970)

	Total Employment		Black Employment		Percent Black	
Officials and Managers	88,301		2,493		2.8	
Professionals	58,756		950		1.6	
Technicians	4,791		269		5.6	
Sales Workers	12,113		404		3.3	
Mgmt.		5,814		114		2.0
Non-Mgmt.		6,299		290		4.6
Office and Clerical	359,119		53,765		15.0	
Secretaries (Mgmt.)		4,929		139		2.8
Clerical and Stenog.		141,394		17,309		12.2
Telephone Operators		165,372		31,638		19.1
Supvs./Serv. Assts.		13,440		2,031		15.1
Service Repres.		33,093		2,583		7.8
Other Bus. Off. Empls.		891		65		7.3
Craftsmen	192,328		8,823		4.6	
Operatives	7,437		1,851		24.9	
Service Workers	9,605		3,585		37.3	
Total	732,450		72,140		9.8	

Source:　EEOC W-659

Of 72,000 blacks employed in the System (at the end of 1970) 79 percent were female, while only 53 percent of the white employees were female. In no company were more than 57.6 percent of the white employees female, while in five companies at least 80 percent of the black workers were female.[5]

The relative exclusion of black males from craft jobs in the operating companies was more restrictive than the employment pattern for other companies in the Bell service areas. Although the number of black males in this occupation in the Bell System had doubled between 1968 and 1971, the relative share was still less than five percent of what was a predominantly male area. The number of black males had increased from 5,347 in 1968 to 10,801 in 1971. However, most were still concentrated in the bottom jobs in this occupation.

Few blacks worked as managers in the Bell System, even in those operating companies with good hiring records. As of December 31, 1970, blacks held 2.8 percent

5 *Ibid,* p. 222.

of management jobs in the System nationwide. Table 12.5 shows that for the thirty SMSA's the proportion of blacks in management was slightly higher at 3.4 percent. The entry points for management were craft occupations or college graduates directly hired into management. Blacks were not well represented in either of these "relevant" labor pools. Despite the fact that over a third of all blacks working in the operating companies of the thirty SMSA's were employed in New York and accounted for almost a quarter of all employees, their participation was only 6 percent of all managers. *A Unique Competence* also commented on salary disparities for blacks:

In the 30 SMSA's at the end of 1970, 78.7 percent of all black employees were in jobs paying a maximum basic annual wage of $7,000 or less; only 39.5 percent of all white employees were in jobs having such a low salary.[6]

Hispanics

The Hispanics were described as the "invisible minority" in the Bell System. In none of the twelve SMSA's which had a substantial Hispanic population was their employment by the operating companies at rates near their representation in the work force. See Table 12.2.

Preemployment criteria (paper credentials, test scores, etc.) tended to screen out a disproportionate number of minorities. Chapters 9 and 10 in this volume treat these issues.

Other Testimony

A Unique Competence spelled out in great detail the EEOC position of alleging pervasive and systemic discrimination within the Bell System by sex, race, and national origin. Expert witnesses testified on the economic, psychological, and social aspects of employment discrimination in regulated industries such as the telephone industry. Many of these statements have now been revised and are included in this volume.

The Company Perspective

In August 1972, more than a year and a half after the Federal Communications Commission agreed to hear the case, AT&T presented its testimony. The essential elements of the AT&T position were incorporated in the testimony of its lead witness, John W. Kingsbury, Assistant Vice President for Human Resources Development. A memorandum entitled *The Bell Companies as Equal Employers: A Record of Achievement, A Commitment to Progress* accompanied the Kingsbury materials. In addition, a number of expert witnesses and representatives from the twenty-four Bell operating companies testified. These documents, along with the affirmative action and upgrade and

6 *Ibid*, p. 239

Table 12.5   Blacks in Management (1970)

SMSA	Total Management	Black				
		Management	Level 1	Level 2	Level 3	Above Level 3
Atlanta	2,449	25	25	–	–	–
Baltimore	1,892	66	65	1	–	–
Birmingham	1,304	4	4	–	–	–
Chicago	8,269	390	363	17	9	1
Cleveland	2,933	133	115	16	1	1
Dallas	1,393	9	8	1	–	–
Denver	2,205	22	19	3	–	–
Detroit	4,351	210	199	9	1	1
El Paso	173	1	1	–	–	–
Greensboro	280	1	1	–	–	–
Houston	1,393	20	19	1	–	–
Indianapolis	1,632	44	41	2	1	–
Jacksonville	927	2	2	–	–	–
Kansas City	884	9	9	–	–	–
Los Angeles	7,710	238	215	20	3	–
Memphis	312	2	2	–	–	–
Miami	1,760	4	4	–	–	–
Mobile	180	–	–	–	–	–
New Orleans	1,095	13	13	–	–	–
New York	19,280	1,165	1,123	37	4	1
Newark	3,359	86	71	13	1	1
Norfolk	311	2	2	–	–	–
Philadelphia	4,453	111	100	9	1	1
Phoenix	1,139	5	4	1	–	–
Richmond	1,124	13	11	2	–	–
St. Louis	2,280	29	29	–	–	–
San Antonio	689	4	4	–	–	–
San Diego	1,850	18	15	3	–	–
San Francisco	6,940	157	144	13	–	–
Washington	4,034	178	171	5	1	1
30 SMSA Totals	86,601	2,961	2,779	153	22	7

Source: EEOC Exhibit 1, Charts and Tables, pp. 393–423.

transfer plans that were developed by a special task force of company managers, presented the salient issues of the AT&T position.

Kingsbury testified that the Bell System, as well as all American industry, should be unequivocally committed to the elimination of discrimination on the basis of race, religion, sex or national origin in its employment policies. Furthermore, he noted that the Bell companies (as all employers, including the federal government) still had much progress to make in eliminating discrimination.

Kingsbury strongly disagreed, however, with the EEOC's allegations of past discrimination, and noted that the EEOC had consistently asked the FCC to measure the Bell System's past policies and actions by 1971 standards. Since the passage of the Civil Rights Act of 1964, the definitions of discrimination had changed considerably. Examples of this were the legality of state protective laws for women workers and the impact of Title VII on sex-segregated help-wanted newspaper advertising. Although the requirement that federal contractors take affirmative action to insure against sex discrimination was imposed in October 1968 (Executive Order 11375), specific regulations including the setting of goals and timetables for women (Revised Order No. 4) were not forthcoming until December 4, 1971.

Contrary to the charges made by the EEOC, AT&T denied that their system discriminated against qualified applicants. The Company maintained that the EEOC sought to have Bell lower its standards in order to admit women and minorities into the better jobs. The utility insisted that the standards the operating companies employed were necessary to provide efficient and economical service to their customers.

Furthermore, in its zeal in trying this case against the Bell System, the EEOC has failed to recognize that the primary reason that the Bell System exists is to provide communications service to the American public, not merely to provide employment to all comers, regardless of ability. We cannot ignore our responsibility to continue to provide good communications services at the lowest reasonable cost. If the Bell companies were to act upon the EEOC's contention that they should require less skills or abilities of those whom they hire, it would be difficult to continue to provide quality service. By its very nature ours is a business with many technically oriented jobs. If the people filling those jobs are not qualified to perform adequately, the communications services we provide will reflect it.

The EEOC argues that we should be able to continue to provide our companies with qualified employees by imparting all the necessary skills and abilities in our training programs. What the EEOC fails to recognize is that unless we maintain relevant hiring standards our training costs would soar astronomically and these costs would necessarily be passed on to our customers. For example, adding one day to our current training program for operators would cost an additional $1.4 million a year. The EEOC has made its arguments with no regard for cost and service.

In addition, in some of our job categories there are very real obstacles that stand in the way of providing immediate employment to anybody who has not gained necessary experience in entry-level jobs—obstacles which the EEOC refuses to recognize. These are the technically oriented higher craft jobs which have traditionally been held by men. These jobs involve such responsibilities as installing and repairing complex PBX facilities and necessarily must be filled from the lower craft jobs. Thus, until significant numbers of interested women can be brought into these lower level craft jobs it is not realistic to talk in terms of filling the higher level craft jobs with significant numbers of women immediately.

A significant number of our salaried and management jobs require engineering background. Traditionally, few minorities or women have studied engineering. For example, over 99 percent of the degrees awarded in engineering in 1969 were to males. In 1971 blacks received less than one percent of the B.S. degrees awarded in the field. Thus, until our engineering schools are graduating significantly more minorities and women the relevant labor market for engineers will continue to be almost exclusively white and male.

Thus it should be clear that our hiring and promotion of women and minorities is not done in a homogeneous society as portrayed by the EEOC's statisticians. We must necessarily hire and promote all kinds of people—people from all educational levels, people with definite job preferences.[7]

Past Efforts and Achievement

Kingsbury noted that the Bell System had made earnest efforts to contribute to the national goal of equal employment opportunity. He cited Bell's participation in Plans for Progress, a program emphasizing affirmative action to increase employment opportunities for minorities. Also, the company participated in the National Alliance of Businessmen (NAB) and its allied program, Job Opportunities in the Business Sector (JOBS). Over 17,000 disadvantaged persons were employed by Bell, and, of these, 76 percent were black and 11 percent were Spanish surnamed.

In an attempt to reach more minorities outside the program focusing on the disadvantaged, Kingsbury noted that the companies undertook special recruiting efforts to reach minorities, such as advertising in the minority media, recruiting at predominantly black schools, maintaining partnership arrangements with high schools having a high minority enrollment, and participating in work-study arrangements.

Kingsbury cited remarks made at a recent AT&T annual meeting by the president of AT&T, Robert D. Lilley:

We believe our record shows that we have been a leader among institutions in the effort to promote equal opportunity. We were in the vanguard of those who first came forth to cooperate with and endorse programs at various levels of government to encourage opportunities for minorities.

We are realistic enough, however, to realize that times and conditions do change. The emphasis in the past has been on minorities. Now we are witnessing a significant evolution both in the status and the aspirations of women. I am confident we will meet this new challenge.

In short, our policy has always been right and clear: to treat every employee with dignity; to extend to every employee the fullest measure of opportunity. The programs we're evolving now are designed to assure in very specific ways that that policy will be implemented to the extent that it is humanly possible to do so in a business of this size.[8]

7 Testimony of John W. Kingsbury, FCC Docket No. 19143 (August 1, 1972), pp. 3–5.
8 *Ibid,* p. 13.

Overview of the Data

Kingsbury reviewed statistics mainly on new hires to indicate the results of equal employment efforts by the Bell companies from 1965 to 1971. Hire rates for minorities and women in certain occupations had to be high initially to increase their proportions in these occupations. During 1969–1971 minorities accounted for about one-quarter of all new Bell Company hires.

Other data from the appendices to Kingsbury's testimony showed levels of employment by sex and minority group during this period (see Table 12.6). For example, women increased more than seven-fold in the craftsmen category between 1965 and 1971, yet they still made up only a little more than one percent of all craftsmen. In 1971, there were 215,841 male craftsmen employed by Bell, and 2,971 female craftsmen. It is indeed true that it takes time to change sex and minority ratios in a company where more than half the employees were hired prior to 1964.

Affirmative Action Steps

Kingsbury cited as examples of affirmative action steps:

1. Development during the late 1960s of urban orientation training programs to assist management in the assimilation and supervision of newly hired employees previously classified as "disadvantaged";
2. A special task force that examined the utilization of women in Bell System management positions was established at the beginning of 1970;
3. Compliance reviews as an ongoing internal activity which examined the companies' application of various personnel practices;
4. The companies' evolving response to state protective laws and the Bona Fide Occupational Qualification (BFOQ) provision in Title VII
5. The development of special programs to improve the employability and utilization of Spanish-surnamed Americans;
6. An innovative effort of "Early Identification" of potential to accelerate the upward mobility of minority and female employees;
7. The job enrichment programs aimed at improving the quality and worth of Bell System jobs.[9]

Kingsbury stated that a Bell task force had analyzed the sex and race profile of the present employee work force for some fifteen major job categories and determined the number of job openings expected in 1972 and the next five years for each of these categories. The company examined the labor market that would supply the people to fill those jobs, and established numerical goals for women and minorities.[10]

---

9 *Ibid*, p. 120.
10 *Ibid*, pp. 151–55.

Table 12.6 Bell System Employment, by Occupation (1968, 1971)

	Total	Male	Female	Female Percent of Total
Total employment				
1968	697,620	307,690	389,930	55.9
1971	795,992	370,062	425,930	53.5
Officials and Managers				
1968	81,758	48,491	33,267	40.7
1971	97,712	58,829	38,883	39.8
Professionals				
1968	55,285	44,635	10,650	19.3
1971	70,098	55,379	14,179	20.2
Technicians				
1968	7,082	4,152	2,930	41.4
1971	7,838	4,141	3,697	47.2
Sales Workers				
1968	11,447	8,987	2,460	21.5
1971	13,760	10,281	3,479	25.3
Office and Clerical				
1968	345,049	10,941	334,108	96.8
1971	369,542	12,419	357,123	96.6
Craftsmen (skilled)				
1968	179,953	178,774	1,179	0.7
1971	218,812	215,841	2,971	1.4
Operative (semi-skilled)				
1968	6,545	6,485	60	0.9
1971	7,921	7,773	148	1.9
Service Workers				
1968	10,497	5,221	5,276	50.3
1971	10,308	5,398	4,910	47.6

Source: Appendices Kingsbury Testimony, Tables 6-13.

Table 12.6   Continued

	Nonwhite [a]	Nonwhite Male	Nonwhite Female	Nonwhite Percent of Total
Total employment				
1968	57,425	11,462	45,963	8.2
1971	83,999	19,706	64,293	10.6
Officials and Managers				
1968	1,373	258	1,115	1.7
1971	3,526	867	2,659	3.6
Professionals				
1968	616	325	291	1.1
1971	1,610	855	755	2.3
Technicians				
1968	238	99	139	3.4
1971	504	199	305	6.4
Sales Workers				
1968	309	162	147	2.7
1971	633	312	321	4.6
Office and Clerical				
1968	43,545	1,005	42,540	12.6
1971	59,988	1,575	58,413	16.2
Craftsmen (skilled)				
1968	5,861	5,725	136	3.3
1971	11,866	11,607	259	5.4
Operative (semi-skilled)				
1968	1,561	1,557	4	23.9
1971	2,073	2,048	25	26.2
Service Workers				
1968	3,919	2,328	1,591	37.3
1971	3,798	2,242	1,556	36.8

[a] Includes Blacks, Orientals, American Indians.

The AT&T's model affirmative action program and transfer and upgrade plan were submitted to the Administrative Law Judge conducting the public hearing in April 1972. Many of the provisions of these plans were later incorporated in the memorandum of agreement signed in January 1973.

Upgrade and Transfer Plan

To insure continued progress in providing better opportunities for women and minorities, AT&T developed an upgrade and transfer plan that would allow each nonmanagement employee to request a transfer or upgrade into other nonmanagement jobs in the Bell Companies. Procedures were spelled out for the handling of promotions, lateral moves, or even downgrades to jobs in every department in the company. The plan incorporated and expanded on the existing transfer arrangements of several operating companies. It not only provided a mechanism for processing requests, but also involved the encouragement of employees to initiate transfer requests. Incumbent employees would have priority over new hires when vacancies occurred. Moreover, the plan focussed on company rather than departmental seniority. A centralized placement bureau would handle all requests and would match employees with available opportunities. Kingsbury stated that the expansion of lateral and promotional opportunities would enhance both intra- and inter-departmental mobility of women and minority employees, have a good effect on employee attitudes and morale, and, it was hoped, reduce force losses. The central purpose of the plan would be to establish resource pools to provide significant numbers of women and minorities for jobs where they now may be underrepresented.[11]

Expert Witnesses

In addition to Kingsbury's testimony, several expert witnesses responded to the EEOC allegations of discrimination in the Bell companies. I present below brief summaries of the testimony of: Dr. Valerie K. Oppenheimer, Sociologist from the University of California, Los Angeles; Dr. Lewis J. Perl, Economist from Cornell University; Dr. Hugh Folk, Economist from the University of Illinois, Urbana-Champaign; Dr. Leona Tyler, Psychologist from the University of Oregon; and Dr. Jules Cohn, Political Scientist from the City University of New York. Transcripts of these testimonies were submitted to the FCC as Bell exhibits on August 1, 1972.
Dr. Valerie K. Oppenheimer. From her studies of sex-segregated occupations Oppenheimer found that women were not evenly distributed across occupations, but clustered in specific areas. In 1960, for example, 81 percent of the female labor force was found in employment where women were overrepresented. In studying the telephone and telegraph industries, Dr. Oppenheimer found that in 1960 practically all the employed women (90 percent) were in occupations where 80 percent or more

11 *Ibid*, pp. 156–58.

of the workers were female. However, she contended that jobs which were sex-segregated in Bell were segregated in other industries as well.

Dr. Oppenheimer gave a number of reasons for the sex segregation in occupations:

1. Women have usually been a cheap, available source of labor.
2. Female dominated occupations historically have had low wages for the skills required.
3. The need for cheap but educated labor in certain occupations tended to promote reliance upon women.
4. Early industry could benefit from "feminine" skills (spinning, weaving, etc.).
5. Jobs requiring strength necessitated males.
6. Employers assumed women had more manual dexterity.
7. Sex appeal was considered important in some jobs.
8. Women's labor force participation has tended to be intermittent.
9. Tradition has been important in the sex-labeling of occupations
10. Men dominate jobs where there is career continuity.
11. Women tend to be secondary breadwinners.
12. Women frequently have low occupational aspirations.[12]

Dr. Lewis J. Perl. Perl criticized Oaxaca's testimony, and stated that the Oaxaca model implicitly assumed that, after controlling for certain personal and demographic characteristics, men and women represented essentially homogeneous inputs into the labor market. Other differences such as the quality of education and experience might account for observed differences in earnings even in the absence of discrimination. Also, Professor Oaxaca's assumption that the quality of male and female education is the same was held to be questionable since men score much higher than women on tests of quantitative and technical ability, and women generally attend the less prestigious colleges. College men and women also differ in their fields of study, with men emphasizing technical areas more. Perl also stated that Oaxaca's model underestimates the difference in experience between men and women by not accounting for child-bearing.

Perl believed that the models of Oaxaca, Ashenfelter, and Bergmann were seriously flawed by the failure to control for the differences in ability and scholastic achievement. As a result of this omission, their estimates of the extent of discrimination against blacks may be upwardly biased by an indeterminate but possibly large amount.[13]

Dr. Hugh Folk. Folk accused the EEOC of presenting statistics in a misleading fashion and of biasing the sample by using too many southern SMSA's. He refuted the EEOC charges against Bell by indicating that the charges assume that only employer demand is important in the labor market, and not employee supply. Earlier

12 Testimony of Valerie K. Oppenheimer, FCC Docket No. 19143, August 1, 1972.
13 Testimony of Lewis J. Perl, FCC Docket No. 19143, August 1, 1972.

Folk had developed a model for predicting the available labor supply in a community. By 1971 the Community Labor Market Information System (COLMIS) had been used by a half dozen or more of the Bell operating companies.

Folk claimed that it is Bell's arbitrary grouping of employees that is the reason women appear to be concentrated in certain occupations. In addition, he noted that a very large proportion of women consider the operator's job to be a very good one. Folk further contended that Bell's record in employing minorities was good and that much of the occupational segregation within Bell was due to employee preference.[14]

Dr. Leona Tyler. Tyler contended that the EEOC charges against the Bell companies ignored well-known patterns of occupational interests, preferences, and preparations of women resulting from such things as education, parental influences, and peer group pressures. The most widely accepted explanation of sex differences, she said, is in terms of cultural sex roles. Most women show distinct preferences for the feminine occupations (e.g., housewife, nurse, secretary, teacher).

Tyler believed that these role models could change, but that this would take time. She asserted that sex segregation in AT&T was the result of these well-developed role preferences. A period of 15 to 20 years would be needed in order to modify interests and motivations. Tyler believed that getting women into craft jobs would be even slower than getting women into management.[15]

Dr. Jules Cohn. Cohn noted Bell's good record of participation in programs for the disadvantaged, especially the National Alliance of Business (NAB) jobs. In 1969 Cohn had evaluated some of these programs for the AT&T. He concluded by stating:
1. The telephone companies have fulfilled, and even sometimes exceeded, their pledges under the JOBS program of the NAB.
2. Bell's programs are of high quality.
3. Bell's programs, perhaps because they are decentralized, have been creative and varied.
4. Bell programs have minimized the temptation to "cream"[16] [to select only the best or "overqualified" of program participants].

14 Testimony of Hugh Folk, FCC Docket No. 19143, August 1, 1972.
15 Testimony of Leona Tyler, FCC Docket No. 19143, August 1, 1972.
16 Testimony of Jules Cohn, FCC Docket No. 19143, August 1, 1972.

13 The Consent Decrees

Phyllis A. Wallace

This chapter discusses the Consent Decree and memorandum of agreement that brought the Bell companies into compliance with Title VII of the Civil Rights Acts of 1964 as amended, the Equal Pay Act of 1963, and the requirements of Executive Order 11246. The AT&T model affirmative action program, upgrading and transfer plan, and job briefs and qualifications were accepted by the Department of Labor (OFCC) as consistent with the requirements of Revised Order No. 4. The EEOC declared that these programs constituted a bona fide seniority or merit system within the meaning of Section 703 (h) of Title VII. The Bell Companies are permanently enjoined from violating the Equal Pay Act on those issues dealing with the promotion pay plan and the pay adjustments.[1]

No attempt will be made to compare the earlier versions of the AT&T programs with the final affirmative action and upgrade and transfer plans incorporated in the consent decree. The Bell model should greatly expand the utilization of women and minorities in all occupational levels. The achievement of this objective would appear to depend heavily on major modification of personnel procedures. Nearly a year after the agreement a Bell official noted,

We in the Bell System are very comfortable with our agreement and the consent decree. We came out with the right to manage our business in fact an improved personnel program, and made a quantum jump in equal opportunity which bodes well for society, minorities, for women, and the Bell System.[2]

Affirmative Action Plan

AT&T's Affirmative Action Plan (AAP) specifies that:

The equal employment objective for the Bell System is to achieve within a reasonable period of time, an employee profile, with respect to race and sex in each major classification, which is an approximate reflection of proper utilization. . .

This objective calls for achieving full utilization of minorities and women at all levels of management and non-management and by job classification at a pace beyond that which would occur normally; to prohibit discrimination in employment, because of race, color, religion, national origin, sex or age; and to have a work environment free of discrimination.[3]

1 *Equal Employment Opportunity Commission, James Hodgson, Secretary of Labor, United States Department of Labor, and United States of America vs. American Telephone and Telegraph Company* (January 18, 1973, Civil Action No. 73–149) (hereafter referred to as Consent Decree), p. 3.
2 Address by Daniel Davis, EEO Personnel Manager For AT&T, *Bureau of National Affairs Inc.* Washington, D.C. 20037, November 21, 1973.
3 "A Model Affirmative Action Program For The Bell System," American Telephone and Telegraph Company.

Goals for each of these protected groups that had been underutilized were to be set for fifteen major job classifications in more than 600 Bell System establishments. The 1973 consent decree endorsed goals for males in two predominately female occupations, operator and clerical jobs. In addition, intermediate targets would be set for one-, two-, and three-year time frames, and at the end of the three-year period the goals would be reevaluated and adjusted or eliminated as appropriate.

The company's affirmative action efforts were designed to be "the quickest possible and least disruptive paths to the objectives of full utilization of minorities and women at every level of the business." Goals are derived from work force analyses determined in accordance with the criteria of Revised Order No. 4.[4]

Guidelines For Intermediate Targets and Time Frames

Goals and intermediate targets were to be established on the basis of projected job opportunities and relevant labor pools for those job classifications in which there had been underutilization. For entry-level jobs, ratios from the external labor market would be applied. Since the aforementioned entry-level jobs would be filled mainly by employees from lower-level job classifications, the traditional Bell System policy of promotion from within was reaffirmed.

The Bell AAP had recommended that if, in any given year, the representation of any protected group in entry-level jobs was less than the percentage derived from utilization analysis, the latter percentage multiplied by one-and-a-half times would determine the appropriate job opportunity percentage. In no case would the goal set for total minorities or for total women exceed fifty percent of direct hires. For above entry-level jobs the goals would be set so that each protected group would be at least as well represented as it was in the relevant employee pool for that job classification.

Under selected conditions, an affirmative action override might be used to promote the protected group employees at higher percentages than they were in the employee pools. The affirmative action override for promoting women and minorities is applied in the following manner: (1) if the job category percentage is 50 percent or less that of the employee pool, promotions are made at twice the percentage in the pool; (2) if the job category percentage is from 51 to 79 percent that of the employee pool, promotions are made at one-and-a-half times the percentage in the pool. An AT&T official described the affirmative action override as a novel technique "which permits the transfer bureau to override seniority and best qualified if an establishment is not making its targets."

Progress toward the intermediate targets will be measured and evaluated by (1) comparing race and sex composition in each job classification at the end of the year with those for the preceding year, (2) comparing the percent of job opportunities

4 *Ibid.*

filled during the year by each race and sex with what had been forecast. The intermediate targets are subject to close and continuing scrutiny by a government coordinating committee.

The success of the AAP will depend on many actions within the Bell System. Systematic monitoring relies on an extensive manpower information system. At least seven types of reports are maintained by minority and sex designations. The quarterly reports include (1) employment office activity (applicant and hire flow, referrals and hires, and reasons for rejections of applicants), (2) placement, upgrade, and promotions, (3) resignations and dismissals, (4) transfer plan activity, (5) training class attendance, (6) progress of company subunits toward goals and intermediate targets, and (7) projected number of job opportunities by major titles for the balance of the year.[5] Part of the good faith effort may be that the operating companies will evaluate the performance of all management employees on the basis of equal employment efforts and results as well as other job related criteria.

Upgrading and Transfer

Full utilization of women and minorities can be achieved mainly through greater mobility of Bell employees. The AT&T upgrading and transfer plan included in the January 1973 Consent Decree and memorandum of agreement specifies procedures to be followed in handling of nonmanagement promotion, laterals, and downgrades. The plan stipulated that "to ensure equal opportunity for mobility, employees shall be informed of all nonmanagement jobs within their companies, the qualifications required for these jobs, and how to apply for another job." In order to obtain an unbiased selection system a centralized interdepartmental placement group, the Transfer Bureau was established in the Personnel Department.

The Transfer Bureau will make all selections for jobs normally considered "entry level" nonmanagement positions, and final selections from all other nonmanagement jobs will be made by the department with the vacancy. Employees meeting certain minimum length of service in their current jobs may request to be transferred. The employee initiated transfer plan can be very supportive of the interests of both management and employees, providing eligible candidates for consideration by the former and job counseling to the latter. This allows for a free flow of employees across departmental lines.

Each Bell Company agreed to offer "its female and minority employees in nonmanagement, noncraft jobs who had four or more years of net credited service on July 1, 1971, and who expresses a desire for transfer—to a job in AAP job classification 9 or 10 (craft, semi-skilled) an opportunity to compete therefor with other employees on the basis of net credited service and basic qualifications—if females or

5 *Ibid.*

minorities currently are underutilized in such AAP classification 9 or 10 and such employee is a member of the group which is underutilized."[6]

In filling vacancies at the craft skilled level (AAP job classification 6 or 7), "candidates for promotion shall be evaluated on the basis of net credited service and best qualified, unless a lower standard of qualification is provided in a collective bargaining agreement or pursuant to Bell Company practices. However, if any Bell Company is unable to meet its intermediate targets within the stated time frames using these criteria, it will use only the criteria of net credited service and a basic qualified criterion and if necessary will seek new hires who meet at least the basic qualified criterion."[7]

The "net credited service" or seniority for purposes of transfer and promotion has been expanded to mean length of service with the operating company instead of within a department or unit. System-wide seniority will continue to be used for other purposes. The issue of departmental versus company seniority was very important because of sex segregation of the lines of progression. When women transferred from the traffic department to craft jobs, they had to start at the bottom of the line because they had no departmental seniority in the new unit even though they might have worked for the company for many years.

In addition the Consent Decree stipulated an employee information function for the Transfer Bureau. Notices would be provided to nonmanagement employees quarterly on the projected number of job opportunities by major job titles for the balance of the calendar year. Nonmanagement employees would also be informed about the number of jobs filled during the previous quarter with data on the characteristics of the incumbents such as length of services, date of transfers, job title, minority designation, sex, and previous job assignment. Annual summaries of these data will be submitted to the federal compliance agencies.

Pay Adjustments

Most of the considerable publicity on the AT&T settlement involved the $15 million of back pay to 13,00 women and 2,000 minority men and the estimated $23 million to be paid annually to 36,000 minority and female workers as a result of wage adjustments and a new promotion pay policy for nonmanagement jobs. The back pay and pay adjustments were developed at the intensive private negotiations held during 1972. AT&T had a difficult time convincing the operating companies on the back pay issue.

Previously promotion pay scales had been calculated so that employees obtaining promotions to a particular position from "male jobs" received a higher rate of pay than those transferred or promoted to the same position from the "female jobs."

6 Consent Decree, p. 6.
7 *Ibid,* p. 7.

Thus, sex-typing of jobs at differential pay was perpetuated in the promotional procedures. The determinant of the wage of the newly promoted employee was the rate of pay in the previous position. This pay procedure resulted in females and males of the same length of service with the company, occupying the same position following transfer or promotion, but with the women compensated at a lower rate of pay. Consequently, AT&T was not in compliance with the equal pay provisions of the Fair Labor Standards Act (Equal Pay Act of 1963), and automatically was in violation of Title VII and Executive Order 11246. Back pay retroactive up to a maximum of two years was made to 3,000 women already employed in craft jobs. This adjustment would bring these salaries into lines with the new promotion pay plan. More people decided to go into these nontraditional jobs than had been expected.

The new promotion pay plan required that "the employee shall be placed on the step of the new wage table as determined by allowing the employee full wage experience credit"—but on the old wage table, and subject to some restrictions in the more skilled occupations. By the end of the first year of the agreement, the $23 million estimate for pay adjustments had been increased to $30 million with the total cost estimated at $45 million.[8]

The principle of delayed restitution embodied in the Consent Decree noted that in order to compensate for possible delay in promotion in nonmanagement jobs, "lump sum payments shall be made to each female and minority employee in each establishment where there exists in his or her respective job classification an underutilization of the group of which he or she is a member." The criteria for pay of lump sum payments are that the worker: (a) has had four years of net credited service on July 1, 1971, (b) has been or will be promoted from noncraft to craft jobs subsequent to June 30, 1971, and prior to July 1, 1974, and (c) remains in that craft job for a total of more than six months. These lump sum payments, ranging from $100 to $400, were to have been made to at least 10,000 women and minority employees.[9]

An important factor in the increased cost of the implementation of the additional benefits of the decree may have been the equity adjustments paid to incumbent white males—i.e., when women workers had their pay raised under the promotion pay plan, men who had more seniority received increases in salary.

A small proportion of the total payments (approximately $850,000) was to be paid to four-year college graduate female employees hired directly into management other than into the Initial Management Development Program (IMDP) between July 2, 1965, and December 31, 1971. These employees were surveyed to determine their interest in promotion to the third level and above managment positions, assessed at a management center to evaluate their potential for promotion, and, if assessed as satisfactory, had their salary increased by $100 per month. Another $500,000 was to be spent to bring the pay schedules of switchroom helpers (a female job) at Michigan

8 Eileen Shanahan, *New York Times,* May 31, 1974.
9 Consent Decree, pp. 17–18.

Bell into line with the higher-paying frameman job (a male job) in other Bell Companies. In addition, these workers were to receive retroactive pay adjustments for a period of up to two years.

Management Pay Adjustment

A second Consent Decree covering $30 million in back pay and wage adjustments for 25,000 Bell System management employees was signed on May 30, 1974. AT&T agreed to change its system of determining salaries for 175,000 employees in the lower management jobs. Salaries of employees promoted from nonmanagement to lower levels of management or from one management level to another with a higher basic maximum rate of pay were determined by salary received in the lower position. Women employees usually had worked in jobs receiving lower salaries and the differential status was maintained after promotion. Of the 175,000 Bell System level 1 and 2 managers, 63,000 were women.

An estimated $7 million of the total amount will be in the form of back pay to some 7,000 management employees. Wage adjustments amounting to $14.9 million annually will be paid to 17,000 level 1 and level 2 managers. In addition, approximately 8,400 persons (5,000 of them women) will be promoted into these jobs, and they will begin at the new adjusted wage levels. As a result of the settlement, the newly promoted persons are to be paid $7.5 million more a year than previously.[10]

After a job evaluation study, the new policy will provide for a uniform minimum starting salary for all jobs within each salary group in the first two levels of management. The minimum entry rate will be based on the rate for the most favored sex entering that salary category through promotion (higher average rate of pay) during the period July 1, 1972, to June 30, 1973. The decree will be in effect for five years. The minimum entry rates need not apply to employees initially hired into management levels 1 or 2.

In the materials prepared for the public hearings, the EEOC had calculated actual and expected wages by race and sex for Bell employees in thirty selected SMSA's. The data, although grossly estimated, revealed a deficit to females of $422 million a year. On a nationwide basis, the EEOC concluded that "Bell's incumbent female employees, given their age, education and experience, were paid an aggregate of $500 million per year less than males with comparable personal characteristics."[11] This estimate of back pay and pay adjustment for women and minorities may not have been the most precise way of estimating the disparity.

Other Issues

The 1973 Decree included a provision on testing. Although each operating com-

10 EEOC. . . vs. AT&T (May 30, 1974, Civil Action 74–1342). See also Eileen Shanahan, *New York Times,* May 31, 1974.
11 Private correspondence.

pany may utilize test scores on validated tests to assess individual qualifications, it may not rely upon the minimum scores on preemployment aptitude test batteries as a justification for failure to meet intermediate targets. The testing issues are discussed in this volume in Chapters 9 and 10. Bell psychologists Bray and Grant and two expert witnesses Guion and Baxter examined in some detail AT&T testing and test validations.[12]

The parties to the agreement established a procedure for expeditiously resolving the 2,000 or so charges of employment discrimination that were pending before the EEOC. In order to facilitate conciliation of charges filed with EEOC during the six-year life of the decree, the EEOC will provide AT&T with copies of all charges not yet served on Bell companies, and the AT&T or Bell Company involved will propose ways to settle charges and will seek resolution through conciliation. These procedures apparently will reduce if not eliminate litigation and may permit enough time to develop a body of administrative regulations which are the joint efforts of the company and the federal agency. It also may bring the equal employment opportunity models within the framework of the types of bargaining processes that have existed for a number of years in industrial relations.

Whatever may be achieved by the AT&T during the next five years will be done in an atmosphere that is less hostile. The EEOC and the Department of Labor agreed: "That they will not, in any claim, action or proceeding (including rate cases), involving any of the Bell Companies, initiate, encourage, fund, intervene in support of or advocate by *amicus* brief or otherwise, a position inconsistent with the Agreement or the Decree."

By entering into the agreement and accepting the Consent Decree, the Bell companies did not admit that they had engaged in any discriminatory employment practices. The parties agreed that Docket 19143, which was pending before the Federal Communications Commission, would be dismissed. Although the agreement did not require or permit the abandonment of any provision in any Bell Company's collective bargaining agreement except as required to maintain compliance with federal law, the settlement was challenged by the Communications Workers of America (CWA). The union petitioned to block implementation of the decree on the grounds that: (1) it infringed upon their bargaining rights and (2) it was not consulted on areas in which it had a vital interest such as issues affecting wages, hours, and conditions of employment.[13]

12 Dr. Douglas W. Bray, personnel director for Human Resources Development at AT&T, discussed the general methods used in validating aptitude tests. Dr. Donald L. Grant, personnel manager research at AT&T, provided details on the criteria used in validating Bell System employment tests. Dr. Robert M. Guion, an industrial psychologist, evaluated the Bell System tests and its validation studies. Dr. Brent N. Baxter, vice president of the American Institutes for Research, testified on the validity of 15 Bell System employment tests.
13 Decision of U.S. District Court For Eastern Pennsylvania In *Equal Employment Opportunity Commission et al. vs. American Telephone and Telegraph Company et al.* (October 5, 1973).

The International Brotherhood of Electrical Workers (IBEW), a smaller union, had participated in negotiations on the settlement. The right of both unions to negotiate alternatives which comply with applicable federal laws was preserved. The petition by CWA was denied, and on October 5, 1973, the consent decree handed down by the court became unencumbered. CWA appealed the decision, and in December 1974 the Third Circuit Court in Philadelphia ruled that the union would not be permitted to intervene as a plaintiff in the case.[14] The District Court had allowed the union to intervene as a plaintiff only on issues relating to the maternity leave practices of AT&T. CWA might, if requested, intervene as a defendant to protect its interest in its collective bargaining agreements with AT&T by seeking district court modification of those provisions of the Consent Decree which affect those agreements. In March 1975 CWA filed a motion to intervene as a defendent to challenge the decree.

14 Decision of US Court of Appeals for Third Circuit, in the case of *Equal Employment Opportunity Commission et al. vs. American Telephone and Telegraph Company et al., Communications Workers of America, AFL-CIO* (December 19, 1974).

14 What Did We Learn?

Phyllis A. Wallace

When the court denied a petition by the Communications Workers of America[1] to stay the implementation of the AT&T Consent Decree of January 1973, Judge Higginbotham remarked:

When deciding this issue we are approaching uncharted seas without clear markings as to the rights of intervention. Thus in making this ruling I am not attempting to spell out for all time to come any definitive guidelines. . .[2]

Negotiated Settlements

A negotiated settlement of equal employment opportunity issues incorporated in a consent decree strikes a balance between voluntary efforts and court litigation as enforcement procedures. Voluntary compliance may be the preferred means of implementation of the law for those groups most likely to be respondents to charges of discrimination (employers, unions, employment agencies). The affected classes (e.g., persons discriminated against on the basis of race, color, sex, religion, national origin) believe that their statutory rights are more adequately protected under court litigations. The negotiated settlements, with the federal compliance agencies representing the interests of the protected classes, are similar to collective bargaining models.

William Kilberg, Solicitor of Labor, has discussed some of the problems of bargaining with employers and unions on equal employment opportunities settlements:

AT&T raises a question, it seems to me, of how the Government should deal with unions in a settlement situation. . . Clearly, unions have a right to be heard with regard to their legitimate interests in protecting their members. In the AT&T Case we tried to resolve this by setting up parameters for the parties to bargain. Essentially what we did was to agree to the minimums and to the broad framework of what relief was required.

We said, "You can't give any less than this but you can give more."

We did this with regard to seniority. We imposed company-wide seniority. We did not impose system-wide seniority. We said the parties could bargain about that. We set up transfer plans. There were differences we tried to protect, and we carved out things that already were in collective bargaining agreements such as posting notices to protect posting and bidding systems so where they existed they would remain. Where they didn't exist, the parties could bargain about them. We tried to walk a very difficult line: to give neither the employer nor the union something they would not have otherwise obtained through collective bargaining.[3]

---

1 CWA was granted limited intervention to litigate rights for pregnant women.
2 Decision of U.S. District Court For Eastern Pennsylvania in *EEOC et al vs. American Telephone and Telegraph et al.* (October 5, 1973).
3 William J. Kilberg. "Progress and Problems in Equal Employment Opportunity." *Labor Law Journal* 24, No. 10 (October 1973): 656.

Representatives from the telephone company and from the federal compliance agencies negotiated in private sessions simultaneously with the public hearings that were held before the FCC. Issues on remedial and other pay adjustments, transfer, promotion, layoff, recall, testing, and training were resolved during these bilateral discussions and were incorporated in the consent decree. The Communications Workers of America (CWA) the largest union in the telephone industry, elected not to participate in these negotiating sessions.[4] While the CWA contended that the settlement infringed upon its role as sole bargainer for 600,000 telephone employees, the International Brotherhood of Electrical Workers (IBEW), representing employees at the New England Telephone and Telegraph Company, did intervene in the negotiations on behalf of its members. See discussion of litigation by CWA in Chapter 13.

Although consent decrees have since been signed for the steel and trucking industries and for selected companies in banking and airlines,[5] it is too early to determine whether this procedure will be used extensively to remedy institutional discrimination. Considerable publicity surrounds the back pay adjustments of the consent decrees, but the costs of restructuring transfer and promotion systems and revamping personnel and industrial relations systems may total millions of dollars.

The consent decrees signed in the steel industry in April 1974 resulted from negotiations between nine steel companies representing 73 percent of the industry, the United Steelworkers of America, and the federal government. A back pay settlement of $30.9 million to 40,000 minority and female employees, transfer rights, wage rate retention, seniority provisions, and goals and timetables were included in the agreement. An Audit and Review Committee representing the industry, union, and the government was established to review the experience under the decree: "the transfer opportunities, the transfer record of female and minority group members, the progress in achieving stated trade and craft goals, and other Decree related matters." The Audit and Review Committee may propose corrective steps at any plant or facility and only bring matters to the court for final resolution if unanimous agreement cannot be reached.

In June 1974 the banking industry witnessed the announcement of a consent

4 With the exception mentioned in note 1.

5 *United States of America and Equal Employment Opportunity Commission vs. Allegheny-Ludlum Industries Inc. et al.* (Civil Action No. 74-P-339 in the United States District Court for the Northern District of Alabama, Southern Division, April 12, 1974).

Partial Consent Decree In The Trucking Industry, *United States of America vs. Trucking Employers Inc. et al.* (Civil Action 74-453 in the United States District Court For District of Columbia, March 21, 1974). The Justice Department had brought suit against 349 trucking companies and two unions. Seven of the companies threatened by the suit agreed in a partial decree to adopt minority hiring goals.

Wells et al., Equal Employment Opportunity Commission vs. The Bank of America National Trust and Savings Association, US District Court, Northern District of California, July 19, 1974.

Equal Employment Opportunity Agreement Between Delta Air Lines and Labor and Justice Departments, April 30, 1973.

decree settling a class action suit brought against the Bank of America, the largest commercial bank in the world, on behalf of its female employees. The bank not only set affirmative action goals with targets for percentages of women officers at all levels of bank operations by the end of 1978, but also established trust funds totaling $3,750,000 for the benefit of women whose education and employment histories with the bank met certain selection criteria. The expressed purpose of the trusts was to provide an inducement to potential beneficiaries to accept and successfully complete bank management training or, alternatively, for development of their general creative and intellectual capacities through education, travel, or public service. This settlement is of particular interest for its focus was not on back pay as a punitive measure for past discrimination. Instead, it represented an innovative and forward-looking attempt to help women identify themselves as prospects for promotion and to take advantage of opportunities for self-development. If the Bank of America is successful in implementing this settlement, we may look forward to far-reaching change in an industry that is one of the largest nationwide employers of women, but managed nearly exclusively by men.[6]

The steel-industry consent decree raised questions concerning the participants and the agendas for the negotiated settlements in equal employment opportunity. Representatives for women and minority groups are critical of agreements that are negotiated without their participation. The NAACP Legal Defense and Educational Fund, the National Organization for Women (NOW), and a group of minority employees in the steel industry filed a suit to stay the enforcement of those provisions in the decree which stipulate that when back pay awards are offered and accepted employees must sign a release waiving future claims against the company. Their position was turned down by both the district and appellate courts. Prior to the settlement there apparently were some differences between federal compliance agencies over whether back pay should be included.[7]

Implementation of the AT&T Decree

During the two years since the signing of the first telephone consent decree both the federal government and AT&T have institutionalized more effective procedures for handling equal employment opportunity issues. The AT&T case enabled the federal compliance agencies to develop a prototype organization for dealing with patterns of employment discrimination. The task force approach of the several federal compliance agencies for coordinating their efforts and operating as a single compliance review unit is a great improvement over previous ad hoc procedures.

An EEOC representative in each of the ten federal regions has the primary re-

6 Lacey Fosburgh, "Coast Women Win Big Gains at Bank," *New York Times,* June 9, 1974.
7 Philip Shabecoff, "Job Equality Pact In Steel Industry Being Negotiated," *The New York Times,* December 5, 1973.

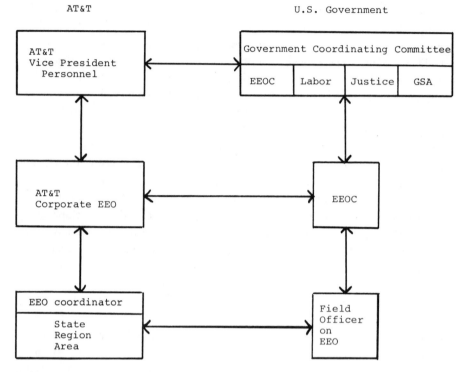

Note:

1) Field office of EEOC processes charges

2) GCC monitors consent decree

Figure 14.1 Monitoring and implementation of the AT&T consent decree

sponsibility of working with the Bell companies in that region. This representative is responsible for processing the charges that had accumulated over the two-year period of the public hearing. The EEOC field personnel had resolved more than 2,400 individual charges by the end of June 1974. This activity did not reduce the backlog of charges of discrimination filed against the Bell companies since many employees filed charges subsequent to the signing of the Consent Decree.[8]

Monitoring of the Consent Decree is done by the Government Coordinating Committee (GCC), a Washington-based group composed of representatives of EEOC, the Departments of Labor and Justice, and the General Services Administration (see Figure 14.1). The GCC is a policy group. To date it has conducted three major activities: (1) review and approval of the goals and timetables of the Bell

8 "Letter from EEOC Chairman Powell to Senators Williams and Javits on Commission Efforts to Improve Title VII Enforcement," *Daily Labor Report,* November 14, 1974. The Bureau of National Affairs, Inc., E-1.

operating companies, (2) negotiation of the second consent decree for low level management (June 1974), and (3) monitoring the compliance with the Consent Decree of January 1973. A team from the GCC has undertaken a major review of each operating company. These on-site visits and discussions with company officials have helped to shape a new institutional framework.

A recent congressional review of EEOC activities revealed that the AT&T settlement also served as a model for a tracking system to utilize fully the investigative and litigative resources of the EEOC. "In enacting the Equal Employment Opportunity Act of 1972, Congress recognized a change in the definition of employment discrimination to include employment systems that perpetuate discrimination."[9] In accordance with this, Track I respondents will be those that have been the subject of individual complaints. Track II respondents included large national companies and unions upon which resolution of charges involving personnel management systems would potentially yield the largest national impact. Such cases may cover multi-unit employers operating within regions who may have a large number of charges pending and/or a history of noncompliance.[10]

It is likely that within the Bell System the personnel process is being modified in order to implement the affirmative action plans. The Consent Decree specifies that the EEOC would notify the companies of all discrimination charges filed. The operating companies would be allowed to conduct their own informal investigations prior to the initiation of formal EEOC investigative procedures. This should provide an opportunity for management to develop internal grievance procedures within which employment discrimination problems may be resolved.

An equal employment opportunity officer in each operating company works closely with the local EEOC representative, and reports to the corporate affirmative action officer at AT&T headquarters. Eventually communication from the field to headquarters should be rapid, and as the different representatives learn to coordinate their efforts, to communicate, and to respect each other, this should be beneficial to all parties. The gains to the compliance agencies could be fewer charges, more effective utilization of resources in nonlitigation activities, and the establishment of a more harmonious relationship with industry and unions. For the companies, the gains might be an opportunity to control their own organizational environments.

Perhaps one of the most significant outcomes of the first years of the consent decree is the wide-ranging impact on other parts of AT&T, other employers, and other groups. In May 1974, a second consent decree covering wage adjustments for persons in the first and second level of management was signed. By September 1974, AT&T's

9 "Joint Letter From Senators Williams and Javits to EEOC Chairman Powell On Title VII Enforcement," *Daily Labor Report,* September 16, 1974. The Bureau of National Affairs, Inc., E-2.
10 *Ibid.* As mentioned in Chapter 12, in December 1970, when the EEOC requested the FCC to investigate the employment practices of AT&T, charges against the telephone company accounted for five to six percent of all charges pending at EEOC.

manufacturing subsidiary (Western Electric) agreed to make back payments of $800,000 to 2,000 hourly female employees and to improve transfer procedures to jobs where there is more promotion without any cut in pay.[11] Also in October 1974, the AT&T and the American Jewish Committee undertook a cooperative effort to recruit Jewish personnel for management.[12] Many employers in both the public and private sector are not in compliance with Title VII on sex discrimination and cautiously are waiting to see how the largest private employer will fully integrate women into all aspects of the workplace.

Both the federal government and the company may have underestimated the effect of powerful social constraints on changing the characteristics of a fairly rigid internal labor market. A congressional report noted in September 1974 that the AT&T settlement had been difficult and expensive to monitor.[13] The company may perceive its primary objective as providing telephone service, securing a fair return on its investment, protecting its markets from firms selling competitive equipment, and adjusting to lower levels of economic activity. John W. Kingsbury, AT&T Assistant Vice President, has noted that

...our managers—and millions of others like them in business after business across the country—did not yet understand the need for some of the specific features required in new, *formalized* procedures, which are necessary in order to speed the upward movement of women and minority group members.

The threat of increased competition from individuals they perceive to be less qualified than themselves is part of the reason for this managerial reluctance. Basic prejudice may be another reason. And some managers may feel they are losing some of their hard-earned management prerogatives. However, the main cause, I submit, is simply a resistance to change. Line managers at all levels of most organizations really don't understand the significance of new equal opportunity regulations, labor laws, OSHA, or a host of other external impingements on their primary responsibilities. And further, they tend not to view these external forces as their problem but as a personnel or legal matter.[14]

Thus, perfecting an effective mechanism whereby AT&T may restructure its personnel and industrial relations activities will not be an easy task. As of January 1975 the government had found AT&T to be in noncompliance with the 1973 Consent Decree on affirmative action and negotiations for both sides were attempting to agree on new terms for remedial relief.[15] Would an external organization jointly funded by the industry and government be able to undertake the basic kind of research that needs to be done as well as to function in an ombudsman role? Such an organization might contribute much to a better understanding of how equal employment opportunity goals can be attained. FOR DEVELOPMENTS TO 1975, SEE APP. D.

11 *Wall Street Journal,* September 30, 1974.
12 *New York Times,* October 27, 1974.
13 See Williams and Javits, *supra.*
14 John W. Kingsbury. "Business Realities and the Law." *The Conference Board Record* 10, No.8 (August 1973) : 55.
15 Daily Labor Report, January 15, 1975, p. A-15–17.

Appendix A

Consent Decree: Equal Employment Opportunity Commission *et al.* v. American Telephone and Telegraph, *et al.*, January 18, 1973

In the United States District Court for the Eastern District of Pennsylvania

Equal Employment Opportunity Commission, James D. Hodgson, Secretary of Labor, United States Department of Labor, and United States of America, Plaintiffs,

    v.

American Telephone and Telegraph Company,
New England Telephone and Telegraph Company,
The Southern New England Telephone Company,
New York Telephone Company,
New Jersey Bell Telephone Company,
The Bell Telephone Company of Pennsylvania
   and the Diamond State Telephone Company,
The Chesapeake and Potomac Telephone Company,
The Chesapeake and Potomac Telephone Company of Maryland,
The Chesapeake and Potomac Telephone Company of Virginia
The Chesapeake and Potomac Telephone Company of West Virginia
Southern Bell Telephone and Telegraph Company,
South Central Bell Telephone Company,
The Ohio Bell Telephone Company,
Cincinnati Bell Inc.,
Michigan Bell Telephone Company,
Indiana Bell Telephone Company, Incorporated,
Wisconsin Telephone Company,
Illinois Bell Telephone Company,
Northwestern Bell Telephone Company,
Southwestern Bell Telephone Company,
The Mountain States Telephone and Telegraph Company,
Pacific Northwest Bell Telephone Company,
The Pacific Telephone and Telegraph Company
   and Bell Telephone Company of Nevada, Defendants.

Civil Action No. 73-149

The Equal Employment Opportunity Commission (hereinafter, EEOC), the Secretary of Labor (hereinafter, the Secretary), and the United States of America having filed their Complaint herein, the EEOC pursuant to Sections 706 (f) (1) and (3) and Section 707 (e) of Title VII, of the Civil Rights Act of 1964, as amended by Public Law 92-261 (March 24, 1972), 42 U.S.C. § 2000e *et seq.* (hereinafter Title VII), the Secretary pursuant to Sections 6 (d), 15 (a) (2) and 17 of the Fair Labor Standards Act of 1938, as amended, 29 U.S.C. § § 201, *et seq.* (hereinafter, the Equal Pay Act), and the United States pursuant to Executive Order 11246, as amended, and the Defendants having filed their Answer denying the allegations in the Complaint and setting forth the extensive affirmative actions they have taken and are taking to provide equal employment opportunity to minorities and women,* and the parties having waived hearing and findings of fact and conclusions of law, the following order is entered without any admission by any of the Defendants or finding by the Court of any violation by any of the Defendants of any of the abovementioned statutes or Executive Order, or any regulations adopted pursuant thereto,

Now therefore it is ORDERED, ADJUDGED AND DECREED as follows:

Part A

I. Affirmative Action Programs

The American Telephone and Telegraph Company's (AT&T's) Model Affirmative Action Program, Upgrading and Transfer Plan, and Job Briefs and Qualifications, attached hereto as Appendices A, B and C, respectively (said three Appendices being referred to herein as the "Model Programs"), subject to the clarifications and amplifications contained in this Decree, are consistent with the requirements of Revised Order No. 4, 29 C.F.R. § § 60-2.1 *et seq.,* issued by the Office of Federal Contract Compliance (hereinafter, OFCC) pursuant to Executive Order 11246, as amended, and constitute a "bona fide seniority or merit system" within the meaning of Section 703 (h) of Title VII. Such Model Programs, if adopted and implemented without material deviation by individual Bell Companies for each of their respective establishments, shall be considered as complying with the requirements of Revised Order No. 4, and employment decisions made in conformity with these Model Programs shall be considered as complying with Title VII. Provided, however, that all individual Company programs embodying material deviations from such Model Programs and any material revisions of such programs resulting from the annual reviews thereof

---

*Defendants contend that venue in the present action is improper as to all Defendants except the American Telephone and Telegraph Company, and The Bell Telephone Company of Pennsylvania. However, all Defendants have waived objections to venue for the limited purpose of the entry of this Decree. By submitting to the jurisdiction of this Court and waiving objections to the venue of this action solely for the purpose of the entry of this Decree, all Defendants preserve their rights to object to the appropriateness of jurisdiction and venue in all other actions brought in the Eastern District of Pennsylvania or any other federal judicial district.

will be submitted to the OFCC and the EEOC prior to implementation by any Bell Company. Such programs shall be deemed accepted unless disapproved by the OFCC within 45 days from the date of submission, consistent with Section 718 of the Civil Rights Act of 1964, as amended.

II. Goals and Timetables

A utilization analysis of each of the fifteen (15) Affirmative Action Program Job Classifications as defined in Section IV of the Model AAP (Appendix A hereto) within each establishment will be conducted pursuant to 41 C.F.R. § 60-2.11. For those job classifications wherein there exists a substantial salary range, such analysis shall specifically include reference to the relative distribution of minorities and women within such salary range. Each factor in 41 C.F.R. § 60-2.11(a) (1) and (2) for which accurate and relevant data are available shall be considered. A goal will be developed for each of the 15 AAP job classifications within each establishment where underutilization is determined to exist pursuant to 41 C.F.R. § 60-2.12. In a good faith effort to meet such goals, each Bell Company will establish intermediate targets for one, two and three-year time frames. At the end of each intermediate three-year time frame, the goal for each classification for which a goal has been set will be re-evaluated to determine whether underutilization still exists, and the goals for each job classification will be adjusted or eliminated as appropriate. All goals and all intermediate targets and time frames for each Company and each establishment must be individually approved by the OFCC, and shall be submitted for approval to the OFCC within 120 days from the date of this Decree, together with the relevant utilization analysis, including worksheets. Such goals, intermediate targets and time frames shall be deemed approved unless disapproved by the OFCC within 90 days of their submission, notwithstanding Section 718 of the Civil Rights Act of 1964, as amended. Worksheets shall include that portion of the goal which each establishment will make a good faith effort to achieve as intermediate targets within stated time frames.

The foregoing utilization analysis, goals, intermediate targets, and time frames shall also be developed for males in the operator and clerical classifications as part of each Bell Company's program.

All goals and all intermediate targets and time frames, as approved by the OFCC, and as adjusted at the end of each intermediate time frame will promptly be submitted by each Bell Company to the appropriate collective bargaining representative of its employees.

III. Transfer, Promotion, Layoff and Recall

A. Each Bell Company shall offer each of its female and minority employees in non-management, noncraft jobs who had four or more years of net credited service on July 1, 1971, and who expresses a desire for transfer as required by the appropriate upgrading and transfer plan or posting and bidding system to a job in AAP job classification 9 or 10, an opportunity to compete therefor with other employees on the basis of net credited service and basic qualifications, as set forth in Appendix C [not reprinted here—ed.], if females or minorities currently are underutilized in such AAP classification 9 or 10 and such employee is a member of the group which is underutilized. For purposes of this Decree, "net credited service" shall mean total length of service with the operating company in which the vacancy occurs. Provided, however, that total length of service within the Bell System shall continue to be used for other purposes, including bridging rights, consistent with the provisions of the applicable Bell Company's collective bargaining agreement(s).

Provided further, each Bell Company and each collective bargaining representative of their employees shall be free to bargain to expand this definition of net credited service, for purposes of this Agreement, to mean total length of service with the Bell System.*

Where the term net credited service is presently defined in applicable collective bargaining agreements as length of service greater than that of the company into which the employee was last hired, definition of that term shall be unaffected by this paragraph.

B. In filling vacancies in AAP job classifications 6 and 7, candidates for promotion shall be evaluated on the basis of net credited service and best qualified, unless a lower standard of qualification is provided in a collective bargaining agreement or pursuant to Bell Company practices. However, if any Bell Company is unable to meet its intermediate targets within the stated time frames using these criteria, it will use only the criteria of net credited service and a basic qualified criterion and, if necessary, will seek new hires who meet at least the basic qualified criterion. Efforts to achieve intermediate targets should be substantially uniform throughout the appropriate time frame. Each Bell Company agrees to notify the appropriate collective bargaining representative of its employees prior to promoting or transferring persons into AAP job classifications 6 and 7 on the basis of net credited service and basic qualifications.

C. Net credited service shall be used for determining layoff and related force adjustments and recall to jobs where nonmanagement female and minority employees would otherwise be laid off, affected or not recalled. Collective bargaining agreements or Bell Company practices shall govern the confines of the group of employees being considered. Provided, however, vacancies created by layoff and related force adjustments shall not be considered vacancies for purposes of transfer and promotion under this Section.

D. Minimum residency (time in title) requirements shall not be greater than the following, in the major job titles noted below:

*Employees returning from maternity leave do not have their service broken (absence in excess of 30 days will be deducted from net credited service).

1. Clerical, six-twelve months time in title;
2. Operator, six-twelve months time in title;
3. Service Representative, fifteen-eighteen months time in title;
4. Lower and Middle Craft, fifteen-eighteen months time in title;
5. Top Craft (Switchman, PBX Installer, PBX Repairman, Toll Test man, etc.), twenty-four-thirty months time in title.

Collective bargaining agreements of company practices which provide lower minimum residency requirements than those outlined above shall continue in effect.

IV. Employee Information Program

A. Each Bell Company shall inform its employees who are affected by the provisions of this Decree, and the appropriate collective bargaining representative of its employees, of the terms thereof in a manner approved by AT&T, EEOC, and OFCC.

B. Each Bell Company will, with respect to each of its transfer bureaus, provide a quarterly notice to nonmanagement employees served by such transfer bureau and to any collective bargaining representative representing such employees of the projected number of job opportunities by the major job titles (*e.g.*, installer, lineman) set forth in the Job Briefs contained in Appendix C hereto, in his or her transfer bureau for the balance of the calendar year and the number of jobs filled during the previous quarter by net credited service date, date of transfer, job title, EEO-1 minority designation, sex, and last previous job assignment.

V. Testing

Each Bell Company may continue to utilize test scores on validated tests along with other job-related considerations in assessing individual qualifications. However, no Bell Company shall rely upon the minimum scores required or preferred on its pre-employment aptitude test batteries as justification for its failure to meet its intermediate targets for any job classification.

VI. Promotion Pay Plan

Each employee promoted from one nonmanagement job to another with a higher basic maximum rate of pay, shall have his or her rate of pay in the higher rated job determined as follows:

The employee shall be placed on the step of the new wage table as determined by allowing the employee full wage experience credit, both in progression and at maximum, on the old wage table, but not to exceed the step down from maximum on the new schedule as listed below:

AAP Classifications	Step from Maximum
15. Service Workers	0
14. Operators	0

AAP Classifications	Step from Maximum
13. Office Clerical—Entry Level	0
12. Office Clerical—Semi-skilled	0
11. Office Clerical—Skilled	6 months
10. Telephone Craft—Semiskilled-Inside	6 months
9. Telephone Craft—Semiskilled-Outside	6 months
8. General Services—Skilled	12 months
7. Telephone Craft—Skilled-Inside	12 months
6. Telephone Craft—Skilled-Outside	12 months
5. Sales Workers	12 months

Notes

1. "Wage experience credit" is defined as the "number of months" step on the wage schedule at which an employee is paid.
2. Moves within an AAP classification shall be at full wage experience credit.
3. Net credited service shall be used instead of the wage experience credit allowance defined above if its use is more favorable to the employee; provided, however, that if the more favorable condition is solely a result of the length of the progression schedule having been shortened in 1970 or 1971 collective bargaining, then the wage experience credit allowance shall be used.
4. Current promotion pay practices which provide more favorable treatment than the procedure outlined above shall continue in effect.
5. Modification of Plan for Promotion from Simple to Complex Line Assigning:

   Employees who have work experience in simple plant line assigning (not including clerks whose duties do not require that they use cable books to locate available cable pairs) and are promoted to complex line assigning (Top or Second Craft) will be treated as follows:
   a. Those with over four years of wage experience credit or net credited service (as provided in note 3 above), at least one year of which is simple plant line assigning experience, upon promotion will receive wage experience credit on the new wage schedule equal to their wage experience credit or their net credited service (as provided in note 3 above).
   b. Employees to whom paragraph 5.a. is not applicable will be accorded promotion pay under the basic promotion pay plan described above.

VII. College Graduate Females Hired Directly into Management

In each Bell Company (other than Cincinnati Bell Inc., which did not have an Initial Management Development Program (IMDP) at any time between July 2, 1965, and December 31, 1971, and The Bell Telephone Company of Pennsylvania, which has heretofore satisfactorily resolved issues respecting female college graduate management hires):

A. Four-year college graduate female employees hired directly into management other than IMDP between July 2, 1965, and December 31, 1971, with the exception of those thereafter placed in IMDP or who were offered placement in IMDP and declined, will be surveyed to determine their interest in promotion to District level (third level) and above management positions. Provided, however, that any Bell Company may during the thirty-day period following the date of this Decree present to the EEOC and OFCC data indicating that an IMDP program was not underutilizing women during any year or years between July 2, 1965, and December 31, 1971. Upon presenting such data, this Section VII shall be inapplicable to four-year college graduate women hired directly into management for those years during which underutilization did not exist in the IMDP program in question. For purposes of this paragraph only, an absence of underutilization shall mean that women constituted 25% of all enrollees in an IMDP program. Failing agreement as to whether an IMDP program or an individual should be excluded from the application of this Section VII.A., such determination shall be submitted to the Court for final and binding adjudication under the Decree.

B. Those employees surveyed pursuant to Section VII.A. who are found to be interested will be scheduled for a two-to-three day assessment at a management center to evaluate their potential for promotion to District level. This assessment process will be conducted under procedures outlined by AT&T and will be completed to the extent possible within twelve months of the date of this Decree. Those employees assessed as satisfactory and who are below second level will be candidates for promotion to second level as vacancies occur and will be added to the District level potential list. Those employees assessed as satisfactory and who are at second level at the date of assessment will be candidates for promotion to District level as vacancies occur. Prior to promotion, both these second level and below second level employees may be reassigned for further developmental experience preparatory to promotion.

C. AT&T shall provide the EEOC and OFCC with descriptions of the criteria employed in making such assessments and on request will provide data at reasonable intervals on the number of persons evaluated and rated satisfactory; provided, however, the foregoing assessment procedure may not be relied upon as a defense by an individual Bell Company for its failure to reach the intermediate targets for those job classifications for which such procedures are used.

D. Those employees evaluated under paragraphs A and B of this Section VII who do not receive a satisfactory rating will return to their current assignments and their assessment rating will not be entered into their permanent personnel file.

VIII. Pay Adjustments
A. **Nonmanagement Jobs.** Employees promoted prior to January 1, 1973, will have

their rate of pay adjusted as of the first pay period after January 1, 1973, to the rate they would have achieved if the Promotion Pay Plan described in Section VI above had been in effect at the time of their promotion.

B. Craft Jobs Only.

1. In recognition of alleged claims of possible discrimination in compensation:

   a. Except for Switchroom Helpers at Michigan Bell Telephone Company (Michigan Bell), back wages shall be accorded those female employees who were resident in AAP classifications 6, 7, 9 and 10 at any time during the period January 1, 1971, to December 31, 1972, as follows:

   Each such employee shall be paid an amount equal to the difference between the amount which was paid to her under the promotion pay plan in effect at that time, and that which would have been paid to her during the period from January 1, 1971, to December 31, 1972, had the promotion pay plan described in Section VI above been in effect at the time of her promotion and for the period of time such employee was resident in a position in AAP classifications 6, 7, 9 or 10.

   b. In order to bring the minimum and maximum rate of pay of Switchroom Helpers at Michigan Bell into the range for the Frameman job in other Bell Companies, the rates for such job will be increased by means of the following formula to be effective the beginning of the first pay period following January 1, 1973:

	Present Minimum Rate	Present Maximum Rate	Proposed Minimum Rate	Proposed Maximum Rate
Zone 1	$124.50	$157.00	$127.50	$169.50
Zone 2	117.00	153.50	119.00	166.00
Zone 3	111.00	151.00	113.50	161.50
Zone 4	109.00	149.50	111.50	159.00

Michigan Bell will establish new wage schedules similar to those in effect for the Frameman job in other Bell Companies to reflect these minimum and maximum rates of pay.

Michigan Bell will pay to Switchroom Helpers who were so classified during any part of the period from January 1, 1971, to December 31, 1972, the difference between what they earned had the wage schedule set forth in the columns "Present Maximum Rate" and "Present Minimum Rate" been in effect during the period January 1, 1971, to December 31, 1972, and what they would have earned had the wage schedules been those set forth in the columns "Proposed Maximum Rate" and "Proposed Minimum Rate."

2. In recognition of alleged claims of possible delay in promotion in nonmanagement jobs because of discrimination, lump sum payments shall be made to each fe-

male and minority employee in each establishment where there exists in his or her respective job classification an underutilization of the group of which he or she is a member, who meets the following criteria:

a. had four or more years' net credited service on July 1, 1971;

b. has been or will be promoted from nonmanagement, noncraft jobs into AAP classifications 6, 7, 9 and 10 subsequent to June 30, 1971, and prior to July 1, 1974; and

c. remain in that job or another job in AAP classifications 6, 7, 9 and 10 for a total of more than six months.

    Those employees meeting the criteria listed in a), b) and c) will receive lump sum payments in accordance with the following schedule (a female minority employee shall be entitled to receive only one lump sum payment).

Promotion Date	Payment
7/1/71 through 12/31/71	$100
1/1/72 through 12/31/72	200
1/1/73 through 12/31/73	300
1/1/74 through 6/30/74	400

    In the event that on July 1, 1974, at least ten thousand (10,000) employees have not received payments pursuant to this Section VIII.B. (2), the Bell Companies will extend the date until 10,000 employees have been paid. All payments after July, 1974, shall be at the rate of $400.

C. **Management Jobs.** Those employees who are assessed as satisfactory pursuant to Section VII above will have their salary increased $100 per month as of their assessment date or September 1, 1973, whichever is earlier.

D. **Limitation on Recovery.** No individual who has received back pay and/or individual relief under a prior settlement agreement, conciliation, or consent decree shall be eligible to receive back pay or individual relief with respect to the same claim of discrimination as a result of this Decree.

Part B

I. Reporting

A. EEOC and OFCC will each receive summaries of the information compiled pursuant to Part A, Section IV.B. compiled by each Bell Company for each of the first two full calendar quarters following the date of this Decree and annually thereafter during the duration of this Decree. These quarterly and annual compilations will be forwarded in duplicate within 45 days subsequent to the second full calendar quarter following the date of this Decree and within 45 days after the close of each calendar year, respectively.

B. During the term of this Decree, except for the requirements of 29 C.F.R. Part 516 and the filing of EEO-1 reports and reports required pursuant to the equal employment rules of the Federal Communications Commission (FCC), 47 C.F.R. §§ 1.815, 21.307, and 23.49, or such other reports of general application which are hereinafter promulgated by EEOC, FCC, or the Department of Labor, the reports required by this Decree will be exclusive, and the Bell Companies shall not be required to file any additional reports or, except as noted below,* submit to any compliance reviews with respect to obligations under any law, regulation or Executive Order concerning equal employment opportunity including Title VII, the Equal Pay Act, Executive Order 11246, as amended.

II. Effect of Decree

A. As to the issues identified in the Complaint and Decree, compliance with the terms of this Decree resolves all remaining questions amongst the parties of the Bell Companies' compliance, for acts or practices occurring prior to the date of this Decree, with the requirements of Title VII of the Civil Rights Act of 1964, as amended, the Equal Pay Act of 1963, as amended, and Executive Order 11246, as amended. Moreover, compliance with the terms of the Decree in the future will constitute compliance with such laws, orders, and regulations as respects those issues dealt with in the Decree.

B. Acceptance by any person of individual relief ordered in Part A. Section VIII of this Decree shall constitute a waiver and release by such person of any claims for alleged violations of Title VII of the Civil Rights Act of 1964, as amended, 42 U.S.C. §§ 1981, 1983, Executive Order 11246, as amended, or any applicable state fair employment practice laws or regulations based upon occurrences prior to the date of this Decree.

C. In the present case, the Secretary's Complaint seeks restraint of any further delay in payment of wages, due under Sections 6 (d) and 15 (a) (2) of the Fair Labor Standards Act, within the meaning of the last sentence of Section 16 (b) of the Act, as to the following class of Defendants' employees:

1. All female employees in nonmanagement jobs who have claims for equal pay violations resulting from the application of the Defendants' promotion pay policies.

2. All Switchroom Helpers employed by Defendant, Michigan Bell Telephone Company, who have claims for equal pay violations resulting from the lower rates paid to Switchroom Helpers by that Defendant than are paid by other Defendants to Framemen.

*The above provision concerning compliance reviews shall not apply to investigations of charges by the EEOC under Section 706(b) of Title VII or to investigations by the Secretary under Section 11 of the Fair Labor Standards Act, and investigations to determine compliance with this Decree. Defendants agree to cooperate with the investigations above described.

D. This Decree shall not be interpreted as requiring the abandonment of any provisions in any Bell Company's collective bargaining agreement(s) except as required to maintain compliance with Federal law, Executive Orders and regulations promulgated pursuant thereto pertaining to discrimination in employment. All of the Bell Companies' obligations in this Decree are required for compliance with Federal law; provided, however, that nothing in this Decree is intended to restrict the right of the Bell Companies and the collective bargaining representatives of their employees to negotiate alternatives to the provisions of this Decree which would also be in compliance with Federal law.

To the extent that any Bell Company has in effect a posting and bidding system, said system shall continue to be used. Provided, however, that such system will be modified to the extent necessary to conform with Part A, Section III of this Decree.

Each Bell Company shall notify all appropriate collective bargaining representatives of the terms of this Decree and of its willingness to negotiate in good faith concerning these terms.

III. Compliance Procedures

A. The government Plaintiffs shall endeavor to coordinate their efforts to assure compliance with this Decree and shall develop such procedures as may be appropriate to this end.

B. The government will promptly notify the Bell Company involved and AT&T of any problems of noncompliance which it believes warrant investigation. Such Company will be given 60 days to investigate the complaint and conciliate with the government regarding the taking of any appropriate corrective action. At the end of this period, the government, if not satisfied, may seek an appropriate resolution of the question by the Court.

IV. Duration of the Decree

A. The Court retains jurisdiction of this action for entry of such orders as are necessary to effectuate the provisions of this Decree. The term of this Decree shall be six years from this date, but as to the issues in Part A, Sections VI, VII and VIII, the Defendants are permanently enjoined from violating the provisions of the Equal Pay Act. Upon certification to this Court that the payment of back wages ordered in Part A, Section VIII, have been made, that portion of this Decree will be dissolved as having been satisfied. Defendants waive none of their rights to move for dissolution or modification of this Decree at any time in addition to those specifically provided for in Section IV.B. (2), below.

B. An essential basis for the agreement of the parties to the entry of this Decree is that the opinion letters from EEOC and the Wage and Hour Administrator to be issued pursuant to the Memorandum of Agreement of the parties which is attached hereto shall remain in full force and effect. Therefore, should either opinion or portion thereof be withdrawn or overruled, the Defendant affected by such withdrawal or overruling may move the Court to dissolve any portion of the Decree which involves the issue or issues with respect to which the opinion letter has been withdrawn or modified and to strike any portion of the pleadings in this action relevant thereto, and such motion shall be granted.

So Ordered:

Leon Higginbotham
Judge, United States District
Court, Eastern District of
Pennsylvania

Consent to the entry of the foregoing Decree is hereby granted.

American Telephone and Telegraph
Company, for itself and on behalf
of its associated telephone companies as set forth herein.

[Signed:]

Charles Ryan,
George E. Ashley,
Harold S. Levy,
Clark G. Redick

American Telephone and Telegraph
Company
195 Broadway
New York, New York 10017

Bernard G. Segal,
Irving R. Segal

Kimber E. Vought
1719 Packard Building
Philadelphia, Pennsylvania 19102

Schnader, Harrison, Segal & Lewis
1719 Packard Building
Philadelphia, Pennsylvania 19102

Of Counsel

Thompson Powers
James D. Hutchinson
Ronald S. Cooper
   1250 Connecticut Avenue, N.W.
   Washington, D.C. 20036

Steptoe & Johnson
1250 Connecticut Avenue, N.W.
Washington, D.C.

Of Counsel

The Equal Employment Opportunity
Commission

William A. Carey
General Counsel

The U.S. Department of Labor

Carin Ann Clauss
Associate Solicitor

The United States of America

By: Robert E. J. Curran
      U.S. Attorney
      Eastern District of
         Pennsylvania

   David L. Rose
      Attorney
      Department of Justice
      Washington, D.C.

Appendix B

Twenty-Five Jobs With Greatest Number of Employees In Thirty SMSA's

Atlanta
Baltimore
Birmingham
Chicago
Cleveland
Dallas
Denver
Detroit
El Paso
Greensboro
Houston
Indianapolis
Jacksonville
Kansas City
Los Angeles
Memphis
Miami
Mobile
New Orleans
Newark
New York
Norfolk
Philadelphia
Phoenix
Richmond
Saint Louis
San Antonio
San Diego
San Francisco
Washington

Atlanta — Southern Bell Tel

Job Title	Grand Total	Males						Females					
		Black	SSA	Ind	Orntl	Anglo	Total	Black	SSA	Ind	Orntl	Anglo	Total
1 Operator	2278	0	0	0	0	0	0	812	3	0	2	1461	2278
2 Installer Repairman	640	36	0	0	0	604	640	0	0	0	0	0	0
3 PBX Installer-Repairman	568	5	1	0	0	562	568	0	0	0	0	0	0
4 Switchman	514	20	0	0	0	485	505	1	0	0	0	8	9
5 Service Representative	406	0	0	0	0	0	0	39	0	0	1	367	406
6 Commercial Clerk	230	0	0	0	0	0	0	52	0	0	0	177	230
7 Frameman	189	11	0	0	0	52	63	1	0	0	0	125	126
8 Cable Splicer	170	2	0	0	0	168	170	0	0	0	0	0	0
9 Processing Clerk	166	0	0	0	0	0	0	49	0	0	2	115	166
10 Lineman	131	11	0	0	0	120	131	0	0	0	0	0	0
11 Secretary	125	0	0	0	0	1	1	0	0	0	0	124	124
12 Cable Repairman	115	0	0	0	0	115	115	0	0	0	0	0	0
13 Test Deskman	109	2	0	0	0	98	100	0	0	0	0	9	9
14 Repair Clerk	107	0	0	0	0	0	0	6	0	0	0	101	107
15 Assistant Engineer	103	0	0	0	1	89	90	0	0	0	0	13	13
16 Assignment Clerk	99	0	0	0	0	0	0	10	0	0	0	89	99
17 Service Assistant	98	0	0	0	0	0	0	23	0	0	0	75	98
18 Central Office Foreman	90	0	0	0	0	89	89	0	0	0	0	1	1
19 Summarization Clerk	87	0	0	0	0	0	0	11	0	0	0	76	87
20 Business Office Supvr	87	0	0	0	0	0	0	2	0	0	0	85	87
21 Stenographer	84	0	0	0	0	0	0	7	0	0	0	77	84
22 Group Chief Operator	84	0	0	0	0	0	0	16	0	0	0	68	84
23 Central Office Clerk	82	0	0	0	0	0	0	2	0	0	0	80	82
24 Installation Foreman	78	0	0	0	0	78	78	0	0	0	0	0	0
25 Supervisor	77	0	0	0	0	43	48	0	0	0	0	29	29
Top Twenty-five Total	6717	87	1	0	1	2509	2598	1031	3	0	5	3080	4119

Baltimore – C & P Tel of Md

Job Title	Grand Total	Males						Females					
		Black	SSA	Ind	Orntl	Anglo	Total	Black	SSA	Ind	Orntl	Anglo	Total
1 Operator	1755	0	0	0	0	0	0	623	1	0	0	1131	1755
2 Central Office Repairman	556	20	0	0	0	535	555	0	0	0	0	1	1
3 Summarization Clerk	520	0	0	0	0	4	4	49	0	0	0	467	516
4 PBX Installer-Repairman	511	3	0	0	0	508	511	0	0	0	0	0	0
5 Installer Repairman	395	25	0	0	1	369	395	0	0	0	0	0	0
6 Service Representative	390	0	0	0	0	2	2	39	0	0	0	349	388
7 Processing Clerk	377	0	0	0	0	3	3	42	0	0	2	330	374
8 Foreman	316	10	0	0	0	306	316	0	0	0	0	0	0
9 Cable Splicer	266	2	0	0	0	264	266	0	0	0	0	0	0
10 Review and Reports Clerk	256	0	0	0	0	0	0	22	0	0	1	233	256
11 Staff Associate	238	6	0	0	0	185	191	1	0	0	0	46	47
12 Test Center Clerk	223	1	0	0	0	1	2	67	0	0	0	154	221
13 Service Order Clerk	188	0	0	0	0	0	0	72	0	0	0	116	188
14 Administrative Assistant	154	1	0	0	0	2	3	1	0	0	0	150	151
15 Service Assistant	146	0	0	0	0	0	0	28	0	0	0	118	146
16 Engineering Assistant	116	0	0	0	0	116	116	0	0	0	0	0	0
17 Frameman	115	31	0	0	0	84	115	0	0	0	0	0	0
18 Lineman	114	4	0	0	0	110	114	0	0	0	0	0	0
19 Staff Assistant	103	0	0	0	0	1	1	2	0	0	0	100	102
20 Assignment Clerk	90	0	0	0	0	0	0	6	0	0	0	84	90
21 Mail and File Clerk	81	1	0	0	0	2	3	16	0	0	0	62	78
22 Drafting Clerk	80	0	0	0	0	0	0	3	0	0	0	77	80
23 Group Supervisor	76	0	0	0	0	3	3	2	0	0	0	71	73
24 Group Chief Operator	72	0	0	0	0	0	0	11	0	0	0	61	72
25 Field Records Clerk	65	0	0	0	0	0	0	5	0	0	0	60	65
Top Twenty-five Total	7203	104	0	0	1	2495	2600	989	1	0	3	3610	4603

Birmingham – South Central Bell Tel

Job Title	Grand Total	Males						Females					
		Black	SSA	Ind	Orntl	Anglo	Total	Black	SSA	Ind	Orntl	Anglo	Total
1 Operator	829	0	0	0	0	0	0	334	1	0	0	494	829
2 Switchman	195	5	0	0	0	190	195	0	0	0	0	0	0
3 Installer Repairman	190	12	0	0	0	178	190	0	0	0	1	0	0
4 Service Representative	142	0	0	0	0	0	0	4	0	0	0	137	142
5 PBX Installer-Repairman	126	1	0	0	0	125	126	0	0	0	0	0	0
6 Processing Clerk	117	0	0	0	0	0	0	14	0	0	0	103	117
7 Stenographer	115	0	0	0	0	0	0	6	0	0	0	109	115
8 Secretary	100	0	0	0	0	0	0	1	0	0	0	99	100
9 Lineman	73	10	0	0	0	63	73	0	0	0	0	0	0
10 Summarization Clerk	72	0	0	0	0	0	0	5	0	0	0	67	72
11 Cable Splicer	68	1	0	0	0	67	68	0	0	0	0	0	0
12 Assistant Engineer	61	1	0	0	0	45	46	0	0	0	0	15	15
13 Supervisor	58	0	0	0	0	35	35	0	0	0	0	23	23
14 Traffic Results Clerk	55	0	0	0	0	0	0	7	0	0	0	49	55
15 Central Office Clerk	53	0	0	0	0	0	0	3	0	0	0	50	53
16 Service Assistant	51	0	0	0	0	0	0	5	0	0	0	46	51
17 Group Chief Operator	50	0	0	0	0	0	0	1	0	0	0	49	50
18 Stenographic Clerk	47	0	0	0	0	0	0	3	0	0	0	44	47
19 Directory Clerk	46	0	0	0	0	0	0	5	0	0	0	41	46
20 Cable Repairman	43	0	0	0	0	43	43	0	0	0	0	0	0
21 Unit Supervisor	40	0	0	0	0	0	0	3	0	0	0	40	40
22 Teller	39	0	0	0	0	0	0	3	0	0	0	36	39
23 Service Foreman	38	0	0	0	0	38	38	0	0	0	0	0	0
24 Accounting Supervisor	38	0	0	0	0	0	0	0	0	0	0	38	38
25 Frameman	36	4	0	0	0	7	11	0	0	0	0	25	25
Top Twenty-five Total	2682	34	0	0	0	791	825	391	1	0	1	1464	1857

Chicago – Illinois Bell

Job Title	Grand Total	Males						Females					
		Black	SSA	Ind	Orntl	Anglo	Total	Black	SSA	Ind	Orntl	Anglo	Total
1 Operator	5907	1	0	0	0	0	1	1675	64	2	5	4160	5906
2 Communications Mtnceman	1750	69	7	0	1	1658	1735	5	0	0	0	10	15
3 Service Representative	1714	1	0	0	0	0	1	371	12	0	2	1328	1713
4 Communications Serviceman	1600	94	8	0	0	1498	1600	0	0	0	0	0	0
5 Installer Repairman	1252	217	24	0	1	1009	1251	0	0	0	0	1	1
6 PBX Installer	1195	19	1	0	0	1175	1195	0	0	0	0	0	0
7 Service Order Clerk	726	2	0	0	0	3	5	136	7	0	0	578	721
8 Engineer	639	8	0	0	0	615	623	0	0	0	1	15	16
9 PBX Instln Apprentice	499	59	10	0	0	430	499	0	0	0	0	0	0
10 Processing Clerk	475	5	2	0	1	20	28	102	12	0	0	332	447
11 Frameman	474	95	16	0	3	279	393	21	2	0	0	58	81
12 Cable Splicer	471	16	4	0	0	451	471	0	0	0	0	0	0
13 Supervisor	442	13	1	0	0	92	106	26	3	1	0	307	336
14 Asst Staff Supervisor	433	5	1	0	0	335	341	3	0	0	0	88	92
15 Senior Plant Assigner	403	3	2	0	0	386	391	0	0	0	0	12	12
16 Staff Supervisor	383	3	0	0	0	351	354	0	0	0	0	29	29
17 Central Office Clerk	376	1	0	0	0	0	1	68	4	0	1	302	375
18 Lineman	370	22	6	0	0	342	370	0	0	0	0	0	0
19 Clerk	346	0	0	0	0	4	4	19	4	0	0	319	342
20 Central Office Foreman	341	7	0	0	0	334	341	0	0	0	0	0	0
21 Business Office Supvr	341	2	0	0	0	0	2	37	2	0	0	300	339
22 Group Chief Operator	316	0	0	0	0	0	0	37	3	0	0	274	316
23 Communications Consultant	308	16	1	0	0	269	286	3	0	1	0	19	22
24 District Staff Assistant	303	0	0	0	0	0	0	20	3	0	0	279	303
25 General Clerk	284	1	0	0	0	4	5	110	4	0	0	165	279
Top Twenty-five Total	21348	659	83	0	6	9255	10003	2635	120	4	10	8576	11345

Cleveland – Ohio Bell Tel

Job Title	Grand Total	Males						Females					
		Black	SSA	Ind	Orntl	Anglo	Total	Black	SSA	Ind	Orntl	Anglo	Total
1 Operator	1498	0	0	0	0	0	0	588	0	0	2	908	1498
2 Foreman	579	15	0	0	1	557	573	0	0	0	0	6	6
3 Central Office Repairman	453	30	1	0	1	420	452	0	0	0	0	1	1
4 Splicer	420	24	1	1	0	394	420	0	0	0	0	0	0
5 Service Representative	364	0	0	0	0	2	2	38	0	0	0	324	362
6 PBX Installer	350	11	0	0	0	339	350	0	0	0	0	0	0
7 PBX Repairman	334	6	0	0	0	328	334	0	0	0	0	0	0
8 Installer	312	38	2	0	1	271	312	0	0	0	0	0	0
9 Supervisor	296	1	0	0	0	13	14	23	0	0	0	259	282
10 Utility Clerk	293	1	0	0	0	0	1	79	0	0	0	213	292
11 Apparatusman	285	53	1	0	0	225	279	1	0	0	0	5	6
12 Accounting Clerk	279	0	0	0	0	0	0	89	0	0	0	190	279
13 Repairman	241	20	0	0	0	220	240	1	0	0	0	0	1
14 Deskman	187	10	0	0	0	177	187	0	0	0	0	0	0
15 Directory Clerk	161	0	0	0	0	0	0	70	0	0	0	91	161
16 Assignment Clerk	148	0	0	0	0	0	0	37	1	0	0	110	148
17 Assistant Analyst	143	4	0	0	2	51	57	4	0	1	0	81	86
18 Engineer	142	3	0	0	0	135	138	0	0	0	0	4	4
19 Service Assistant	140	0	0	0	0	0	0	36	0	0	0	104	140
20 Engineering Assistant	137	3	0	0	0	128	131	1	0	0	0	5	6
21 Project Engineer	128	1	1	0	0	125	127	0	0	0	0	1	1
22 Repair Clerk	124	0	0	0	0	1	1	35	1	0	0	87	123
23 Records Supervisor	124	0	0	0	0	0	0	15	0	0	0	109	124
24 Senior Utility Clerk	114	0	0	0	0	0	0	22	0	0	0	92	114
25 Lineman	114	12	0	0	0	102	114	0	0	0	0	0	0
Top Twenty-five Total	7366	232	6	1	5	3488	3732	1039	2	1	2	2590	3634

Dallas — Southwestern Bell

Job Title	Grand Total	Males						Females					
		Black	SSA	Ind	Orntl	Anglo	Total	Black	SSA	Ind	Orntl	Anglo	Total
1 Operator	2235	0	0	0	0	0	0	631	62	4	0	1538	2235
2 Switchman	436	5	2	1	0	474	437	0	0	0	0	4	4
3 Service Representative	301	0	0	0	0	1	1	13	4	1	1	281	300
4 Station Installer	271	8	2	0	0	261	271	0	0	0	0	0	0
5 PBX Installer	231	1	1	0	0	229	231	0	0	0	0	0	0
6 Directory Compilation Cl	183	0	0	0	0	0	0	3	6	0	0	147	183
7 Exchange Repairman	171	0	0	0	0	171	171	0	0	0	0	0	0
8 Frameman	145	11	4	1	0	116	132	0	0	0	0	13	13
9 Records Clerk	124	0	0	0	0	0	0	6	0	0	0	119	124
10 Central Office Clerk	123	0	1	0	0	0	0	6	0	0	0	117	123
11 Cable Splicer	113	3	0	0	0	109	113	0	0	0	0	0	0
12 Service Assistant	104	0	1	0	0	0	0	5	2	0	0	97	104
13 Secretary	101	0	0	0	0	0	0	3	0	0	0	101	101
14 Lineman	82	5	0	0	0	77	82	3	0	0	0	0	0
15 Deskman	71	0	0	0	0	66	66	0	0	0	0	5	5
16 Reports Clerk	67	0	0	0	0	0	0	0	0	0	0	66	67
17 Senior Engineer	67	0	0	0	0	67	67	0	0	0	0	0	0
18 Group Chief Operator	67	0	0	0	0	0	0	4	1	0	0	61	67
19 Business Office Supvr	61	0	0	0	0	0	0	0	2	0	0	61	61
20 Directory Representative	59	0	0	1	0	56	56	0	0	0	0	3	3
21 House Serviceman	56	44	0	0	0	11	56	0	0	0	0	0	0
22 Senior Stenographer	56	0	0	0	0	0	0	0	0	0	0	56	56
23 PBX Repairman	55	0	0	0	0	55	55	0	0	0	0	0	0
24 Installation Foreman	53	0	0	0	0	53	53	0	0	0	0	0	0
25 Chief Switchman	53	0	0	1	0	52	53	0	0	0	0	0	0
Top Twenty-five Total	5285	77	10	4	0	1748	1839	695	77	5	1	2668	3446

Denver – Mountain Bell

Job Title	Grand Total	Males						Females					
		Black	SSA	Ind	Orntl	Anglo	Total	Black	SSA	Ind	Orntl	Anglo	Total
1 Operator	1319	1	0	0	0	9	10	94	154	2	3	1056	1309
2 Accounting Clerk	404	1	2	0	0	22	25	33	33	2	0	311	379
3 Communications Serviceman	377	2	2	0	0	373	377	0	0	0	0	0	0
4 Analytical Clerk	371	0	0	0	0	0	0	9	23	0	1	338	371
5 Service Representative	334	0	0	0	0	2	2	8	2	1	0	321	332
6 Installer Repairman	282	7	13	0	1	261	282	0	0	0	0	0	0
7 Central Office Repairman	276	4	5	1	0	266	276	0	0	0	0	0	0
8 Service Foreman	207	1	0	0	0	206	207	0	0	0	0	0	0
9 Cable Splicer	200	1	8	0	1	190	200	0	0	0	0	0	0
10 Plant Reports Clerk	191	0	0	0	0	0	0	5	19	1	1	165	191
11 Lineman	173	7	6	0	0	160	173	0	0	0	0	0	0
12 Facilities Planner	166	0	1	0	0	154	155	0	0	0	0	5	5
13 Frameman	115	6	5	0	1	93	105	0	0	0	0	0	0
14 Technical Clerk	89	0	0	0	0	0	0	4	13	0	1	71	89
15 Service Assistant	88	0	0	0	0	0	0	3	3	0	0	82	88
16 Engineering Technician	86	0	0	0	0	75	75	0	0	0	0	11	11
17 Secretary	82	0	0	0	0	0	0	0	0	0	0	82	82
18 Business Office Supvr	82	0	0	0	0	0	0	0	0	0	0	82	82
19 Unit Supervisor	78	0	0	0	0	71	72	1	0	0	0	77	78
20 Staff Technician	78	1	0	0	0	70	70	0	0	0	0	6	6
21 Test Deskman	70	0	0	0	0	70	70	0	0	0	0	0	0
22 Central Office Clerk	70	0	0	0	0	0	0	4	2	0	0	64	70
23 Data Systems Specialist	68	1	2	0	0	51	54	0	0	0	0	14	14
24 Staff Assistant	67	0	0	0	0	0	0	0	2	0	0	65	67
25 Account Representative	66	0	0	0	0	0	0	3	3	0	0	60	66
Top Twenty-five Total	5337	32	44	1	3	2003	2083	164	254	6	6	2824	3254

Detroit – Michigan Bell

Job Title	Grand Total	Males						Females					
		Black	SSA	Ind	Orntl	Anglo	Total	Black	SSA	Ind	Orntl	Anglo	Total
1 Operator	3092	0	0	0	0	0	0	1159	15	6	3	1909	3092
2 Switchman	1078	73	5	0	3	990	1071	1	0	0	0	6	7
3 Service Representative	871	0	0	0	0	0	0	146	0	0	0	725	871
4 Station Installer	727	100	2	0	1	624	727	0	0	0	0	0	0
5 Splicer	686	34	1	2	0	649	686	0	0	0	0	0	0
6 PBX Installer	523	23	0	0	0	500	523	0	0	0	0	0	0
7 Station Repairman	431	61	0	0	0	370	431	0	0	0	0	0	0
8 Switchroom Helper	388	2	0	0	0	12	14	127	1	0	0	246	374
9 PBX Repairman	384	17	0	0	1	366	384	0	0	0	0	0	0
10 Staff Supervisor	343	3	0	0	1	312	316	0	0	0	0	27	27
11 Sec to District Dept Head	244	0	0	0	0	0	0	24	1	0	1	218	244
12 Test Center Clerk	241	0	0	0	0	0	0	90	1	0	1	149	241
13 Lineman	241	22	0	0	0	219	241	0	0	0	0	0	0
14 Service Assistant	225	0	0	0	0	0	0	71	1	0	0	153	225
15 Senior Operator	204	0	0	0	0	0	0	92	2	0	0	110	204
16 Processing Clerk	203	0	0	0	0	0	0	32	1	1	0	169	203
17 Testman Local	199	8	0	0	0	184	192	1	0	0	0	6	7
18 Installation Order Clerk	190	1	0	0	0	0	1	52	1	0	0	136	189
19 Project Engineer	190	0	1	0	1	186	188	0	0	0	0	2	2
20 Group Chief Operator	180	0	0	0	0	0	0	37	1	1	1	140	180
21 Business Office Supvr	172	0	0	0	0	1	1	22	3	0	1	145	171
22 General Commercial Clerk	169	0	0	0	0	0	0	44	0	0	0	125	169
23 Senior Clerk	167	0	0	0	0	0	0	47	1	0	0	119	167
24 Plant Engineer	151	2	0	0	0	149	151	0	0	0	0	0	0
25 General Clerk	138	0	0	0	0	0	0	42	0	0	0	96	138
Top Twenty-five Total	11437	346	9	2	7	4562	4926	1987	28	8	7	4481	6511

El Paso – Mountain Bell

Job Title	Grand Total	Males						Females					
		Black	SSA	Ind	Orntl	Anglo	Total	Black	SSA	Ind	Orntl	Anglo	Total
1 Operator	277	0	0	0	0	0	0	13	92	0	1	171	277
2 Communications Serviceman	62	0	5	0	0	57	62	0	0	0	0	0	0
3 Installer Repairman	58	2	5	0	0	51	58	0	0	0	0	0	0
4 Service Representative	49	0	0	0	0	0	0	1	11	0	0	37	49
5 Central Office Repairman	44	0	1	0	0	43	44	0	0	0	0	0	0
6 Analytical Clerk	40	0	0	0	0	0	0	0	9	0	0	31	40
7 Service Foreman	35	1	0	0	0	34	35	0	0	0	0	0	0
8 Central Office Clerk	30	0	0	0	0	0	0	0	9	0	0	21	30
9 Cable Splicer	29	3	3	0	0	23	29	0	0	0	0	0	0
10 Frameman	26	0	6	0	0	19	25	0	0	0	0	1	1
11 Lineman	19	0	2	0	0	15	17	0	0	0	0	2	2
12 Facilities Planner	18	0	0	0	0	16	16	0	0	0	0	2	2
13 Service Assistant	17	0	0	0	0	0	0	0	5	0	0	12	17
14 Engineering Technician	17	0	2	0	0	14	16	0	0	0	0	1	1
15 Service Order Clerk	13	0	0	0	0	1	1	0	1	0	0	11	12
16 Engineering Records Clerk	13	0	0	0	0	1	1	1	5	0	0	6	12
17 Order Center Reviewer	12	0	0	0	0	0	0	0	2	0	0	10	12
18 Group Chief Operator	12	0	0	0	0	0	0	0	5	0	0	7	12
19 Plant Dispatcher	11	0	0	0	0	0	0	0	1	0	0	10	11
20 Test Deskman	10	0	0	0	0	10	10	0	0	0	0	0	0
21 Plant Reports Clerk	10	0	0	0	0	0	0	0	2	0	0	8	10
22 Plant Repair Service Clerk	10	0	0	0	0	0	0	0	1	0	0	9	10
23 Janitor	9	5	4	0	0	0	9	0	0	0	0	0	0
24 Teller	9	0	0	0	0	0	0	0	0	0	0	9	9
25 Technical Clerk	9	0	0	0	0	0	0	0	3	0	0	6	9
Top Twenty-five Total	839	11	28	0	0	285	324	15	146	0	1	353	515

Grnsbro – Wnst – SLM – Southern Bell Tel

Job Title	Grand Total	Males						Females					
		Black	SSA	Ind	Orntl	Anglo	Total	Black	SSA	Ind	Orntl	Anglo	Total
1 Operator	642	0	0	0	0	0	0	222	0	0	0	420	642
2 Installer Repairman	117	2	0	0	0	115	117	0	0	0	0	0	0
3 PBX Installer-Repairman	83	0	0	0	0	83	83	0	0	0	0	0	0
4 Service Representative	78	0	0	0	0	0	0	3	0	0	0	75	78
5 Switchman	76	0	0	0	0	76	76	0	0	0	0	0	0
6 Service Assistant	47	0	0	0	0	0	0	7	0	0	0	40	47
7 Group Chief Operator	35	0	0	0	0	0	0	1	0	0	0	34	35
8 Cable Splicer	33	0	0	0	0	33	33	0	0	0	0	0	0
9 Lineman	32	0	0	0	0	32	32	0	0	0	0	0	0
10 Service Foreman	32	0	0	0	0	32	32	0	0	0	0	0	0
11 Frameman	29	4	0	0	0	4	8	0	0	0	0	21	21
12 Cable Repairman	26	0	0	0	0	26	26	0	0	0	0	0	0
13 General Office Clerk	26	0	0	0	0	0	0	0	0	0	0	26	26
14 Assignment Clerk	25	0	0	0	0	0	0	1	0	0	0	24	25
15 Dispatching Clerk	19	0	0	0	0	0	0	1	0	0	0	18	19
16 Repair Clerk	17	0	0	0	0	0	0	0	0	0	0	17	17
17 Central Office Foreman	16	0	0	0	0	16	16	0	0	0	0	0	0
18 Business Office Supvr	16	0	0	0	0	0	0	0	0	0	0	16	16
19 Toll Testcard Man	14	0	0	0	0	14	14	0	0	0	0	0	0
20 Outside Plant Clerk	14	0	0	0	0	0	0	0	0	0	0	14	14
21 Engineering Clerk	14	0	0	0	0	0	0	1	0	0	0	13	14
22 Communications Advisor	14	0	0	0	0	13	13	0	0	0	0	1	1
23 Assistant Engineer	14	0	0	0	0	12	12	0	0	0	0	2	2
24 Test Deskman	13	0	0	0	0	12	12	0	0	0	0	1	1
25 Service Order Typist	13	0	0	0	0	0	0	2	0	0	0	11	13
Top Twenty-five Total	1445	6	0	0	0	468	474	238	0	0	0	733	971

Houston — Southwestern Bell

Job Title	Grand Total	Males Black	Males SSA	Males Ind	Males Orntl	Males Anglo	Males Total	Females Black	Females SSA	Females Ind	Females Orntl	Females Anglo	Females Total
1 Operator	992	0	0	0	0	0	0	192	0	0	0	800	992
2 Switchman	277	22	1	0	1	253	277	0	0	0	0	0	0
3 Station Installer	270	1	0	0	0	269	270	0	0	0	0	0	0
4 Service Representative	211	22	0	0	0	189	211	0	0	0	0	0	0
5 PBX Installer	209	0	0	0	0	0	0	13	0	0	0	196	209
6 Frameman	196	0	0	0	0	0	0	12	0	0	0	184	196
7 Exchange Repairman	161	0	0	0	0	1	1	17	0	0	0	143	160
8 Cable Splicer	132	10	0	0	0	122	132	0	0	0	0	0	0
9 Records Clerk	128	0	0	0	0	0	0	4	0	0	0	124	128
10 Service Assistant	120	9	0	0	0	109	118	0	0	0	0	2	2
11 Lineman	115	1	0	0	0	114	115	0	0	0	0	0	0
12 Cable Splicers Helper	111	0	0	0	0	0	0	15	0	0	0	96	111
13 Telephone Repeaterman	110	1	0	0	0	2	3	21	0	0	0	86	107
14 Deskman	94	0	0	0	0	94	94	0	0	0	0	0	0
15 PBX Repairman	80	27	0	0	0	52	79	0	0	0	0	1	1
16 Secretary	76	0	0	0	0	0	0	3	0	0	0	73	76
17 Central Office Clerk	73	8	0	0	0	65	73	0	0	0	0	0	0
18 Group Chief Operator	73	0	0	0	0	1	1	13	0	0	1	58	72
19 Business Office Supvr	72	0	0	0	0	2	2	20	0	0	0	50	70
20 Installation Foreman	71	0	0	0	0	9	9	2	0	0	0	60	62
21 Cable Repairman	68	1	0	0	0	66	67	0	0	0	0	1	1
22 Equipment Clerk	68	0	0	0	0	0	0	0	1	0	0	67	68
23 Chief Switchman	65	5	0	0	0	58	63	2	0	0	0	0	2
24 Senior Stenographer	63	0	0	0	0	0	0	6	0	0	0	57	63
25 Stockman	58	1	0	0	0	1	2	1	0	0	0	55	56
Top Twenty-five Total	**3893**	**108**	**1**	**0**	**1**	**1407**	**1517**	**321**	**1**	**0**	**1**	**2053**	**2376**

Indianapolis — Indiana Bell

Job Title	Grand Total	Males Black	Males SSA	Males Ind	Males Orntl	Males Anglo	Males Total	Females Black	Females SSA	Females Ind	Females Orntl	Females Anglo	Females Total
1 Operator	2110	0	0	0	0	0	0	896	135	2	1	1076	2110
2 Switchman	428	22	11	0	0	381	414	0	0	0	0	14	14
3 Exchange Repairman	397	23	8	0	0	366	397	0	0	0	0	0	0
4 Installer Repairman	372	0	0	0	0	0	0	17	17	0	0	338	372
5 Service Representative	321	2	2	0	0	317	321	0	0	0	0	0	0
6 Plant Clerk	197	24	11	0	1	144	180	0	0	0	0	17	17
7 Utility Clerk	191	6	2	0	0	183	191	0	0	0	0	0	0
8 Cable Splicer	143	2	1	0	0	140	143	0	0	0	0	0	0
9 Departmental Assistant	125	2	0	0	0	2	4	13	9	0	0	99	121
10 Assistant Engineer	116	0	0	0	0	0	0	12	7	1	0	96	116
11 Project Engineer	115	7	4	0	0	104	115	0	0	0	0	0	0
12 Repair Clerk	105	7	1	0	0	97	105	0	0	0	0	0	0
13 General Clerk	102	1	0	0	0	94	95	0	0	0	0	7	7
14 Service Supervisor	100	0	1	0	0	90	91	1	0	0	0	8	9
15 Frameman	92	0	0	0	0	92	92	0	0	0	0	0	0
16 Staff Assistant	82	0	0	0	0	0	0	0	2	0	0	80	82
17 Lineman	82	0	0	0	0	0	0	4	4	1	0	73	82
18 Special Clerk	82	0	0	0	0	0	0	7	7	0	0	68	82
19 Machine Clerk	80	0	0	0	0	0	0	2	0	1	0	77	80
20 Accounting Clerk	70	0	0	0	0	70	70	0	0	0	0	0	0
21 Testman	65	1	0	0	0	64	65	0	0	0	0	0	0
22 Senior Accounting Clerk	61	0	0	0	0	0	0	1	7	0	0	53	61
23 Dial Office Clerk	59	0	0	0	0	59	59	0	0	0	0	0	0
24 Cable Repairman	54	0	0	0	0	0	0	3	4	0	0	47	54
25 Administrative Assistant	53	19	2	0	0	32	53	0	0	0	0	0	0
Top Twenty-five Total	5602	116	43	0	1	2235	2395	956	192	5	1	2053	3207

Jacksonville — Southern Bell Tel

Job Title	Grand Total	Males						Females					
		Black	SSA	Ind	Orntl	Anglo	Total	Black	SSA	Ind	Orntl	Anglo	Total
1 Operator	665	0	0	0	0	0	0	228	0	0	0	437	665
2 Installer Repairman	223	5	0	0	0	218	223	0	0	0	0	0	0
3 PBX Installer-Repairman	143	0	0	0	0	143	143	0	0	0	0	0	0
4 Service Representative	140	0	0	0	0	0	0	4	0	0	0	136	140
5 Switchman	136	1	0	0	0	130	131	0	0	0	0	5	5
6 Directory Clerk	91	0	0	0	0	0	0	3	0	0	0	88	91
7 Assistant Engineer	87	1	0	0	0	79	80	0	0	0	0	7	7
8 Lineman	76	15	0	0	0	61	76	0	0	0	0	0	0
9 Cable Splicer	73	4	0	0	0	69	73	0	0	0	0	0	0
10 Cable Repairman	70	0	0	0	0	70	70	0	0	0	0	0	0
11 Engineering Clerk	63	0	0	0	0	0	0	5	0	0	1	57	63
12 Service Assistant	62	0	0	0	0	0	0	3	0	0	0	59	62
13 Traffic Results Clerk	61	0	0	0	0	0	0	5	0	0	0	56	61
14 Processing Clerk	61	0	0	0	0	0	0	6	0	0	1	54	61
15 Frameman	53	3	0	0	0	29	32	0	0	0	0	21	21
16 Engineering Associate	52	0	1	0	0	51	52	0	0	0	0	0	0
17 Group Chief Operator	41	0	0	0	0	0	0	0	0	0	0	41	41
18 Special Clerk	40	0	0	0	0	0	0	0	0	0	0	40	40
19 Test Deskman	39	0	0	0	0	38	38	0	0	0	0	1	1
20 Secretary	37	0	0	0	0	0	0	0	0	0	0	37	37
21 Stenographic Clerk	35	0	0	0	0	0	0	0	0	0	0	35	35
22 Stenographer	34	0	0	0	0	0	0	0	0	0	1	33	34
23 Accounting Supervisor	34	0	0	0	0	0	0	0	0	0	0	34	34
24 Repair Clerk	33	0	0	0	0	1	1	1	0	0	0	31	32
25 Central Office Clerk	33	0	0	0	0	0	0	1	0	0	0	32	33
Top Twenty-five Total	2382	29	1	0	0	889	919	256	0	0	3	1204	1463

Kansas City – Southwestern Bell

Job Title	Grand Total	Males						Females					
		Black	SSA	Ind	Orntl	Anglo	Total	Black	SSA	Ind	Orntl	Anglo	Total
1 Operator	1227	0	0	0	0	0	0	341	22	1	1	862	1227
2 Switchman	275	4	0	0	0	269	273	0	0	0	0	2	2
3 Service Representative	246	0	0	0	0	0	0	8	1	0	0	237	246
4 Exchange Repairman	212	0	1	0	0	211	212	0	0	0	0	0	0
5 Station Installer	206	8	1	0	0	197	206	0	0	0	0	0	0
6 PBX Installer	150	0	0	0	0	150	150	0	0	0	0	0	0
7 Frameman	137	34	7	0	0	92	133	0	0	0	0	4	4
8 Service Assistant	102	0	0	0	0	0	0	11	5	0	0	86	102
9 Records Clerk	92	0	0	0	0	0	0	6	1	0	0	85	92
10 Cable Splicer	91	2	0	0	0	89	91	0	0	0	0	0	0
11 General Office Clerk	80	0	0	0	0	0	0	5	1	0	0	74	80
12 Deskman	65	0	0	0	0	65	65	0	0	0	0	0	0
13 Secretary	61	0	0	0	0	0	0	0	0	0	0	61	61
14 Lineman	55	7	0	0	0	48	55	0	0	0	0	0	0
15 Business Office Supvr	52	0	0	0	0	0	0	0	0	0	0	52	52
16 Telephone Repeaterman	50	0	0	0	0	50	50	0	0	0	0	0	0
17 Group Chief Operator	48	0	0	0	0	0	0	0	2	0	0	46	48
18 Draftswoman	44	0	0	0	0	0	0	3	0	0	0	41	44
19 Teletypeman	39	0	0	1	0	38	39	0	0	0	0	0	0
20 Teller	39	0	0	0	0	0	0	5	0	0	0	34	39
21 Service Order Writer	39	0	0	0	0	0	0	4	1	0	0	34	39
22 Stockman	38	18	0	0	0	20	38	0	0	0	0	0	0
23 Chief Switchman	38	0	0	0	0	38	38	0	0	0	0	0	0
24 Reports Clerk	34	0	0	0	0	0	0	2	2	0	0	30	34
25 Telephone Saleswoman	30	0	0	0	0	0	0	2	0	0	0	28	30
Top Twenty-five Total	3450	73	9	1	0	1267	1350	387	35	1	1	1676	2100

Los Angeles – Pacific Tel

Job Title	Grand Total	Males						Females					
		Black	SSA	Ind	Orntl	Anglo	Total	Black	SSA	Ind	Orntl	Anglo	Total
1 Operator	8005	4	5	0	2	55	66	1518	589	9	68	5755	7939
2 Cent Ofc Equipment Man	1675	83	107	0	30	1451	1671	1	0	0	0	3	4
3 Staff Clerk	1552	5	2	1	0	6	14	242	212	4	48	1032	1538
4 Service Representative	1370	2	3	0	0	6	11	167	57	2	8	1125	1359
5 PBX Installer	1128	58	56	2	14	598	1128	0	0	0	0	0	0
6 Plant Service Clerk	1095	20	10	0	3	26	59	309	142	5	30	549	1036
7 PBX Repairman	791	21	36	3	14	717	791	0	0	0	0	0	0
8 Station Installer	728	99	85	0	9	533	726	0	0	0	0	2	2
9 Frameman	697	100	89	2	13	467	671	3	1	0	0	22	26
10 Reports Clerk	686	0	0	0	0	0	0	81	54	0	18	533	686
11 Splicer	682	35	34	0	1	612	682	0	0	0	0	0	0
12 Office Clerk	611	3	1	0	7	8	19	151	75	2	30	334	592
13 Transmission Man	609	18	38	2	33	518	609	0	0	0	0	0	0
14 Central Office Clerk	581	0	0	0	0	0	0	76	38	1	6	460	581
15 Engineer	550	6	14	0	4	448	472	0	2	0	0	76	78
16 Service Assistant	532	0	1	0	0	0	1	74	47	1	4	405	531
17 Plant Reports Clerk	491	0	0	0	1	1	2	64	39	1	10	375	489
18 Marketing Representative	474	3	5	0	0	17	25	41	39	0	8	361	449
19 Communications Consultant	443	11	13	0	2	386	412	1	0	0	0	30	31
20 Senior Engineer	437	0	8	0	4	414	426	0	0	0	0	11	11
21 Assistant Tffc Opertng Mg	432	0	0	0	0	0	0	33	15	0	1	383	432
22 Reconciliation Clerk	416	3	2	0	0	6	11	102	53	2	11	237	405
23 Compilation Clerk	411	14	6	0	4	12	36	145	56	3	8	163	375
24 Deskman	376	10	11	0	2	353	376	0	0	0	0	0	0
25 Line Assigner	374	3	6	0	4	148	161	24	22	0	7	160	213
Top Twenty-five Total	25146	498	532	10	147	7182	8369	3032	1441	31	257	12016	16777

Memphis — South Centrl & Southwestern Bell

Job Title	Grand Total	Males Black	Males SSA	Males Ind	Males Orntl	Males Anglo	Males Total	Females Black	Females SSA	Females Ind	Females Orntl	Females Anglo	Females Total
1 Operator	291	0	0	0	0	0	0	142	0	0	0	149	291
2 Installer Repairman	208	20	0	1	0	187	208	0	0	0	0	0	0
3 Switchman	180	3	0	0	0	174	177	0	0	0	0	3	3
4 Service Representative	164	0	0	0	0	0	0	19	0	1	0	144	164
5 PBX Installer-Repairman	123	0	0	0	0	123	123	0	0	0	0	0	0
6 Cable Splicer	71	3	0	0	0	68	71	0	0	0	0	0	0
7 Frameman	59	7	0	0	0	33	40	1	0	0	0	18	19
8 Processing Clerk	52	0	0	0	0	0	0	4	0	0	0	48	52
9 Lineman	45	5	0	0	0	40	45	0	0	0	0	0	0
10 Cable Repairman	42	0	0	0	0	42	42	0	0	0	0	0	0
11 Repair Clerk	36	0	0	0	0	0	0	14	0	0	0	22	36
12 Central Office Clerk	36	0	0	0	0	0	0	3	0	0	0	33	36
13 Test Deskman	35	0	0	0	0	29	29	0	0	0	0	6	6
14 Assignment Clerk	35	0	0	0	0	0	0	9	0	0	0	26	35
15 Unit Supervisor	34	0	0	0	0	0	0	0	0	0	0	34	34
16 Central Office Foreman	30	0	0	0	0	30	30	0	0	0	0	0	0
17 Service Order Typist	27	0	0	0	0	0	0	2	0	0	0	25	27
18 Dispatching Clerk	25	0	0	0	0	0	0	0	0	0	0	25	25
19 Installation Foreman	25	0	0	0	0	25	25	0	0	0	0	0	0
20 Communications Advisor	20	0	0	0	0	20	20	0	0	0	0	0	0
21 Group Chief Operator	19	0	0	0	0	0	0	1	0	0	0	18	19
22 Special Clerk	18	0	0	0	0	0	0	0	0	0	0	18	18
23 Service Assistant	18	0	0	0	0	0	0	3	0	0	0	15	18
24 Summarization Clerk	17	0	0	0	0	0	0	1	0	0	1	15	17
25 Stenographer	16	0	0	0	0	0	0	0	0	0	1	15	16
Top Twenty-five Total	1626	38	0	1	0	771	810	199	0	1	2	614	816

Miami – Southern Bell Tel

Job Title	Grand Total	Males Black	Males SSA	Males Ind	Males Orntl	Males Anglo	Males Total	Females Black	Females SSA	Females Ind	Females Orntl	Females Anglo	Females Total
1 Operator	2133	0	0	0	0	0	0	600	76	0	2	1455	2133
2 Installer Repairman	796	18	46	0	5	727	796	0	0	0	0	0	0
3 PBX Installer-Repairman	571	6	21	0	0	544	571	0	0	0	0	0	0
4 Service Representative	445	0	1	0	0	8	9	39	29	0	1	367	436
5 Switchman	370	14	27	0	2	308	351	0	0	0	0	19	19
6 Cable Splicer	273	16	15	0	0	242	273	0	0	0	0	0	0
7 Frameman	265	15	21	0	3	112	151	5	0	0	1	108	114
8 Test Deskman	153	0	2	0	0	130	132	3	0	0	0	18	21
9 Repair Clerk	153	0	0	0	0	2	2	26	5	0	0	120	151
10 Cable Repairman	140	2	2	0	0	136	140	0	0	0	0	0	0
11 Assistant Engineer	138	1	5	0	0	127	133	0	0	0	0	5	5
12 Assignment Clerk	130	0	0	0	0	1	1	24	8	0	1	96	129
13 Lineman	127	12	4	0	1	110	127	0	0	0	0	0	0
14 Service Assistant	127	0	0	0	0	0	0	17	1	0	0	109	127
15 Group Chief Operator	117	0	0	0	0	0	0	1	1	0	0	115	117
16 Directory Clerk	115	0	1	0	0	0	1	3	12	0	1	98	114
17 Installation Foreman	114	0	0	0	0	114	114	0	0	0	0	0	0
18 Central Office Clerk	110	0	0	0	0	0	0	10	11	0	0	89	110
19 Summarization Clerk	106	0	0	0	0	0	0	7	11	0	1	87	106
20 Engineering Clerk	99	0	0	0	0	1	1	8	16	0	1	73	98
21 Dispatching Clerk	93	0	0	0	0	0	0	25	7	0	0	61	93
22 Plant Assigner	90	0	0	0	0	30	30	0	0	0	0	60	60
23 Service Clerk Typist	88	0	0	0	0	1	1	7	18	0	0	62	87
24 Business Office Supvr	88	0	0	0	0	0	0	0	2	0	0	86	88
25 Central Office Foreman	87	0	0	0	0	87	87	0	0	0	0	0	0
Top Twenty-five Total	6928	84	145	0	11	2680	2920	775	197	0	8	3028	4008

Mobile — South Central Bell Tel

Job Title	Grand Total	Males Black	SSA	Ind	Orntl	Anglo	Total	Females Black	SSA	Ind	Orntl	Anglo	Total
1 Operator	358	0	0	0	0	0	0	38	0	0	0	320	358
2 Installer Repairman	100	3	0	0	0	97	100	0	0	0	0	0	0
3 Service Representative	62	0	0	0	0	0	0	1	0	0	0	61	62
4 Switchman	60	0	0	0	0	60	60	0	0	0	0	0	0
5 PBX Installer-Repairman	43	0	0	0	0	43	43	0	0	0	0	0	0
6 Toll Testcard Man	31	0	0	0	0	31	31	0	0	0	0	0	0
7 Cable Splicer	26	1	0	0	0	25	26	0	0	0	0	0	0
8 Central Office Clerk	25	0	0	0	0	0	0	0	0	0	0	25	25
9 Lineman	24	7	0	0	0	17	24	0	0	0	0	0	0
10 Cable Repairman	22	0	0	0	0	22	22	0	0	0	0	0	0
11 Service Assistant	21	0	0	0	0	0	0	0	0	0	0	21	21
12 Group Chief Operator	19	0	0	0	0	0	0	0	0	0	0	19	19
13 Test Deskman	15	0	0	0	0	14	14	0	0	0	0	1	1
14 Stenographer	15	0	0	0	0	0	0	0	0	0	0	15	15
15 Service Order Typist	15	0	0	0	0	0	0	0	0	0	0	15	15
16 Repair Clerk	14	0	0	0	0	0	0	0	0	0	0	14	14
17 Frameman	13	2	0	0	0	11	13	0	0	0	0	0	0
18 Unit Supervisor	13	0	0	0	0	0	0	0	0	0	0	13	13
19 Service Foreman	12	0	0	0	0	12	12	0	0	0	0	0	0
20 Assistant Engineer	11	0	0	0	0	11	11	0	0	0	0	0	0
21 Assignment Clerk	10	0	0	0	0	0	0	0	0	0	0	10	10
22 Service Order Clerk	9	0	0	0	0	0	0	0	0	0	0	9	9
23 Central Office Foreman	5	0	0	0	0	9	9	0	0	0	0	0	0
24 Plant Assigner	8	0	0	0	0	8	8	0	0	0	0	0	0
25 Installation Foreman	8	0	0	0	0	8	8	0	0	0	0	0	0
Top Twenty-five Total	943	13	0	0	0	368	381	39	0	0	0	523	562

Newark – New Jersey Bell Tel

Job Title	Grand Total	Males Black	Males SSA	Males Ind	Males Orntl	Males Anglo	Males Total	Females Black	Females SSA	Females Ind	Females Orntl	Females Anglo	Females Total
1 Operator	1960	0	0	0	0	0	0	828	21	0	1	1110	1960
2 Installer	645	63	8	0	0	574	645	0	0	0	0	0	0
3 Service Representative	496	0	0	0	0	0	0	55	3	0	0	438	496
4 Switchman-Central Office	410	8	0	0	0	402	410	0	0	0	0	0	0
5 Records Clerk	369	0	0	0	0	1	1	88	8	0	5	267	368
6 Repairman	301	15	3	0	0	283	301	0	0	0	0	0	0
7 Rcds Clk-Assignment Bur	282	0	0	0	0	1	1	85	8	0	4	184	281
8 Staff Assistant	275	8	1	0	0	186	195	2	0	0	0	78	80
9 Splicer	258	19	0	0	0	239	258	0	0	0	0	0	0
10 Service Assistant	251	0	0	0	0	0	0	71	1	0	0	179	251
11 Frameman	207	26	2	0	0	179	207	0	0	0	0	0	0
12 Clerk-Other	197	0	0	0	0	0	0	40	4	0	1	152	197
13 Lineman	192	23	1	0	1	167	192	0	0	0	0	0	0
14 Svc Order Reviewing Clerk	179	0	0	0	0	0	0	33	2	0	1	143	179
15 Assistant Engineer	178	4	0	0	0	169	173	0	0	0	0	5	5
16 Engineer	176	0	1	0	0	174	175	0	0	0	0	1	1
17 Machine Clerk-Key Punch	164	0	0	0	0	0	0	87	22	1	2	52	164
18 Plant Serviceman	142	26	18	0	2	96	142	0	0	0	0	0	0
19 Senior Records Clerk	141	0	0	0	0	0	0	12	1	0	0	128	141
20 Directory Review Clerk	131	0	0	0	0	0	0	12	1	0	0	118	131
21 Staff Analyst	130	1	0	0	0	108	109	1	0	0	0	20	21
22 Supervising Clerk	128	0	1	0	0	3	4	2	1	0	1	120	124
23 Deskman	120	1	1	0	0	118	120	0	0	0	0	0	0
24 Reports Clerk	109	0	0	0	0	0	0	36	1	0	1	71	109
25 Records Clerk-Computer	109	5	1	0	1	18	25	32	0	0	0	52	84
Top Twenty-five Total	7550	199	37	0	4	2718	2958	1384	73	1	16	3118	4592

New Orleans – South Central Bell Tel

Job Title	Grand Total	Males						Females					
		Black	SSA	Ind	Orntl	Anglo	Total	Black	SSA	Ind	Orntl	Anglo	Total
1 Operator	1361	0	0	0	0	0	0	432	2	0	2	925	1361
2 Installer Repairman	300	13	1	0	0	286	300	0	0	0	0	0	0
3 Service Representative	265	0	0	0	0	0	0	21	0	0	0	244	265
4 Switchman	228	7	1	0	1	219	228	0	0	0	0	0	0
5 PBX Installer-Repairman	199	0	0	0	0	199	199	0	0	0	0	0	0
6 Directory Clerk	93	0	0	0	0	0	0	13	1	0	0	79	93
7 Group Chief Operator	85	0	0	0	0	0	0	3	0	0	0	82	85
8 Assistant Engineer	74	1	0	0	0	50	51	2	0	0	0	21	23
9 Unit Supervisor	72	0	0	0	0	0	0	2	0	0	0	70	72
10 Frameman	67	11	0	0	0	56	67	0	0	0	0	0	0
11 Service Order Typist	66	0	0	0	0	0	0	8	0	0	0	58	66
12 Processing Clerk	64	0	0	0	0	0	0	9	0	0	1	54	64
13 Assignment Clerk	63	0	0	0	0	0	0	0	0	0	0	63	63
14 Service Assistant	61	0	0	0	0	0	0	9	0	0	0	52	61
15 Cable Repairman	58	1	1	0	0	56	58	0	0	0	0	0	0
16 Summarization Clerk	58	0	0	0	0	0	0	5	0	0	0	53	58
17 Engineering Clerk	57	0	0	0	0	0	0	5	0	0	0	52	57
18 Central Office Clerk	56	0	0	0	0	0	0	6	0	0	0	50	56
19 Engineer	56	0	0	0	0	56	56	0	0	0	0	0	0
20 Test Deskman	54	1	0	0	0	53	54	0	0	0	0	0	0
21 Cable Splicer	52	2	0	0	0	50	52	0	0	0	0	0	0
22 Traffic Results Clerk	48	0	0	0	0	0	0	2	0	0	0	46	48
23 Repair Clerk	42	0	0	0	0	0	0	4	0	0	0	38	42
24 Stenographer	40	0	0	0	0	0	0	3	0	0	0	37	40
25 Supervisor	40	1	0	0	0	30	31	0	0	0	0	9	9
Top Twenty-five Total	3559	37	3	0	1	1055	1096	524	3	0	3	1933	2463

New York – New York Tel

Job Title	Grand Total	Males						Females					
		Black	SSA	Ind	Orntl	Anglo	Total	Black	SSA	Ind	Orntl	Anglo	Total
1 Operator	15877	0	0	0	0	0	0	8719	487	1	40	6630	15877
2 Installer	5897	504	193	0	33	5166	5896	0	1	0	0	0	1
3 Switchman	4171	336	117	0	70	3587	4110	2	0	0	0	59	61
4 Representative	3744	58	16	0	4	197	275	650	76	0	13	2730	3469
5 Repairman	3740	413	169	0	11	3145	3738	1	0	0	0	1	2
6 Service Clerk	3066	171	49	0	36	253	509	894	118	0	30	1515	2557
7 Cable Splicer	2771	283	86	0	7	2394	2770	0	0	0	0	1	1
8 Frameman	2533	505	200	0	37	1786	2528	0	0	0	0	5	5
9 Service Foreman	1904	25	2	0	1	1876	1904	0	0	0	0	0	0
10 Deskman	1601	148	57	0	7	1389	1601	0	0	0	0	0	0
11 Processing Clerk	1361	64	15	0	17	100	196	420	87	1	14	643	1165
12 Service Assistant	1140	0	0	0	0	0	0	583	10	0	0	547	1140
13 Engineer	1032	6	0	0	4	1006	1016	0	0	0	0	16	16
14 Repair Service Attendant	992	40	7	0	1	71	119	310	22	0	2	539	873
15 Secretary	941	0	0	0	0	3	3	68	25	0	7	838	938
16 Central Office Foreman	945	19	2	0	2	922	945	0	0	0	0	0	0
17 Dial Office Clerk	857	6	0	0	2	7	15	380	41	0	3	418	842
18 Lineman	768	48	10	0	2	708	768	0	0	0	0	0	0
19 Staff Assistant	730	11	1	0	1	378	391	26	4	0	0	309	339
20 Building Serviceman	717	364	91	0	8	254	717	0	0	0	0	0	0
21 Business Office Supvr	705	0	1	0	0	8	9	79	8	0	2	607	696
22 Assistant Engineer	646	16	6	0	12	567	601	0	1	0	1	43	45
23 Group Chief Operator	640	0	0	0	0	0	0	215	3	0	0	422	640
24 Clerk	617	3	0	0	0	7	10	202	27	0	7	371	607
25 Service Order Typist	588	0	0	0	0	1	1	148	19	0	7	413	587
Top Twenty-five Total	57983	3020	1022	0	255	23825	28122	12697	929	2	126	16107	29861

Norfolk – C & P Tel of Va

Job Title	Grand Total	Males Black	Males SSA	Males Ind	Males Orntl	Males Anglo	Males Total	Females Black	Females SSA	Females Ind	Females Orntl	Females Anglo	Females Total
1 Operator	677	0	0	0	0	0	0	76	0	0	1	600	677
2 Central Office Repairman	186	3	0	0	0	183	186	0	0	0	0	0	0
3 Installer Repairman	183	10	0	0	0	173	183	0	0	0	0	0	0
4 Technical Clerk	161	0	0	0	0	0	0	3	0	0	0	158	161
5 PBX Installer-Repairman	146	0	0	0	0	146	146	0	0	0	0	0	0
6 Service Representative	119	0	0	0	0	0	0	4	0	0	0	115	119
7 Foreman	97	0	0	0	0	96	96	0	0	0	0	1	1
8 Records Clerk	71	0	0	0	0	0	0	5	0	0	1	65	71
9 Cable Splicer	68	1	0	0	0	66	67	0	0	0	0	1	1
10 Engineering Assistant	39	0	0	0	0	39	39	0	0	0	0	0	0
11 Lineman	30	0	0	0	0	30	30	0	0	0	0	0	0
12 Building Attendant	29	28	0	0	0	1	29	0	0	0	0	0	0
13 Frameman	28	2	0	0	0	26	28	0	0	0	0	0	0
14 Group Chief Operator	28	0	0	0	0	0	0	0	0	0	0	28	28
15 Summarization Clerk	27	0	0	0	0	0	0	0	0	0	0	27	27
16 Service Assistant	24	0	0	0	0	0	0	1	0	0	0	23	24
17 Central Office Clerk	19	0	0	0	0	0	0	0	0	0	0	19	19
18 Service Supervisor	18	0	0	0	0	0	0	0	0	0	0	18	18
19 Foreman Supervisor	17	0	0	0	0	17	17	0	0	0	0	0	0
20 Staff Assistant	16	1	0	0	0	0	1	1	0	0	0	14	15
21 Administrative Assistant	13	0	0	0	0	0	0	0	0	0	0	13	13
22 Control Clerk	12	0	0	0	0	0	0	0	0	0	0	12	12
23 Group Supervisor	12	0	0	0	0	0	0	0	0	0	0	12	12
24 Coin Telephone Collector	11	1	0	0	0	10	11	0	0	0	0	0	0
25 Staff Associate	11	0	0	0	0	8	8	0	0	0	0	3	3
Top Twenty-five Total	2042	46	0	0	0	795	841	90	0	0	2	1109	1201

Philadelphia – Bell Tel of Pa & NJ Bell Tel

Job Title	Grand Total	Males Black	Males SSA	Males Ind	Males Orntl	Males Anglo	Males Total	Females Black	Females SSA	Females Ind	Females Orntl	Females Anglo	Females Total
1 Operator	3761	0	0	0	0	0	0	1182	8	0	3	2568	3761
2 Senior Clerk	996	0	0	0	0	0	0	129	0	0	0	867	996
3 Switchman	950	47	2	0	3	897	949	0	0	0	0	1	1
4 Service Representative	930	0	0	0	0	0	0	102	1	1	1	825	930
5 PBX Installer	679	17	0	0	0	662	679	0	0	0	0	0	0
6 Splicer	570	21	3	0	0	546	570	0	0	0	0	0	0
7 Station Installer	549	79	0	0	0	470	549	0	0	0	0	0	0
8 General Clerk	504	0	0	0	0	0	0	94	1	0	0	409	504
9 Processing Clerk	418	0	0	0	0	0	0	75	1	0	1	342	418
10 PBX Repairman	391	7	0	0	0	384	391	0	0	0	0	0	0
11 Frameman	362	95	1	0	0	258	354	1	0	0	0	7	8
12 Service Foreman	345	1	0	0	0	344	345	0	0	0	0	0	0
13 Field Clerk	337	0	0	0	0	0	0	63	1	0	0	273	337
14 Lineman	335	29	1	0	0	305	335	0	0	0	0	0	0
15 Engineering Associate	327	3	0	0	0	304	307	0	0	0	0	20	20
16 Records Clerk	307	0	0	0	0	0	0	27	0	0	0	280	307
17 Deskman	304	7	0	0	0	296	303	0	0	0	0	1	1
18 General Field Clerk	297	0	0	0	0	0	0	47	1	0	0	249	297
19 Staff Associate	261	4	0	0	1	157	162	0	1	0	0	98	99
20 Station Repairman	250	15	0	0	0	235	250	0	0	0	0	0	0
21 Installer	247	13	1	0	0	233	247	0	0	0	0	0	0
22 Supervisor	237	0	0	0	0	0	0	51	0	0	0	186	237
23 Senior Accounting Clerk	212	0	0	0	0	0	0	4	0	0	0	208	212
24 Attendant	198	104	5	0	0	89	198	0	0	0	0	0	0
25 Business Office Supvr	195	0	0	0	0	0	0	11	0	0	1	183	195
Top Twenty-five Total	13962	442	13	0	4	5180	5639	1786	13	1	6	6517	8323

Phoenix — Mountain Bell

Job Title	Grand Total	Males						Females					
		Black	SSA	Ind	Orntl	Anglo	Total	Black	SSA	Ind	Orntl	Anglo	Total
1 Operator	1029	0	0	0	0	0	0	94	70	9	3	853	1029
2 Installer Repairman	309	8	11	0	0	290	309	0	0	0	0	0	0
3 Communications Serviceman	295	2	4	1	0	288	295	0	0	0	0	0	0
4 Accounting Clerk	288	2	1	1	0	17	21	13	27	0	1	226	267
5 Service Representative	249	0	0	0	0	0	0	3	3	1	0	242	249
6 Cable Splicer	249	8	14	2	0	225	249	0	0	0	0	0	0
7 Analytical Clerk	206	0	0	0	0	0	0	3	8	1	0	194	206
8 Central Office Repairman	194	0	2	0	0	188	190	0	0	0	0	4	4
9 Lineman	186	8	9	0	0	169	186	0	0	0	0	0	0
10 Service Foreman	159	0	2	1	0	155	158	0	0	0	0	1	1
11 Plant Reports Clerk	98	0	0	0	0	1	1	4	9	0	0	84	97
12 Frameman	94	4	7	0	0	66	77	1	1	0	0	15	17
13 Foreman	89	1	2	0	0	86	89	0	0	0	0	0	0
14 Service Order Clerk	82	0	0	0	0	0	0	1	4	0	0	77	82
15 Engineer	76	0	0	0	0	76	76	0	0	0	0	0	0
16 Central Office Clerk	70	0	0	0	0	0	0	3	11	1	0	55	70
17 Business Office Supvr	70	0	0	0	0	0	0	0	0	0	0	70	70
18 Account Representative	69	0	0	0	0	0	0	1	0	0	0	68	69
19 Facilities Planner	64	0	0	0	0	63	63	0	0	0	0	1	1
20 Order Center Reviewer	60	0	0	0	0	0	0	0	3	1	1	55	60
21 Communications Consultant	55	1	0	0	0	53	54	0	0	0	0	1	1
22 Service Assistant	54	0	0	0	0	0	0	1	3	0	0	50	54
23 Directory Review Clerk	54	0	0	0	0	0	0	2	3	1	0	48	54
24 Teller	51	0	0	0	0	0	0	1	1	0	0	49	51
25 Unit Supervisor	48	0	0	0	0	1	1	0	0	0	0	47	47
Top Twenty-five Total	4198	34	52	5	0	1678	1769	127	143	14	5	2140	2429

Richmond – C & P Tel of Va

Job Title	Grand Total	Males						Females					
		Black	SSA	Ind	Orntl	Anglo	Total	Black	SSA	Ind	Orntl	Anglo	Total
1 Operator	651	0	0	0	0	0	0	326	0	0	0	325	651
2 Technical Clerk	540	0	0	0	0	1	1	25	0	0	0	514	539
3 Staff Associate	252	2	0	0	0	188	190	0	0	0	0	62	62
4 Installer Repairman	191	10	0	0	0	181	191	0	0	0	0	0	0
5 Summarization Clerk	179	1	0	0	0	14	15	38	0	0	0	126	164
6 Central Office Repairman	165	4	0	0	0	161	165	0	0	0	0	0	0
7 Processing Clerk	137	0	0	0	0	11	11	39	0	0	0	87	126
8 Administrative Assistant	115	0	0	0	0	1	1	0	0	0	0	114	114
9 Service Representative	111	0	0	0	0	0	0	12	0	0	0	99	111
10 Foreman	107	2	0	0	0	105	107	0	0	0	0	0	0
11 PBX Installer-Repairman	98	0	0	0	0	98	98	0	0	0	0	0	0
12 Records Clerk	79	0	0	0	0	1	1	20	0	0	0	58	78
13 Engineer	68	0	0	0	0	68	68	0	0	0	0	0	0
14 Cable Splicer	66	0	0	0	0	66	66	0	0	0	0	0	0
15 Control Clerk	63	2	0	0	0	0	2	13	0	0	0	48	61
16 Staff Assistant	56	0	0	0	0	4	4	0	0	0	0	52	52
17 Unit Supervisor	51	1	0	0	0	4	5	0	0	0	0	46	46
18 Drafting Clerk	49	0	0	0	0	2	2	2	0	0	0	45	47
19 Mail and File Clerk	46	0	0	0	0	3	3	13	0	0	0	30	43
20 Directory Clerk	44	0	0	0	0	0	0	3	0	2	0	39	44
21 Typist	43	0	0	0	0	0	0	10	0	0	0	33	43
22 Order Supervisor	37	0	0	0	0	1	1	0	0	0	0	36	36
23 Engineering Assistant	36	0	0	0	0	35	35	0	0	0	0	1	1
24 Frameman	34	4	0	0	0	30	34	0	0	0	0	0	0
25 Posting Clerk	34	0	0	0	0	5	5	11	0	0	0	18	29
Top Twenty-five Total	3252	26	0	0	0	979	1005	512	0	2	0	1733	2247

Saint Louis – Southwestern & Illinois Bell

Job Title	Grand Total	Males						Females					
		Black	SSA	Ind	Orntl	Anglo	Total	Black	SSA	Ind	Orntl	Anglo	Total
1 Operator.	1983	0	0	0	0	0	0	599	6	0	0	1378	1983
2 Service Representative	513	0	0	0	0	0	0	34	2	0	0	477	513
3 Switchman	507	18	2	0	0	485	505	0	0	0	0	2	2
4 Station Installer	329	12	0	0	0	317	329	0	0	0	0	0	0
5 Frameman	285	53	0	0	0	205	258	6	0	0	0	21	27
6 Records Clerk	257	0	0	0	0	1	1	20	0	1	0	235	256
7 PBX Installer	251	0	0	0	0	251	251	0	0	0	0	0	0
8 Exchange Repairman	246	8	0	0	0	238	246	0	0	0	0	0	0
9 Cable Splicer	184	4	0	0	0	180	184	0	0	0	0	0	0
10 Secretary	175	0	0	0	0	0	0	2	0	0	0	173	175
11 Central Office Clerk	160	0	0	0	0	0	0	17	0	0	0	143	160
12 Service Order Writer	150	0	0	0	0	0	0	30	0	0	0	120	150
13 Service Assistant	129	0	0	0	0	0	0	19	0	0	0	110	129
14 Deskman	125	6	0	0	0	112	118	0	0	0	0	7	7
15 Cable Repairman	104	0	0	0	0	104	104	0	0	0	0	0	0
16 Business Office Supvr	102	0	0	0	0	0	0	3	0	1	0	98	102
17 Directory Compilation Clerk	100	0	0	0	0	0	0	15	0	0	0	85	100
18 Telephone Repeaterman	89	6	0	0	0	82	88	0	0	0	0	1	1
19 Service Order Clerk	88	0	0	0	0	0	0	6	0	0	0	82	88
20 Group Chief Operator	82	0	0	0	0	0	0	10	0	0	0	72	82
21 PBX Repairman	81	0	0	0	0	81	81	0	0	0	0	0	0
22 Chief Switchman	73	0	0	0	0	73	73	0	0	0	0	0	0
23 Teller	72	0	0	0	0	0	0	6	0	0	0	66	72
24 Senior Stenographer	72	0	0	0	0	0	0	3	0	0	0	69	72
25 Draftswoman	69	0	0	0	0	0	0	5	0	0	0	64	69
Top Twenty-five Total	6226	107	2	0	0	2129	2238	775	8	2	0	3203	3988

San Antonio — Southwestern Bell

Job Title	Grand Total	Male Black	Male SSA	Male Ind	Male Orntl	Male Anglo	Male Total	Female Black	Female SSA	Female Ind	Female Orntl	Female Anglo	Female Total
1 Operator	803	0	0	0	0	0	0	63	289	1	1	449	803
2 Station Installer	146	5	43	0	0	98	146	0	0	0	0	0	0
3 Service Representative	136	0	0	0	0	0	0	7	17	0	2	110	136
4 Switchman	122	5	12	0	0	105	122	0	0	0	0	0	0
5 PBX Installer	74	0	3	0	0	71	74	0	0	0	0	0	0
6 Exchange Repairman	65	0	4	0	0	61	65	0	0	0	0	0	0
7 Records Clerk	60	0	0	0	0	3	3	1	16	0	0	40	57
8 Cable Splicer	58	2	2	0	0	54	58	0	0	0	0	0	0
9 Telephone Repeaterman	55	6	5	0	0	44	55	0	0	0	0	0	0
10 Service Assistant	53	0	0	0	0	0	0	0	12	0	1	40	53
11 Secretary	53	0	0	0	0	0	0	0	5	0	0	48	53
12 Frameman	51	6	31	0	0	14	51	0	0	0	0	0	0
13 Central Office Clerk	37	0	0	0	0	0	0	1	8	0	0	28	37
14 Senior Stenographer	35	0	0	0	0	0	0	0	11	0	1	23	35
15 Senior Engineer	35	0	0	0	0	35	35	0	0	0	0	0	0
16 Lineman	34	1	12	0	0	21	34	0	0	0	0	0	0
17 Deskman	32	0	1	0	0	31	32	0	0	0	0	0	0
18 Directory Representative	32	0	0	0	0	32	32	0	0	0	0	0	0
19 Business Office Supvr	31	0	0	0	0	0	0	3	3	0	0	25	31
20 Group Chief Operator	29	0	0	0	0	0	0	2	1	1	0	25	29
21 Cable Repairman	26	1	0	0	0	25	26	0	0	0	0	0	0
22 Reports Clerk	26	0	0	0	0	0	0	0	11	0	0	15	26
23 Engineering Clerk	25	0	0	0	0	0	0	0	13	0	0	12	25
24 Engineering Associate	23	0	2	0	0	21	23	0	0	0	0	0	0
25 Directory Sales Clerk	22	0	0	0	0	0	0	0	1	0	0	21	22
Top Twenty-five Total	2,063	26	115	0	0	615	756	77	387	2	5	836	1307

San Diego – Pacific Tel

Job Title	Grand Total	Male						Female					
		Black	SSA	Ind	Orntl	Anglo	Total	Black	SSA	Ind	Orntl	Anglo	Total
1 Operator	1388	0	0	0	0	2	2	138	117	3	4	1124	1386
2 Staff Clerk	341	0	0	0	0	0	0	11	16	0	5	309	341
3 Cent Ofc Equipment Man	309	10	10	0	3	285	308	0	0	0	0	1	1
4 Service Representative	301	0	0	0	0	1	1	12	6	0	1	281	300
5 Station Installer	259	17	35	0	1	206	259	0	0	0	0	0	0
6 Engineer	255	1	4	1	3	226	235	0	0	0	0	20	20
7 Splicer	250	10	13	0	0	227	250	0	0	0	0	0	0
8 Records Clerk	217	0	0	0	0	0	0	4	7	0	3	203	217
9 PBX Installer	206	2	4	0	1	199	206	0	0	0	0	0	0
10 Senior Engineer	178	1	1	0	0	173	175	0	0	0	0	3	3
11 Transmission Man	154	2	5	1	2	144	154	0	0	0	0	0	0
12 PBX Repairman	143	0	2	2	0	139	143	0	0	0	0	0	0
13 Plant Service Clerk	138	0	0	0	0	0	0	9	4	0	0	125	138
14 Frameman	132	6	11	0	0	105	122	0	0	0	0	10	10
15 Line Assigner	131	2	2	0	0	70	74	0	2	0	0	55	57
16 Lineman	122	4	14	0	1	103	122	0	0	0	0	0	0
17 Central Office Clerk	122	0	0	0	0	0	0	5	4	1	1	111	122
18 Station Repairman	109	6	7	0	2	94	109	0	0	0	0	0	0
19 Service Assistant	96	0	0	0	0	0	0	7	5	0	1	83	96
20 Plant Reports Clerk	96	0	0	0	0	0	0	3	4	0	1	88	96
21 Statistical Clerk	86	0	0	0	0	0	0	7	7	0	0	72	86
22 Deskman	76	1	2	0	0	73	76	0	0	0	0	0	0
23 Installation Foreman	73	2	0	0	0	71	73	0	0	0	0	0	0
24 Special Assistant	69	0	0	0	0	0	0	1	1	0	0	67	69
25 Engineering Aide	64	0	0	0	0	0	0	2	2	0	1	59	64
Top Twenty-five Total	5315	64	110	4	13	2113	2309	199	175	4	17	2611	3006

San Francisco – Pacific Tel

Job Title	Grand Total	Male						Female					
		Black	SSA	Ind	Orntl	Anglo	Total	Black	SSA	Ind	Orntl	Anglo	Total
1 Operator	4568	13	3	0	6	92	114	729	238	26	192	3605	4854
2 Staff Clerk	1977	2	0	1	9	5	17	242	98	11	183	1426	1960
3 Cent Ofc Equipment Man	1328	75	68	12	39	1125	1319	1	0	0	0	8	9
4 Service Representative	857	0	0	0	1	10	11	47	16	0	13	770	846
5 Splicer	725	37	29	3	5	651	725	0	0	0	0	0	0
6 Plant Service Clerk	708	1	2	1	2	4	10	91	40	10	81	476	698
7 PBX Installer	683	18	21	5	9	630	683	0	0	0	0	0	0
8 PBX Repairman	572	6	17	2	4	543	572	0	0	0	0	0	0
9 Installer Repairman	512	23	28	0	7	454	512	0	0	0	0	0	0
10 Frameman	500	53	43	9	20	338	463	1	1	0	0	35	37
11 Office Clerk	492	1	2	0	3	7	18	58	26	7	52	331	474
12 Transmission Man	466	25	8	0	27	405	465	0	0	1	1	1	1
13 Engineer	401	2	5	0	9	350	366	1	0	0	1	32	35
14 Service Assistant	397	0	0	0	0	1	1	64	19	0	8	305	396
15 Central Office Clerk	366	0	0	0	0	0	0	48	17	7	8	291	366
16 Plant Reports Clerk	324	1	0	0	0	7	8	21	16	0	16	263	316
17 Senior Engineer	322	1	5	0	1	299	306	0	1	0	0	15	16
18 Reports Clerk	305	0	0	0	2	0	2	22	16	4	35	226	303
19 Reconciliation Clerk	300	1	0	1	1	1	3	30	26	3	26	212	297
20 Line Assigner	278	4	4	1	0	109	118	13	7	3	5	132	160
21 Chief Equipment Man	275	6	6	0	3	260	275	0	0	0	0	0	0
22 Marketing Representative	269	0	0	0	1	2	3	21	3	0	8	234	266
23 Assistant Trfc Opertng Mg	257	0	0	0	0	1	1	30	9	0	7	210	256
24 Compilation Clerk	256	0	1	0	7	3	6	45	16	10	33	146	250
25 Deskman	242	0	6	0	2	231	239	0	0	0	0	3	3
Top Twenty-five Total	17780	269	248	34	158	5529	6237	1464	549	77	668	8785	11542

Washington — C & P Tel of DC, Md & Va

Job Title	Grand Total	Male Black	Male SSA	Male Ind	Male Orntl	Male Anglo	Male Total	Female Black	Female SSA	Female Ind	Female Orntl	Female Anglo	Female Total
1 Operator	3262	0	0	0	0	0	0	1460	1	0	1	1800	3262
2 Installer Repairman	1442	147	1	0	1	1293	1442	0	0	0	0	0	0
3 Central Office Repairman	1303	86	1	0	4	1208	1299	0	0	0	0	4	4
4 PBX Installer-Repairman	1034	15	0	0	1	1018	1034	0	0	0	0	0	0
5 Service Representative	913	7	0	1	0	15	22	194	3	1	2	691	891
6 Foreman	733	7	0	0	0	726	733	0	0	0	0	0	0
7 Cent Ofc Clerk Grade 1	543	7	0	0	0	6	13	254	0	0	1	275	530
8 Staff Associate	541	12	0	0	1	337	350	49	0	0	1	142	191
9 Review and Reports Clerk	493	0	0	0	0	0	0	86	0	0	0	407	493
10 Cable Splicer	464	16	0	0	0	448	464	0	0	0	0	0	0
11 Frameman	444	114	1	0	0	370	435	0	1	0	0	9	9
12 Processing Clerk	379	3	0	0	0	4	7	135	0	0	2	235	372
13 Administrative Assistant	281	0	0	0	0	1	1	29	1	0	0	250	280
14 Staff Assistant	244	4	0	0	1	32	37	12	0	0	0	195	207
15 Service Order Clerk	239	2	0	0	0	0	2	85	1	0	1	149	236
16 Service Assistant	215	0	0	0	0	0	0	55	0	0	0	160	215
17 Plant Field Clerk	185	0	0	0	0	1	1	52	1	0	0	131	184
18 Cent Ofc Clerk Grade 3	180	1	0	0	0	1	2	34	0	0	0	144	178
19 Group Supervisor	176	0	0	0	0	3	3	14	0	0	0	159	173
20 Group Chief Operator	168	0	0	0	0	0	0	35	0	0	0	133	168
21 Lineman	161	13	0	0	0	147	161	0	0	0	0	0	0
22 Foreman Supervisor	141	0	0	0	0	140	140	0	0	0	0	1	1
23 Service Supervisor	136	0	0	0	0	7	7	15	0	0	0	114	129
24 Storekeeper	133	49	0	0	0	84	133	0	0	0	0	0	0
25 Mail and File Clerk	129	18	0	0	0	18	36	37	0	0	2	54	93
Top Twenty-five Total	13938	501	3	0	8	5810	6322	2505	7	1	10	5093	7616

Appendix C

Consent Decree: Peter J. Brennan, Secretary of Labor, United States Department of Labor, Equal Employment Opportunity Commission, and United States of America v. American Telephone and Telegraph, *et al.* May 30, 1974

In the United States District Court for the Eastern District of Pennsylvania

Peter J. Brennan, Secretary of Labor, United States Department of Labor, Equal Employment Opportunity Commission, and United States of America, Plaintiffs,
   v.
American Telephone and Telegraph Company,
New England Telephone and Telegraph Company,
The Southern New England Telephone Company,
New York Telephone Company,
New Jersey Bell Telephone Company,
The Bell Telephone Company of Pennsylvania
   and the Diamond State Telephone Company
The Chesapeake and Potomac Telephone Company,
The Chesapeake and Potomac Telephone Company of Maryland,
The Chesapeake and Potomac Telephone Company of Virginia,
The Chesapeake and Potomac Telephone Company of West Virginia,
Southern Bell Telephone and Telegraph Company,
South Central Bell Telephone Company,
The Ohio Bell Telephone Company,
Cincinnati Bell Inc.,
Michigan Bell Telephone Company,
Indiana Bell Telephone Company, Incorporated,
Wisconsin Telephone Company,
Illinois Bell Telephone Company,
Northwestern Bell Telephone Company,
Southwestern Bell Telephone Company,
The Mountain States Telephone and Telegraph Company,
Pacific Northwest Bell Telephone Company,
The Pacific Telephone and Telegraph Company
   and Bell Telephone Company of Nevada, Defendants.

Civil Action No. 74-1342

The Equal Employment Opportunity Commission (hereinafter, EEOC), the Secretary
of Labor (hereinafter, the Secretary), and the United States of America having filed
their Complaint herein, the EEOC pursuant to Sections 706(f)(1) and 707 (e) of
Title VII, of the Civil Rights Act of 1964, as amended, 42 U.S.C. § 2000e *et seq.*
(hereinafter, Title VII), the Secretary pursuant to Sections 6 (d), 15 (a) (2) and 17
of the Fair Labor Standards Act of 1938, as amended, 29 U.S.C. § § 201 *et seq.*
(hereinafter, the Equal Pay Act), and the United States pursuant to Executive Order
11246, as amended (hereinafter, the Executive Order), and the Defendants having
filed their Answer denying the allegations in the Complaint,[1] and the parties having
waived hearings and findings of fact and conclusions of law, the following order is
entered without any admission by any of the Defendants or finding by the Court
of any violation by any of the Defendants of any of the above-mentioned statutes or
Executive Order, or any regulations adopted pursuant thereto.

Now, therefore, it is ORDERED, ADJUDGED AND DECREED as follows:

Part A

I. Management Promotion Pay Plan
Definitions:
1. "Salary Band" is a category with a stated minimum and a stated maximum
   salary rate which includes a number of management positions determined by
   the respective Company to be of comparable value for compensation purposes.
2. "Salary Zone" is a geographic area of a Company's operation within which
   compensation rates are separately determined.
3. "Most favored sex" means the sex having the higher average rate of pay on
   promotions to a salary band (or job for back pay determinations) during the
   respective study periods (July 1, 1972 to June 30, 1973;[2] or June 1, 1972
   through May 31, 1974).
4. "Least favored sex" means the sex having the lower average rate of pay on
   promotions to a salary band (or job for back pay determinations) during the
   study period.
5. "Through Promotion" limits the employees included in the calculation required to establish a minimum entry rate, and the employees entitled to back
   pay pursuant to Section II, C., below, to those employees entering a manage-

1 Defendants assert that venue in the present action is improper as to all Defendants except the
Long Lines Department of the American Telephone and Telegraph Company, and The Bell
Telephone Company of Pennsylvania. However, all Defendants have waived objections to venue
for the limited purpose of the entry of this Decree. By submitting to the jurisdiction of this
Court and waiving objections to the venue of this Decree, all Defendants preserve their rights to
object to the appropriateness of jurisdiction and venue in all other actions or as to any other
claims brought in this or any other federal judicial district.
2 For establishing the minimum entry rate for each salary band, the study period with respect
to New England Telephone and Telegraph Company shall be January 1, 1973 to June 30, 1973.

ment band as a result of a promotion[3] from any position or band with a lower maximum rate.[4] Neither calculation shall include employees entering as new hires, entering through lateral transfer, or temporarily promoted.

6. "Temporarily Promoted" means a promotion in which the employee does not assume all the duties and responsibilities of the assigned position or a promotion for a specific period of time which is not a permanent assignment.

A. In each Operating Telephone Company, A.T.&T. Long Lines, and A.T.&T. General Departments, job evaluation is the primary vehicle by which management positions (excepting certain professional or other specialized positions) are classified into various salary bands.[5]

B. No later than June 30, 1975, each Company will have completed its job evaluation study in management levels 1 and 2 (as described in A above) and shall have placed each position in the salary band for which it qualifies, based on the evaluation results. Upon placement in a new salary band, salaries of employees below the minimum (dollar) entry rate, as described below, of the band will be brought to the minimum (dollar) entry rate.

C. Within each Operating Telephone Company, A.T.&T. Long Lines, and A.T.&T General Departments, a minimum (dollar) entry rate shall be established for each salary band in management levels 1 and 2 for each salary zone, based on a study of entry rates paid in all salary zones (converted into percentages of zone maximum rates at the time of promotion) to the most favored sex entering that salary band through promotion during a study period between July 1, 1972 and June 30, 1973. The minimum (dollar) entry rate for each salary band shall equal the average salary rate of the most favored sex who entered the band through promotion during the study period of July 1, 1972 to June 30, 1973. The minimum entry rate shall be a separate dollar amount for each salary zone. Where fewer than five employees of each sex were promoted to a salary band during the study period, the study period shall be expanded in the following manner so that the base of employees studied shall include five employees of each sex: (1) first, to post-study periods in chronological order up to the date of this Decree; and (2) if necessary, to pre-study periods in reverse chronological order, not to exceed two years prior to July 1, 1972. Where no reasonable sex-mix (minimum of five of each sex) can be obtained by expanding the base period, the minimum entry rate

3 In Wisconsin Telephone Company and The Ohio Bell Telephone Company "promotion" includes only reassignments which entitle the employees to a promotional salary increase consistent with the promotion pay practices of those Companies.

4 Maximum rates means the highest attainable salary rate for completely satisfactory performance and does not include salary rates attainable only for outstanding performance.

5 Defendants note that their purpose in establishing minimum entry rates by salary bands rather than jobs is based on salary administration and personnel reasons, and Defendants deny that these bands are required for compliance with the Equal Pay Act, Title VII or the Executive Order.

for any salary band shall be established as described above, providing at least one employee of each sex was promoted to the band in question. When a study discloses no promotion of employees of one sex, the minimum entry rate shall be established at 85% of the maximum rate for the salary zone expressed in dollars. In no instance shall the minimum (dollar) entry rate established for a salary band by any method exceed 85% of the maximum rate for the salary zone.

D. In each Operating Telephone Company, A.T.&T. Long Lines, and A.T.&T. General Departments, salaries of employees below the minimum (dollar) entry rate in any salary band in management levels 1 and 2 shall be adjusted upward to the minimum rate as of the first day of the first full calendar month following the date of this Decree.

E. In each Operating Telephone Company, A.T.&T. Long Lines and A.T.&T. General Departments, no employee entering a given salary band in management levels 1 and 2 through promotion in the future shall be paid a salary less than the minimum (dollar) entry rate, upon promotion to that band.

F. When and if a salary structure (the combined salary bands in a management level) in management levels 1 and 2 are revised in any Company covered by this Decree, the minimum (dollar) entry rates for the salary bands in the revised structure shall conform to the greatest extent possible with the pattern of rates established in the salary bands existing on the date of this Decree.

The minimum (dollar) entry rate for each new salary band shall be at least as high as the minimum rate of the band in which the majority of the employees in the new band were previously located, subject to the 85% limitation described in C above. Minimum (dollar) entry rates established under this Decree shall not be decreased in corresponding salary bands in the revised structure as a result of such restructuring.

G. Except as specifically modified by the Management Promotion Pay Plan set forth herein, the management pay practices of any Operating Telephone Company, A.T.&T. Long Lines or A.T.&T. General Departments are not affected by this Decree.

Exceptions:

1. The minimum (dollar) entry rate for the applicable salary band and salary zone need not apply to an employee initially hired into management levels 1 or 2. However, within two years from an employees' initial employment in management levels 1 or 2, a Company shall compensate such employee at least at the minimum rate established for the applicable salary band and salary zone.

2. In the Ohio Bell Telephone Company, Illinois Bell Telephone Company, the Long Lines Department of the American Telephone and Telegraph Co, and The Pacific Telephone and Telegraph Company (and Bell Telephone Company of Nevada), which have implemented management promotion pay plans which

the parties agree are at least as favorable to employees as the promotion pay plan set forth above, continued use of their respective plans complies with the requirements of Title VII, the Equal Pay Act, and the Executive Order, provided that either their own promotion pay plan, a combination of their own plan and the plan set forth above, or the plan set forth above, is applicable to management levels 1 and 2.

3. The minimum (dollar) entry rate for the applicable salary band and salary zone shall not apply to employees temporarily promoted; provided, however, that where an employee has occupied a position for more than sixty calendar days, the promotion shall no longer be considered temporary and the employee shall be brought to the applicable minimum entry rate.

II. Back Pay

In each Operating Telephone Company, A.T.&T. Long Lines and A.T.&T. General Departments, back pay awards shall be granted to certain employees under this Decree (limited as noted, Section II, E, below). Such awards shall be limited to situations and time periods in which employees in management levels 1 and 2, of both sexes have been engaged in performance of equal work; that is, jobs involving substantially the same duties, the performance of which require equal skill, effort and responsibility, and which are performed under similar working conditions.

A. Such awards shall be based on an examination in each Company of entry rates in positions within the same salary band which have the same first two digits of Bell System status codes and the same Bell System job duties codes (as revised and verified by each Company) on a Company-wide basis,[7] during the period from the first day of the first full calendar month following the date of this decree to two years prior to that date. Within 90 days from the date of this Decree, each Company shall furnish the government Plaintiffs with a list of all positions in management levels 1 and 2, which are in the same salary bands, have the same first two digits of the Bell System status codes and the same Bell System job duties code, and which the Company contends do not involve "equal work," as defined above. For each group of such management positions on the list furnished to the government Plaintiffs, each Company will provide a summary of the bases on which it has determined that such positions do not involve "equal work." The government Plaintiffs shall within 60 days from the receipt of such lists, review the listings and conduct such investigations as they deem appropriate to verify the information provided and the accuracy of the Company's determination. In the event of a dis-

7 Defendants note that their agreement herein to pay back and establish minimum entry rates on a "Company-wide" basis by Defendants is based on salary administration and personnel reasons and Defendants deny that jobs in different "establishments" or "locations" may be compared under the Equal Pay Act, Title VII, or the Executive Order. [Footnotes have been numbered as in the original copy, which does not include a note 6–Editor.]

agreement as to any determination made by any Company, the government Plaintiffs shall follow the procedure provided in Part B, Section II, C, below. As to any management positions for which the procedures of Part B, Section II, C, below are invoked, the payment of back pay shall be made within 30 days of the final resolution of such procedures.

B. Each Company shall calculate a minimum (dollar) entry rate for each job (as determined in Section II, A, above) into which employees of both sexes have been promoted, in management levels 1 and 2. The calculation shall be made in the same manner as provided in Section I,C, above. The minimum rate shall be a separate (dollar) amount for each salary zone.

C. Any employee who entered a job in management levels 1 or 2 through promotion, who was a member of the least favored sex as defined above, and who was employed in such a job after two years prior to the first full calendar month following the entry of this Decree at a rate of pay below the minimum (dollar) job entry rate calculated for the job pursuant to Section II, B, above, shall receive an amount equal to the difference between the minimum job entry rate for the applicable job and the individual's salary rate(s).

D. Back pay awards shall be granted for the period of time such employee has been performing a job which qualifies for an award since two years prior to the first day of the first full calendar month following the entry of this Decree.

E. Back pay awards for The Pacific Telephone and Telegraph Company (including Bell Telephone Company, The Mountain States Telephone and Telegraph Company, The Ohio Bell Telephone Company, the Long Lines Department of the American Telephone and Telegraph Company, and Illinois Bell Telephone Company, which have introduced alternative entry rate plans shall be limited to the period of time and management level(s) to which such plans did not apply during the period provided in C and D above.

Part B

I. Effect of Decree

A. As to the specific issues identified in the Complaint and Decree, compliance with the terms of this Decree resolves all existing questions among the parties of the Bell Companies' compliance, for acts or practices occurring prior to the date of this Decree, with the requirements of Title VII of the Civil Rights Act of 1964, as amended, the Equal Pay Act of 1963, as amended, and Executive Order 11246, as amended. Moreover, compliance with the terms of the Decree in the future will constitute compliance with such laws, orders, and regulations as respects those issues specifically dealt with in the Decree.

B. Acceptance by any person of individual relief ordered in Part A, Section II of this Decree shall constitute a waiver and release by such person of any claims for alleged violations of Title VII of the Civil Rights Act of 1964, as amended, 42 U.S.C. §§ 1981, 1983, Executive Order 11246, as amended, or any applicable state fair employment practice laws or regulations based upon occurrences prior to the date of this Decree as respects those issues dealt with in the Decree.

C. As to the specific issues resolved in this Decree, the parties agree to continue the procedures and agreements implemented pursuant to Part B, Section I, A–B, of the Memorandum of Agreement of January 19, 1973, entered between these same parties with respect to non-management employees.

D. The Plaintiffs further agree:

1) That they will not, in any claim action or proceeding (including rate cases), involving any of the Defendants, initiate, encourage, fund, intervene in support of or advocate by *amicus* brief or otherwise, a position inconsistent with this Decree.

2) That EEOC will advise its Regional and District offices, as well as state and local agency grantees, and the Department of Labor will advise its Regional and District offices and contract compliance agencies, that the Decree will bring the Bell Companies into compliance with Title VII, the Equal Pay Act, and the Executive Order requirements as to the specific issues identified in the Decree and that, to the limit of EEOC's contractual power to insure such a result, such Companies shall not be the subject of enforcement programs funded by EEOC, as to the matters covered herein.

3) That any actions taken by EEOC Regional or District offices or Department of Labor Regional or District offices or OFCC field offices which any Bell Company believes to be inconsistent with the terms of this Decree may be brought to the attention of the national headquarters of the EEOC, Department of Labor, or OFCC, as appropriate, and such national headquarters shall become the party with whom such Bell Company may resolve such compliance issues.

II. Compliance Procedures

A. The government plaintiffs shall endeavor to coordinate their efforts to assure compliance with this Decree and shall develop such procedures as may be appropriate to this end.

B. As to the issues resolved in this Decree, the parties agree that Defendant Companies shall provide the following reports within 8 months of the date of this Decree:

1) By each Company, a list of employees by race and sex paid back wages under Part A, Section II, and the amount paid to each;

2) By each Company, a list of employees by race and sex accorded wage
raises pursuant to Part A, Section I, D.

Nothing in this Decree shall limit the right of the Department of Labor to make
investigations under Section 11 of the Fair Labor Standards Act nor the right of
EEOC to investigate charges pursuant to Section 706 (b) of Title VII.

C. The government will promptly notify the Bell Comapny involved and A.T.&T.[9]
of any problems of noncompliance with this Decree which they believe warrant
investigation. Such Company will be given 60 days to investigate the complaint and
conciliate with the government regarding the taking of any appropriate corrective
action. At the end of this period, the government, if not satisfied, may seek an
appropriate resolution of the question by the Court.

III. Duration of the Decree

A. The Court retains jurisdiction of this action for entry of such orders as are necessary to effectuate the provisions of this Decree. The term of this Decree shall be
five years from this date, but as to the specific issues dealt with herein, the Defendants
are permanently enjoined from violating the provisions of the Equal Pay Act, Title
VII, and the Executive Order. Upon certification to this Court that the payment of
back wages ordered in Part A, Section II, has been made, that portion of this Decree
will be dissolved as having been satisfied. Defendants waive none of their rights to
move for dissolution or modification of this Decree at any time in addition to those
specifically provided for in Subsection B below.

B. Opinion letters have been issued by the General Counsel of EEOC and the
Wage and Hour Administrator and are attached hereto as Exhibits A and B, respectively. Should either opinion or portion thereof be withdrawn or overruled, the
Plaintiffs will, at the request of the Defendant(s) affected by such withdrawal or
overruling, join such Defendant(s) in moving the Court to dissolve any portion of
the Decree which involves the issue or issues with respect to which the opinion
letter has been withdrawn or modified, and to strike any portion of the pleadings
in this action relevant thereto, and such motion shall be granted.

So Ordered: Leon Higginbotham
                   Judge, United States District Court

---

9 The responsibility of A.T.&T., apart from responsibility for the compliance of its own departments, shall be limited to: (1) in case of an irreconcilable conflict between the government and
an individual Bell Company, to use its good offices to aid in achieving a resultion of such
conflict; (2) the provision of advice to its associated telephone companies as to the meaning of the
Decree and the procedures for compliance; and (3) the coordination of reports required by
PART B, Section II, B. [Footnotes have been numbered as in the original copy, which does not
include a note 8–Editor.]

Consent to the entry of the foregoing Decree is hereby granted.

AMERICAN TELEPHONE AND TELEGRAPH
COMPANY, for itself and on behalf of its associated telephone companies as set forth herein.

[Signed:] Charles Ryan
Clark G. Redick
American Telephone and Telegraph Company
195 Broadway
New York, New York 10017

Bernard G. Segal
Irving R. Segal
Kimber E. Vought
1719 Packard Building
Philadelphia, Pennsylvania 19102

Schnader, Harrison, Segal & Lewis
1719 Packard Building
Philadelphia, Pennsylvania 19102

Of Counsel

Thompson Powers
James D. Hutchinson
Ronald S. Cooper
1250 Connecticut Avenue, N. W.
Washington, D.C. 20036

Steptoe & Johnson
1250 Connecticut Avenue, N. W.
Washington, D.C. 20036

Of Counsel

William A. Carey
General Counsel

William L. Robinson
Associate General Counsel

Isabelle R. Cappello
Assistant General Counsel

Ethel Ollivierre
Attorney

C. Daniel Karnes
Attorney

Equal Employment Opportunity Commission

William J. Kilberg
Solicitor of Labor

Carin Ann Clauss
Associate Solicitor

Karl W. Heckman
Attorney

United States Department of Labor

J. Stanley Pottinger
Assistant Attorney General

David L. Rose
Attorney

James S. Angus
Attorney

Robert E. J. Curran
United States Attorney

United States Department of Justice

Appendix D

Addendum 1975. Summary of Supplemental Agreement, May 13, 1975

On May 13, 1975, the federal government and AT&T modified the January 1973 Consent Decree because reviews of company performance revealed that the 1973 intermediate targets were not met for many job classifications in many companies (Tables D.1, D.2). The Supplemental Agreement[1] provides for new procedures for priority hiring and promotion of women and minorities in order to eliminate 1973 deficiencies. Some of the difficulty in implementing the original Consent Decree was perhaps due to the late submission of 1973 intermediate targets thereby delaying the joint (government and AT&T) on-site reviews of the Bell System companies. These reviews were not started until April 1974, some fourteen months after the signing of the Consent Decree. The initial monitoring mechanisms were found to be ineffective and neither the "affirmative action override" nor aggressive recruitment had been utilized to meet race, sex, and ethnic-group intermediate targets.

Many of the problems encountered in 1973 were minimized to such an extent in 1974 that on a system-wide basis the Bell companies had achieved more than 90 percent of their intermediate targets. Thus, the Government Coordinating Committee (GCC) recommended and AT&T agreed to an aggregation of 1973, 1974, and 1975 targets into a supplemental action program. "Good faith efforts" supported by documentation warranted some reduction of these deficiencies. A carry-forward procedure based on priority placement of minorities and women reserves 50 percent of projected job opportunities for them.

The Supplemental Order provides that the shortfalls in the targets of specific establishments that have not been eliminated by December 31, 1976 may be prorated by the operating companies to other establishments. Thus, an element of flexibility has been introduced into the system through the distribution of deficiencies to establishments elsewhere in the operating system where job vacancies exist. The supplemental order also requires payment of specified sums (ranging from $125 to $1500) to certain employees whose hiring or promotions were delayed by company employment practices. Each company will contribute to a Bell System Affirmative Action Fund, to be administered by the Human Resources Development Department of AT&T for such programs as: (1) studies designed to examine equipment used in craft positions which has been an obstacle to women's performance; (2) management training programs to determine technical skills and knowledge required for second and third level management; (3) feasibility study on the value of awareness training packages for supervision of minorities and female managers.

1 Supplemental Agreement, *Equal Employment Opportunity Commission, James D. Hodgson, Secretary of Labor, United States Department of Labor and United States of America,* May 13, 1975, Civil Action No. 73–149.

Both sides have recognized the difficulties of implementing a complex consent decree. The federal government has defined a "good faith effort" especially for hiring and promoting women to outside craft jobs. If the detailed actions for recruiting, selection, plant training, and placement of women in these nontraditional jobs are undertaken, the company has met the good faith efforts requirement and is in compliance with respect to these obligations. Many companies had complained that it was exceedingly difficult to meet the 19 percent goal for women in outside craft jobs. Now they only need to demonstrate that they have taken those "efforts which a reasonably prudent manager would have foreseen and undertaken in furtherance of a legal objective."

The federal agencies also clarified the "affirmative action override" principle. The 1973 Consent Decree provided for application of affirmative action override of contractual seniority provisions in cases where intermediate targets in nonmanagement jobs (classifications 5-15) were not being achieved. The companies are permitted to evaluate candidates for promotion and hiring on the basis of applicable selection criteria provided in collective bargaining agreements or pursuant to Bell System operating company practices. However, to the extent that any operating company is unable to meet its intermediate targets in job classifications 5-15 using these criteria, the Decree requires (except for some special situations in job classifications 9 and 10) that the selections will be from among any "at least basically qualified candidates" from the deficient groups.[2]

The companies apparently were discouraged from using the "affirmative action override" in 1973 by the filing of grievances. The Communications Workers of America (CWA), The International Brotherhood of Electrical Workers (IBEW), and the Alliance of Independent Telephone Unions have challenged the decree and supplemental order in court. Their main objection is that the seniority provisions of collective bargaining agreements can be overridden where necessary to meet intermediate targets. The company seems pleased that some of the 1973 deficiencies in nontraditional jobs were reduced as a result of "good faith efforts." Since final goals and interim targets for job classifications may be modified in the future through negotiation, the managerial prerogatives of the company are intact.

2 Appendix C of Supplemental Agreement, May 13, 1975.

Table D.1 Employment Performance of Bell System, 1973–1974 (From Supplemental Agreement 73–149)

Job Categories	Employment Profile 12/31/74	Net Gains in 1973 and 74	Percent Increase
Women, Second level management and above	7,570	2,402	46
Women, craft jobs	14,032	7,625	119
Blacks, second level management and above	921	415	82
Blacks, craft jobs	14,073	1,778	14
Spanish-surnamed Second level management and above	379	183	93
Spanish-surnamed craft jobs	7,082	1,815	34
Other minorities (all jobs)	8,397	2,572	44
Males, clerical and operator jobs	25,456	15,146	147

Table D.2 Deficiencies, by Operating Companies, 1973–1974 (From Supplemental Agreement 73-149)

Numbers indicated in parenthesis are those portions of the deficiencies attributable to 1973 and subject to the provisions of subsection I, B of the supplemental order.

AAJC	Race/Sex/Ethnic Group	Deficiency
	A. American Telephone and Telegraph Company, General Departments	
2	Spanish-surnamed American (SSA) males	4 (2)
4	Black females	10 (6)
	SSA females	2
11	White males	8
12	White males	9
	B. American Telephone and Telegraph Company, Long Lines Division (New York establishment only)	
3	Black males	2 (1)
	SSA males	4
4B	Black males	1
	Black females	1
8	White females	1
	Black females	1
11	SSA males	1
	SSA females	2
15	White females	3
	C. The Bell Telephone Company of Pennsylvania	
3	Black males	16
	Black females	7
4	Black females	35
6	Black males	11 (7)
	White females	5
8	White females	35
9	White females	13 (8)
	Black females	5
12	White males	1
	Black males	12
	D. The Chesapeake and Potomac Telephone Company of Virginia	
2	Black males	3
	Black females	2
3	Black males	1
	Black females	8
4	Black females	6
5	Black males	2
	Black females	1
6	Black males	7
7	Black males	5
8	White females	1
	Black females	7
9	Black males	1
	Black females	1
11	Black females	14
12	Black males	1
13	White males	2
	Black males	9

AAJC	Race/Sex/Ethnic Group	Deficiency
	E. Cincinnati Bell, Inc.	
2	White females	2
4	Black males	1
12	White males	1
	F. The Diamond State Telephone Company	
2	White females	2
3	White females	3
4	Black females	1
6	White females	1
7	White females	2
8	Black females	1
9	White females	3
	G. Illinois Bell Telephone Company	
1	White females	2
2	White females	20 (10)
3	Black males	19 (16)
	SSA males	8 (4)
	SSA females	6 (2)
4	White males	3
5	Black males	2
6	Black males	57 (24)
	SSA males	20 (11)
	White females	38 (10)
	Black females	21 (4)
7	Black males	13 (7)
8	White females	27
	Black females	13 (11)
9	White females	15
11	SSA females	32 (16)
12	White males	31
	Black males	35
13	White males	22
14	SSA females	17
15	White males	4
	White females	4
	H. Indiana Bell Telephone Company, Incorporated	
1	White females	1
3	White females	20
	Black females	3
6	White females	2 (1)
12	Black males	1

Table D.2 (continued)

I. Michigan Bell Telephone Company

1	Black males	2	
	White females	2	
3	White females	53	
5	Black females	2	
6	Black males	12	
	Black females	2	
7	Black females	6	(5)
8	White females	77	(53)
9	White females	43	(15)
	Black females	2	
10	White males	46	(33)
12	White males	26	
13	White males	7	

J. The Mountain States Telephone and Telegraph Company

2	White females	32	(26)
	Black females	2	(1)
	SSA females	4	
3	SSA males	9	(5)
	SSA females	13	
4	White males	1	
	SSA females	3	
6	White females	52	(50)
	Black females	2	
	SSA females	4	
7	White females	83	(69)
	Black females	2	
	SSA females	17	
	Asian American (AA) females	1	
9	White females	18	
	Black females	2	
	SSA females	11	(9)
	American Indian (AI) females	1	
11	SSA males	11	
12	White males	12	
	SSA males	8	
13	White males	17	
15	White females	8	

K. New England Telephone and Telegraph Company

2	White females	55	(43)
3	Black males	15	(13)

L. New Jersey Bell Telephone Company

2	White females	87	(79)
3	Black males	41	
	SSA males	16	(10)
4	White males	3	
5	SSA males	4	(3)
7	SSA males	6	
8	White females	29	(27)
9	White females	34	
	Black females	16	(14)
	SSA females	2	(1)
10	White females	28	
12	White males	13	
13	White males	1	
15	White females	3	

M. New York Telephone Company

2	Black males	3	
	SSA females	1	
3	Black males	5	
	SSA males	4	
	Black females	28	
	SSA females	10	
4	SSA females	1	
5	Black males	6	
	SSA males	3	
6	White females	2	
8	White females	16	
9	White females	11	
14	SSA females	1	

N. The Ohio Bell Telephone Company

2	White females	61	(37)
	Black females	8	(6)
3	Black males	36	(23)
6	Black males	9	(7)
8	White females	40	
	Black females	7	
9	White females	11	
	Black females	1	
12	White males	7	
13	White males	14	
	Black males	6	
15	White females	10	

O. The Pacific Telephone and Telegraph Company and Bell Telephone Company of Nevada

2	Black males	1	
	SSA males	8	
	AA males	2	
	SSA females	5	(3)
3	Black males	12	
	SSA females	50	
	AA females	1	
4	White males	6	
	Black males	3	
	SSA males	10	
	AA males	3	
5	SSA males	11	(8)
	SSA females	8	(5)
7	Black males	9	
	SSA males	11	
	SSA females	8	(5)
8	SSA females	4	
	AA females	6	
9	AA males	18	
	SSA females	32	(21)
11	AA females	6	3)
	White males	30	
	Black males	26	
	SSA males	31	
	SSA females	137	(81)
12	White males	39	
	Black males	36	
	SSA females	20	
	SSA males	61	(53)
13	White males	104	
14	AA females	43	(34)

P. South Central Bell Telephone Company

2	Black males	12	(9)
	White females	65	

Table D.2 (continued)

3	Black males	53
	Black females	89 (79)
4	Black females	12
5	White females	1
6	Black males	99 (98)
	White females	34 (32)
	Black females	4 (3)
7	Black males	90
8	White females	4
	Black females	40 (31)
9	White females	135
	Black females	78 (72)
10	Black females	13
12	White females	10
	Black males	36 (35)
15	White females	3

Q. Southern Bell Telephone and Telegraph Company

1	White females	9
2	White females	132 (122)
	Black females	9
	SSA females	4
3	Black males	100 (85)
	SSA males	1
	Black females	44
	SSA females	4
4	White males	5
	SSA males	1
	Black females	26
5	Black males	2
	Black females	1
	SSA females	3
6	Black males	91
	SSA males	25
	White females	21
	Black females	9 (6)
	SSA females	3
7	Black males	144
	SSA males	4
8	White females	36 (29)
	Black females	12
	SSA females	5
9	White females	171 (164)
	Black females	52
	SSA females	14 (12)
10	SSA females	7
11	Black males	1
	Black females	25
12	White males	13
	Black males	74 (62)
	SSA males	19
13	White males	4
14	SSA males	7
	SSA females	126
15	White females	1

R. The Southern New England Telephone Company

1	White females	2
2	Black males	1
4	White males	4
	Black males	1
8	White females	15 (11)
10	White females	1
15	White males	2

S. Southwestern Bell Telephone Company (Houston establishment only)

1	White females	2
2	White females	21 (8)
	Black females	7 (2)

	SSA females	6 (2)
3	Black males	16
	SSA males	1
	SSA females	1
4	SSA females	2
5	Black males	7 (6)
	SSA males	2
6	Black males	19
	SSA males	1
	White females	2 (1)
7	Black males	10
8	SSA males	3
	Black males	6
9	Black males	6
	White females	14
10	Black males	8
	SSA females	3
12	White males	1
	Black males	5
	SSA males	3

T. Wisconsin Telephone Company

2	White females	1
3	Black males	3 (2)
	SSA males	1
	AI males	1
	White females	14
	Black females	5
7	White females	10
8	White females	15 (13)
9	White females	4
12	White males	2

Index